W9-DDB-304

Social Anthropology

Canadian Perspectives on Culture and Society

Social Anthropology

Canadian Perspectives on Culture and Society

by Edward J. Hedican

CSPI Toronto

Social Anthropology: Canadian Perspectives on Culture and Society
by Edward J. Hedican

First published in 2012 by
Canadian Scholars' Press Inc.
180 Bloor Street West, Suite 801
Toronto, Ontario
M5S 2V6
www.cspi.org

Copyright © 2012 Edward J. Hedican and Canadian Scholars' Press Inc. All rights reserved. No part of this publication may be photocopied, reproduced, stored in a retrieval system, or transmitted, in any form or by any means, electronic, mechanical, or otherwise, without the written permission of Canadian Scholars' Press Inc., except for brief passages quoted for review purposes. In the case of photocopying, a licence may be obtained from Access Copyright: One Yonge Street, Suite 1900, Toronto, Ontario, M5E 1E5, (416) 868-1620, fax (416) 868-1621, toll-free 1-800-893-5777, www.accesscopyright.ca.

Every reasonable effort has been made to identify copyright holders. CSPI would be pleased to have any errors or omissions brought to its attention.

Canadian Scholars' Press Inc. gratefully acknowledges financial support for our publishing activities from the Government of Canada through the Canada Book Fund (CBF).

Library and Archives Canada Cataloguing in Publication

Hedican, Edward J.
Social anthropology : Canadian perspectives on culture and society / Edward J. Hedican.—1st ed.

Includes index.
ISBN 978-1-55130-407-6

1. Ethnology—Canada—Textbooks. 2. Ethnology—Textbooks. I. Title.

GN316.H43 2012   306.0971   C2011-907290-4

Text design by Brad Horning
Cover design by Colleen Wormald
Cover image ©Eduardo Rivero/Shutterstock

Printed and bound in Canada by Webcom

For my grandsons Hadrian and Tomas,
may you both live long and prosper in this world

Men make their own history, but they do not make it just as
they please; they do not make it under circumstances chosen
by themselves, but under given circumstances directly encountered and inherited from the past.

Karl Marx,
The Eighteenth Brumaire of Louis Bonaparte
(1978 [orig. 1852]): 9.

Table of Contents

Preface

Choose a job you love, and you will never have to work a day in your life.

Confucius

The Cree know that anthropologists vary: that some do better studies than others. They know that the knowledge that anthropologists collect is useful knowledge—for all the work over the past decade [1971–1981] has been used by the Cree.

Richard Salisbury,
A Homeland for the Cree (1986: 156)

Canadians tend to neglect the study of their own heritage, sometimes allowing others to define their sense of history, culture, and identity. And so it is in this spirit that this book on anthropology was written, as an exploration of our own rich social and cultural heritage. It is evident that anthropology in Canada has a long and varied history. This history ultimately is about the relationships that anthropologists have developed with local peoples, and the contributions that anthropology makes to the store of knowledge about human cultures.

Richard Salisbury, an anthropologist who was formerly the dean of Arts at McGill University, has indicated in the quote above that the relationship between the Cree of Quebec and anthropologists was a mutually beneficial one. During the James Bay Hydroelectric Project the Cree were displaced from their ancestral home, and anthropologists studied the impact of the resulting relocation. The Cree used the anthropologists' social impact studies as evidence that their hunting way of life was harmed by the flooding of rivers in their territory, and the anthropologists learned much through such studies about the effects of large-scale development projects on indigenous populations.

The first modern field studies in anthropology date from the research of Franz Boas among the Inuit of Baffin Island during the 1880s. Boas lived with the Inuit, learned their language, and travelled throughout their hunting territories with them, participating as much as possible in their way of life. Boas's monograph, *The Central Eskimo* (1888), is considered by many to be the first modern study in anthropology based on first-hand fieldwork. Later, during 1897–1898, Boas conducted additional field research among the Kwakiutl and Bella Coola First Nations of the British Columbia coast, contributing further to the scientific development of anthropology. Over the ensuing century and into this new millennium anthropologists have worked with many Aboriginal First Nations in Canada, documenting their traditional ways of life, providing evidence for land claims disputes, in addition to numerous other topics.

While studies involving First Nations have provided a core research area of anthropology in Canada, many other social and cultural settings have been the subject of research as well. There have been studies, for example, of religious sects such as the Hutterites of Alberta, identity among the Jewish community of Toronto, the impoverished condition of Blacks in Nova Scotia, as well as rural agricultural villages in Quebec. Anthropologists have also made important theoretical contributions to the concept of multiculturalism, a mainstay of modern Canadian society. Identity issues and political conflicts, such as those experienced by the Métis, have also been an object of research, contributing to our knowledge of social adjustment and change in a modern nation-state, especially one comprising numerous ethnic minorities. Canada has also witnessed large-scale development projects, such as the previously mentioned James Bay Hydroelectric Project. Anthropologists have been in these localities studying the effects of such projects on indigenous lifeways.

The purpose of this book is to provide what is, I believe, the first introductory text that focuses on social anthropological research using Canadian examples and perspectives. To date, what has been available have been expensive textbooks from south of the border that are called "Canadian editions," which basically amounts to some Canadian material spliced into an existing American text using their own perspectives. It is regretable that so far, in the history of anthropology, Canadian research has not been considered important enough for someone to write a text using the perspectives and research of this country.

The present text covers the basic conceptual building blocks of anthropology based, where appropriate, utilizing Canadian examples. The first goal is to provide introductory students with a solid background into the conceptual and research aspects of anthropology, while at the same time exploring the rich history of the discipline in a Canadian context. It is about time that this valuable resource is used in anthropology classrooms in Canadian universities as part of our national heritage. It is also appropriate that we tell our own story, rather than have others do it for us. My hope is that this is just the beginning of many such studies to follow in the future.

It must be realized, however, that anthropology is a discipline with a global perspective. Even though the emphasis in this text is on Canadian examples, various supplemental examples are also included from other parts of the world as a way of illustrating the cultural diversity of the world's population and anthropology's holistic point of view. These examples of global perspectives are presented in special boxes set apart from the regular flow of the text in order to introduce students to various classic ethnographic cases in the history of anthropology, such as the Trobriand Island Kula Ring, and as a way of presenting biographical material on such influential figures as Margaret Mead and Bronislaw Malinowski. There are also special boxes devoted to profiles of important Canadian anthropologists in Chapter 2.

The seminal ideas that formed the basis for a book on Canadian anthropology were first realized in my initial introductory classes as an undergraduate student at Lakehead University over 40 years ago. Since then I have been a graduate teaching assistant involved in introductory classes at McMaster and McGill universities. Over the succeeding years I have taught numerous anthropology students at the universities of Guelph, York, and Brandon in the areas of social anthropology, kinship and social organization, Aboriginal issues, community development, research methods, as well as other topics. Through these varied classroom experiences I have come to know what sorts of questions students are likely to ask about cultural and social variation, and what tends to spark their interest concerning the human condition. For these many student questions and interests I am truly grateful because they have contributed to an immeasurable degree to my development as a teacher.

Among my own colleagues I am indebted to several professors who were particularly helpful in my formative years and who are, unfortunately, no longer with us, namely, Ken Dawson (Lakehead University), Jud Epling (University of North Carolina at Chapel Hill), and my Ph.D. supervisor, Richard Salisbury (McGill University). I also wish to thank my long-time friend and colleague Stan Barrett (professor emeritus, University of Guelph) for his help, both academic and personal, on numerous occasions. A special thanks also to Christine Elsey, University of the Fraser Valley, for her constructive comments on earlier drafts of this manuscript.

I also wish to express my gratitude to the following luminaries who were willing to discuss anthropology with me when I was a fledgling grad student: Margaret Mead, Marvin Harris, Clifford Geertz, Max Gluckman, Kim Romney, Bea Medicine, Ruth Landes, and Sir Edmund Leach.

Edward J. Hedican
University of Guelph

1 The Scope of Anthropology

Glad to meetcha...
"The pleasure is mine, Thorby. Call me 'Margaret.'
My title doesn't count here anyhow... Do you know
what an anthropologist is?"
"Uh, I am sorry, ma'am—Margaret."
"It's simpler than it sounds. An anthropologist is a
scientist who studies how people live together."
Thorby looked doubtful. "This is a science?"

      —Robert Heinlein,
     Citizen of the Galaxy (1957: 77)

About 3 or 4 million years ago, a small bipedal creature, barely over a metre tall, scurried furtively away from her group. She had remembered seeing a cluster of berry bushes several days before and was curious to find out if the fruit had ripened. Normally she would not dare to stray away from the protection of her family, but food was in short supply at this time of year on the East African savannah. Hunger drove her to take chances. To her delight the berries were a brilliant red, and she could hardly contain herself with avid anticipation of tasting this succulent treat.

The last thing this creature, whom we now call an australopithecine, saw in life was a dark shadow sweep over her view of the sun. It was all over in a matter of seconds. With a flash of breathtaking speed, a large tiger sunk its sabre-like canines into the skull of this unwary, hapless forerunner of humanity. The tiger looked around for signs of any competitors, and then dragged the limp body of its prey into a short, nearby tree. After the tiger had enjoyed its meal, the bones fell into a deep crevice below the tree.

Many millenniums later, a paleontologist would hoist up the same skull, examine the large, grotesque puncture holes on the top of the australopithecine's skull, and shudder at such a violent death. No longer members of a hominid group who scurried about in a heightened state of continual fear, the descendants of those small australopithecines, at the time of the archaeological investigation that uncovered the punctured skull, now rule the Earth and every creature on it.

Today we are apt to wonder how such puny creatures, so lacking in strength, speed, or any other of the traits favouring survival, could have attained such lofty heights in the animal kingdom. Today, humans number in the billions, and their survival is threatened only by their very success. Even though *Homo sapiens*, and all their predecessors before them—*Homo erectus*, *Homo habilis*, and Neanderthals—lacked the qualities of strength, agility, and ferociousness that made other animals successful competitors for food and shelter, humans possess three important characteristics that ensure success more than all the other abilities combined—their cunning, intelligence, and, most of all, their curiosity. Even so, the creatures we were then are the creatures we are now, one contained in the other, harbouring the same fears, ambitions, and need for security that we had when we lived in that primeval world so long ago.

■ Curiosity and Innovation

Human beings are probably the most curious creatures on the planet. Even after their basic requirements for food, clothing, and security are met, humans are nonetheless still curious about so many things. They are curious about where they came from, what their neighbours are doing, and about the bright lights in the sky at night. Humans were curious about what would happen when they played around with fire, something no other creature would ever do. They were like Pythagoras, who saw in the varied shapes of nature angles and geometric designs. These creatures were curious about what would happen when they banged rocks together and chips flew off. Maybe they could tie these sharp chips to the end of a stick, they thought, and scare away the creatures that haunted them in the night. This curiosity about practically everything humans encountered on the planet is no doubt the foremost reason for the species' success. It is also the single most important reason why we have gone from being prey for tigers to travellers in the nighttime sky.

As far as the origins of anthropology are concerned, it is certainly rooted in curiosity. Curiosity may have killed the cat, and in some cases a curious australopithecine as well, but its advantages to the human species have certainly outweighed its disadvantages. Some scholars have suggested that anthropology really originated with the ancient Greeks, such as Pythagoras, Plato, and Archimedes, whose curiosity about the natural world led to important discoveries in mathematics, philosophy, and physics. Socrates, for example, is reputed to have said that "the unexamined life is not worth living." What we can take from this is that we should not be just living our lives, but looking at it in an objective sense, apart from ourselves. If we do this, then we are apt to ask important questions concerning our origins, how we are related to others, and the meaning of the various stages in our lives.

However, in anthropology the concern is more than just a preoccupation with ourselves; we also seek to understand people who live lives different from our own. As Clifford Geertz (1983: 5) has so eloquently phrased it, the task of anthropology is to "somehow understand how it is we understand understandings not our own." This curiosity about other societies goes back to the Middle Ages when travellers came back to

Figure 1.1: Cultural innovations may have unexpected rewards.

Europe with strange and, from our perspective today, ludicrous tales of people who had their feet on backwards, or had their faces on their chests. Of course much of this curiosity about other societies was based on an exploitive element—how to facilitate trade, acquire slaves, or save the souls of the heathen. It became obvious that other societies could be exploited more effectively when their internal characteristics and dynamics were better understood.

Later, when many of these societies began to die out because of European disease, overexploitation of natural resources, or outright slaughter, some intellectuals became interested in documenting these societies before they disappeared all together. For many years in the 1800s there was a flurry of research activity of the anthropometric variety—measuring skulls and other body parts—and in collecting the vanishing people's material culture—weapons, strange gods, and the like. These interests became supplanted in later years with an interest in kinship ties, family organization, leadership patterns, and religious life—what is today called *ethnographic research*. Of course the guiding theoretical orientation of this cultural collecting era was a strict adherence to a unilinear evolutionary frame of reference, which is to say that all cultures change along the same line of development. From this perspective there was no questioning that Europeans were the civilized peoples, while the others were primitive, or at least barbarians. In this context there was hardly any room for an objective view of the "other," or of cultures different from one's own.

■ The Fields of Anthropology

Anthropology today has evolved into a multifaceted discipline with a diversity of subcomponents or fields. The field of *physical* or *biological* anthropology is based on the fact that human beings are mammals and biological members of the animal kingdom. There are several important areas of study in this field and the research covered is quite diverse. We have previously mentioned paleontologists, for example, who are interested in the various stages of human evolution. Many people have heard about Louis Leakey and his skeletal discoveries in the Olduvai Gorge region of East Africa, and the australopithecine, "Lucy," supposedly the ancient progenitor of us all.

Primatologists recognize that humans are primates who are closely related to the other great apes such as chimpanzees, gorillas, and orangutans. All the members of this group in the hominid family share many common characteristics. In fact, humans and chimps share over 90 percent of the same DNA, and the blood of chimps is virtually the same as humans, attesting to our close ancestry. All primates have stereoscopic vision, which allows for depth perception, and see in colour, which is an important adaptive advantage in sorting out the variety of edible fruits that were an exclusive part of our diet in the past. We also have long arms, referred to as brachiaters, because we all swung in the trees at some point in the past, and our flexible hands all have five digits to facilitate grasping of tree limbs and other items.

The gestation period for primates is also relatively long, allowing for a more prolonged period of development than is common in other animals. There is also a long period of mother-child dependency in primates, which allows for the passing on of learning and skills. Most importantly, primates are gregarious creatures, meaning that they tend to rely on their social group for protection, support, and food sharing, although there are some relatively rare exceptions, such as the solitary orangutan.

Medical anthropology is a field of physical anthropology that combines biological, social, and cultural factors. It is an aspect of anthropology that studies health, nutrition, illness, and disease, and recognizes that in most cultures there is already an indigenous medical system of practices and beliefs. Medical anthropology, in recognition of indigenous beliefs, seeks not simply to impose Western scientific medicine on local peoples, but to synchronize the two in some manner that brings about effective results without simply usurping local health care with an external one.

The Canadian Association for Medical Anthropology was founded in 1982, and this field has grown steadily ever since. Much of this field concerns research on health-related issues, such as Shkilnyk's (1985) study of the effects of mercury pollution in the northern Ontario Ojibwa communities of White Dog and Grassy Narrows. There has also been research concerning Aboriginal treatment practices in a modern context, such as Turner's (1989) study of Inuit shamans and their healing performances, epidemiological perspectives (Waldram, Herring, and Young 1995), and Aboriginal spirituality and symbolic healing in Canadian prisons (Waldram 1997). These studies complement those conducted on health care in the central Subarctic (Young 1988), and the story of a Cree healer (Young, Ingram, and Swartz 1989). Speck's (1987) study, *An Error in Judgement*, is a focus on the politics of medical care in British Columbia. Anthropologists have also taken an active interest in food, diet, and nutrition (Hedican 1990c; Fiet 2004).

Szathmary, Ritenbaugh, and Goody (1987) studied the effects of dietary change on incidences of diabetes among Aboriginal peoples. Their focus was on a comparison of Athapaskan (or Dene) hunters of the Northwest Territories and more southern-based Aboriginal populations. They found that diabetes was more prominent among Aboriginal peoples in the larger, southern-based urban centres, where they consumed a diet heavy in low-cost carbohydrates. In the northern areas where Aboriginal peoples continued to practise traditional hunting and fishing, their diet was high in nutritious protein, with a low intake of carbohydrates, and consequently diabetes occurred much less frequently in these northern areas than in the south. These sorts of studies effectively illustrate the interaction of health and nutrition as these relate to wider social and economic community patterns.

Another example of Canadian medical anthropology focused on the study of mental health issues among Greek women in Montreal (Lock and Wakewich-Dunk 1990). The women in this study suffered from a condition that they referred to as "Nerva," which could not be diagnosed using conventional medical concepts. The Greek women complained of dizziness and chest pains, and related this illness to feelings of isolation or problems in their work. Lock and Wakewich-Dunk interpreted this condition as resulting from a confusion that the Greek women felt over their new role in Canada. The conclusion of this study is that mental health issues need to be placed in a social context in order to be more effectively understood.

Forensic anthropology is an exciting new field that combines aspects of physical anthropology, archaeology, and crime-scene investigation. Forensic anthropologists are specialists in the identification of human skeletal remains for legal and criminological purposes. Quite often the crime scenes that forensic anthropologists are asked to investigate are not new or recent ones. This involves the remains of peoples missing for some time, or those who have died as a result of accidents or murder many years before. Often the only

Box 1.1: Emoke J. Szathmary (1944–): Member of the Order of Canada (2003)

Emoke Szathmary was born in Hungary and earned a Ph.D. in biological anthropology in 1974 from the University of Toronto. Her research, which addressed the genetics of Aboriginal peoples in North America, focuses on type 2 diabetes, and the microevolution of Subarctic and Arctic populations. She was named distinguished lecturer by the American Anthropological Association in 1998, which is the highest recognition given by the anthropological discipline for a lifetime of exemplary service.

Dr. Szathmary has also received five honorary doctorates in recognition of her contributions to higher education and her research. She is an elected fellow of the Arctic Institute of North America (1989), the American Association for the Advancement of Science (1995), and the Royal Society of Canada (2005). In 2007 she was awarded the lieutenant governor's medal for excellence in public administration in Manitoba. In addition, she was made a member of the Order of Manitoba (2009) and the Order of Canada (2003).

Emoke Szathmary also has had a very extensive career in university administration. Her first administrative post was as chair of the Department of Anthropology at McMaster University, a position Szathmary left to become dean of the Faculty of Social Science at the University of Western Ontario. She was then named the tenth president and vice-chancellor of the University of Manitoba in 1996, a position she held until 2008. Prior to this she served as provost and vice-president (academic) at McMaster University in Hamilton, Ontario. In 2004, she was named one of Canada's top 100 most powerful women by the Women's Executive Network and the Richard Ivey School of Business (*Winnipeg Free Press*, 3 November 2009; www.utoronto.ca/alum-dev/profiles/emoke_szathmary).

Photo 1.1: St. Paul's High School honours past president and vice chancellor of the University of Manitoba, Emoke Szathmary, with a tribute dinner in 2009. (Source: Winnipeg Free Press, 3 November 2009)

materials left at the crime scene are the bones themselves, sometimes scattered by foraging animals. In such cases the anthropologist is asked to help identify the sex, age, and possible racial origins of the deceased person. Frequently the bones unearthed in such investigations also provide clues to a person's health and nutrition status, or the diseases or accidents that have been suffered during the victim's lifetime. This is the sort of valuable information that is not often available to police departments or medical examiners through the normal course of their criminal investigations.

Applied anthropology has a long history in Canada, although its organizational form did not emerge until the foundation of the Society of Applied Anthropology in Canada in 1981 (Hedican 2008; Ervin 2005, 2006a, 2006b). This field of study's central concern is applying anthropological knowledge to the understanding and possible solution of various human problems. An example of this sort of research involved assessing the impact of the flooding of northern Quebec rivers and the subsequent construction of dams on the Cree of northern Quebec (Salisbury 1986). Anthropologists and graduate students from McGill's Programme in the Anthropology of Development (PAD) worked with the Cree to assess possible impacts on their traditional hunting, fishing, and trapping. They also studied the effects of community relocation that the flooding would necessitate. The director of PAD, Richard Salisbury, also appeared as a witness on behalf of the Cree in their court appearance during the negotiations of the James Bay Agreement of 1975.

Another example of applied anthropology involves my own role as an intermediary between the Whitesand First Nation near Lake Nipigon in northern Ontario and the Department of Indian Affairs in Thunder Bay (Hedican 2008: 91–108). In this case I was asked by Indian Affairs as part of a research team from the Rural Development Outreach Project (RDOP) at the University of Guelph to help the Whitesand band to reach a decision in a land claims problem. The original reserve of the Whitesand people on Lake Nipigon had been flooded many years before, in the 1940s, and the band was negotiating with Indian Affairs for a new reserve. My own role was less of a researcher in this situation and more of an advocate of the Aboriginal people's position, which is trying to explain the concerns of the Whitesand band to Indian Affairs and their consultants. At times I therefore also acted in an intermediary role between the conflicting parties in this situation. The lesson that I learned from this experience is that anthropologists can become involved in situations that are confusing in terms of the role or roles that they are expected to play. This is especially true with research that is in the applied area and not of the conventional variety.

Archaeology in anthropology is another significant sub-field. Its goals are not so much the retrieval of material culture from the past, but to understand the adaptive patterns and environmental adjustments of past societies. An archaeological investigation is conducted in a rigorous scientific procedure. Great care is taken to document the exact location of artifacts, both spatially at the once-living floor, and also in terms of the soil depth as well, using the principle of *stratigraphy*. The goal is to reconstruct the location of artifacts back at the archaeology lab, hence the precision in the excavation techniques employed during the investigation. In Canada a vast grid is employed that covers the whole country, so that the geographical location of artifacts can be identified with a high degree of accuracy. Various scientific techniques for dating artifacts are also employed, such as the Carbon-14 method, which determines a date when a once-living organism was alive using the principle of radioactive degradation (the half-life principle). Most archaeological investigations in Canada concern the Aboriginal inhabitants, tracing their lives from the period of big-game hunting during the *Paleolithic* period just after the end of the last ice age (about 10,000 years ago), through to the so-called *Archaic* period, and then through the *Woodland* period, when the Iroquoian peoples in southern Ontario began to domesticate their own crops.

Anthropologists are also interested in the study of human languages, or *linguistics*, because the methods of verbal and written communication are such an important aspect of human social life—we would hardly be human without some form of linguistic communication. The study of anthropological linguistics basically entails two primary areas. The first of these is *descriptive linguistics*, which concerns the way languages are put together in terms of their sound units and grammatical structures. *Phonology* comprises the basic sound units in a language, not to be confused with the letters of an alphabet. The sound /*ch*/, for example is a *phoneme*, yet comprises two letters in the English language.

For the most part, human languages utilize a very limited number of basic sounds, or phonemes, usually about 25 or so, which is amazing considering the complexity of human speech. In all languages, phonemes—basic units of sound—are put together into more complex patterns of meaning, called *morphemes*, of which our use of the term "word" is a rough approximation. *Syntax* refers to the grammatical rules that are employed in all languages for correct speech. Anthropologists feel that syntax becomes embedded in our brains as we learn a language during our developmental stages to form a deep structure. This might account for the fact that we are usually aware immediately when a basic rule of syntax is broken in our language without being able to identify the precise grammatical rule that is broken. For example, if someone tells you that "John and Mary to the movies went," we intuitively know that there is something wrong here, but may not be sure exactly what.

Historical linguistics is the second major area of language study that focuses mainly on the manner in which languages change—in other words, it is primarily comparative in terms of its orientation. *Philology* is one such area of study. Few people realize that the Grimms brothers of fairytale fame actually collected their European stories so that they could try to find out if there were regularities in the way languages change. In the process of these studies, they formulated the *Law of Phonetic Change*, which is a basis for the idea that all human languages change in regular, predictable patterns rather than in accidental or haphazard ways. For example, *brother, bruder, frater*, and *brat* are all *cognates* of one another because they are descended from the same source, *bhrata* in Sanscrit, the original language of the Indo-European language family. It was also discovered that when words in Latin were incorporated into the Germanic languages, a whole series of regularities are evident, such as /*p*/ changing to /*f*/, or /*t*/ to /*th*/, hence *pater* becomes "father."

Later, in the 1950s, linguists also discovered that they could date with precision the times when languages separated from one another using the technique of *lexico-statistical* dating, or *glottochronology* as it is also sometimes called. Using this method of historical linguistics it was discovered that the Navajo of the southwestern United States are actually Dene or Athapaskan speakers who migrated southward from the Great Slave Lake area about 800 years ago.

Anthropologists often find that they have to learn a new language in order to conduct their research. Frequently this involves a non-written language so that preparation beforehand is not always practical—one learns the language during the course of one's research by being immersed in the language. As an example of what is involved for the anthropologist, I conducted a study of an Ojibwa, or *Anishenabe* as they call themselves, community called Collins, which is about 30 kms west of the Whitesand band discussed before in northwestern Ontario (Hedican 1986a, 2001a, 2001b). Collins is situated in the bush about 300 kms north of Thunder Bay. At the time of my research, the people lived in log cabins heated by wood stoves, did not drive cars or trucks, and hunted and fished for their food.

There was some English spoken in the community, but for the most part everyday conversations were in their Aboriginal language of Ojibwa, one of the Algonquian languages. I was lucky to find a dictionary with rules of grammar, published in the 1800s, although it was still relevant for my purposes (Wilson 1874). Each morning a young man in the community visited me in my cabin to teach me pronunciation, go over vocabulary, and instruct me in short phrases. I also kept a list of words that I had heard used in conversation by people in the community, and studied these before my instructor arrived. What I found interesting were the words the Ojibwa residents used for things that were new to their culture. For example, their word for "train" is *shkoote-tabaun*, which literally means "fire-sled." *Tabaun* is their word for "toboggan," so I imagined the early coal-burning locomotives shooting out a stream of smoke and sparks as they chugged down the railway tracks.

At one time I also heard the word *kokoosh*, which was their name for "pork," and this made me realize that they had borrowed the French word *cochon* because this was not an item originally in their culture. I also heard them used the term *kitchi-mokauman*, which literally means "long knives," for Americans and was puzzled how this usage had filtered up into northern Ontario since I was sure that they had never seen a Western movie. It was also interesting that the Ojibwa divide all of their nouns, not in classes of male and female as the French do, but into two groups as to whether the noun refers to an object that is alive or in motion (animate), or not moving (inanimate). They also have the habit of forming noun and verbal structures together to produce long phrases, such as *kaween anishenabemose*. *Kaween* indicates a negative, ending with *se*, like *ne pas* in French. *Anishenabe* means Ojibwa or "the people," and *mo* is first-person singular for "speak." These are the sorts of linguistic matters that many anthropologists have to learn while they are conducting their research.

The fourth major field of anthropology is social (or cultural) anthropology. While many texts use the term *social anthropology*, some use *cultural anthropology*, while others combine the two into *socio-cultural* anthropology. The reason for this diversified terminology is that in Britain anthropology evolved as an offshoot of sociology, where for a time it was referred to as comparative sociology and, later, social anthropology. In this context the division of academic labour was that social anthropology studied other cultures, and sociology focused on modern, mostly urban society. Anthropology's intellectual roots in Britain therefore can be traced to such prominent sociologists of the late nineteenth and early twentieth centuries as Emile Durkheim and Max Weber.

There is a stronger preference for the term "cultural anthropology" in America because in this case, anthropology emerged more out of a museum and, later, a university setting not directly tied to sociology. The term "cultural anthropology" also reflects an American emphasis on the concept of culture, with an emphasis on learned behaviour, while in Britain more importance has traditionally been placed on the study of social structure and organization. However, most anthropologists today see the concepts of culture and social structure as equally important, such that the terms "cultural anthropology" and "social anthropology" are often used interchangeably. As Barrett (1996: 9) explains: "Many prominent anthropologists ... see little purpose in separating social and cultural anthropology ... [They] use the terms social and cultural anthropology interchangeably, or simply socio-cultural."

■ Ethnography and Fieldwork

The data-gathering stage of social anthropology is referred to as *ethnography*, which is a basic description of a particular culture. The person conducting such a study is known as an *ethnographer*. An ethnographer could be considered a cross-cultural translator, one who interprets different ideas and customs in a familiar language. Usually the ethnographer spends a fairly long period of time, often a year or so, living with a group of people whom he or she can get to know on a first-hand basis. This research stage is called *fieldwork* and the people who provide information in field studies are referred to as *informants*. Fieldwork usually involves participating where possible in local activities, observing behaviour, or interviewing people who are knowledgeable in certain areas important to the ethnographer's area of interest. It is important to indicate, however, that ethnographic settings can exhibit great variety, from a small jungle village in a remote part of South America, to drug use in New York City slums.

Ethnographic fieldwork can therefore be considered a type of *inductive* method of inquiry in that general inferences are made from particular instances. A *deductive* approach is more common in disciplines such as sociology, in which the investigator initially proposes a hypothesis about a certain situation and then proceeds to test the hypothesis to find out if it is valid. While ethnography is largely descriptive in nature, social anthropologists often engage in *cross-cultural comparisons* whereby certain traits in one society are compared with comparable traits in another. *Ethnology* is the term applied to this comparative work, which is often aimed at arriving at generalizations or theory building. The goal of ethnology is to find out about the similarities and differences among cultures to gain a better understanding of the wider commonalities of human behaviour.

Figure 1.2: Social anthropologists conducting ethnographic fieldwork attempt to conduct themselves in the role of objective observers, but sometimes personal bias may creep in.

■ The Culture Concept

The *concept of culture* has played a major role throughout the history of the discipline. Although the concept of culture has been defined in various ways—Kroeber and Kluckhohn (1952), for example, claimed to have found more than 500 phrasings and uses of the culture concept—many anthropologists today would still agree with one of the original definitions formulated by nineteenth-century British anthropologist Sir Edward Tylor. In *Primitive Culture* Tylor indicated that culture can be regarded as "that complex whole which includes knowledge, belief, art, law, morals, custom and any other capabilities and habits acquired by man as a member of society" (1871: 1). My own working definition of culture does not depart in any significant way from that espoused

---

Box 1.2: Amazon Journey: Fieldwork among the Mekranoti of Brazil

The Mekranoti live in a heavily forested region of the Amazon jungle. Like many of their neighbours in this region, they grow a variety of crops, such as sweet potatoes, corn, and pumpkin, using the slash-and-burn horticulture technique. The planting and maintenance of the crops are tasks performed by the women, while men engage in hunting the pig-like peccaries, monkeys, and the occasional jaguar. While relatively peaceful themselves, the Mekranoti appear to live in constant fear of attack from warlike tribes roaming the jungle. A feeling of camaraderie among the men is enhanced by their separate sleeping quarters in a men's house, away from the women and children. Villages are moved frequently because of the depletion of soil fertility and the apparent threat of attack.

An anthropologist conducting fieldwork under these conditions has many difficulties to overcome. One of the main problems is the isolation caused by the difficulty of learning the Mekranoti's language. There are also feelings of claustrophobia because one's view is almost always blocked out by the forest cover, the dangers of being stung by scorpions, and the ever-present threat of attack by hostile neighbours. However, as time goes on over the succeeding months, the fieldworker begins to adjust to the local conditions. Kinship studies are begun and the language is learned slowly through vocabulary lessons given by an agreeable informant. In addition, the physical threat of attack is minimized when it is learned that the most feared of the Mekranoti's neighbours had mostly died out from a smallpox epidemic.

Dennis Werner ends his ethnography of the Mekranoti with this insightful view of anthropological fieldwork:

> Probably most anthropologists feel as ambivalent as I do about their jobs, caught between orderly caution and romantic abandon; between scientific rigor and human empathy. It may be this ambivalence is what attracts us to the profession. Few fields accommodate so easily our wavering spirits. (1990: 196)

Fieldwork in anthropology is probably the most challenging endeavour in the social sciences. This is not just because of the practical problems of food and shelter, learning a strange language, and adapting at times to inscrutable customs, but because of the isolation and "culture shock" that comes with adapting to another way of life away from the anthropologist's familiar world.

---

by Tylor, which is to say that culture can be seen as the set of learned values, behaviours, and beliefs characteristic of a particular society.

An emphasis on *learned behaviour* is a key element of the culture concept. Anthropologists today do not generally believe that most behaviour is biologically determined, although there is a strong emphasis on the physical components of behaviour among *socio-biologists*, who believe that many aspects of human behaviour can be explained by basic physical and genetic processes, as opposed to learned behaviour. The so-called nature versus nurture controversy was played out years ago, such that the nurture or learning aspects of human life are considered far more of a factor in accounting for the behaviour of human beings than their biological impulses. As such, for the most part, studies in anthropology today suggest that human behaviour is primarily a learned phenomenon. Through the process called *enculturation* people learn as they grow up from the cultural traditions, knowledge, and skills that are passed on from generation to generation. The enculturative process provides a valuable adaptive advantage for humans, especially in problem solving, since successful solutions can be incorporated into the fabric of a culture, and less useful traits phased out. This essentially means that better ways of doing things can be accumulated, rather than invented anew with each successive generation.

This idea of culture allowing for the recycling of more adaptive ideas, and relinquishing those that do not work as well, suggests that the changing aspects of culture are significant characteristics as well. Studies in anthropology demonstrate than there are no stagnant cultures and that all cultures are in a constant state of transition, although it is recognized that culture change occurs more rapidly in some societies than others, or in certain time periods of the same society. Cultures change because of two intermingling processes. Change results, on the one hand, from the internal dynamics of invention and innovation as new ideas are internally generated and spread throughout a culture. Another process accounting for culture change involves contact with other societies, or *culture borrowing*, as new ideas and ways of doing things diffuse from one society to another. The process of *diffusion*, however, is usually a selective one as most people more readily borrow such things as new tools and technology, which may make their lives easier, but are more resistant to borrowing items that could fundamentally change their core system of beliefs or world view.

Acculturation is a term that is applied to situations of culture contact on a first-hand basis between societies that are quite different from one another in size, power, and influence. A certain amount of coercion or force is often applied to the smaller, less powerful society to accept the ways of the more dominant one. A situation of forceful culture change was a prominent pattern of interaction between Canada's indigenous populations and the Europeans who colonized the country. In the early part of Canada's history the Hudson's Bay Company was responsible for massive changes in the economic practices of (mainly) northern First Nations who underwent a transformation from subsistence hunting and fishing to a commercial integration into the fur-trapping economy. Aboriginal peoples, though, were not hapless victims of the fur trade. They did receive valuable items through the trading process, such as copper pots, steel traps, guns, blankets, and other items, which helped their life in the northern bush. Aboriginal trappers were also able at times to successfully negotiate terms of the trade favourable to them, especially during periods of competition, such as occurred between the rival Hudson's Bay Company and the North West Company in the early 1800s.

In many other areas of this *assimilation process* the results were very detrimental to Aboriginal populations, such as the missionary work that undermined traditional religious beliefs and the authority of First Nation elders. The residential school system was one of the most destructive of these coercive assimilative changes as Aboriginal children were removed from their homes, often by forceful means, and placed in an institutional structure that separated them from their parents and elders, forbade them from using their Native language, and at times subjected such children to sexual and physical abuse. From these examples we can see that culture change is a multifaceted phenomenon that involves internal dynamics of change, as well as those that result from the borrowing or diffusion of cultural elements from one society to another, or the forced change of acculturation that results when a dominant society uses coercion to manipulate the culture change of the less powerful one. This sort of situation could be called *internal colonialism*, which occurs when minority groups within a nation-state are subjected to intense pressure to conform to the norms and values held by the members of the dominant society.

The sorts of problems of culture contact, such as those just described involving force-ful assimilation and colonialism, often result when the members of one society regard themselves as superior in some manner to other societies, and consequently attempt to force their beliefs and attitudes on the members other societies so that the other people will change their ideas, beliefs, behaviour, and cultural practices. The notion of superior-ity that is integral to these attitudes is what is referred to as *ethnocentrism*. Ethnocentrism is a belief that one's own culture is superior in some fundamental sense to that of another culture or group of cultures. It essentially involves viewing another culture only through the lens of one's particular cultural vantage point, resulting usually in a distortion of interpretation or misjudgment of the cultural practices of other people. Ethnocentrism also provides a moral basis for regarding some cultures as inferior to one's own, and thereby treating the members of these cultures unfairly, or in ways that advantage the members of a dominant group.

A further distinction of importance concerns the difference between culture and soci-ety. If we regard a culture as the sum total of learned behaviour traits characteristic of the members of a society, then does that mean that society and culture represent the same thing? The answer is sometimes, but not always. A *society* can be defined as an aggrega-tion of human beings, i.e., a population, living as a distinct entity in a fairly well-defined territory and possessing social, economic, and political institutions that unite them in some larger sphere, such as a nation. Thus, we can refer to Canadian society, but this society comprises a diversity of different cultures, such as various Aboriginal cultures, French Canadian culture, or the Hutterite culture in Alberta, to name a few. In the Canadian case, then, the term "society" encompasses a much larger scope of population than does any one particular culture.

In some other situations, a culture may be spread across the borders of particular nations, such as the Kurdish culture, situated in Iraq and Turkey. Or a nation may be comprised of several virtually separate societies such as existed in the former country of Yugoslavia with the Serbs, Croatians, and Bosnians. Alternatively, the cultures of North and South Korea are not significantly different from one another yet, because of political reasons, inhabit two separate nations. In Canada, Aboriginal First Nations wish to have their nationhood

Figure 1.3: Attempts to change religious and cultural beliefs of people in another society are not always successful.

recognized along with their rights to self-determination within the Canadian state. All in all, the terms "culture," "society," and "nation" can be quite separate entities.

Box 1.3: The Yanomamo and the Culture of Violence

The concept of culture in anthropology, with its emphasis on learned behaviour and adaptation, would seem to suggest that most societies are fundamentally the same. There are no doubt many cross-cultural similarities around the world, but there is also a very wide range of habits, customs, norms, and values. The Yanomamo, who live in southern Venezuela and adjacent portions of northern Brazil, illustrate some of the extremes of human behaviour, especially in their preoccupation with warfare and interpersonal violence.

From most outward appearances, the Yanomamo live a conventional village life in the jungle habitat of South America. They clear the forest using the swidden or slash-and-burn horticultural technique, and grow crops of bananas and manioc in small garden plots. They also engage in an elaborate system of marriage involving brother-sister exchange such that kinship groups become interdependent pairs of woman-exchanging kin groups. However, despite these apparent cultural regularities, the Yanomamo also engage in forms of violence in a graded series of aggressive activities. This behaviour ranges from inter-village raiding parties, chest-pounding duels, and club fights in which contestants try to hit each other on the head with long poles, resulting in lacerated skulls and broken fingers.

The plight of women among the Yanomamo is particularly hazardous. If a man and his wife are caught in the forest by an enemy group on a raiding party, the wife is apt to be abducted and her husband killed. The captured woman is then raped by all the men in the raiding party, and possibly also by the men in the village. Even within her own village, a woman may be subjected to physical violence. In one instance, a wife was punished by her husband, who cut off both her ears with his machete. As anthropologist Napoleon Chagnon indicates, "I describe the Yanomamo as 'the fierce people' because that is the most accurate single phrase that describes them. That is how they conceive themselves to be, and is how they would like others to think of them" (1968: 1). As such, one of the challenges of social anthropology is placing such societies as the Yanomamo in the wider context of human behaviour in which there are also many societies of a more peaceful nature.

Another important term, along with "society," is that of *social structure*, by which we mean the ways in which groups and individuals are organized and relate to one another. Social structure is commonly seen as the social relations that hold groups together, such as family and kinship, political organization, law, and economic activities. However, the term "social structure" is somewhat ambiguous. As Barrett (1996: 8–9) explains, "What is the difference between social structure and society, between social structure and social organization? Is social structure a real thing? Is it concrete or merely an abstraction? In other words, is there a social structure out there to discover, or does the investigator simply impose a structure on the data in order to simplify chaos?"

British social anthropologist Edmund Leach (1982: 237) attempted to provide some degree of clarification on the concept of social structure by acknowledging that social structure is an "expression used by social and cultural anthropologists in a variety of senses.... The society as a whole is envisaged as a kind of organism in which the various institutions are articulated together to form a functioning whole. The social structure is the persisting framework of such a self-perpetuating system. An approximate analogy is that the relationship between the social structure and the society as a whole is comparable to the relationship between the bony skeleton of a living mammal and its total bodily form." However, Barrett (1996: 9) also explains that the concept of social structure in British social anthropology has lost ground because of a renewed interest in cultural studies, especially in America, and a "switch in emphasis from social structure to 'meaning,'" which began to take place in the mid-1980s.

◼ Cultural Relativism

In social anthropology it is recognized that most people of the world regard their own culture as superior in some way to others; that they take pride in their own beliefs and traditions; and, because of their individual acculturative processes, find it difficult to view other cultures on their own terms or in an objective sense. If anthropologists, however, were to adopt only ethnocentric points of view, then cross-cultural understanding would be entirely impossible. In order to counteract these non-productive attitudes, and to promote understanding across cultural boundaries, anthropologists have adopted the concept of *cultural relativism*. Cultural relativism means that a society's customs and ideas should be understood in the context of that society's problems and opportunities, culture, and environment.

The philosophy of cultural relativism can therefore be thought of as an intellectual antidote to ethnocentrism. Cultural relativism encourages an objective, inside view of other cultures, something that is referred to as an *emic* perspective in anthropology, in contrast to an *etic* or outside point of view. It is important to point out that, despite its merits, cultural relativism as a guiding principle in anthropological research is not without its difficulties. There is a considerable debate in anthropology today concerning the continued usefulness of cultural relativism, especially as it concerns this concept's role as a main philosophical underpinning of social anthropological research (see, for example, Zechenter 1997).

There is no doubt that cultural differences are central to the curiosity that anthropologists hold concerning other peoples. This curiosity is founded to a large degree on a tolerance of these cultural differences and, even more, on an attitude that various cultural patterns have an intrinsic worth in their own right. On the other hand it is unavoidable that anthropologists, because they are human beings with their own individualistic acculturative tendencies, are apt to make ethical judgments concerning different sorts of cultural patterns. Certain topics, such as poverty, sexual abuse, or discrimination, for example, could be seen as a fundamental detriment to humans' well-being and therefore pre-empt an objective point of view. It would be difficult, if not impossible, to conduct an anthropological study of genocide while at the same time maintaining that this phenomenon should be accorded the same relativistic status as, say, a belief in a polytheistic universe. The two situations are not just comparable, either ethically, morally, or culturally.

Box 1.4: Genital Mutilation: The Relativist Dilemma

The concept of cultural relativism holds that each culture must be evaluated in its own terms, and not in terms of the standards and values of the anthropologist's own society. Given this axiom, a question arises as to whether or not anthropologists should accept all cultural practices in other societies on an equal basis, or if one's perspectives should be guided by a higher principle such as a universal standard of human rights. The cultural practice of female genital mutilation challenges the anthropological concept of cultural relativism because a powerless group in society—young females—are forced to submit to a painful physical operation in which they are hardly able to exercise their right to object.

There is probably no other cultural practice that has caused greater outrage among feminists, social activists, or even the general public at large than female circumcision. This operation involves the removal of a female's external genitalia. It can be as drastic as excising the entire clitoris, known as clitoridectomy, or the removal of the labia. In such an operation, the cut tissue can be stitched with thorns or other material, leaving only a small opening.

Such practices as genital mutilation are widespread in Africa, with both Islamic and Christian countries allowing this operation. Incidences of this practice are found in Middle Eastern and Far Eastern Islamic nations, such as Indonesia and Malaysia, as well as in over 30 other countries. Possibly as many as 130 million women have undergone some form of female genital operation around the world.

The justification for continuing such a practice may vary from country to country. However, generally speaking, an explanation is often offered that it is part of a long cultural tradition that should continue into the future. In some countries a woman's role as mother or wife can be linked to such practices, since a man may refuse to marry a woman who has not undergone such an operation. Religious beliefs may also be cited as justification for this practice, although there have been differences of opinion among Islamic scholars regarding a belief that the Prophet Mohammed commanded such a practice.

Attempts to abolish the practice of female genital mutilation have been met with only limited success. The World Health Organization and UNICEF have attempted to pressure various governments to ban this practice, and a few African governments have complied with this request. Both Canada and the United States have granted political asylum for women who might face this procedure if returned to their homeland. In Canada, the practice of female genital mutilation is illegal; however, as more and more immigrants enter this country from societies where this practice is common, medical and judicial officials are faced with a dilemma. Should medical operations be performed in Canada where safe facilities can be provided, or should a compromise be considered that takes into consideration human rights? As far as anthropology is concerned, there is a professional dilemma in this discipline as well. One of the most fundamental principles of anthropology concerns an attitude of cultural relativism. Given this axiom, should such practices as genital mutilation be acknowledged or accepted as a valid cultural tradition, or should it be considered as a violation of universal human rights? Daly (2000), for example, accuses anthropologists of ignoring this ritual and attempting to remain neutral because of a mistaken attempt to avoid cultural judgments.

What this situation suggests is there is a continuum in the application of the cultural relativism concept when it comes to such issues as human rights. Anthropological research can be at the hub of such difficulties when such research might leave open the possibility of even greater exploitation of indigenous populations than might have existed previous to the research. There are those who might ask if there is any real possibility for a truly neutral or objective research agenda. If this is the case, then maybe anthropologists should abandon their long-held relativistic stance and embrace the idea of promoting certain cultural changes and discouraging others. This would mean an entirely different sort of anthropology than what presently exists, one with a social conscience, or even a political agenda. As Barak (1988: 101) expressed the issue: "the self-determination and emancipation of anthropology's subject peoples is as much (if not more) contingent upon the recognition of their common experiences as of their differences."

Organizations such as the World Council of Indigenous People, which has a very strong presence among the Canadian Aboriginal population (see Manuel and Posluns 1974), have been founded as much on the commonalities of their shared colonial experience than on their members' recognition of their cultural differences. These shared commonalities of experience are also largely responsible for a more resurgent and politically active Aboriginal response to colonial pressures. For anthropologists who become involved in this struggle against colonial pressures, or at least act as sympathetic bystanders, this sort of advocacy role becomes problematic in a relativistic context if anthropology espouses a neutral observer position.

Even for those anthropologists who do not conduct their research in the contemporary Aboriginal scene, such as those involved in *ethnohistorical* studies, the concept of cultural relativism poses a problem. McGill anthropologist Bruce Trigger (1986), who has conducted extensive research on the Huron of southern Ontario, coined the term *historical relativism* in recognition of the idea that past cultures should be understood in the context of particular historical time periods, and should be studied in a holistic manner.

A *holistic perspective* is an important component of anthropological research, whether conducted in contemporary or past societies. This fundamental principle of social anthropology recognizes that all cultural institutions, whether these institutions are economic, religious, or political, relate to one another in an overall system of behaviour and institutions. As such, a holistic approach engenders a culturally relativistic orientation because it encourages a fuller appreciation of the complexities of Aboriginal societies, especially in terms of how the various actions, beliefs, and cultural practices relate to one another.

Such a perspective, from the distance of many centuries, as is the case with Trigger's studies of the Huron, however, poses even greater difficulties than if a more contemporary society was the focus of study. Not only is the seventeenth-century Huron cultural and social behaviour difficult to understand because of the great time gap, there is the problem of the limited and culturally biased, documentary evidence provided by *The Jesuit Relations*, which were the various reports and letters that were documented at the time. In other words, not only does it take an immense historical effort to attempt an explanation of behaviour separated by several centuries from contemporary Euro-Canadian culture, there is also the difficulty of trying to understand the Jesuits as well.

As Trigger explains, "I found that trying to understand the mentality of seventeenth-century Jesuit missionaries required almost as great an act of anthropological imagination as did understanding the perceptions of the Huron of that period" (1986: 67).

Despite these challenges, the concept of cultural relativism nonetheless continues to have a great influence on the conduct of anthropological research, both in historical and contemporary contexts. The wider issue that cultural relativism raises is that we continually need to be reminded that anthropology ultimately is involved in the search for the source and nature of knowledge. Anthropologists are not just the collectors of cultural facts. They are also interpreters of the reality in which they exist, and this question of existence—or, one might say more precisely, the interpretation of existence—is a core facet of what the work of anthropology is all about.

■ Multiculturalism in Canada

As far as the practice of anthropology in Canada is concerned, the concept of cultural relativism provides a useful context for understanding Canada's official *policy of multiculturalism* (Fleras and Elliot 2002; Turner 1993). The Canadian government passed the Multiculturalism Act in 1988, making it the first country to adopt multiculturalism as an official policy. Under this policy, cultural groups in Canada such as Italians, East Indians, or First Nations peoples do not have to abandon their cultural identities. The policy of multiculturalism as a fundamental ideology promotes cultural pluralism, tends to counteract processes that lead to a homogeneous world culture, and rejects bigotry and racism. It therefore allows for more than one culture to exist in a society, allows for the social and political interaction of people with different ways of living, and promotes respect for the cultural traditions of other peoples.

Canadians are justifiably proud that they have not tried to force all ethnic and cultural groups in the country into a common mould, into a large melting pot, in which everyone ends up the same. We value cultural differences, and across Canada there are many celebrations attesting to this view, from Kitchener's Oktoberfest, to Toronto's annual Aboriginal powwow at the Rogers Centre. Does this mean that Canada is a more tolerant nation than most others? According to Barrett's study of racism and the right wing, entitled *Is God a Racist?*, he concludes that "Canada is unexceptional in both its right-wing tendencies and its tolerance. The organized right wing is substantial, but not out of proportion with that in other countries; nor is the radical right's racist thrust incompatible with the nation's wider setting and institutions" (1987: 355).

What we might summarize from such a statement is that Canadians should reflect on what they think their country is about, and what it is *really* like, in the face of persistent racial and cultural intolerance (Hier 2000) and in recognition of the "sameness of all humanity" (Argyrou 1999). There are some deep questions about how Canadian society is perceived by its inhabitants. For example, what is the reality of life for people of colour in Canada? Is Canada an ideal model on which to construct a more equitable country?

Box 1.5: Multiculturalism in Other Countries

In Canada a policy of multiculturalism stems from Canadians' desire to recognize the special rights of the three founding peoples—Aboriginal First Nations, English, and French—while at the same time respecting the distinctive cultural traditions of more recent immigrants to this country. In other parts of the world, attaining cultural pluralism and tolerance has been a difficult goal to achieve, especially when religious values clash. Sectarian violence, for example, has long been a part of Irish history because of the apparently irreconcilable differences between Catholics and Protestants, or in Iraq, where conflicts between Sunni and Shiite Muslims are at the root of much social and political strife.

Cultural pluralism and multi-ethnic tolerance, however, can be found in various parts of the world. In Belgium the Flemish and French Walloons have their own cultural heritages, yet live in peaceful coexistence. The same can be said of Switzerland, where German, Italian, and French cultures exist close to one another in relative harmony. In both these countries pluralism and tolerance would appear to stem from the fact that even though the members of these diverse cultural groups speak different languages, they nonetheless have a common European cultural heritage.

This would suggest that cultural pluralism tends to have a greater chance of success when the various cultural traditions are less divergent from one another. It is also worth recognizing that even within state structures, distinctive groups have rights, at least according to the United Nations' Covenant of Human Rights, passed in 1966, which states, in part, that "In those states in which ethnic, religious or linguistic minorities exist, persons belonging to such minorities shall not be denied the rights, in community with other members of their group, to enjoy their own culture, to profess and practice their own religion or to use their own language" (quoted in Bodley 1990: 99). As such anthropologists have an opportunity to support such laudable goals by working with indigenous groups to help protect their cultural rights and to speak out against the injustice and suppression of ethnic minorities that may be encountered during the course of their research.

In historical terms, we should not forget that an unentrenched Bill of Rights was not adopted in Canada until 1960, and that the current Charter of Rights and Freedoms was enacted only in 1982, more than 150 years after the U.S. version. In addition, Aboriginal peoples (with Indian status) were not allowed to vote in federal Canadian elections until the 1960s. The original British North America Act of 1867 actually made no specific mention of human rights, aside from provisions to protect the English and French languages, and did not recognize Aboriginal rights at all. The Indian Act, passed in 1876, is primarily a restrictive and coercive piece of legislation rather than an emancipatory one, prompting Kallen to comment that "Among the most pernicious pieces of legislation was the Indian Act, whereby Indians were virtually denied all of the fundamental rights" (1982: 43).

Photo 1.2: Celebrating a tea dance at Treaty time, Battleford, Saskatchewan. (Source: University of Saskatchewan Library, c. 1880–1900)

One would think that anthropologists would be forerunners in providing informed commentary on Canada's multiculturalism policy. After all, anthropologists are supposed to be the experts on matters pertaining to culture, and there are many who believe that the *raison d'être* of the discipline is to grapple with cultural issues. Yet, "what culture consists of is something that has troubled the social sciences, particularly scholars working in anthropology, for more than a century" (Beck 1980: 10). This is not to suggest that anthropology has failed as a discipline because it has not provided the definitive voice on the concept of culture and Canada's multicultural policy, but to indicate that the social sciences, and anthropology in particular, need to engage more actively in a discussion of social issues in the country.

■ Ethics of Research

An issue that has become extremely important within the discipline of social anthropology itself concerns the *ethics of research*. In recent years there has been an increased concern with the ethical aspects of research that involves living human beings who could be detrimentally impacted by the research of anthropologists. As a result, researchers have become more concerned with the rights of individuals to their privacy (Hedican 2008: 34–38; Warry 1998: 150). In several ways anthropologists' interest in the ethical considerations of people who are participating in their studies is similar to that of issues found in journalism because "we go to the informed source and offer confidentiality and accuracy in exchange for information and the consent to use it" (Price 1987: 36).

The Society of Applied Anthropology in Canada (SAAC) formulated a code of ethics in the mid-1980s in an attempt to deal with issues of confidentiality and informed consent of research subjects. *Informed consent* is a principle that requires researchers collecting information to inform the participants of research about the intentions of the research project and possible risks and effects that such participation could involve. This principle also requires that the researcher make every effort to protect the anonymity of the people in the study unless permission is otherwise granted by the subjects to reveal their identities (Fluehr-Lobban 1994).

Obtaining informed consent can be a difficult practical matter in anthropological research because much of the research takes place among people who speak a language different from that of the ethnographer and are probably not familiar with what is being asked of them. Many people in other cultures have probably never heard of anthropology, and while they may have some familiarity with answering questions for government officials or health care workers in their home area, they may not be aware that they have a right to refuse to give information or have the right to not participate in the research in the first place. Obviously it would be a breach of research ethics if the researcher applied coercive threats or other measures to obtain information in such areas of the world where such threats are customarily applied to force people to tell certain things that they might not otherwise divulge to strangers. There are also problems of translation here when attempts are made to explain in a language that does not have analogous terms for "research," "informants," or "social science."

An important ethical issue in anthropology therefore arises from the fact that much ethnographic research takes place in cross-cultural settings in which the subjects or participants of this research are apt to be unclear about or unaware of factors pertaining to their involvement as information givers. Such factors that might need to be explained could involve the ethnographer's reasons for conducting the research, and the responsibilities that the researcher could have toward his or her sponsors, such as granting agencies, with regard to the publication of reports. There is also the possibility that personal conflicts could arise between researchers and their informants. There is the potential here for serious ethical problems to occur during fieldwork, which could become aggravated because the researcher frequently becomes closely involved in a community as a result of the long-term nature of the research. As such, researchers in anthropology, often conducting research in distant places and working in cultures where values and behaviour differ significantly from that of their own society, could face more severe ethical dilemmas than are encountered by researchers in other social sciences.

This all means that contemporary anthropology, as far as the ethics of research are concerned, faces far greater scrutiny today than at any other time in the past. This scrutiny is apt to begin even before the ethnographer begins fieldwork—it can begin when the initial grant proposal is originally submitted to a funding agency. Most of the time grant proposals are subject to a lengthy review process in which competent scholars both inside, and even possibly outside, one's discipline assess the merits of scholarly research. This assessment process is evaluated on the potential of the research to generate new knowledge in a particular field of study, but also as to the potential practical difficulties that could be encountered along the way.

It is possible, for example, that anthropologists might wish to conduct research in an area that would endanger themselves or the subjects involved because of conflicts between warring factions, drug trade activities, or other such issues. The research might not be funded because of these dangerous aspects of the research milieu even though the scholarly merits of the research might in themselves be sound.

It is also very common today for research proposals to be examined by university ethics committees. Such committees are increasingly interested in the extent to which a researcher is able to obtain consent, usually in writing, from the local people involved in the research. As far as anthropology is concerned, obtaining this sort of written consent may pose a problem because people may feel that they could be placed in compromising situations when signing written documents, aside from the practical matter of translating the document into an idiom that makes sense in the local language. This is all compounded by problems of accessibility—a researcher is probably not able to just hop on a plane, travel to a remote place many thousands of miles away, obtain the necessary written permission to satisfy a university ethics committee, and then return home.

Another ethical issue concerns the possibility that untrained individuals could pose as qualified researchers. This is a serious issue for anthropology because it could undermine the credibility of the discipline. As a result of the potential danger in such situations, and in an attempt to prevent the unscrupulous use of anthropological studies, some anthropologists are attempting to protect themselves. One suggestion is to require practising anthropologists to become certified in some manner so that they become linked with a parent professional organization. This was proposed several years ago during the annual meeting of the parent organization, the Canadian Anthropology Society, in which a draft paper was circulated, entitled "Towards the Certification of Canadian Anthropologists" (Tremblay, Freeman, and Ervin 1990). This document explains that there is a concern with "recent examples of unqualified or unethical individuals making claims of possessing anthropological expertise in their practice as consultants or expert witnesses. Protection of the public, the reputation of the discipline and the employment opportunities of properly qualified practicing anthropologists were all considered at issue" (1990: 1).

With all of these efforts to acquire informed consent, to protect a subject's identity throughout the different phases of a research project, and to protect the reputation of anthropologists, research subjects could now be considered equal partners in the research process. This implies that research subjects should also have access to the results of the research project, which may involve royalty payments for books or other publications. Research subjects should therefore also have the right to preview journal articles and books before they are published, in order to ensure their accuracy and to make sure that the subjects' views are properly represented.

A related matter pertinent to a discussion of ethics in the social sciences concerns the issue of speaking out when injustices are uncovered during the course of research. The participants in anthropological research are often rural people who have been subjected to colonial pressures, manipulated and coerced into selling their lands, or had their lands subjected to pollution, deforestation, or other forms of environmental degradation. Since anthropologists are often able to see these results on a first-hand basis, a question concerns whether they have a responsibility to inform the larger public of these incidents. In this regard, the code of ethics for Canadian applied anthropologists makes it clear that they have "the obligation to speak out publicly in areas of their professional expertise, thereby contributing to the understanding upon which public opinion and policy are derived" (Price 1987: 41).

Speaking about the research of anthropologists in Canada's Northwest coast, Effrat and Mitchell (1974) have suggested that there should be a contractual relationship between Aboriginal First Nations and social scientists. Since anthropological research often involves a long-term association between the researcher and the Aboriginal community, the suggestion is that researchers should be required to sign a legal contract before they are allowed to work in the community. One of the reasons why this issue of possible contractual obligations has become so prominent has to do with the publication of Mary Lee Stearn's book *Haida Culture in Custody* (1981). Members of the Masqet First Nation had apparently not given their approval for the publication of Stearn's study, which the Haida leaders claimed presented their community in an unfavourable light. As a consequence, Stearn's anthropological study was banned from the Masqet community because its residents did not want their social problems publicly known.

If community members, as research participants, wish to modify the contents of a study or forbid its publication altogether because they might be embarrassed by its contents, would this amount to a form of censorship? If publication is to be denied on non-academic grounds, how much control should research participants have over the whole process of the dissemination of research findings? Anthropologists have been known to disparage government agencies, if their policies are unfavourable to First Nations' interests, or private industry, if it impacts negatively on ethnic minorities. If anthropologists say only certain things in their publications in order to avoid criticism and legal complications from ethnic and Aboriginal groups, then this could lead to a distortion of the ethical dimension of anthropological research. There are evidently several unresolved aspects pertaining to the ethical dimensions of research in anthropology. Probably this is all for the better because it illustrates anthropology's evolving, dynamic nature.

In summary, the different fields of anthropology explore a wide range of characteristics of human beings. Physical anthropology recognizes that we are mammals and share traits with others in the animal kingdom, have had a long period of physical evolution that is still continuing, and are closely related to other primates. We are also perceiving and communicating creatures that use a distinctive pattern of verbal skills that we call language, differing in major ways from the cues and calls of other living organisms. Humans are also gregarious creatures who live in social groups as members of particular societies, which allows for mutual support of its members and the sharing of the food, protection, and other necessities of life. Culture is another characteristic of humans that is primarily a symbolic medium through which common traits are learned and passed down through the generations. Anthropology is a scientific discipline that collects and analyzes knowledge about human beings, and provides comparative insights about humans in a general sense, rather than by the narrow scope of one's own culture or society.

2 Anthropology in Canada

Canadian anthropology, eh?
I suggest that Canadian anthropologists at the Millennium can and should use their ethnographic expertise to link the complexity and ambiguity of the Canadian experience to the possibility of proud and self-confident national identity.
　　　　　　　　　　　　　—Regna Darnell (2000: 167)

■ Jesuits and Fur Traders

Anthropology in Canada now has a history that is at least a century old, and even longer than this if we include the observations on Aboriginal life provided by the Jesuits in the seventeenth century (Cole 2000). The development of anthropology in Canada owes its intellectual heritage less to any European scholarly influences than it does to the Jesuit missionaries (McFeat 1980). The black-robed priests produced a prodigious collection of notes and letters that comprised 73 volumes of material called *The Jesuit Relations and Allied Documents* (Thwaites 1896–1901), primarily pertaining to the life of the Huron, or Wyandot as they called themselves. The Jesuits' correspondence provided the inspiration for a considerable body of ethnohistorical research focusing on the social, religious, and political life of the Iroquoian peoples of southern Ontario and neighbouring Algonquian-speaking peoples such as the Ottawa, Mississauga, and Ojibwa (Heidenreich 1971; Trigger 1969, 1976, 1985; Tooker 1964). *The Jesuit Relations* also provided the inspiration for studies of the fur trade, family hunting territories, and the impact of European influences on Aboriginal life (Bailey 1937; Leacock 1954).

The Jesuit Relations is a chronicle of missionary activity among the Huron between the years 1634–1650. In the early part of this period, the reports were written by Father Jean de Brebeuf and Father Francois le Mercier. As Trigger indicates, both men were gifted writers, and their descriptions of Huron culture are often of superb quality. The Jesuits were careful to record not only their general conclusions about the Huron, but also many of the observations on which these conclusions were based (Trigger 1969: 4–5).

Box 2.1: The Jesuit Relations: Controversial Documents

The Jesuit Relations, known also as *The Relations des Jesuites de la Nouvelle-France*, are a compilation of early documents pertaining to the Jesuit missions in New France (Thwaites 1896–1901). They cover a period of approximately 200 years, beginning in 1611 and appearing thereafter on an annual basis, beginning in 1632. The material covers various aspects of the Huron or Wyandot peoples living in the Huronia region of the Bruce Peninsula of southern Ontario, as well as other northern Iroquoian and Algonquian cultures. *The Jesuit Relations* have been used extensively as ethnohistorical sources by such notable anthropologists and historians as Elizabeth Tooker (1964), Bruce Trigger (1969, 1976, 1985), and Conrad Heidenreich (1971).

The use of *The Jesuit Relations* as research sources for ethnographic accounts of Aboriginal peoples raises certain controversial issues for social anthropology. On the one hand, it could be argued that since there is little surviving ethnographic material from the seventeenth century in this region of Canada, then their use is justified on this basis, allowing for due caution. Alternatively, it can be argued that these sources are such biased, ethnocentric, and prejudicial accounts of Aboriginal life during this time period that their anthropological or historical value is practically worthless. After all, it is quite evident that the Jesuits regarded the Aboriginal peoples as backward (from a European perspective) and possessing primitive customs that would be in their best interests to change. The Jesuits were interested primarily in saving souls, in converting the Aboriginal peoples to Christianity, and it was widely regarded that undermining Aboriginal cultural practices was an effective means to this end.

As Daniel Richter (1985: 1) warns, the fact that such "printed reports [as *The Jesuit Relations*] were designed to raise money for the mission suggests a need for caution." Furthermore, Allan Greer (2000: 14) questions the claim that *The Jesuit Relations* represent accurate eyewitness accounts or unadulterated testimony. The letters from the Jesuit missionaries were brought down from Huron country by the summer canoe brigades, then "the superior at Quebec would compile and edit these letters, paraphrasing some parts, copying others verbatim, and forwarding the whole package to France."

The Jesuits were not, evidently, particularly interested in ethnographic accuracy, especially when it interfered with attempts to gain capital to continue the missions in New France. *The Jesuit Relations* were also edited, often quite heavily, by various people so that the original documents, by the time they finally reached France, could contain information quite different from that originally intended or described. It is also evident that the Huron themselves were guarded about what they told the Jesuits, and maintained a state of relative hostility toward the missionaries. At least from what one can glean from Trigger's (1976) careful reading of the documents, the Huron widely resented the fact that fur traders in Quebec insisted that trade would not occur unless the Huron allowed the Jesuits to reside in their villages. What followed were many internal conflicts, especially between the Huron who converted to Christianity and those who wished to maintain their traditional beliefs and rituals. The Huron were also a proud people who resented the characterization of their ways in the derogatory manner in which the Jesuits described them.

Box 2.2: Bruce G. Trigger (1937–2006): Ethnohistorical Perspectives

As described in his obituary in *The [London] Times* of 7 December 2006, "Bruce Trigger was a leading expert in three distinct fields of archaeology: as a historian of the discipline, as an Egyptologist, and as an authority on the aboriginal cultures of ancient North America. He placed archaeology as an academic discipline and a practice within a broader context of social and cultural evolution."

Bruce Trigger was born in Preston, Ontario, and studied as an undergraduate student at the University of Toronto, receiving a doctorate in archaeology in 1964 from Yale University. After spending a year teaching at Northwestern University, he then joined the Department of Anthropology at McGill University in Montreal, where he remained for the rest of his academic career.

It could be argued that Trigger's greatest work is his two-volume study of the Huron entitled *The Children of Aataentsic* (1976), for which he was adopted into the Huron-Wendat nation as an honourary member. A subsequent work, *Natives and Newcomers: Canada's "Heroic Age" Reconsidered* (Trigger 1985), attempted to address a wider audience. Trigger's conclusion is that in "the whole of Canadian history," Native peoples have "long been ethnocentrically regarded" (p. xi). He then went on to marshal evidence indicating that Canadian Aboriginal societies prior to European colonization possessed sophisticated cultural systems that were not inferior to any other societies. Trigger's attempt in putting forth such ideas was to counteract Euro-American and Canadian stereotypes that regarded First Nations cultures in North America as inherently static and less developed than other cultures. These ideas, he argued, were essentially false and motivated by political interests designed to disinherit Aboriginal populations of their ancestral lands.

Bruce Trigger earned many accolades during his career. He was made a fellow of the Royal Society of Canada and won the Innis-Gerin Medal in 1985. The Society for American Archaeology (SAA) dedicated a special session to his research in 2004. Trigger was made an officer of the National Order of Quebec in 2001, and in 2005 was made an officer of the Order of Canada (Williamson and Bisson 2006).

Photo 2.1: Bruce G. Trigger, McGill University, Montreal.

Another anthropologist, Elizabeth Tooker, tends to agree with Trigger's assessment of the Jesuits' ethnohistorical contributions. As she notes that, "although these documents should not be read uncritically, the cautions are few. By omitting the obvious biases of the writers ... a probably quite accurate picture of the Huron is obtained" (Tooker 1964: 7). We should not, however, regard the Jesuit accounts of Aboriginal life as unbiased studies equivalent to modern ethnographic studies—"They were works of propaganda first and works of history only second" (Trigger 1969: 5).

Aside from *The Jesuit Relations*, another major source of information pertaining to Aboriginal life in Canada from a historical perspective relates to the records kept by the Hudson's Bay Company, beginning in 1660. Europeans were interested in the riches to be gained by bartering the Natives' furs for their manufactured goods. The merchants (or factors) of the Hudson's Bay Company built numerous fur trading posts in the northern areas of Canada, then called Rupert's Land, resulting in a network of trade and exploration that was to have a profound influence on the future economic and political development of the country. As far as the Aboriginal peoples were concerned, the fur trade resulted in an almost complete transformation of the social and economic lifestyle as they began to abandon their former subsistence-based life in favour of hunting and trapping for trading purposes (Bishop 1974; Francis and Morantz 1983; Krech 1984; Ray 1974; Yerbury 1986).

Figure 2.1: A scene depicting the now extinct Beothuk trading furs with John Guy and his men in Newfoundland, possibly near Bull Arm, c. 1612, by German engraver Theodore de Bry. (Source: Memorial University, Centre for Newfoundland Studies)

The records kept by the HBC traders provide a wide range of material on Aboriginal life. As Bishop explains, "These documents give detailed continuous accounts of the Indians, the country, and the fur trade kept in the form of day-to-day post journals, district reports, account books and correspondence files" (1974: ix). Unfortunately, he does not provide an assessment of the records as far as their possible biases are concerned, or in terms of their general validity from a modern ethnographic perspective as Trigger and Tooker had done with *The Jesuit Relations*.

As far as the ethnographic value of the HBC records is concerned, it must be remembered that the fur traders were interested in the Aboriginal populations only to the extent that they were a source of furs and, of course, profit for the company's shareholders. Despite this caveat, and recognizing that comparable accounts are mostly not available, we should no doubt be grateful that the company traders took the time they did to provide for posterity the only sources we now have on the early contact period in Canadian history.

■ Early Academic Predecessors

Sir Daniel Wilson, a professor of English and history at the University of Toronto, has been described as Canada's first anthropologist (Trigger 1966a). Although anthropology was only in its infancy at this time, and could be described more as an amateur curiosity than a true academic discipline, Wilson did produce a commendable body of anthropological studies, most notably *Prehistoric Man* (Wilson 1862), and collected some first-hand ethnographic information on the Aboriginal peoples of the Great Lakes area.

Another nineteenth-century scholar, George Mercer Dawson, also played an important role in the early development of anthropology in Canada. Dawson secured an appointment with the Geological Survey of Canada in 1875, and then proceeded to conduct an extensive survey of the British Columbia shoreline. During the course of this survey work, he detailed records of the Aboriginal peoples in this area, especially the Haida of the Queen Charlotte Islands and the Shuswap of the interior plateau region. His records provide the first attempts to accurately describe the Northwest coast people's religious ceremonies, language, and subsistence patterns. As Dawson believed that Aboriginal life was deteriorating because of the settlement of Europeans in the area, he urged the Canadian government to establish a museum to preserve the Aboriginal peoples' arts, crafts, and material culture (Trigger 1966b; Van West 1976).

■ The Boasian Influence

The period of modern, professional anthropology in Canada can rightly be said to begin with the studies of Franz Boas (1858–1942). Boas had originally been trained in Germany as a physicist, but changed his field to anthropology during a scientific expedition to the Canadian Arctic during 1883–1884. After the expedition returned

"There goes civilization as we know it."

Figure 2.2: The meaning of terms such as "civilization" often depends upon one's point of view.

home to Germany, Boas stayed behind to study the life of the Inuit of Baffin Island. He travelled with the Inuit, learned their language, produced detailed maps of the territory, and recorded their family and social groups. One could say that his report, entitled *The Central Eskimo* (1888), was the first published ethnographic monograph of the modern era. Its most important characteristic is that Boas's information was collected on a first-hand basis, using the fieldwork technique of *participant observation* rather than relying on second-hand accounts of travellers and missionaries, which was common during the previous "armchair period."

Box 2.3: Franz Boas (1858–1942): Separating Race and Culture

One of the greatest contributions that anthropology has made to social scientific knowledge is the separation of race from the culture concept. This separation of race and culture was largely due to the indefatigable efforts of Franz Boas, who stressed that all culture is learned rather than biologically inherited. Prior to Boas, many people mistakenly believed that there was a direct relationship between culture and race. One of the reasons for this belief is that individuals who share a culture tend to marry within their society and therefore come to share similar physical characteristics. The problem with this reasoning is that human physical characteristics vary so much from one population to another that it is virtually impossible to associate any one of these with aspects of human behaviour. A second problem is that many human physical characteristics—such as skin colour, for example—may represent biological adaptations to environmental or climatic conditions and therefore have nothing to do at all with people's intelligence or cultural inventiveness.

Boas was one of the leading North American scientists to initiate a public protest against racial bigotry (Harris 1968: 292–297). In his study of immigrants to the United States in the early 1900s, Boas successfully demonstrated that human physical types were hardly stable entities because they fluctuated from one generation to another because of such environmental conditions as food and nutrition, and the availability of health practitioners or adequate housing (Boas 1948). His goal in such studies was to demonstrate that race itself was a concept with little academic or intellectual merit, especially when it was linked to human behaviour as a determining or causal mechanism. In fact, the Boasians rejected all explanations of social and cultural differences that were based on any deterministic principles whatsoever.

The Boasian attack on racist theories coincided with the rise of Nazi race intolerance in Germany and elsewhere in the world. Boas was a member of an immigrant minority and had himself suffered discrimination because of his religion in his native Germany, a factor that made him unwilling to concede that any one particular social or racial group was inherently superior to any other. Boas and his pupils attempted to replace an ideology of intolerance with the idea of cultural relativism, with a belief in a multiracial democracy, which stressed individual freedom of expression. However, as Barrett (1996: 25) summarizes, "The concept of culture emerged as a counterweight to biological explanations of social life, and to the prevailing racial theories of the times. Yet it would be a mistake to assume that academic racism—what we call scientific racism—abruptly disappeared." Evidently there is still much academic work to be done in combating intolerant attitudes in modern society, despite the pioneering work of Franz Boas and his students.

A second important characteristic of Boas's study is that he was able to separate culture from environment. Up until Boas's time, there was a strong belief among scientists that the physical environment was a determining or at least a strongly influencing factor in cultural development. Cultures, it was believed, were shaped or formed by the environments in which they were situated. Boas was determined to counteract this argument by demonstrating that among the Inuit, who live in one of the world's harshest environments, cultural factors develop independent of environmental determinism. This does not mean that cultures are not influenced in certain ways by the environments in which they are situated; it is just that the role of environment, in Boas's mind, played more of a selective role in shaping a culture, but did not determine it outright.

In later years Boas refined his methods of ethnographic research on the Northwest coast with his studies of the Kwakiutl (1897) and Bella Coola (1898). Furthermore, in 1884, a special committee of the British Association for the Advancement of Science was instituted to investigate the hardships endured by British Columbia's Aboriginal population as a result of the encroachment of Europeans. Boas was hired to head this investigation four years later, which laid the foundation for the establishment of the new Ethnographic Bureau of Canada (Darnell 1992). As such, these Northwest coast ethnographic origins based on Boas's scholarly reputation were instrumental in the subsequent professionalization of anthropology in North America and "paved the way for

Photo 2.2: Franz Boas stressed the primacy of culture over biology and environment. In this scene Boas is posing as a Kwakiutl hamatsa dancer for a museum display.

his dominance in Canadian anthropology" (Cole 1973: 41). Incidentally, the first North American Ph.D. awarded in anthropology under Boas was a Canadian, Alexander Francis Chamberlain from Peterborough, Ontario, in 1894 from Clark University, where Boas taught before moving to Columbia University. Chamberlain had previously earned his M.A. from the University of Toronto in 1889.

An Anthropological Division of the Geological Survey of Canada was created in 1911. Its staff consisted initially of Edward Sapir, perhaps Boas's most gifted student (Preston 1980), Diamond Jenness, and Marius Barbeau. Sapir was largely responsible for establishing the Anthropological Division as the pre-eminent research institution in Canada, spread across anthropology's major sub-fields of ethnography, linguistics, physical anthropology, and archaeology (Darnell 1975, 1976). Jenness, originally from New Zealand and an Oxford graduate, conducted ethnographic studies of the Inuit and Athapaskans of the Northwest Territories. His research was published in *The Indians of Canada* (Jenness 1932), for many years the most prominent text on Aboriginal First Nations in Canada and still considered as an authoritative reference work in the field of Native studies. Barbeau, also an Oxford graduate, conducted ethnographic studies of the Tsimshian of British Columbia's Northwest coast and on folklore in rural Quebec.

The Anthropological Division was incorporated in the 1920s into the National Museum of Canada, which today is called the Canadian Museum of Civilization. The National Museum was largely responsible for most of the anthropological research conducted in Canada for most of the early part of the twentieth century. With Sapir's departure in 1926, Diamond Jenness was appointed the National Museum's curator (Richling 1989; S.E. Jenness 2008). Over Jenness's lengthy career he conducted fieldwork among the Copper Inuit of the central Arctic, and the Carrier, Ojibwa, Sekani, and Salish. Jenness's five-volume work, *Eskimo Administration* (1964), remains a testimony to his concern for the plight of the Canadian Arctic Inuit population.

The third member of the National Museum's team, Marius Barbeau, joined the museum at its inception in 1911 and enjoyed a remarkable 58-year career (Nowry 1995). Barbeau was the first Canadian recipient of Oxford's prestigious Rhodes scholarship, and in addition to conducting ethnographic research among Northwest coast and Iroquoian cultures, helped to promote the career of Aboriginal artist Emily Carr. Also, his studies of Quebec folklore were instrumental in establishing Euro-Canadian cultural phenomenon as an important focus in anthropology, along with that of the Aboriginal peoples' cultural traditions (Preston 1976).

■ From Museum to University

A more applied emphasis in Canadian anthropology was initiated with a conference held by a group of University of Toronto anthropologists in 1939 with a focus on the contemporary situation of Aboriginal peoples. The result was an important volume entitled *The North American Indian Today*, in which the authors urged government officials to

---

Box 2.4: Diamond Jenness (1886–1969): Museum Anthropology

Diamond Jenness, born in Wellington, New Zealand, was a pioneer of Canadian anthropology and one of the country's greatest early scientists. After graduating with a master's degree from Victoria University College of New Zealand in 1908, he became Oxford University scholar in eastern Papua New Guinea from 1911 to 1912. He then embarked on a long career in Canadian anthropology, beginning as an ethnologist with the Canadian Arctic Expedition from 1913 to 1916, establishing a reputation for his discovery of the Dorset culture (in 1925) and the Old Bering Sea culture in Alaska (1926).

The remainder of his career focused on First Nations (Indian) and administrative studies. Jenness held a distinguished position as chief of anthropology at the National Museum of Canada from 1926 to his retirement in 1948. He accomplished much during this period by expanding the National Museum's various collections and exhibits. In 1941 Jenness joined the war effort, serving in the Royal Canadian Air Force as director of special intelligence until 1944. He also served in the Canadian Department of National Defence in the Topographical Section, which was a forerunner of the Geographical Branch of the Department of Mines and Resources.

Diamond Jenness eventually authored more than 100 ethnographic and archaeological works on Canada's Inuit and First Nations peoples between 1920 and 1970. In 1962 he was awarded the Massey Medal by the Royal Canadian Geographical Society, and in 1968 Jenness was made a companion of the Order of Canada. A peninsula on the west coast of Victoria Island was named after him in 1978 by the Canadian government. In 2008, his son, Stuart E. Jenness, published his memoirs in *Through Darkening Spectacles*, a Canadian Museum of Civilization publication.

Photo 2.3: Diamond Jenness (left) on board the Karluk, 1913, en route with the Canadian Arctic Expedition (1913–1918). Jenness, the expedition ethnologist, was ashore when the ship, caught in pack ice, drifted away and eventually sank. (Source: Photographer Curtis and Miller, Library and Archives Canada)

"plan the broad outlines of an Indian policy for Canada" (Loran and McIlwraith 1943: 18). This book broke new ground with its contemporary concerns, whereas much of the previous anthropological emphasis was with past cultures and traditions.

Thomas McIlwraith, in 1925, was the first anthropologist to receive an appointment at the University of Toronto (Barker 1987). He had initially received his training at Cambridge University in Britain, thus serving to curtail the influence of American anthropology in Canada since the Boasian period. While anthropology was well established at the National Museum, progress of the discipline was slow in becoming part of the university curriculum. It was not until 1936 that Canada's first anthropology department was created—at the University of Toronto—and it did not offer a master's degree until the 1950s. Anthropology departments were subsequently established over the next several decades at McGill University in Quebec and the University of British Columbia (Trigger 1997). It was not until the 1960s that there was a significant surge in the establishment of new universities offering anthropology degrees. Such universities as York, Trent, Simon Fraser, and Lakehead formed anthropology programs in the late 1960s and early1970s. During the 1970s alone, 24 anthropology departments were created in Canada, along with eight additions of anthropology components to existing sociology departments. Today there are about 500 existing academic positions in anthropology at Canadian universities (Darnell 1975, 1998).

A surge of anthropology's expansion in Canadian universities corresponded with the celebrations surrounding Canada's centennial in 1967, and an increased interest in national issues coincident with the Trudeau Liberal government. One of the proposals of the Trudeau government, supported by Jean Chrétien, who was the minister of Indian Affairs in this administration, was that a thorough investigation should be conducted into the situation of Canada's Aboriginal population. The result was a massive undertaking based on research by about 50 ethnologists, directed by Harry Hawthorn at the University of British Columbia and Marc-Adelaid Tremblay at Laval, published in two volumes called *The Survey of the Contemporary Indians of Canada* (Hawthorn 1966–1967).

The Hawthorn Report, as it was more commonly called, contained over 150 recommendations concerning political, economic, and educational needs and policies. The most prominent recommendation, usually referred to as "Citizens Plus," suggested that "in addition to the normal rights and duties of citizenship, Indians possess certain additional rights as charter members of the Canadian community" (Hawthorn 1966–1967: 13). The recommendation was highly controversial at the time, but government practices were changed as a result of it, moving away from an assimilationist policy to one more supportive of Aboriginal self-determination (Cairns 2000: 36–39). It would be hard to imagine such a large mobilization of anthropologists today, but the Hawthorn survey did establish anthropology's relevance in Canadian Aboriginal policy issues and applied initiatives.

■ Anthropology in Quebec

The development of anthropology in Quebec became firmly established with Horace Miner's classic ethnography, *St. Denis: A French Canadian Parish* (Miner [1939] 1967). This work continued a tradition of community studies initiated by Robert Redfield at

Box 2.5: Harry B. Hawthorn (1910–2006): Anthropology at UBC

Harry B. Hawthorn has been referred to as "the father of modern anthropology in British Columbia" (*Globe and Mail*). He was born in Wellington, New Zealand, and after receiving a master's degree in mathematics in 1935 during the height of the Depression, Harry Hawthorn worked in the remote Maori community of Whatawhwhe. It was here that his interest in anthropology began and it eventually took him to Yale University, where he completed a Ph.D. in 1941. Hawthorn then travelled to Canada in 1947, where he secured a teaching position at the University of British Columbia, becoming the university's first anthropologist.

In 1949 Hawthorn began a study of the Doukhobors for the provincial government, which was not released until 1955 (Hawthorn 1955). The Canadian Department of Citizenship and Immigration commissioned an extensive report on B.C.'s First Nations in 1954, later published in 1958 under the title *The Indians of British Columbia* (Hawthorn et al. 1958), and which is still considered a classic in its field. Later, in 1966–1967, Hawthorn, along with Marc-Adelard Tremblay, edited *A Survey of the Contemporary Indians of Canada*, with its famous recommendation that First Nations peoples should be recognized as "Citizens Plus."

Along with his wife and colleague Audrey, Hawthorn was instrumental in establishing the UBC Museum, begun in the 1950s in the basement of the UBC Library. Audrey Hawthorn later recounted it in her book, *A Labour of Love* (A. Hawthorn 1993). Today the museum is housed in a spectacular building designed by Arthur Erickson, overlooking the Pacific Ocean and known across the world for its outstanding collection of Northwest coast artifacts. Harry Hawthorn was awarded the Order of Canada in 1973 for his unparalleled contribution to Canadian anthropology.

Photo 2.4: Harry Hawthorn with museum artifacts, 1949. (Source: UBC Historical Photograph Collection)

Photo 2.5: Totem poles at Totem Park, 1969. (Source: UBC Historical Photograph Collection)

the University of Chicago, which tended to emphasize internal consistency, co-operative efforts, and consensus. A later review of francophone anthropology in the 1960–1980 period by Gold and Tremblay (1983) concluded that "Only a few anthropologists of the sixties were action-oriented. But without exception all the anthropological studies of Quebec communities of this period were to show how the changes of the Quiet Revolution in Quebec were reflected at the regional level.... The anthropology that many students in Quebec's universities wanted in the seventies was *l'anthropologie du Quebec francaise*. Quebec nationalism, and the issue of who controlled the Quebec economy, preoccupied many anthropologists" (1983: 55).

Economic development issues were a prominent aspect of the Quebec political agenda over the next several decades. When the James Bay Hydroelectric Project was announced by Premier Robert Bourassa in the early 1970s, it was seen less in the context of Aboriginal rights than it was of Quebec nationalism and economic independence from anglophone hegemony in the rest of North America. In this context, the James Bay project was seen as an opportunity to assert French identity in Canada, and as a link with the heroic past of the *voyageur* and *coureur de bois*. The appeal was as much to a political audience as an economic one, yet the provision of jobs and industrial development was an important factor as well.

The Cree of northern Quebec had a different point of view. They were still dependent on a traditional economic livelihood of hunting and trapping, so the flooding and dam construction were seen as a definite threat to their way of life. In addition, the Quebec government had not even bothered to negotiate a treaty with them as it was obliged to do when Quebec assumed possession of *Nouveau Quebec* with the Quebec Boundaries Extension Act of 1912. There was an ecological interest in all this as well, with the Sierra Club of San Francisco seeing in the hydro project all the evils of industrial society—ethnic minorities trampled underfoot in the wake of environmental devastation.

Anthropologists in Quebec tended to side with the Cree, and were less sympathetic with the positions of the environmentalists and the Quebec government. The Grand Council of the Cree was locked in a bitter battle with the Quebec government over the lack of a treaty and the costs associated with the inevitable resettlement that would result from the flooding. The historical aspects of research on Aboriginal impacts go back to at least 1960, when Nelson Graburn, of the McGill anthropology department, wrote a master's thesis on the Sugluk community of northern Quebec, later published as *Eskimos without Igloos* (Graburn 1969). The McGill Cree Project was inaugurated in 1964, under the leadership of Norman Chance, whose book, *Conflict in Culture* (1968), points to the dissension between the Cree and the provincial government even before the hydro project was planned.

Richard Salisbury eventually took over as director in 1971, and changed the project's name to the Programme in the Anthropology of Development (Salisbury 1986; Silverman 2004). Under Salisbury's tutelage, a small army of graduate students were mobilized to provide the research that the Cree would need to support their case that the hydro project would produce significant negative impacts in their territory. Examples of this

Photo 2.6: Cree women, 1946, at Fort George, now known as Chisasibi (Great River). Fort George was the original name of the Hudson's Bay Company post, founded in 1803. Today, Chisasibi is one of nine Cree villages in the region and a member of the Grand Council of the Cree. (Source: Photograph by Bud Glunz, National Film Board of Canada)

research included work on the use of subsistence resources, Cree leadership, attitudes to development, and a range of other topics. In all, McGill's research and involvement in the negotiations leading to the James Bay Agreement of 1975 could be seen "as a laboratory for applied anthropology under pressure of the plans to develop dams in northern" Quebec (Price 1987: 3).

Box 2.6: Richard F. Salisbury (1926–1989): Applied Anthropology

Richard Salisbury was born in Chelsea, England, and served in the Royal Marines between 1945 and 1948. He then studied anthropology at Harvard University (A.M. 1955) and the Australian University, where he received a Ph.D. in 1957. In 1962 Salisbury published his oft-quoted study of the Siane, entitled *From Stone to Steel: Economic Consequences of a Technological Change in New Guinea.* In a later work, *Vunamami: Economic Transformation in a Traditional Society*, Salisbury (1970) presented the results of his fieldwork among the Tolai near Rabaul, one of the most prosperous areas in New Guinea. This work touched off a vehement controversy in anthropology over whether so-called primitive or traditional peoples should be studied using a market economy model (the formalist position) or a more socially embedded one (the substantivist position), with Salisbury (1973) clearly espousing the former position.

Richard Salisbury joined the Department of Anthropology at McGill University in 1962, and in 1971 assumed directorship of the Programme in the Anthropology of Development (PAD), which had earlier been founded in 1964 by Norman Chance, known then as the McGill Cree Project. PAD attained a wide reputation for training applied anthropologists, especially concerning impact studies of the Cree during the James Bay treaty negotiations of the mid-1970s, in which Salisbury initiated a pattern of consultant-oriented research. Salisbury played a major role in the formation of the Society for Applied Anthropology in Canada (SAAC) in 1981, contributing further to the training of a new generation of anthropologists with a practical stance to their research.

Richard Salisbury served as McGill's dean of Arts (1986–1989) and was president of five anthropology associations, including the Canadian Sociology and Anthropology Association (1968–1970), the Northeastern Anthropology Association (1968), the American Ethnological Society (1980), the Society for Economic Anthropology (1982), and the Society for Applied Anthropology in Canada (1982). He also served on the board of the Canadian Human Rights Foundation and was a member of the Quebec Commission on Higher Education. Richard Salisbury was elected to the Royal Society of Canada in 1974, and was awarded the prestigious Killam Foundation Research Fellowship for 1980–1982. He died an untimely death at age 62 while at the height of his academic and intellectual power (Hedican 1990d; Silverman 2004).

◼ Western Canada

The 1970s was a period dominated by resource and development issues. While the controversy surrounding the James Bay Hydroelectic Project was unfolding in Quebec, in western Canada the focus was on the Mackenzie Valley Pipeline Inquiry of the Northwest Territories, headed by Thomas Berger, chief justice of the British Columbia Supreme Court. The so-called Berger Inquiry (Berger 1977, 1983) was mandated to examine the impact of the proposed gas pipeline from the Mackenzie Delta to southern Alberta on the Dene or Athapaskan social and economic life. As in the case of the Quebec Cree, the Dene's concern was with the impact of this project on the subsistence hunting and trapping economy of the Northwest Territories. Traditional adversaries began to line up—developers, Aboriginal groups, and environmentalists. Thrown into this mix were the anthropologists, who were called upon to provide their side of the issue based on ethnographic research on traditional economies, community composition, and impact assessment (Ridington 1988; Ryan 1995; Ryan and Robinson 1996).

Berger's report, *Northern Frontier, Northern Homeland* (1977), which recommended a moratorium of 10 years on further pipeline construction in the Mackenzie District, was a source of considerable controversy. As the inquiry moved from community to community along the Mackenzie Valley corridor, it heard from various sectors of the Aboriginal communities involved, such as the elders, trappers, and young people. It was evident that there was a difference of opinion in the Aboriginal communities themselves, with the elders wanting to preserve traditional hunting and trapping, and the younger generation interested just as much in possible jobs that the pipeline might make available to them.

The inquiry also heard from Native specialists (Asch 1982, 1984; Brody 1975) who had diverse opinions about what was going on. As time went on, it became apparent that there was more happening with the inquiry than just the possible impacts of oil and gas issues on the Aboriginal communities; there were wider concerns also expressed about the future development of the northern part of northwestern Canada, aside from the impact issues (Dacks 1981: 125–167). In other words, the Berger Inquiry was a means to explore sensitive Native issues that went back to the time of European contact, such as the political and economic dependency of the Dene people on the larger external society (Coates and Powell 1989; Watkins 1977).

The Berger Inquiry also provoked an underlying controversy in the anthropological community as well, primarily over the whole issue of advocacy, of taking sides in development disputes, and the role of traditional ethnographic research being used to fight political and economic battles. Richard Salisbury (1977), for example, called into question the validity of the research supporting the Berger Inquiry's conclusions. He questioned the scientific nature of the report, asking of the Berger Report, "But is it Social Science?" The larger question at stake here concerned the intellectual integrity of Canadian anthropologists, whether they were becoming pawns for governmental or industrial interests, or possibly the Aboriginal lobby as well. As one anthropologist explained, "While it was extremely expensive, and weak as social science, the Berger Report is in many ways a model of the high road to applied anthropology, combining analysis of engineering, potential ecological damage, and acculturation problems" (Price 1987: 4).

■ The Modern Era

Almost without it being noticed, anthropology in Canada shifted from a pursuit of "pure" research involving traditional community studies characterized by the pre-1970s period, to an engagement in economic and political issues that were not started by

Box 2.7: Joan Ryan (1932–2005): Participatory Research

Joan Ryan was born into an Irish-Canadian family in a poor neighbourhood in Montreal. She completed a B.A. in psychology at Carleton University in 1957. Ryan then travelled to Fairbanks, Alaska, and began a career-long interest in Aboriginal peoples and issues of social justice. She became involved in helping local communities in the areas of land claims, preservation of Aboriginal languages, economic development, and the use of traditional knowledge in the delivery of medicine. While conducting these activities, she became involved in applying anthropological knowledge to help solve local problems, or in what has become known as participatory action research (PAR). In this type of research, community members conduct most of the research and own the information that is gathered (Robinson 2006; Ryan and Robinson 1990, 1996).

From Alaska, Joan Ryan began a career as a teacher with Indian and Northern Affairs Canada in George River and Ungava Bay, Quebec, and Lac La Martre, Northwest Territories (Ryan 1995). Then, in 1964, she enrolled as a Ph.D. student in the Department of Anthropology and Sociology at the University of British Columbia, with Harry Hawthorn becoming her principal mentor. After graduation she was hired in 1967 at the new University of Calgary, eventually becoming the department head (1978–1983) and supervising many M.A. and Ph.D. students in applied anthropology. During this period she wrote her first major work, *Wall of Words: The Betrayal of the Urban Indian* (1978), and was part of a group of scholars who founded the Canadian Anthropology Society.

In 1987 Joan Ryan retired from the University of Calgary as professor emerita and began a new career with the Arctic Institute of North America. At the institute she began her pioneering work into northern participatory action research (PAR) projects in Fort McPherson and Lac La Martre (Ryan 1995). During this time Ryan also worked on PAR projects in Nicaragua and developed a research relationship with the Lubicon Cree in Alberta. In recognition of her lifelong efforts, Joan Ryan received the Weaver-Tremblay Prize for her contributions to Canadian applied anthropology.

Photo 2.7: Joan Ryan, professor emerita, University of Calgary, and Arctic Institute of North America. (Source: Photograph in Arctic, 2006)

their own initiative, but in which the anthropologists were inexorably involved. This is not to imply that traditional anthropological studies were no longer conducted—what Barrett has termed "no-name anthropology" (1996: 179–180)—it is just that as time has gone on, there has been more of an applied emphasis taking hold in the discipline. This means that anthropologists must justify their existence, must justify the expense of their research in ways that they did not have to in the more "ivory tower period," which seemed to come to a dead halt in the 1980s.

Box 2.8: Richard B. Lee (1937–): The Kalahari Research Group

Richard B. Lee, professor emeritus of anthropology at the University of Toronto, was born in New York City and grew up in Toronto. He eventually moved to the University of California at Berkeley, where he conducted doctoral research on the Ju/'hoansi (!Kung San) in Botswana and Namibia in collaboration with Irven DeVore. Lee was co-founder, along with DeVore, of the Kalahari Research Group, which was a multidisciplinary consortium of scholars who were conducting research with the San.

Lee and DeVore published several seminal works in the area of hunter-gatherer studies, such as *Man the Hunter* (Lee and DeVore 1968) and *Kalahari Hunter-Gatherers* (Lee and DeVore 1976), which established their international reputation as pre-eminent authorities in the area of research in social anthropology focused on foraging and band societies. Lee has been past president of the Canadian Anthropology Society and is a fellow of the Royal Society of Canada. Several of the students who worked under his tutelage have also gone on to have successful careers in Canadian anthropology, such as Jacqueline Solway (2003; Solway and Lee 1990) at Trent University, and Renee Sylvain (2005) at the University of Guelph.

Photo 2.8: Richard B. Lee reading to Ju/'hoansi children, 1980. (Source: University of Toronto Libraries)

The Berger Inquiry brought out into the open, probably for the first time, the fact that anthropologists in Canada are not a unified community in terms of their points of view, their research agendas, and where they feel the discipline is or should be heading. Some anthropologists, for example, feel quite comfortable working with anyone who could pay them. Remember that there is a large anthropology workforce that is not directly employed in universities, yet these people still have to make a living without tenure or other job cushions. Some of this work involves consulting jobs on a variety of different sorts of projects—some are related to Aboriginal land claims, while others work on the impact of transportation systems or housing projects. Still others teach on a contractually limited basis, moving from university to university, fluctuating with the ebb and flow of student numbers, existing faculty positions, and university budgets. Many in this labour market must still raise children, pay mortgages, and generally make ends meet in an increasingly competitive work environment.

It would appear quite natural, then, in this world of accountability, labour needs, and contract appointments, that the applied aspects of anthropology by necessity have become more prominent. This trend has become evident by current applied anthropology studies in the area of public policy, advocacy, program evaluation, and self-determination (Asch 2001; Ervin 2006a, 2006b; Gwynne 2003; Hedican 2008). The role of anthropologists as "public intellectuals" is also an important contemporary theme, as attempts are made to apply knowledge gained from anthropological research to aid in solving social problems today (Tsing 2005). This approach is extended, for example, to the topic of human rights in discussions of "the scholar as activist" (Nagengast and Velez-Ibanez 2004). Cultural identity in the modern context of globalization continues to hold the interest of researchers as people grapple with what it is that makes them unique in spite of social and economic homogenizing processes (Nash 2001; Neizen 2004). As the outside world continues to impinge on local areas, it is not surprising, then, that enduring research topics, such as colonialism, continue to be regarded as relevant in today's world (Haig-Brown and Nock 2006; Shewell 2004).

One assessment of contemporary anthropology is that "This is a good time to be an anthropologist. From theoretical to applied work, the discipline is flourishing. Doubts about whether we could survive in a post-colonial world have been laid to rest. Indeed, anthropology has emerged as a leader in the investigation of the forces of globalization" (Barrett 2002: ix). As far as anthropology in Canada is concerned, "Some of it is still oriented toward cultural traditions and ethnohistory, but with much more emphasis on modern issues such as political self-determination and the sociocultural dimensions of Native health and welfare" (Ervin 2001: 20–21).

There are very solid reasons for maintaining a sense of optimism in the continued viability and growth of anthropology in Canada. Its strength would appear that anthropologists in Canada build on the strong research program of its predecessors, especially in the area of Aboriginal studies, while taking a forward-looking stance in which new topics such as policy, identity, hegemony, and globalization are embraced. However, there is no simple answer to the question of what makes anthropology in Canada unique in some manner (Sweet 1976). Thomas McFeat has suggested that "While there were

Box 2.9: Sally M. Weaver (1940–1993): Understanding Aboriginal Policy

Sally Weaver was born in Fort Erie, Ontario, and completed her Ph.D. in 1967 from the University of Toronto, becoming what is believed to be the first Canadian woman who earned a doctorate in anthropology (Abler 1993). She began work at the University of Waterloo in 1966 as its second anthropologist, and served as the chair of the Anthropology department from 1976 to 1979. Weaver also served on the executive of the Canadian Sociology and Anthropology Association from 1970 to 1973. She was instrumental in the founding of the Canadian Ethnology Society (now the Canadian Anthropology Society) in 1974, and served as president of the organization in 1975–1976.

Sally Weaver often served on other panels and boards, such as her position as trustee of the National Museums of Canada (1972–1978), as a member for the program committee of the International Union of the Anthropological Sciences (1980–1983), and as a board member of the United Nations Research Institute for Social Development, Geneva (1985–1988), among other such positions.

Dr. Weaver was the author of an extensive body of work dating back to *Medicine and Politics among the Grand River Iroquois* (1972) and *Making Canadian Indian Policy* (1981). This latter work dealt with the proposal in a 1969 White Paper by the Canadian government under Pierre E. Trudeau to terminate its relationship with Aboriginal peoples. The Social Science Federation of Canada judged the study to be one of the 20 best English-language books in the social sciences written in the past 50 years. "Her anthropological skills," Abler (1993: 119) noted, "allowed her to untangle the exotic tribal behaviour of the Ottawa Bureaucrat." She also compiled and directed, along with Thomas Abler, the Canadian Indian Bibliography Project. The result was an annotated bibliography of over 700 pages, published by the University of Toronto Press in 1974 (Abler and Weaver 1974; Bishop 1979).

In recognition of their contribution, the Weaver-Tremblay Award in Canadian Applied Anthropology has been named after two of Canada's renowned applied anthropologists, the late Sally Weaver and Marc-Adelard Tremblay (Laval), and is administered by the Canadian Anthropology Society.

Photo 2.9: Sally M. Weaver, professor emerita, University of Waterloo, prominent applied anthropologist of the modern era. (Source: Photograph courtesy of David Weaver)

opportunities of a uniquely Canadian anthropology to develop, it did not" (1976: 148). This statement was made a generation ago, and one wonders if he might still have the same opinion today. One anthropologist who has conducted extensive research into the history of anthropology in Canada, Regna Darnell of the University of Western Ontario, suggests that "the national discipline combines features of disciplinary organization and historical context in patterns that *are* unique" (1998: 155). She also offers the opinion, in a later paper, that "In Canada, a critical mass of First Nations languages and cultures maintains them with a saliency in the national forum unparalleled in the United States" (2000: 170). Canada certainly has a history of anthropological research that extends back in time as far as most other countries, and with a diversity of research topics that compares more than favourably with that conducted outside its borders.

3 Explanation, Generalization, and Theory

Now that explains it!
Our consciousness is shaped at least as much by how things
supposedly look to others, somewhere else in the lifeline of the
world, as by how they look here, where we are, now to us.
—Clifford Geertz,
Local Knowledge (1983: 9)

Research without explanation seems rather pointless. Our expectation of good research
is that it allows us a view beyond the immediacy of the present details. Theory, in turn,
can be understood as a form of explanation, or a group of explanations tied together. In
either case general patterns are revealed beyond that which is evident in any particular
case. Of course this process of "revealing beyond" takes a certain leap of imagination.

■ The Nature of Explanation

An *explanation*, in a scientific sense, could be defined as "general abstract propositions
(theories) and specific propositions (hypotheses) that represent how and why reality is
constituted in the manner that it is constituted" (Sidky 2004: 425). Aside from such a
formal representation of the term, in our personal lives, we probably all know intuitively
what makes a good explanation or, alternatively, when an explanation does not help us
understand something very much. Of course there are different types of explanations.
Some just explain what is happening in a particular instance by demonstrating the cause
and effects that lead to a particular result. Other explanations are more general in nature,
leading us to think beyond the parameters of particular cases and into new realms of
thinking that we would not have imagined before.

Scientists have to know what an explanation is, about its characteristics, or otherwise
research would lead nowhere. Research that explains something must add to our understanding. This can be done in several ways, as some types of explanations are better than
others, but most have defects. In all, the following types of explanation can be identified: descriptive, historical, mediating, teleological, and those resorting to general laws
or principles (Beattie 1969).

Box 3.1: Claude Levi-Strauss (1908–2009): French Structuralism

Explanation can take various forms in anthropology. For the French anthropologist Claude Levi-Strauss, for example, cultural behaviour can be explained as a reflection of the basic psychological operations of the human brain. He termed his brand of anthropology "structuralism," by which he means the uniformities that arise from unconscious structures of human thought processes (Levi-Strauss 1967). This view contrasts with the concept of "structural functionalism," by which is meant the role of social practices and institutions in contributing to social stability and the maintenance of the society as a whole, according to British social anthropologist A.R. Radcliffe-Brown (1881–1955).

From the perspective of Levi-Strauss, explanations of social and cultural phenomenon should be sought, not in the understanding of social systems *per se* but in the decoding of the principles according to which the human mind operates. To illustrate this point, he spent a considerable effort in studying myths, which, he argued, reflect the operation of the brain according to its binary patterns. A fundamental example can be found in the culture-nature dichotomy. Levi-Strauss ([1964] 1975) suggests that we cook our food because it transforms such "natural" products into "cultural" ones, thereby also distinguishing human beings from other animals.

In his imaginative study of mythology, Levi-Strauss (1978) suggests that myths are a form of language that stands partway between conventional language and the human brain. He is not concerned so much with the particular details of myths and what they might tell us about the social world, but what an analysis of myths informs us about the workings of the brain. In addition, through his analysis of myths, Levi-Strauss provides insights into fundamental human contradictions, about life and death, male and female, or social and natural. The controversial aspects of Levi-Strauss's version of structuralism have as much to do with his brand of explanation, which tends to contravene the more conventional scientific principle that cause must precede its effect in time, whereas Levi-Strauss proposes that time can proceed both backwards and forwards, leading to a somewhat baffling method of reasoning.

The first type is what could be called a *descriptive explanation*. What is commonly meant when we describe something is that we are told only *how* it happens, rather than *why* things happen. This sort of complaint is not particularly fair because it is meant to diminish the value of such an explanation. In any event, when we are asked to describe how something happens, we are inevitably led into a discussion of causes and effects that is at the bottom of why things occur. Years ago the water pipes burst in the basement of our old and not very well-insulated house. I explained to my children that the pipes burst because they contained water, which, because the basement was so cold, froze. When water freezes, it expands with even greater force than the pipe could contain, and so it split open. As far as science is concerned, this might not be too much of an adequate explanation, but it does in its own descriptive way explain why the pipes burst—at least my children seemed happy with the answer, which led them to the conclusion that we needed a new house.

A second type could be called an *historical explanation*. In this case our explanation is based on some historical factors, or antecedent events, that could reasonably lead to other events, ones that we wish to explain. For example, with regard to the question of why people smoke tobacco, we are immediately led into outlining a series of concatenated historical events—Native American cultivation of tobacco, Sir Walter Raleigh becoming addicted to the nicotine and bringing the plant back to England, and so on. But in the end we really haven't explained why some people took up smoking and others did not, or why some people became addicted and others did not, or why some people smoked even if they were not addicted.

The whole problem with an historical explanation is that it is dependent to a large degree on the necessity of some prior cause that may or may not have occurred in any non-random sort of sequence. Maybe all we need to say is that some people took up smoking because they liked the effects, it gave them comfort, and others did not feel this way so they did not take up the habit. Generally what happens when one resorts to an historical explanation because of the belief that if a particular set of circumstances can be shown to exist at a particular point in time, and there is a need for something to occur, then its occurrence is based on these interrelated factors.

There is a matter of luck here, of course, of a fortuitous merging of circumstances, not to mention individual genius that could lead to an invention, in one spot, but not in another. Take the curious situation of the Mayans and their non-invention of the wheel for regular transportation, such as carts. Other Native groups might have used a *travois* and dragged their gear behind a dog or horse, so there was probably no chance of the wheel diffusing into Mayan culture from other areas of North America. Regardless of these extenuating circumstances of possible diffusion, the Mayas knew about the wheel because it is known that they used these in their children's toys. They were also very bright people who knew about cosmology, advanced construction techniques, and other civilized achievements. So resorting to an historical explanation doesn't get us very far, except to say that the weight of tradition is the cause, which is to say that people will continue to do what they do unless there is a strong motivation to change. In this case we will never know because we cannot go back and ask them, and even if we could we might not get very far because humans do all sorts of seemingly irrational things, or so they seem to outsiders, but not to themselves. Anyway, there is always this matter of the inscrutable nature of the human psyche.

A third type of explanation is based on *mediating factors*. In this case an explanation is attempted by demonstrating a connection between things or events thought to be separate in some regard. This is the basis of most *functional* theories, which rely on a correlation of things in space or time. Take the famous French sociologist, Emile Durkheim, and his study of suicide ([1897] 1951). In a very lengthy book, and after years of collecting statistics on suicide, he came to the conclusion that religion was at the basis of different suicide rates in Europe. The Roman Catholics, who had the lowest incidence of suicide, were integrated into society because of their many rituals—that is, they suffered less from *anomie*. Protestants were more prone to suicide because they were more disconnected. There is a lot more to this sort of explanation than I can outline here, but there is also as much psychology in Durkheim's explanation of suicide as sociology, such as his idea of a collective conscience, which makes it difficult to keep all the mediating variables straight. As with many functional explanations, or ones based on mediating factors, it is difficult to determine which came first or, in Durkheim's case, how suicide, religion, marital status, and psychological tendencies are linked historically as cause and effect.

A *teleological explanation* is a fourth type. In this case there is a resorting to some ultimate end or purpose. In other words, this is more of a converse of an historical explanation because the reasoning proceeds from a cause to an effect, whereas historical explanations rely on an effect resulting from a cause. That is, a certain consequence is brought about because of a quality inherent in that which is to be explained. In social anthropology this sort of explanation often involves social ends served by institutions: "essential to it is the notion that what is explained has causal implications for some kind of complex, comprehended as a working system, and having some kind of value, such as utility or efficiency, attached to it ... [for example] a man is slaughtering a goat with the object of providing a feast" (Beattie 1969: 119).

Finally, in a fifth type of explanation, one resorts to *general laws or principles*. This kind of explanation is not so much explanatory as it is classificatory because all it does is suggest that a certain thing to be explained falls into a particular class or category in which it also possesses the characteristics by which the class is defined, or has characteristics with other members of that class with which it is invariably associated. An association is therefore drawn, from the thing which we have sought to explain, to a general class of similar phenomenon, without ever along the way providing an actual explanation in some other terms outside of this closed system. In other words, resorting to a general law or principle as a mode of explanation, without explicating how this general law or principle operates, or the conditions under which it exists, leads to a *tautology* because the thing to be explained is inherent in the explanation itself—like a dog chasing its tail in a circular fashion, and around and around we go.

■ Generalization and Social Facts

There are some similarities to the conduct of ethnography and seashell collecting. We go along the beach picking up this pretty shell, and then another, according to our fancy, then bring them home in a bag. Once there we lay them out on a table and try to organize them in some way, according to type, shape, or colour. We may attempt a classification of some sort, but first we must decide on some criterion for selection. In ethnography, or fieldwork, we roam around inside another culture (usually) picking up raw data or social facts, according to some general idea as to why we are there in the first place. Sometimes the anthropologist finds a whole new set of facts that are more interesting than originally anticipated and completely changes the project. Rarely is the project as initially conceived ever carried through according to the original design or intentions. People and social facts intervene in the mean time. It is like the adage, "life takes place while we are making other plans."

There is a problem with this procedure and it is not that good science cannot result in this way; the problem is that we collect so many items that we do not know what to do with them all. This could lead to a lot of wasted effort. As we have previously indicated, studies in social anthropology are usually built from the ground up or through *induction*, which is reasoning from the particular to the general, rather than *deduction*, by which one starts with a general principle and then goes to the ground to test it out (Bernard 1969). Neither method is inherently better than the other, or necessarily more scientific.

So the fact of life in social anthropology is that we are stuck with what we have in this inductive approach, with what we are used to, and the way we have mostly been. This does not alleviate anthropologists from the burden of producing generalizations because without them, data collection becomes a meaningless exercise, devoid of any meaningful purpose, and so a waste of time. What we really mean when we talk about deduction and induction has to do with *levels of abstraction*. A low level of abstraction is closely tied to the data, and therefore explains somewhat less than a higher level of abstraction, which includes more data, and consequently explains more. This is also what we mean by the *explanatory power* of our mode of reasoning.

In its most basic form, a *generalization* "is a proposition that relates two or more classes of phenomena to each other. An important logical property of generalizations is that they make claims that go beyond what has been observed or recorded" (Kaplan and Manners 1972: 11–12). As such there are different types or forms of generalizations, mostly based on how much data on human societies they take into consideration. For example, an *empirical generalization* refers to relationships occurring among the same kind of phenomena, in a restricted number of cases, which hold under certain specified conditions. *Theoretical generalizations*, on the other hand, refer to highly abstract relationships under which empirical generalizations can be subsumed as special cases; they "lead us to new facts and open up new lines of research" (Kaplan and Manners 1972: 12).

So what is evident from this discussion is that ethnography specifically, and social anthropology more generally, rely fundamentally on empirical rather than theoretical modes of inquiry. As Barrett explains, "While empirical generalizations are widely employed by anthropologists, and justifiably so, given the largely inductive nature of fieldwork, the same cannot be said about propositions and laws; indeed, most anthropologists would be hard pressed to come up with a dozen propositions in the literature, let alone a single law" (1996: 41). This means that anthropology's claim to the status of a science is a particularly problematic one.

■ Characteristics of Theory

One may find different *definitions of theory* in the literature of anthropology. Theory, according to Kaplan and Manners, "is knowledge organized so that facts are subsumed under general principles" (1972: 31). Similarly, Barrett defines theory as "an explanation of a class of events, usually with an empirical referent, providing insights into how and what is going on, and sometimes explaining why phenomena exists" (1996: 40). The philosopher of science, Abraham Kaplan, suggests that a "theory is a way of making sense of a disturbing situation so as to allow us most effectively to bring to bear our repertoire of habits and, even more important, to modify habits or discard them altogether, replacing them by new ones as the situation demands" (1964: 295).

A theory is also then a type of generalization because it organizes facts in a highly abstract manner, suggesting "why"—and not just "how" or "what"—and a mode of explanation that informs us about why certain effects are brought about by certain causes. When a theory works, we are presented with a view of the world that is systematic and orderly.

There is some preference in the earlier literature to distinguish between *macro-theory* and *middle-range (or micro-) theories* (Kaplan 1964: 299–300; Harris 1968: 3–4), but there is not a definitive division that can be made between the two. Macro-theory illuminates the big picture, the vast expanse of history, Einstein's relativity, Darwin's natural selection, or Hegel's dialectic. Macro-economics, for example, focuses on the characteristics and internal dynamics of the economy as a whole, while micro-economics is concerned with the behaviour of individual participants in this economy. This would suggest that the macro and micro distinction is a matter of scale, or the extensiveness of the events under consideration, rather than kind, which is to say that they are intrinsically different.

As far as anthropological theory is concerned, Harris suggests that middle-range theories do not offer much more than a "piecemeal approach … there is little to commend the idea of middle-ground theory" (1968: 3). Given the variability of human behaviour and cultural practices around the world, it is not likely that a theory will emerge that accounts for all things cultural or social relating to human beings, thus limiting the range over which any particular theory has explanatory power. Humans have a certain freedom of choice, even to be irrational in their choices, which is an ability that atoms do not have. It is never easy to predict in any consistent manner what humans will do, even under controlled circumstances. There are certain cultural and physical factors that, of course, influence choice making, but never to the point of determining these decisions.

It seems to make more sense then to talk about the *probability* that a person will behave in a certain way under a specified set of conditions, rather than to try to predict exactly what will occur as a result of human decision making. This approach could also be called a *statistical generalization*, even though in anthropology the precise statistical probability that an event will occur cannot be specified with the sort of precision found in the natural sciences. A related form of explanation could be called a *pattern theory*. In this case certain configurations, regularities, or patterns are identified and then extrapolated into an explanation of the phenomena under study. It could also be expected "that certain elements of the pattern are more central, crucial, or strategic than others in determining the overall configuration. Moreover, since we mean by *patterning* the way the various elements relate to each other to form a larger system, we can see no reason why these relationships cannot be expressed in propositional form, either statistical or universal in nature" (Kaplan and Manners 1972: 16).

This reference to explanations and theories of a particular pattern or statistical configuration essentially mean that what we are talking about is a form of *prediction*. But is prediction really a form of explanation? The two are certainly linked because if I can tell you what could reasonably be expected in the future, given certain conditions, then I must have also explained the phenomena in some manner that would allow for that prediction in the first place. In other words, explanation and prediction are to a large extent inseparable as far as theory formation is concerned. The reason is that when we use a particular theory to explain something, we are also at the same time setting out certain expectations—predictions, if you will—about what will tend to happen under similar circumstances in the future. Prediction is important because it allows one to anticipate, and therefore prepare for upcoming circumstances.

As far as anthropology is concerned, there are special problems associated with this area of inquiry that makes theorizing, searching for generalization, and predicting a difficult matter, thereby influencing the manner in which anthropological knowledge is formed and accumulated. It is a fact that every society has its own system of knowledge that explains human origins, and all of the aspects of the world in which we live. There are also hundreds, even thousands, of human languages that conceptualize human experiences in a multitude of ways. Cultural diversity, past and present, adds another layer of complexity. So as far as theory formation in anthropology is concerned, there is almost too much of a burden to explain everything about human behaviour and experience. For this reason, many anthropologists prefer a term that is burdened with fewer expectations, in terms of a rigorous mode of explanation, than the word "theory."

This alternative term is *theoretical orientation*, which means a particular school of thought that is distinctive in some ways from other scholarly traditions. Functionalism (which stresses the interrelatedness of parts of a social system) could be called a theoretical orientation, as could evolutionism (stressing social progress or development), because they each have their own conceptual territory, their own particular modes of explanation and assumptions, and their own methods of analysis. Theoretical orientations do not have to be mutually exclusive modes of reasoning because some overlap can be expected in their conceptual territory. In addition, some theoretical orientations operate at a higher level of abstraction than others, such that one school could be subsumed under another. Evolutionism, for example, has various subtypes (unilineal, multilineal, specific, or universal), and each operates in some independent manner, but are ultimately tied to one another in a larger, overarching scheme of inquiry.

■ Epistemology: Positivism and Phenomenology

Whichever theoretical orientation anthropologists choose to organize their fieldwork data largely is a matter of preference based on the assumption of a certain philosophical perspective. *Epistemology* is the study of how knowledge is organized, or how it is that we understand the world around us. As such, a *paradigm* is a conceptual framework that guides a scientific inquiry with a certain research strategy

(Kuhn 1962: 43; Sidky 2004: 19–22). As Kuhn suggests in *The Structure of Scientific Revolutions* (1970), scientific knowledge does not necessarily grow and accumulate. Instead, scientific knowledge changes because of paradigmatic shifts in the underlying assumptions that guide research agendas, such that a new paradigm explains what a previous one could not, and helps to resolve anomalies that were unaccounted for in previous paradigms.

The term *model* is a somewhat more general term than "paradigm," meaning the way reality is described in some analogous fashion. A model is not reality, but a representation of the empirical universe. It could be called a *heuristic device*, which is used to help understand the essential form and characteristics of complex phenomenon. Max Weber, a nineteenth-century sociologist, used the term *ideal-type*, which could be used as a guide or model in research (it had all the ideal characteristics that one was looking for), but was not actually found in the natural world. An ideal-type specifies something "with which the real situation or action is compared and surveyed for the explication of certain of its significant components" (Weber 1949: 93).

From Kuhn's perspective, all knowledge is problematic since it depends upon cultural and linguistic factors, underlying assumptions, agreed-upon sets of meaning, and acceptable research methodologies. Yet for practical purposes, we can identify two broad spectrums of beliefs or philosophies: positivism and phenomenology.

Positivism refers to the view that the social world is patterned and orderly. It is based on the doctrine that scientific knowledge pertains only to empirical experience and is built up through the generation of propositional (testable) knowledge (Sidky 2004: 435). This philosophy has been attributed to Auguste Comte, hailed as the father of sociology (Harris 1968: 64), as set out in his *The Positive Philosophy* (published in 1896). The essential aspect of Comte's philosophy of positivism is that reality can be apprehended objectively, and that explanation in the social sciences can and should be as objective and empirical as in the natural sciences. In other words, a positivist view assumes that the social world is highly structured, and that it is amenable to measurement by techniques comparable to those used in the hard sciences (Barrett 1984b: 3). An associated term, *empiricism*, means that research is grounded in data, in concrete facts, that exist in the real world. In addition, *nomothetic inquiry* refers to the search for regularities and laws; the assumption is that such laws are discoverable in the natural and social worlds.

Positivism received its strongest backing in sociology by Emile Durkheim (1858–1917), who borrowed Comte's perspective, or at least fundamentally agreed with it, when he posits in *The Rules of Sociological Method* ([1895] 1938) that "the first and most fundamental rule is: *Consider social facts as things*" (1938: 14; emphasis in the original). Durkheim explains further: "social phenomena are things and ought to be treated as things.... [I]t is unnecessary to philosophize on their nature.... It is sufficient to note that they are the unique data of the sociologist. To treat phenomena as things is to treat them as data, and these constitute the point of departure in science" ([1895] 1938: 27).

Durkheim's ideas exerted a serious influence on the development of early social anthropology in Britain through A.R. Radcliffe-Brown (1881–1955). Radcliffe-Brown

Box 3.2: Thomas Kuhn (1922–1996): "Scientific Revolutions" in Anthropology?

Even though Thomas Kuhn's thesis on scientific revolutions was formulated a half-century ago, it is still as controversial today as it ever was. The reason for the controversy pertains to his attack on the conventionally held opinion that growth in scientific knowledge takes place incrementally, with small discoveries added to other small discoveries. The conventional wisdom also holds that scientific growth maintains a steady progression from ignorance to enlightenment in a cumulative manner.

Kuhn's proposal throws all of this conventionally held knowledge upside down. Scientific knowledge, Kuhn claims, is not necessarily cumulative or even progressive. It proceeds in fits and starts around commonly held beliefs that together form a model or paradigm about how the universe operates. Eventually a new paradigm overthrows the old in a revolutionary manner, causing scientific endeavours to start almost from scratch again.

There was much criticism of this approach at the time of Kuhn's initial publication, and it is still the subject of debate (Shapere 1964; Barrett 1984b: 53–62). Sidky (2004: 19–21), for example, refers to Kuhn as an "irrational philosopher," suggesting that if science operates as he suggests, then there could not be any growth or accumulation in scientific knowledge at all. Furthermore, Kuhn's position is "highly implausible for the simple fact that more is known today than was known ten years ago, fifty years ago, a century ago, and so forth" (2004: 19).

As far as anthropology is concerned, Kuhn's proposals do not seem to have much to offer in understanding the development of this discipline. For one thing, anthropology has apparently never had in its entire history, going back at least a century and a half, the sort of all encompassing paradigm that is so important to Kuhn's view of science. Leaving aside for the moment the question as to whether or not anthropology is even a "science" at all, during the unilineal evolutionary period, with its one model or scheme fits all approach, there were dissenters. One could argue that anthropology is still in a "pre-paradigmatic" stage, to use Kuhn's term, but even then one wonders why there is so such theoretical diversity in anthropology inhibiting the development of the overarching paradigms that Kuhn claims exist in "true" sciences. Even when one looks at anthropological theory in terms of its major theoretical orientations—unilineal, historical particularism, neo-evolutionism, cultural materialism, and so on—there are in anthropology's history many more theoretical proposals, some complementing those just listed, and a myriad of others that are quite opposing them in terms of fundamental principles.

Further discussion on the issue of scientific knowledge is, of course, always welcome, but one is led to wonder if the problem is not so much with anthropology's theories or competing paradigms, but with Kuhn's suggestions. Of course it is also a debatable matter as to whether anthropological knowledge is cumulative, since even some of its founding principles, such as culture or cultural relativism, have their detractors. But, nonetheless, one hopes that certain matters hold open the possibility that thoughtful progress has been made in anthropology over the previous decades, such as an increase in the value of human diversity and an increase in tolerance and understanding.

was not an armchair theorist as he had conducted fieldwork during 1906–1908 in the Andaman Islands west of Thailand. His goal was to remake anthropology into a natural science of society, at a par with sociology, and free from anthropology's earlier speculative evolutionary period (Radcliffe-Brown 1952).

Lacking the controlled laboratory experiment of the physical sciences, Radcliffe-Brown regarded anthropology's comparative method as an essential alternative. His assumption was that cross-cultural comparisons would eventually yield the generalizations that would put anthropology on a solid scientific footing. Unfortunately for Radcliffe-Brown's aspirations for anthropology, as fieldwork became more common in the discipline and was regarded as the rite of passage to a graduate degree, it became increasingly evident that the natural science model of society, at least Radcliffe-Brown's version, was unable to cope with the complexities of social life, and that perhaps a more subtle model was required (Barrett 1996: 64).

The problem with a positivistic or natural science view of society is that the social world of human beings is a messy one that defies the formation of strict rules and laws. People often do not behave in predictable ways. They say one thing, but do another. Humans have options that atoms do not. The complexity of the social world poses an immense challenge to social scientists, which suggests that the limitations of positivism infer a need for an alternative philosophy, one with a more subjective orientation.

Phenomenology is frequently contrasted with positivism, as if the two approaches occupy distinct or mutually exclusive conceptual territories—I will argue later that they do not. A phenomenological approach indicates that an adequate understanding of social phenomena requires that we understand the subjective meanings that people attach to social facts and the ways in which people actively create these social facts. Similarly, it has been defined as an approach "that is primarily oriented towards description, not theory formation, and in which the vantage point of subjectivity ... is of first importance" (Goldstein 1968: 98).

Phenomenology, thus conceived, is essentially a relativistic approach in that it emphasizes the particular and the unique. In this regard culture can be seen as a complex of individual interpretations and meanings, some overlapping others, and some discrete unto themselves This relativistic orientation also blends well with the idea that customs should be understood in their own specific cultural context, which is the essence of cultural relativism.

This does not necessarily mean, however, that cross-cultural comparisons are deemed impossible, or at least undesirable, from a relativistic perspective. It simply means that such comparisons need not overlook or minimize the individualistic, subjective meanings associated with cultural phenomenon. The problem is that cross-cultural comparisons must necessarily be selective—you cannot compare everything—and so the particularistic aspects that make individual cultures unique are diminished or even eliminated altogether.

■ Anthropology: Art or Science?

A question that is inevitable in any discussion pertaining to a discourse of positivism versus phenomenology has to do with: "Is anthropology art or science?" (Carrithers 1990).

Box 3.3: A.R. Radcliffe-Brown (1881–1955): Nomothetic Inquiry

Although Bronislaw Malinowski played a key role in developing fieldwork in early British social anthropology, it was A.R. Radcliffe-Brown who eventually emerged as the major theoretician of this period. Radcliffe-Brown's theoretical approach, known as structural functionalism, was much more sophisticated than that espoused by Malinowski (Barrett 1996: 60–64; Sidky 2004: 183–199).

Radcliffe-Brown, born in Birmingham, England, studied anthropology at Trinity College, Cambridge. He conducted fieldwork from 1906 to 1908 in the Andaman Islands, off the coast of Burma in the Bay of Bengal, although his work was not published until much later (Radcliffe-Brown 1922). From 1910 to 1912 Radcliffe-Brown (1918) undertook fieldwork among the Aboriginal peoples of western Australia, during which time he abandoned his earlier diffusionist perspective on culture change and began to develop a more sophisticated approach that combined the functionalist theory of sociologist Emile Durkeim with his ideas on social structure. As Edmund Leach (1982: 237) explains, "social structure is the persisting framework of a self-perpetuating system. An approximate analogy is that between the bony skeleton of a living mammal and its total bodily form."

Radcliffe-Brown is also known for the years that he spent teaching at the University of Chicago (1931–1936), during which time he was able to offer American anthropologists a theoretical alternative to the prevailing Boasian perspective of historical particularism. The Chicago anthropologists formed the first non-Boasian school in the United States committed to a more positivistic or "nomothetic" orientation (Adams 1998: 352). In this regard Radcliffe-Brown helped to build a bridge between British and American anthropology.

The nomothetic approach is defined by Radcliffe-Brown as the "theoretical or nomothetic study of which the aim is to provide acceptable generalizations.... A nomothetic enquiry ... has for its purpose to arrive at acceptable general propositions" (1952: 1). In Radcliffe-Brown's approach, then, the goal of social anthropology should be to develop a scientific understanding of social systems and to generate explanatory laws that would account for cultural similarities and differences. Eventually, though, Radcliffe-Brown's orientation began to have a diminished influence, especially in American anthropology, as more humanistic, interpretive styles began to emerge during the 1960s. However, by the 1970s, scientific explanations for socio-cultural phenomenon in the form of cultural materialistic approaches began to gain currency as championed by Marvin Harris, which provided at least a partial vindication of Radcliffe-Brown's nomothetic orientation in the history of social anthropology.

The essential concern is this: "How are we to represent anthropology as a serious activity to ourselves and to those with whom we are engaged if it is so nebulous?" (Carrithers 1990: 263). Anthropology could be made less nebulous, in the view of some, if it became more rigorous in a methodological sense—that is, in terms of its techniques of investigation and its overall philosophical approach. As Renner (1984: 540) explains, "the absence of an empirically convincing theory and methodology has as its consequence the fact that there can be no program for the direction in which research should proceed."

"It is my hope that these images will generate a huge number of academic journal papers and theses on the Palaeolithic period."

Figure 3.1: Art can have many purposes, such as aesthetic or utilitarian ones.

Clifford Geertz was asked to comment on Carrither's (1990) article about art and science in an issue of *Current Anthropology*. Geertz wrote that "I do not believe that anthropology is not or cannot be a science, that ethnographies are novels, poems, dreams, or visions, that the reliability of anthropological knowledge is of secondary interest, or that the value of anthropological works inhere solely in their persuasiveness" (Geertz 1990: 274). In other words, Clifford Geertz is suggesting that the question about anthropology being an art or science depends on the context in which cultural information is placed. In some instances this information can be regarded in a scientific context, but in other instances it is more appropriate to adopt a humanistic perspective as a way of understanding cultural material.

Box 3.4: Clifford Geertz (1926–2006): Thick Description

Clifford Geertz has been one of the most influential and controversial anthropologists of the last generation. For some he was considered "for three decades … the single most influential cultural anthropologist in the United States" (Geertz, Shweder, and Good 2005: 1). Yet, there are those who "find here cryptic excuses for a vacuous paradigm and reparation for an ethnographer's failure to do a thorough job … 'thick descriptions' are theoretically useless" (Sidky 2004: 332).

Clifford Geertz was born in San Francisco, California, and received his Ph.D. from Harvard University in 1956. He was on the anthropology staff of the University of Chicago from 1960–1970, and eventually retired as professor emeritus at the Institute for Advanced Study at Princeton, New Jersey (*New York Times*, 1 November 2006). He was considered a founder of interpretive, or symbolic, anthropology, and his literary flair distinguished him from most theorists and ethnographers. In *The Interpretation of Cultures*, for example, Geertz explained that "man is an animal suspended in webs of significance he himself has spun" (1973: 5).

While the controversial aspects of Geertz's work extend into many areas, such as his view that ethnographic reality does not exist apart from anthropologists' written versions of it, his approach to ethnography, which he termed "thick description," is the source of much debate within anthropology. As Geertz explains, the idea behind his version of anthropology is to probe deeper and deeper into the domain of meaning and the layers of significance that constitute the symbolic worlds humans construct (Bohannan and Glazer 1988: 530). "What the ethnographer is faced with," Geertz (1988b: 536) suggests, "is a multiplicity of complex conceptual structures, many of them superimposed upon or knotted into one another, which are at once strange, irregular, and inexplicit."

The appeal of Geertz's anthropology for many stems from his assertion that the important question about cultural phenomena is not about what they do, but what they mean. Culture for Geertz is not easily defined across cultural or social boundaries because what it means to be human lies in cultural peculiarities, in their oddities, and in "the pattern of meanings embodied in symbols" (1973: 89). It is in the symbolic world that humans find a reference to understand reality. It is therefore through "thick description" that anthropologist attempt in their fieldwork to explain, with as much detail as possible, the reasons behind human behaviour, and through which one can uncover the "system of inherited conceptions expressed in symbolic forms by means of which people communicate, perpetuate, and develop their knowledge about and attitudes toward life" (Geertz 1973: 89).

Those who would agree with the essence of Geertz's statement would probably also support the idea that anthropology should become more explicitly a humanistic discipline. For example, supporters of a humanistic approach would see in this version of anthropology an admirable alternative to "the reductionism and ethnocentrism of traditional science" (Scholte 1972: 542). The question concerning whether or not anthropology is an art or science is therefore regarded by many anthropologists as one without a firm conclusion.

Robin Ridington, a long-established ethnographer of the Dene or Athapaskan of Canada's Northwest Territories, echoes similar sentiments to those Geertz expressed. Ridington, in comments concerning Dene knowledge and power concepts, argues that long-term fieldwork is a crucial aspect of understanding cultural phenomena, since "the careless and uncritical application of ideas from academic traditions to the thought worlds of Subarctic people may produce bizarre and ethnocentric results" (1988: 98). As an example, Ridington points to the "uninformed ethnocentrism" that dominated much of the debate about the causes of the windigo psychosis among eastern Subarctic Aboriginal peoples.

The references above equating science with ethnocentrism would probably refer to the idea that interpretations of people's behaviour that are formulated outside a particular cultural area and then imposed from above, as in a deductive approach, are apt to lead to misunderstandings. Although not everyone would agree that science and anthropology are not a good mix, a more reasoned approach is that "a thorough historical and political understanding under which epistemology in relation to fieldwork takes place is, therefore, an important part of cross-cultural understanding" (Ulin 1984: 22).

There are equally strong supporters of a positivistic or scientific point of view in anthropology. As Lett indicates, it is all a matter of "epistemological responsibility" as his stance is that the phenomenological argument is doomed" (1987:19) because of "its lack of explicit theoretical and methodological guidelines" (1987: 117). The positivist perspective is better suited to studying cultural phenomenon because it is more rigorous in explaining the relationship between cause and effect, whereas phenomenology shies away from this sort of explanation.

One of the most prominent proponents of positivism in modern anthropology is Marvin Harris. His theoretical position is commonly referred to as *cultural materialism*, which is to say that cultural variation can be attributed to technology, economics, and environment—in other words, the material conditions of social life are seen as causal factors. In Harris's words, when anthropologists ignore causal viewpoints, "their flat rejection of scientific truth as a goal of ethnography results in fragmentary, contradictory, and essentially nihilistic notions about the human condition" (1991: 405).

We have then, as far as anthropology is concerned, somewhat of a philosophical conundrum. On the one hand, if we follow the road of science and its positivistic orientation, we are apt to destroy the individualistic flavour that makes each culture special in its own right. On the other, the phenomenological or relativistic orientation, taken to an extreme, makes comparison nearly impossible. What do we choose?

Well, for one thing, do we really want a discipline that comprises hundreds, or eventually even thousands of specific ethnographies? What we would be craving for, if that were the case, is for some general understanding of what it is to be human. Individualism is fine, but we can rejoice as much in our unique qualities as much as in our commonalities. One of the central problems in anthropology, then, is how to explain the tremendous variability in human cultures and languages with the essential homogeneity of the human species. Clifford Geertz has articulated this issue in an incisive manner: "the great natural variation of cultural forms is, of course, not only anthropology's great (and wasting) resource, but the ground of its deepest theoretical dilemma: how is such variation to be squared with the biological unity of the human species?" (1973: 22). The fundamental problematic in anthropology is therefore the simultaneous notion of cultural uniqueness and the underlying similarity of *Homo sapiens*.

■ Reconciling the Paradigms

Positivism wants us to look over the broad landscape of human variation and draw similarities, generalizations, and even possibly laws of human society. Phenomenology wants us to look within or, as Geertz instructs us, "the essential task of theory building ... [is] not to generalize across cases but to generalize within them" (1973: 26). The question then becomes: Is it possible to reconcile these disparate paradigms of positivism and phenomenology? Or, to put it another way, can the two paradigms be made more commensurate with one another?

There are those who believe that reconciliation is not only possible, but essential, if anthropology is to make any theoretical progress. For example, Leon Goldstein, a professor of philosophy commenting on anthropological theory, argues that "far from opposing one another, these two approaches—positivism and phenomenology—are complementary and both of them necessary if we are to have a full account of the phenomenon in question. Each does a different job, and there is no reason why we cannot have both" (Goldstein 1968: 98). This perspective, which suggests that both positivism and phenomenology are acceptable approaches, allows anthropology to break out of its current impasse.

There could be some validity to Goldstein's suggestion that positivism and phenomenology are not mutually exclusive, but complementary to each other. There is emerging, for example, the idea of a culturally based science. The idea is that science is not necessarily a Western, or European-based activity of discovery. Other cultures have their ways of explaining what goes on in the universe, and even though one culture's science does not always match up with any other culture's science, this does not mean that each is not valid in its own right. What we have, then, is a multiplicity of sciences, each with its own basic assumptions and methodologies for discovering facts about the world we live in.

Rather than choosing sides, as we are apt to presently do, Goldstein's suggestion is that we look at the different jobs that each paradigm does, and then see how they might fit together in the overall whole, rather than seeing one to the exclusion of the other. In other words, join them together in some manner, as if they are two sides of the same coin. In any event, it all starts with ethnographic description, derived from fieldwork, as social anthropology's inductive (bottom-up) point of departure (Hedican 1994). Then, on the basis of the fieldwork investigation, one can initiate a search for categories of comparison that are relevant to one's topic of investigation.

This approach of seeking complementarity rather than injunctions or divisions provides a basis for widening the research, employing some well-defined categories of culture. These categories have been already worked on for at least the last 50 years, using a compilation of cultural characteristics called the Human Relations Area Files (HRAF). To explain how this is done must await our discussion of methodology. In order to remain consistent with the themes of the present chapter, we should proceed with a discussion of the history of anthropological thought and the various theoretical orientations that have been adopted over the decades.

4 From Evolutionism to Feminist Anthropology

Bad day at the office, Dear?
Although deconstructionists make valid points ... their flat rejection of scientific truth as a goal of ethnography results in fragmented, contradictory, and essentially nihilistic notions about the human condition.

—Marvin Harris,
Cultural Anthropology (1991: 405)

A common perception that many people have is that life just keeps getting better and better. They point to the advances in medical technology, human lifespans are increasing, and we have more relief from drudgery than ever before. Of course what is missing in this optimistic view are the drawbacks to modern civilization: much of the world's people go to bed hungry at night, authoritarian regimes seem to be on the rise, there is genocide occurring unabated, pollution, and so on. In other words, it is necessary to temper our sense of reality with the obvious negative aspects as well.

Much the same can be said for a social scientific perspective on theory. Many see theory as a series of advances, as a steady progression of more sophisticated and refined ideas. What is often overlooked is that each new theory has significant drawbacks, despite the initial euphoria accompanying its introduction. Another issue is that theoretical advance in a straight-line progression from the past until today is largely a myth. In reality, theories form a complex web, some advancing and gaining acceptance while others are in decline. Some theories spawn a number of offshoots, while other theories are rediscovered or reclaimed from the almost forgotten past. There is much more to the story about how theories change, so it is worthwhile considering this aspect of social scientific history before we embark on a discussion of the actual theories themselves.

■ How Theories Change

Thomas Kuhn, as was indicated earlier in our discussion of paradigms, proposed a convincing argument about the history of scientific revolutions. He largely disagreed with the notion that scientific advancement could be characterized by a steady growth, by an accumulation of good ideas. Alternatively, Kuhn suggested that science proceeds in a herky-jerky sort of manner. Or, put more precisely, scientific development is a succession of tradition-bound periods punctuated by non-cumulative breaks.

Kuhn begins with the notion of a *paradigm*, which he defines as "universally recognized scientific achievements that for a time provide model problems and solutions to a community of practitioners" (1962: viii). After a particular paradigm becomes entrenched in the scientific community, normal science begins to occur: "normal scientific research is directed to the articulation of those phenomena and theories that the paradigm already supplies" (Kuhn 1962: 24). Things go along pretty well for a period of time, but as normal science proceeds, an increasingly greater number of anomalies begin to occur that cannot be accounted for by the original paradigm. New and unsuspected phenomena are repeatedly discovered by scientific research, which eventually creates a sense of crisis.

The existing paradigm ultimately begins to collapse under the weight of its own inconsistencies and inability to account for the increasing number of anomalies. With any luck, a new paradigm is discovered and articulated in such a manner that resolves the previous anomalies, and normal science once again takes place for a period of time as new problems are discovered that need resolution. In time, this paradigm, too, collapses and a new one emerges.

This whole process of paradigm shifts was inspired by the so-called Copernican Revolution. The orthodoxy that insisted the sun revolved around the earth became so obviously false with Galileo's discovery of the telescope that a new interpretation of planetary movements was needed to account for the observations that were becoming increasingly apparent. The Copernican view of planetary motion became the new paradigm, replacing entirely the previous one, which saw the sun revolving around the Earth.

If we can accept the basic premise of Kuhn's argument, then the question becomes: Is this approach applicable to anthropology in particular, and the social sciences in general? First, we need to consider the nature of paradigms, and then decide if anthropology has ever had one. There is much dispute among anthropologists about this. A paradigm, in Kuhn's sense, implies a common framework of research conducted under common assumptions, such as Einstein's theory of relativity. Barrett has argued that "the label 'paradigm' must be reserved for disciplines that lend themselves to nomothetic inquiry. Only twice has anthropology come close to attaining this status: First, in the social-fact approach of Durkheim and, second, in the cultural-materialist approach" (Barrett 1984b: 4). Even during times when these two cases were in vogue, social scientists, and anthropologists in particular, have conducted their research using multiple paradigms.

Kuhn's proposals have drawn many criticisms. For example Sidky writes that if science operates as Kuhn suggests, "then there could not be any growth or accumulation of scientific knowledge. This position, however, is highly implausible for the simple fact that more is known today that was known 10 years ago, 50 years ago, a century ago, and so forth" (Sidky 2004: 19). However, I'm not sure that Kuhn's use of paradigm shifts renders implausible, or is incompatible with, the idea of an accumulated growth of knowledge, as Sidky suggests.

There are other possibilities. Consider Georg Hegel's (1770–1831) *dialectic* as an alternative to Kuhn's abrupt breaks in paradigmatic knowledge. In Hegel's philosophy, change results from the resolution of opposites. A central *thesis* is opposed by its opposite (*antithesis*), resolved in a *synthesis*, which becomes a new thesis generating an antithesis, and so on. Later, Karl Marx (1881–1883) and Friedrich Engels (1820–1895) expanded on Hegel's idea of progression by sequential stages with their proposal of *dialectical materialism* in which social transformations are construed as the results of inherent internal contradictions and conflicts arising out of opposing interests in socio-cultural systems (Sidky 2004: 423).

Robert Murphy adapted these ideas to anthropology in his book, *The Dialectics of Social Life* (1971). He explains his approach by stating that his "dialectical approach is simple in the extreme, for it requires only that the analyst of society question everything that he sees and hears.... It requires us to also look for paradox as much as complementarity, for opposition as much as accommodation. It portrays a universe of dissonance underlying apparent order and seeks deeper orders beyond the dissonance" (1971: 117).

The formulations of both Thomas Kuhn and Robert Murphy portray a steady, cumulative progression in scientific ideas. For Kuhn, the progression is one of discrete stages, in which paradigms come and go. For Murphy, the progression switches back and forth in a dialectic fashion. Another alternative is that there has not been much progress, at least in the sense of a direct progression. As far as anthropology is concerned, Barrett has argued that the notion of progress is a fallacy, in which he argues for the "non-cumulative nature of anthropological theory. There has been little significant advance in the field since the writings of Marx, Weber, and Durkheim, who laid the basis for a positivistic science of society" (Barrett 1984b: 3).

My purpose in the foregoing discussion is not to unnecessarily confuse readers. The purpose is to portray the variety of opinions in the discipline concerning anthropological theory, and to give readers some basis for arriving at their own conclusions regarding the cumulative or non-cumulative, lineal or dialectical nature of the progression of ideas.

■ Early Evolutionism

In the nineteenth century anthropology was an amateur endeavour. Men with enough independent financial means to sit in their libraries, speculating on the nature and evolution of the human species, pored over the published reports of explorers, missionaries, and traders. This is what is commonly referred to as the *armchair period*. The anthropologists of the time did not collect their own data on non-European peoples, but relied mainly on the usually biased ideas of travellers, who were often prone to exaggeration.

Charles Darwin (1809–1882) was a different sort of scholar. He actually sailed around the world in *The Beagle*, collecting his own information and then, using his observations, formulated a theory, based on the idea of evolution through natural selection. In *The Origin of Species* (1859), Darwin's ideas accounted for the continuity of past and present life forms and had a dominating effect on the intellectual climate of the period.

Box 4.1: Lewis Henry Morgan (1818–1881): Early Evolutionism

In his time, Lewis Henry Morgan was an early American anthropologist who made important contributions to the study of Iroquois society (*League of the Ho-de-no-sau-nee, or Iroquois*, 1851), kinship and social organization (*Systems of Consanguinity and Affinity of the Human Family*, 1870), and cultural evolution (*Ancient Society*, 1877). Morgan's anthropology is particularly noteworthy because he actually conducted field-work, unlike most "armchair" evolutionary thinkers of this period, prepared question-naires, and collected data in a systematic manner, thus setting a precedent for the field-work of Boas and Malinowski.

Although Morgan was never affiliated with any university, he did act as an intellectual mentor to John Wesley Powell, who became head of the American Bureau of Ethnology in 1879 at the Smithsonian Institution. Morgan was also elected president of the American Association for the Advancement of Science in 1879, and was a member of the National Academy of Sciences. His reputation began to spread with the publication of *Ancient Society*. Karl Marx was reputed to have been enamoured with his work because of Morgan's emphasis on the role of technology and society, and wanted to dedicate his major work *Das Kapital* to him, but Morgan declined the honour (Moses 2009).

His *Ancient Society* (1877) is considered an anthropological classic. Morgan pro-posed three stages of cultural evolution, divided further into various subtypes, then tied this scheme to stages of development of marriage and the family, and three classes of kinship terminology. Morgan also proposed that kinship terminology be divided into two types: classificatory (terms applied to several relatives) and descriptive (terms refer-ring to one individual, or a restricted range of individuals), which is a system still in use today in social anthropology.

Contemporary assessment of Morgan's work, despite several of his favourable contribu-tions, is not particularly flattering. Marvin Harris, for example, refers to Morgan as a racist: "Morgan, his respect for the virtues of barbarism notwithstanding, did not consider the American Indian the equal of the European.... Morgan's life-long appreciation and defence of the American Indian was coupled with a strong prejudice against Negroes" (1968: 138–139). Furthermore, as Barrett explains, "For Morgan, like Tylor, the transition from a lower to a higher stage meant progress, not only in technological sophistication but also in moral-ity. This helps to explain his racist bent" (1996: 50–51).

In Morgan's defence, there are still contemporary scholars who draw inspiration from his evolutionary schemes. Marvin Harris, in particular, is drawn to the attention that Morgan gave to technological innovations as a basis for the development of human culture. Harris no doubt would discount Morgan's specific evolutionary stages as base-less in fact, but nonetheless the overall evolutionary framework that Morgan proposed appears to continue today, with such derogatory terms as "savage" and "barbarian" being replaced with the more acceptable "hunter and gatherer" and "horticulturalist." Thus, minus the racist undertones in his work, Morgan's basic evolutionary framework

apparently continues under the neo-evolution-
ary guise of Julian Steward's "multi-linear" evolutionism or Harris's "cultural materialism."

Photo 4.1: Lewis H. Morgan, pioneering American
anthropologist and social theorist.

While Darwin's ideas of evolutionary selection and survival of the fittest pertained
to non-human life forms, his theory had an impact on those who saw in human society
similar principles at work. Herbert Spencer (1820–1903), for example, in *Principles of
Sociology* (1876), drew a parallel inspired by Darwin's theory between biological and
social evolution. Spencer put forward the idea that human society is characterized by an
evolutionary progression from simple to complex in which there is struggle and progress.

Spencer's ideas of social progress were central to the early evolutionary thinkers. A
unilinear line of development was the prevailing assumption of the time in which all
cultures were thought to go through the same stages of evolution, from primitive to
barbarism to civilization. Of course there is more than a tinge of ethnocentrism in this
scheme since civilization, the pinnacle of the evolutionary scale, culminated in English
and other European societies.

Edward Tylor (1832–1917) could be regarded as the most influential anthropologist
of the nineteenth century. His book, *Primitive Culture* (1871), was widely read. In it he
proposed the first definition of culture, and suggested the three-part stages of cultural
evolution. He also set out a famous definition of religion—a belief in spiritual beings—
and set out a version of the comparative method based on what he termed *survivals,*
cultural elements that persisted or survived from previous stages of evolutionary development. Tylor was also involved in an interesting methodological issue in early anthropology, now commonly referred to as *Galton's Problem*, when he presented a paper to
the Royal Society of Britain in 1889. In this paper Tylor presented a thesis, which stated
that given the same level of technological conditions, residence patterns following marriage would be the same. Francis Galton, a statistician sitting in the audience, wanted
to know if the individual societies for which Tylor had data on the residence patterns
were actually discrete examples, or had diffusion and cultural borrowing contributed to

the observed patterns. Anthropologists to this day have grappled with this problem in formulating cross-cultural comparisons.

Another important anthropologist of the early evolutionary period was Lewis Henry Morgan (1818–1881) from the United States. Although Morgan was a lawyer by training, he had a strong interest in the Aboriginal populations of America, and had represented the Iroquois Five Nations in a land claim case. He noticed in his discussions with the Iroquois that they had a kinship system based on tracing relatives through the female line, which differed remarkably from his own system of tracing descent. Out of this curiosity regarding different ways in which people might be related to one another, Morgan sent out questionnaires to practically everyone he knew (missionaries, traders, explorers, government administrators) who would have contact with cultures in various parts of the world. He wanted these people to record the culture's kinship systems for him, and on this basis produced one of anthropology's most important studies of any period, *Systems of Consanguinity and Affinity of the Human Family* (1870).

From today's perspective, the early evolutionary period was fundamentally flawed because of its ethnocentric orientation. Despite some important ideas upon which anthropology was to develop in later periods, such as Tylor's concept of culture, or Morgan's comparative study of kinship, the idea of inevitable progress in human society common to thinkers of this period has been shown to be a faulty assumption. First, there are many societies and cultures in the world, so that placing them all on one evolutionary scheme is not an acceptable basis of comparison. Societies also change at different rates, as some become more complex in time, while others regress. Look at the great empires of history—for example, such as the Egyptians, the Romans, or the Mayans. They all achieved remarkable success for a period of time, but could not maintain this complexity and eventually regressed into simpler (more primitive?) units. There is obviously a lesson to be learned here for our modern Western civilization, with its attitude of superiority: the good times do not last forever.

■ Historical Particularism

Historical particularism is an anthropological perspective commonly associated with Franz Boas (1858–1942) and several of his students, such as Margaret Mead (1901–1978). It was founded on an aversion to speculative, armchair theorizing common during the early evolutionary period of anthropology, and stressed the particularistic or unique aspects of each culture, which were thought to result from random historical processes. The philosophy of *cultural relativism* is an important foundation of this approach, founded on the idea that each culture should be evaluated in its own terms, rather than by invidious comparisons with other cultures. A *holistic* approach is also an important aspect of the research promoted by Boas, such that a culture is studied in as comprehensive manner as possible, including the ways in which the different parts relate to one another. As Stocking (1974: 18) summarizes, it was out of an extension of "Boas's critique of evolutionary assumptions that certain of the most fundamental orientations of modern American cultural anthropology derive ... the elaboration of the concept of culture as a relativistic, pluralistic, holistic, integrated and historically conditioned framework for the study of the determination of human behaviour."

When Boas embarked on his seminal research among the Inuit of Baffin Island, his attitude was that cultures should be studied in as much depth as possible. This meant long-term ethnographic fieldwork using the technique of *participant observation*. By using this technique, anthropologists immerse themselves in another culture, joining the people in their day-to-day activities and learning as much of their language as possible. This was the research technique that Boas developed in his Baffin Island and later West coast studies, which revolutionized the manner in which anthropologists collected data on other cultures, transforming anthropology from a speculative curiosity to a science based on sound research techniques.

As a theory, however, historical particularism has its deficiencies because it is less concerned with studying the comparative or developmental basis by which cultures change than it is in documenting their particularistic qualities. At times Boas's research reports seemed chaotic to his contemporaries because of the lack of generalized statements that could be used to draw the ethnographic material together in a coherent manner. Robert Lowie's (1920: 441) famous comment on culture, no doubt made in reference to Boas's research, was that of "a planless hodgepodge," a "thing of shreds and patches." Another anthropologist commented that even though "Boas wrote over 5,000 pages on the Kwakiutl, he was never able to write a coherent ethnographic monograph on the subject" (Sidky 2004: 128).

Even though his ethnographic work has been criticized by those who were not in agreement with his concept of historical particularism as a research agenda, probably Boas's most significant contribution concerns his role in the professionalization of anthropology in North America, transforming it from the museum context of collecting material culture to establishing anthropology's role in the university curriculum (Darnell 1998). From 1889 to 1892, Boas taught at Clark University in Worcester, Massachusetts, where he supervised the first North American Ph.D. in anthropology, awarded in 1892 to a Canadian, Alexander Chamberlain (1865–1914), from Peterborough, Ontario, who had previously received his M.A. in 1889 from the University of Toronto.

Later, during Boas's time at Columbia University, he was responsible for training a generation of anthropologists who spread out across North America, and who themselves created new departments of anthropology. One prominent student was Edward Sapir (1884–1934), a noted linguist, who became head of the Anthropological Division of the Geological Survey of Canada from 1910 to 1925, a period generally recognized as the beginning of professional anthropological research in Canada. Sapir utilized Boas's cultural relativistic perspective in his linguistic studies, formulating the idea of *linguistic relativity* based on the thesis that culture and language are interrelated. He also formulated an important principle in anthropological linguistics referred to as the *Sapir-Whorf Hypothesis*, which states that language conditions our thoughts and perceptions, thus determining or at least strongly influencing our sense of reality.

Box 4.2: Ruth Benedict (1887–1948): Culture and Personality

Ruth Benedict was trained by Franz Boas and in her time became one of the most famous anthropologists in the world. Marvin Harris (1968: 398), for example, claimed that Benedict's *Patterns of Culture* (1934) was the best-selling anthropology book of all time. Her pronouncement in *Patterns* was equally dramatic: "Cultures ... are individual psychology thrown large upon the screen, given gigantic proportions and a long time span" (1934: 24). There are few quotes in the history of anthropology as famous as this one.

Benedict was born in New York City and graduated from Columbia University with a Ph.D. in anthropology in 1923. She was a close friend of Margaret Mead and other young scholars who studied under Franz Boas, and who promoted the cultural relativist perspective in their work (Lapsley 1999). Benedict was president of the American Anthropological Association and an active member of the American Folklore Society. She was also elected a fellow of the American Academy of Arts and Sciences in 1947. A U.S. postage stamp was released in her honour in 1995.

Her work *Patterns of Culture* is generally regarded as one of the forerunners of anthropology's culture and personality school, which could be considered an offshoot of Boas's historical particularism. From Benedict's perspective, each culture tends to be characterized by the leading personality traits of the people living in that culture. The Pueblo Indians of the American Southwest, for example, place an emphasis on restraint, which she described as "Apollonian." At the other extreme are the Kwakiutls of the Northwest coast, who are described as "Dionysian" or "megalomaniacs" because of their apparently unrestrained gift-giving and status achievement in celebrating the potlatch.

Benedict continued her research into culture and personality in *The Chrysanthemum and the Sword* (1946), a study of Japan based on her wartime investigations. This work is a study of a society through its literature, films, newspapers, and other "distant" research. Her aim was unabashedly to aid the war effort by seeking to understand Japan's militaristic aggression under Emperor Hirohito, and thereby also uncover Japan's possible weaknesses. Benedict's research helped to understand the role of the emperor of Japan in Japanese culture, leading to President Roosevelt's decision to allow for the continuation of the emperor's reign after the war.

It could be expected that there would be criticisms of Benedict's work because of its controversial nature and the claim that most of her ideas were based on library research (Sidky 2004: 149–150). Harris (1968: 402) described *Patterns of Culture* as "a way out of the diffusionist cul de sac, [but] its contribution to the explanation of cultural differences and similarities was miniscule." However, "Because of its great popularity, it served as the most important single source of recruitment for anthropology as a profession" (1968: 406). "It is tempting to conclude," Barrett (1996: 58) suggests, "that it [the culture and personality school] left little of value as its legacy." In perhaps a more sympathetic view, Sidky (2004: 157) suggests that "Benedict's work, regardless of its serious shortcomings, was influential in pointing out to anthropologists the importance of considering personality as an aspect of the cultures they studied." Even Harris (1968: 409) was to admit that "The artful presentation of cultural differences to a wide professional and lay public by Mead and Benedict must be reckoned among the important events in the history of American intellectual thought."

Photo 4.2: Ruth Benedict, author of Patterns of Culture, one of the best-selling anthropology books of all time.

Ruth Benedict (1887–1948) was also an influential anthropologist trained by Boas, most notable for her widely read book, *Patterns of Culture* (1934), and for her involvement in a psychological orientation to ethnography, known as the *culture and personality school*. From Benedict's perspective, it was possible to characterize entire cultures around several psychological traits. As she explains, "Cultures from this point of view are individual psychology thrown large upon the screen, given gigantic proportions and a long time span" (1932: 24). One of her more famous comparisons of personality types was to characterize the Kwakiutl of Canada's Northwest coast as Dionysian or megalomaniacs, and the Pueblo of New Mexico as unemotional and passive. The Zuni, on the other hand, were described as *Apollonian*, or serene and peaceful.

Thus, according to Benedict, each culture has its own distinct emotional and psychological configuration. This perspective became known as *configurationalism*, by which is meant the unconscious underlying psychological patterns or configurations that account for observable cultural patterns (Sidky 2004: 421). The implication of this configurationist approach is that if culture determines personality, then each culture is unique unto itself and therefore not comparable or commensurate with any other culture. This perspective fits well with Boas's cultural relativistic perspective, but also suffers from many of the same defects, which is to say it inhibits cross-cultural generalization. There are methodological difficulties with Benedict's work as well. As Harris (1968: 405) suggests: "It is now generally agreed that Benedict's sketch of the Apollonian way of life achieved its beautiful symmetry only as a result of the omission or selective de-emphasis of nonconforming data." Similarly, "where psychological theories of cultural phenomena contain reference to such essentially hidden, non-observable entities and processes ... one is bound to encounter serious methodological problems in the validation of such theories" (Kaplan and Manners 1972: 142). Put another way, since empirical evidence is not presented in support of the existence of distinct psychological entities that are distinct or independent of the behaviour from which the entities are constructed in the first place, then these sorts of explanations are essentially tautological in nature because the phenomenon that one seeks to explain (i.e., variations in personality or psychological types) is inherent in the explanation itself (i.e., culture determines personality).

Margaret Mead (1901–1978), a student of both Boas and Benedict (who was Boas's teaching assistant), became famous for her research in Samoa when she published the popular *Coming of Age in Samoa* (1928) and *Growing up in New Guinea* (1930). Mead's research brought a contemporary relevance to anthropology since she attempted to demonstrate that the period of adolescence was trouble-free for teenage girls in Samoa, unlike the experiences of teenagers in the United States. She attributed this difference to variability in cultural child-rearing practices, thus demonstrating the importance of the role of culture in determining behaviour over biological factors; in other words, the conclusion is that "nurture" is more significant than "nature" in explaining social behaviour. In her later years, Mead became a prominent figure on the international stage, criticizing the war in Vietnam and promoting the rights of women, among other issues.

Mead's Samoan ethnography was also later severely attacked by an Australian anthropologist, Derek Freeman (1916–2001), in a book entitled *Margaret Mead and Samoa: The Making and Unmaking of an Anthropological Myth* (1983). In what was to become known as the *Mead-Freeman Controversy*, Derek Freeman suggested that Mead's Samoan ethnography was severely flawed. Freeman has argued that the Samoans were aggressive, puritanical, and sexually inhibited, rather than the tension-free experience of Samoan youth portrayed by Margaret Mead. Freeman also accused Mead of forming her theory before she actually started the fieldwork, and then just found examples to support her preconceived notions. This controversy has caused anthropologists to re-examine some of the important historical underpinnings of their discipline, and to acknowledge that misinterpretations are possible even by some of the icons of anthropology.

In evaluating the school of thought known as historical particularism, one is drawn to a singularly identifying characteristic, which is an almost obsessive documenting of cultural details, in Boas's case at least, to the neglect of an attempt to draw generalizations on the basis of fieldwork. In the end one is left with cultural descriptions that are not much more than shreds and patches, to use Lowie's term. In fact, it is not really accurate to describe historical particularism as a theory per se, since there is no articulation of any overarching principles by which the field data can be organized to demonstrate some general explanation.

It is almost as if the aversion to the speculation of the early evolutionists created a sort of paranoia of drawing general conclusions in any form. In addition, the ever increasing portrayal of cultural uniqueness and individuality created an explanatory dead end; the greater the ethnographer delved into the individualistic aspects of particular cultures, the less one can see what is held in common with other cultures. Boas's attempt to make anthropology more scientific could not be based on a program of empirical data collection alone. One also needs hypotheses that could be tested and some attempt to formulate generalizations that could be evaluated cross-culturally. The research agenda of the Boasians was particularly deficient in this regard.

■ Structural Functionalism

Structural functionalism is a theoretical orientation which states that cultures consist of social parts that are integrated and function to maintain the structural whole. The integrated nature of these social wholes suggests that changes in one element produce a corresponding change in other social elements. This formulation is associated with British social anthropology, in particular anthropologists Bronislaw Malinowski (1884–1942) and A.R. Radcliffe-Brown (1881–1955). The inspiration for this approach was derived from the French sociologist Emile Durkheim's (1858–1917) formulations of functionalism, which is to say that social phenomena consist of integrated relationships that function to maintain the society as a whole and to promote group solidarity. However, in the adaptation to British anthropology, the concept of functionalism was reformulated to mean that social institutions function to serve the basic biological needs of individuals in society. In this context, *social structure* could be understood to refer to the ways in which groups and individuals are arranged and related to one another in a functioning entity that is society.

Malinowski was born in Poland, where he received a Ph.D. in mathematics and physics. Like Franz Boas, Malinowski eventually turned from physics to anthropology. In 1914 Malinowski embarked on a field trip to Australia, which coincided with the outbreak of the First World War, and eventually began a period of intensive research among the people in a group of islands called the Trobriands. Malinowski believed that it was important for the ethnographer to become proficient in the local language, so he immersed himself in the day-to-day activities of the Trobriand residents, a technique that we now know as *participant observation*. On this basis the claim is made that Malinowski is the inventor of modern fieldwork (Kuper 1999: 9).

Although a similar claim could be made for Boas's fieldwork among the Inuit of Baffin Island, what sets the two apart is Malinowski's functionalist theoretical perspective. In his classic ethnography, *Argonauts of the Western Pacific* (1922), it is evident on practically every page that he attempts to explain the ethnographic facts that he is gathering in terms of wider principles and to develop the connection between the two. Malinowski, for example, articulates these connections in *Argonauts* in the following manner: "ethnographic sources are of unquestionable scientific value, in which we can clearly draw the line between, on the one hand, the results of direct observation and of native statements and interpretations and, on the other, the inferences of the author, based on his common sense and psychological insight" (1922: 3). Explained in another way, Malinowski's emphasis on rigorous data gathering, involving the detailed analysis of the systematic linkages between cultural elements in a documented manner, was not an end in itself. He sought to go beyond description in order to produce useful generalizations about socio-cultural phenomena (Sidky 2004: 170).

It is from Malinowski's ethnographic observations of the Trobriand islanders that we are given such classic institutions as the *avunculate* and the *kula*. The Trobriand people trace their kinship linkages through the female line only, which we refer to as *matrilineal descent*. Among the Trobriand, the *avunculate* refers to the special relationship that

Box 4.3: The Kula Ring of the Trobriand Islands

The Kula Ring of the Trobriand Islands, located to the east and north of New Guinea, is perhaps the most famous ethnographic description in all of social anthropology. First described by Bronislaw Malinowski in his monumental work, *Argonauts of the Western Pacific* (1922), the kula is a system of ritual exchange uniting certain island residents in a pattern of trading partnerships. The partners in kula exchange relationships circulate cowry shell armbands (*mwali*) in a counter-clockwise direction among the Trobriand Islands, and red shell necklaces (*soulava*) in a corresponding clockwise manner.

The Kula Ring is commonly thought of in anthropology as a system of ceremonial or reciprocal exchange, suggesting that not all trade is undertaken for purely practical purposes or motivated by economic considerations. While men on the kula voyages may trade for other goods as well, the circulating armbands and necklaces are highly sought-after items in themselves and are possessed, even for a short period of time, with great pride and prestige among the owners. Thus, the possessors of these treasured items can gain considerable fame and influence for themselves, as well as for the entire island population of which they are residents. Malinowski's interpretation of the Kula Ring reflects his functional theoretical orientation since he suggested that such a circulating system of exchange links a widely disparate network of relationships that tends to promote peace and harmony, rather than discord and conflict.

Photo 4.3: Bronislaw Malinowski in this famous photograph taken during his fieldwork among the Trobriand islanders.

develops between a boy and his maternal uncle, to the point in which the boy's mother's brother plays more of a socializing role than his own biological father, who is in a different kinship group than his own biological son. This special relationship is further reinforced by a post-marital residence pattern called *avunculocal residence*, in which the newly married couple take up residence with or near the groom's maternal uncle. Thus, Malinowski was able to demonstrate that the peculiarities of Trobriand kinship had a wider applicability in understanding the special institutional characteristics of many societies practising matrilineal descent.

The *kula* refers to a Trobriand Island economic institution that consists of special trading partnerships through which special ceremonial objects—such as white shell armbands, which circulate in a counter-clockwise direction around the islands, and red shell necklaces, which circulate in the opposite direction. This sort of trading is referred to as an example of *balanced reciprocity* and involves long-distance voyages between the various islands. The kula results in the development of tight social bonds between the trading partners and, as Malinowski argues, increases social solidarity because it replaces a situation of potential hostility and warfare with one of mutual support and friendship. Utilitarian objects and materials, such as stone axes, fish, and sweet potatoes, are also exchanged on these voyages, thus demonstrating Malinowski's thesis concerning social institutions functioning to serve basic needs.

The structural functional approach dominated British social anthropology until the early 1960s. Malinowski's students continued using his approach, specializing in particular in fieldwork in West African societies, while at the same time attempting to rectify some of the functionalist flaws. Chief among structural functionalism deficiencies is a difficulty in explaining how societies change. Since a culture was seen as an integrated whole, with a functional interdependence among its various parts, change is difficult to accommodate in a positive way because it is apt to be seen as disruptive and therefore dysfunctional. Yet African societies were undergoing great upheavals as colonialism was coming to an end, and various nations were establishing their own autonomy separate from external pressure.

Max Gluckman (1911–1975) had attended Malinowski's seminar at the London School of Economics, but his scholarly approach was also influenced indirectly by Radcliffe-Brown and Durkheim. In one of Gluckman's prominent studies, *Order and Rebellion in Tribal Africa* (1963), he attempted to reconcile the philosophy of functionalism (a concern with 'order') with a perspective on social upheaval and change (rebellion). What emerged from this attempt is what has been termed an *equilibrium model*. According to this perspective, societies are seen to go through relatively long periods of order and tranquillity, followed by a burst of turmoil and change, returning thereafter to a renewed period of stability. As Gluckman explains in *Custom and Conflict in Africa* ([1956] 1970: 47–48): "So it is clear, to me at any rate, that our studies show that social life breeds conflict, and societies by their customary arrangements (which I accept as given) accentuate conflicts. The conflicts in wider ranges compensate one another to produce social cohesion."

While most anthropologists laud Gluckman's attempt to deal with conflict in a functional paradigm, there are many who would see in this endeavour a failed attempt to account for social change. In other words, one might suggest that Gluckman's approach is not a real theory of conflict at all, but an attempt to keep functionalism afloat without fundamentally changing it. Another issue pertains to Britain's colonial heritage in Africa, with the accusation that British social anthropologists did not actively criticize colonialism and therefore exercised complicity in their muted response to it. One assessment is that "functionalist equilibrium models were indeed problematic and they did emphasize system stability ... but it does not automatically place proponents of structural functionalist models into the camp of the handmaidens of imperialism" (Sidky 2004: 190).

■ Transactional Models

From the 1960s onward, British social anthropology continued to grapple with the vexing problem of explaining social change. The Gluckman equilibrium model was not much more than functionalism in disguise. It was evident that a new approach was necessary to explain change and conflict, one that did not rely on a functionalist underpinning. The new approach that eventually emerged is commonly called a *transactional model*, which is to say that social change can be explained by the choices people make in the constant competition over scarce resources, and the transactions, negotiations, and exchanges that are involved in the decision-making process (Hedican 1986c). Fredrik Barth's *Models of Social Organization* (1966) is a concise statement of the transactional approach. He discusses the ethnographic example of a Norwegian fishing fleet in which decisions about where to fish are in constant flux as a result of the ebb and flow of the decisions made by other boat captains. What emerges from Barth's study is a view of society in which individuals are understood as manipulating creatures, constantly looking out for their own self-advantage. However, the choices people make are also governed or constrained by various parameters, such as norms and values, and the distribution of scarce resources, so Barth's suggestion is that social organization is best understood in terms of underlying processes that eventually result in, or generate, the social organization itself.

Another influential study of the post-functionalist period in Britain is F.G. Bailey's *Stratagems and Spoils* (1969), which has an explicit focus on the exercise of power and the politics of social interaction. Bailey's principle point is that individuals in society are constantly manipulating the world around them to get what they want, and are willing to transgress rules of the normative in order to satisfy their needs. People often say one thing, but do another, if it is to their advantage. The view of society that emerges is one of individualistic self-interest in which everyone is calculating the costs and benefits of almost every action he or she takes.

This pragmatic approach to social organization goes a long way in explaining social change, especially in terms of people's varying opportunity costs of the actions they take, and in this sense it is an innovative work that takes anthropology beyond the static offering of functionalism. Yet, perhaps the case for individualistic self-interest as the chief

---

Box 4.4: Political Leadership among Swat Pathans, Pakistan

In one of the most influential monographs in social anthropology, Fredrik Barth (1959) describes the leadership patterns of the Pathans of the Swat valley in the Northwest frontier province of Pakistan. Among the Swat Pathans there are small local groups that maintain internal order through coercive authority, often supported by physical force. As Barth (1959: 2) explains, "Each individual is born into a particular structural position, and will accordingly give his political allegiance to a particular group or office-holder. In Swat, persons find their place in the political order through a series of choices, many of which are temporary or revocable."

Thus, Barth's contribution to the study of political anthropology is that the leadership structure in Swat is not so much based on predetermined patterns or traditions set in place for long periods of time, but on a fluidity of choice making in which each individual assesses his or her own options in terms of the benefits that might be derived from one particular leader or another. However, these choices also take place within a social structure that provides a framework such that the existing social organization may be seen to be the result of a multitude of choices or transactions that take place within a system of wider constraints and options that are available to a person at any one particular point in time.

Among the Swat Pathans, this interaction between social structure, on the one hand, and choices available to a person, on the other, involves a complex combination of factors such as birth and residence, patrilineal descent groups, and a social system of roughly 10 hierarchically ordered hereditary castes. Members of the landowning Pakhtun caste have the most power and serve as the political patrons for all members of the lower castes. Yet there is no predetermined pattern of political allegiances or dominance over any specific person belonging to one of the lower castes because followers have an opportunity to bargain their services in order to take advantage of benefits that could be offered by office holders, such as occupational contracts, membership of men's houses, and religious tutelage.

Ties between leaders and followers develop on an individual or dyadic basis and, as such, political action among the Pathans sorts itself out through a manipulation of these relationships into a viable body of supporters. In addition, both landowners and people of holy descent are active in attempts to attract a political following so that two different types of political groups emerge. The primary groups that are formed on the basis of these dyadic or contractual relationships also combine to form a wider political system comprised of two large, internally coordinated alliances or blocs. Ultimately, then, the form of these blocs results from the regularities in the choices made by individual leaders and their followers, rather than from a political system defined by a set of formal structural positions.

---

characteristic of the human conditions is overstated. People also have altruistic motives for their behaviour, and society as we know it would fall apart if people were not willing, for the most part, to follow rules and social conventions even though these may not be to their immediate advantage.

■ Cultural Ecology and Multilinear Evolution

While anthropologists in Britain were putting their research efforts into seeking ways out of the functionalist bind of explaining social change, in North America the efforts of anthropologists were being directed at providing coherence to the concept of culture, aiming at something more than the shreds and patches approach inherited from Franz Boas. One of the most significant of these attempts is the approach termed *cultural ecology*, which pertains to the relationship between human cultures and their environments.

Alfred Kroeber (1876–1960) was the first of Boas's students to receive a Ph.D. from Columbia University, but he eventually became dissatisfied with his mentor's reluctance to formulate generalizations beyond the particularistic view of culture. Kroeber's approach was to look beyond the individualistic characteristics of culture by examining ecological relationships that tie humans to their environmental settings. In *Cultural and Natural Areas of Native North America* (1939), Kroeber formulated what he called the *culture area concept*. The basic idea of this concept is that cultures within a particular geographical area, such as the Great Plains or the Northwest coast, tend to be similar to one another because of the similar adaptive processes that occur within these areas. In other words, Kroeber suggests a coherent mechanism to explain why cultures change, through the process of environmental *adaptation*, and some of the mechanisms by which this change occurs.

What Kroeber suggested was that social groups moving into a new geographical area begin to adapt their social and economic system to take advantage of the new opportunity for procuring food in the new environment. The emerging adaptive process for each new group entering the area will be more or less the same for each group; hence over time what emerges is a similarity in cultural forms regardless of the characteristics of the original cultures. If we take as an example the Great Plains area, when horses became available, surrounding Aboriginal First Nations began to flood into the area because of the availability of buffalo hunting that the new mobility provided. Some groups were originally Algonquian hunters and gatherers from the Great Lakes area, such as the Comanche. Some, such as the Mandan, were horticulturalists living a marginal Plains life, while others, such as the Sioux, originated in the Carolinas, where they split from their Iroquoian relatives.

A multiplicity of different cultural groups entered the Plains with differing backgrounds. Yet, over time and through a similarity in the adaptive processes involved and cultural borrowing from each other, the cultures became virtually indistinguishable from each other. Characteristics of the Great Plains culture area included the skin teepee, Sun Dance ceremony, sweat lodges, horse pastoralism, and so on. At least these outward appearances would suggest a basic similarity across the entire culture.

While Kroeber's culture area concept, especially its adaptive aspects, provides an explanation for culture change beyond the Boasian paradigm of historical particularism, it probably goes too far, or is not sufficiently precise enough. Are all aspects of a culture, for example, similarly affected by the ecological adaptation process? There is much that is hidden beyond the appearance of tools, technology, and economic systems. How about kinship systems, religious beliefs, and rituals? Are they affected in a similar manner to the economic realm?

It was these sorts of questions that led another of Boas's students, Julian Steward (1902–1972), to refine the cultural ecological approach and merge it with a revitalized version of the earlier unilineal evolutionary perspective. As Steward set out in his *Theory of Culture Change* (1955), a culture can be understood as comprising two significant aspects: its *core* (techno-economics) and *superstructure* (ideology), with each of these affected in a different manner by environmental influences. The *core* comprises the technological and economic aspects of a cultural system, while the *superstructure* comprises such aspects as art, religion, folklore, and politics, which are not directly related to environmental factors. Thus, Steward's scheme provided a refinement on Kroeber's ecological approach of the culture area concept by identifying more precisely the parts of a social and cultural system that are impacted in various ways by changing ecological factors.

Steward's methodology called for a three-part approach: first, examine the tools and technology of a society; second, study the behavioural patterns resulting from the use of this technology; and third, analyze the extent to which the behaviour patterns affect other sectors of a society. This scheme is based on the belief that not all areas of a culture have the same status in terms of causal relationships. He then attempted to operationalize this ecological approach in an effort to understand the way cultures change or evolve.

Rather than suggest that all cultures are apt to change in the same manner or on the same course, as suggested by the unilineal evolutionists, Steward put forward the idea of *multilinear evolution*, by which he meant that cultural evolutionary change can be understood to occur along a number of lines depending upon the influence of particular environmental areas. Thus, Steward was able to avoid the untenable position of the earlier nineteenth-century evolutionists who held to the idea of one fixed pathway for all cultures, while still allowing for a model of evolution that could accommodate particular cultural circumstances and a variety of environmental settings.

■ Northern Plainsmen and Adaptive Strategies

As time went on, further refinements were made to the ecological approach in anthropology, although not always tying these advances to any particular evolutionary scheme. In *Northern Plainsmen* (1969), John Bennett conducted fieldwork in southern Saskatchewan in a region he called Jasper. This area has a complex socio-cultural mix of Hutterites, farmers, ranchers, and Cree Indians. Bennett introduced several innovative approaches to the study of cultural ecology. He pointed out, for example, that cultures are not just directly influenced by environmental settings in a one-way process of interaction, but that the reverse is also true; humans are constantly changing the ecosystem as well.

This idea of a mutual interaction between culture and environment is an important distinction because it improves on earlier ecological studies, such as that of Kroeber or Steward, because it introduces the notion of a *reciprocal feedback* between humans and

Photo 4.4: Threshing crew and machinery near Smiley, Saskatchewan. Notice that many of the men posing for the camera are riding oxen, which are in harness; date not indicated. (Source: University of Saskatchewan Library, Special Collections)

the settings in which they live. There is certainly an adaptation that cultures must make to ecological conditions, but cultures also modify these conditions as well. A second strength of Bennett's approach is that he emphasizes the role of *adaptation*. However, unlike earlier ecological studies, he focuses on the ways in which the different cultural groups in Jasper adapt to each other, along with an adaptation to environmental conditions.

Bennett's concept of adaptation is further refined by introducing the concept of *adaptive strategies*. Each of the four different groups in the Jasper area—Hutterites, farmers, ranchers, and Cree—live in close proximity to each other and must adapt to the courses of action that each of the other groups follows. Members of each of the different groups attempt to adjust to what members of the other groups are doing by adopting their own strategy, which might allow them to take advantage of the interaction that takes place.

The Hutterites, for example, have adapted life on the Northern Plains by developing certain strategies that give them distinct advantages over other groups in the area. One of the most effective of these strategies is purchasing large tracts of land, which they farm on a communal basis. This allows the Hutterites to benefit from an economy of scale, since larger tracts of land are often farmed on a more cost-effective basis. By pooling their labour, buildings, and machinery on a communal basis, the Hutterites also avoid the cost of duplicating many of their farming expenses. In addition, unlike other similar religious groups, such as the Amish or Mennonites, the Hutterites are not averse to adopting modern farming technology,

Photo 4.5: Mennonite settler returning to his farm for dinner after discing. Taken near Colonsay, Saskatchewan; date unknown. (Source: Canadian Department of Interior, Library and Archives Canada)

Photo 4.6: Edenbridge Hebrew Colony, Saskatchewan, celebrating their twenty-fifth anniversary, 1906–1931. (Source: Photograph by Louis Rosenberg, Library and Archives Canada)

Box 4.5: Karl Marx (1818–1883): Materialist Anthropology

It would be hard to imagine a social theorist who has had a greater impact on anthropology and the social sciences in general than Karl Marx. Marx was a German philosopher, historian, and political economist who remained relatively unknown during his lifetime, but his ideology of Marxism began to have a major impact following his death. Two of his most notable works were *The Communist Manifesto* ([1848] 1888) and *Capital* ([1867] 1909), which set out his theory of *historical materialism*. In the preface to his *Contribution to the Critique of Political Economy* ([1859] 1904), Marx explained that "the mode of production in material life determines the general character of the social, political, and spiritual processes of life. It is not the consciousness of men that determines their existence, but, on the contrary, their social existence determines their consciousness" (10–11). A controversial aspect of Marx's theory is that he argued for revolutionary action on the part of underprivileged people to topple capitalism (Sidky 2004: 336–338).

Marx's influence has been felt in many areas of social anthropology. Leslie White (1900–1975), for example, visited Russia in 1929 and later suggested that Marx's theoretical perspective had great possibilities for anthropology. White's theory of "universal evolution" suggests that culture advances according to the increase in the amount of energy per capita per year of a society (1949, 1959). Thus, cultural evolution is directional and progressive, which is a view similar to that proposed by Marx.

Marx's theories are also an important cornerstone of later cultural materialist perspectives in American anthropology, especially those associated with Marvin Harris and others in the cultural ecology field. Harris (1991, 2001) was to build on the work of such "neo-evolutionists" as Leslie White and Julian Steward (1955) by refining the cultural evolutionary approach with the addition of Marx's concept of *mode of production* (the manner in which the techno-economic factors are organized) and the *mode of reproduction* (technologies that affect population size).

Another important area of Marxian influence in anthropology concerns what has been termed "conflict theory." From Marx's perspective, society is divided into competing interest groups—proletariats and capitalists, for example—and that conflicts of interest are the underlying force of social change. Much scholarly investigation in anthropology and sociology has therefore focused on class analysis and the manner in which divisions of labour in society illustrate the divergent interests of wage-earners and the owners of the means of production in capitalist societies (Barrett 1996: 97–98).

Photo 4.7: Karl Heinrich Marx, German philosopher and revolutionary socialist, famous for The Communist Manifesto ([1848] 1888) and other influential writings.

which strengthens their competitive edge. In other words, "Bennett laid to rest the simplistic notion that for each set of ecological conditions there can only be a single cultural response" (Barrett 1996: 90).

■ Cultural Materialism and the Riddles of Culture

The last major contributor to the ecological *cum* evolutionary perspective in social anthropology is Marvin Harris's concept of *cultural materialism*. In several highly provocative books—such as *Cows, Pigs, Wars, and Witches: The Riddles of Culture* (1975) and a later widely used introductory anthropology text that espouses the principles of cultural materialism (Harris 2001)—Harris attempts to explain why humans engage in such inscrutable behaviour as instituting a religious ban on killing cows in a country such as India, where many of its population are either starving or severely malnourished.

Harris's basic explanation is that such religious doctrines as *ahimsa* (the Hindu principle of the unity of life, of which a sacredness of cattle is a principal symbol) is really a cover-up to secure certain economic advantages. Harris marshals an impressive array of statistics on the Indian economy to illustrate the major economic advantages that cows provide—millions of tons of cow dung used for cooking fuel and fertilizer, traction for ploughing fields in place of expensive tractors, leather for sandals, and a host of other products. The list goes on and on: cows do not require much upkeep since they eat grass along the roadways and other marginal areas, and they provide a source of protein (for certain castes) when they eventually die.

The conclusion is then obvious: cows are protected in India because of their immense economic value. If one were to introduce Western-style agricultural production in India, as many development agencies would suggest, the economic consequences would lead to a major catastrophe. Perhaps the people are malnourished in some areas, yet it would bankrupt the Indian economy if a majority of the cows were culled from the countryside and replaced by expensive tractors and fertilizer with no obvious increase in agricultural proficiency. *Ahimsa* therefore prevents the relinquishment of this major economic asset in the Indian economy. The sacred cattle complex, rather than being irrational, plays a positive and critical economic role in India.

Similar arguments are developed to explain why there are religious prohibitions against eating pigs in the Middle East (it is not cost effective to raise them, given the arid climate), or why the same animals are revered as ancestors in New Guinea (it costs almost nothing to raise pigs in this temperate climate, where they largely forage for themselves in the surrounding forest). The general argument suggests that as human economic history developed over the millennia, "there was an incentive to keep the most useful animal species and eliminate those that were too costly to maintain" (Sidky 2004: 380).

Beyond these specific details of cows and pigs and the ecological advantages and disadvantages of raising or not raising them in particular cultures, Harris presents a wider

---

Box 4.6: The Tsembaga Maring of Papua New Guinea

The Tsembaga Maring live in the highlands of central New Guinea. Their principle mode of subsistence is based on slash-and-burn horticulture in which they grow taro, yams, and sweet potatoes. The Tsembaga also raise domesticated pigs, which are sometimes fed refuse yams, or the pigs forage for food around the village and in the surrounding forest. The Tsembaga also engage in periodic warfare with neighbouring tribes, not for the acquisition of additional land, but to avenge earlier raids that may have killed or injured one of their kinsmen.

Ethnographer Roy Rappaport (1967, 1984) has made a systematic study of Tsembaga subsistence patterns that leads him to suggest there is a complex system of cyclical relationships involving inter-village conflicts and alliances, the raising of pigs, and wider ecological factors pertaining to population density among the highland tribes of New Guinea. He suggests, for example, that the cycle begins with the establishment of a period of peaceful relations among otherwise hostile villages, a period symbolized by the planting of a sacred *rumbin* tree.

As long as this special tree is growing and remains healthy, war between the hostile neighbours is not likely to occur. Over time, though, the pig population, which had previously undergone a drastic reduction because of a period of feasting with allied neighbours, once again begins to proliferate. An increasing pig population causes stress among village members because the swine begin to forage in people's gardens, causing interpersonal conflicts. Eventually village residents begin to remember old scores that should be settled with their previous hostile neighbours. As tensions rise, village residents may also begin to renew alliance with the members of friendly tribes, eventually holding a series of feasts in which large numbers of pigs are slaughtered and the meat distributed among the guests.

According to Rappaport, the village warriors become energized by this gorging of protein, eventually leading to renewed hostilities. The *rumbin* tree is uprooted, and a new cycle of violence takes place. Generally this cycle of growth in the pig population, rising village tensions, hosting of feasts for allies, and renewed hostilities with enemy tribes takes between five and 10 years to complete, after which a new cycle begins.

The suggestion in Rappaport's analysis is that the Tsembaga pig-warfare cycle is not so much an example of ecological adaptation but of equilibrium and system maintenance. Ritual mediates between the Tsembaga people and their environment. Ritual regulates competition for scarce resources between people and pigs, and is the guiding hand behind warfare. When the pig population builds up, which threatens the equilibrium between people and pigs, warfare erupts, leading to a decimation in the population of both people and pigs. In this way a balance is restored so that the carrying capacity of the local environment is no longer overtaxed or exceeded. Thus, the cycle of fighting and feasting keeps the balance among humans, land, and animals.

---

argument. *Cultural materialism* can be defined as a theory of cultural causation in which the independent variables of economics, technology, and environment interact with one another. It is a research strategy that accounts for cross-cultural differences and similarities in the material constraints on human behaviour.

Furthermore, Harris builds on or refines Steward's distinction between core and superstructure by dividing these further into a three-part system. *Infrastructure* is divided into *mode of production* (the technology and practices of food production) and *mode of reproduction* (practices employed for expanding, limiting, and maintaining population size). *Structure* is seen in two parts: *domestic economy* (basic production, exchange, and consumption patterns, along with the division of labour), and *political economy* (political organizations, taxation, law and order, police, and military). The third part of Harris's scheme, the *superstructure*, is comprised of art, music, literature, religious rituals, and sports.

These are the components of what Harris refers to as the *universal pattern* by which he means this pattern is applicable to all societies. These components are also to be seen as a hierarchical pattern, with infrastructure at the bottom and superstructure at the top, such that there is an ascending order or relationship in terms of environmental influences. In other words, the infrastructure, which refers to the basic subsistence production practices, is most closely tied to environmental influences, while those components higher up, such as the superstructure of sports and religion, is least influenced by the environment.

A pertinent question as far as anthropological theory is concerned would be: is cultural ecology (and cultural materialism) with its emphasis on causality and objective conditions, especially technology and environment, a better alternative to historical particularism in understanding the human condition? A balanced answer would be that both approaches have their strengths and weaknesses, but they complement each other in a certain manner because each fulfills a role in explaining cultural phenomenon that the other does not do very well.

Historical particularism, with its emphasis on detailed fieldwork, is an inductive approach, which is in close touch with cultural details. The evolutionist and cultural materialist orientation is more of a deductive approach in which the anthropologist comes armed with theoretical principles already in mind. One, historical particularism, is burdened by (excessive) cultural detail, and lacks the ability to generalize beyond specific cases. The other, cultural materialism, with its narrow focus on environment and technology, is apt to miss the rich details of cultural life that make human societies so interesting. Contemporary social anthropology has shown a decided preference for the former (a subjective, inductive orientation), rather than the latter (objective, deductive).

■ The Fundamentals of Postmodernism

By the mid-1980s the type of science epitomized by cultural materialism was becoming increasingly scrutinized and criticized. The old macro-micro dilemma, one of social anthropology's most persistent themes and seemingly insoluble issues, was beginning to re-emerge after a period of suppression by the scientific, objective orientation of cultural materialism and its allied approaches. One of the most vexing issues in the history of anthropology is the one of positivism versus relativism or, as Barrett (2002: 24) phrases it, "how does one pull off a study that is rich in local detail, and yet integrated into the broader historical and structural setting?"

Efforts to resolve the micro-macro issue did not take place in the late 1980s; instead, anthropology plunged headlong into a post-positivist era, commonly known as postmodernism. *Postmodern anthropology* can be defined as an anti-science, subjective, literary perspective, which rejects the idea of universally valid objective knowledge and focuses on culture as open-ended negotiated meanings and stresses the examination of how ethnographies are written (Sidky 2004: 436). During this postmodernist period, anthropologists saw science itself as artificial and not in touch with cultural realities, and some even regarded it as imperialistic and obscene.

Postmodern anthropologists "vehemently oppose science and scientific perspectives and instead advocate approaches based upon local insights and the view of the social actors as individuals" (Sidky 2004: 393). In this light, postmodernism is a return to a relativistic perspective and a culturally constructed view of reality, rather than an attempt at reconciling the positivistic and relativistic themes in anthropology. The theoretical pendulum in anthropology at the start of the twenty-first century clearly has swung back toward an orientation very much reminiscent of Boas's historical particularism, with an emphasis on interpretation and meaning (Geertz 1973, 1983).

There are two works of the postmodern genre that most vociferously attack the pillars of traditional science. In *Writing Culture: The Poetics and Politics of Ethnography*, the point is made that "all constructed truths are made possible by powerful lies of exclusion and rhetoric ... [postmodern] social scientists have recently come to view good ethnographies as 'true fictions'" (Clifford and Marcus 1986: 6–7). We are told that anthropology is in an "experimental moment" and, furthermore, that the solution to the problem that anthropologists face in accurately representing other cultures lies in creating new forms of ethnographic writing. It is founded on the belief that "writing has emerged as central to what anthropologists do both in the field and thereafter" (1986: 2).

From this perspective, the value of an ethnography does not adhere in its scientific value, which is seen as largely fictitious, based on "lies of exclusion," but as a literary text, as a form of writing. Clearly the postmodernist suggestion is to move ethnography out of the realm of science and into the humanities, where it can be studied as a literary art form (Geertz 1988a). The postmodernist dissatisfaction with conventional "scientific ethnography," aside from whether or not it should be art or science, also stems from a concern with what some regard as an unacceptable *anthropological authority*.

Their point is that it is exceedingly arrogant that anthropologists should be presumptuous enough to think that they can adequately represent the cultural lives of people in other societies. It is furthermore suggested that anthropologist are agents of colonialism because of the differential power between Western societies (the home of the anthropologists, generally) and the rest of the world. Postmodernist anthropologists use the term *dialogical approach*, which is to say that fieldwork consists of a dialogue between the "Other," or natives, and the ethnographer. Another term sometimes also used is *polyvocal*, meaning that the voices of the research subjects should be combined with that of the ethnographer in such a way that the latter's voice does not dominate the former.

In a related work, *Anthropology as Cultural Critique*, it is suggested that "the contemporary debate is about how an emergent postmodern world is to be represented as an object for social thought in its various disciplinary manifestations" (Marcus and Fischer 1986: vii). The idea promoted in this work is that anthropology should have a political mission, such that ethnography would document cultural differences with a view to encouraging a more tolerant Western society. Marcus and Fischer (1986: 141) explain that for this reason, "a major task of the epistemological critique offered by anthropology is to deal directly and in novel ways with the materialist or utilitarian bias of Western thought in explanations of social life."

In all, the postmodern perspective in social anthropology can be summed up by identifying the following characteristics. First, postmodernism represents a turn away from objective science, which emphasizes causality and generalization, toward a focus on meaning and relativist interpretations. Second, postmodernism promotes a challenge to the ethnographer's authority as the sole voice, such that it advocates a polyvocal approach in which the native's point of view is heard in combination with the fieldworker. And third, the idea of an ethnography consisting of a scientific document is replaced with an emphasis of ethnography as a literary text or a type of writing that one can study, as one studies a novel, poem, or other work of fiction.

■ Feminist Anthropology

Feminist anthropology shares several characteristics with the postmodernist perspective, with several additional concerns. It shares with postmodernism a subjective, inductive approach, an emphasis on meaning and interpretation rather than causality and positivistic perspectives, and a concern with ethnographic authority. In addition, feminist anthropologists are concerned with a perceived male bias in ethnography, and are interested in the gendered aspects of social relationships (Lamphere, Rayna, and Rubin 2007; Milton 1979; Stacey 1988; Strathern 1987; Warren 1988; Whittaker 1994).

Judith Stacey asks the rhetorical question: "Can there be a feminist ethnography?" (1988). She begins with the observation that "Most feminist researchers, committed, at a minimum, to redressing the sexist imbalances of masculinist scholarship, appear to select their research projects on substantive grounds. Personal interests and skill meld, often mysteriously, with collective feminist concerns" (1988: 21). Feminist anthropology is a personal matter, since most social relationships have an important gendered aspect to them, which influences one's research interests. Stacey also points out a fundamental perspective: "Feminist scholars evince widespread disenchantment with the dualisms, abstractions, and detachment of positivism, rejecting the separations between subject and object, thought and feeling, knower and known, and political and personal" (1988: 21).

As far as the answer to her question about feminist anthropology is concerned, Stacey suggests that there cannot be a fully feminist ethnography because there can

Box 4.7: Margaret Mead (1901–1978): Storm over Samoa

Margaret Mead may not have been solely responsible for a feminist perspective in anthropology, but she certainly played a major role in enhancing the role of women ethnographers in the discipline. When her mentor, Franz Boas, suggested that it was too dangerous for a woman to conduct research in the Polynesian islands, Mead rebuffed the warning. Boas suggested she conduct her research closer to home, among an American Aboriginal culture, as her teaching assistant Ruth Benedict had done among the Zuni.

As Mead explained in her autobiography, *Blackberry Winter*, "I had a chance to do field work in Samoa, where I wanted to go, instead of working with an American Indian tribe, which was what my professor Franz Boas, wanted me to do" (1972: 39). And then, "Three years later, after my return from Samoa, when I submitted my manuscript of *Coming of Age in Samoa* [1928], he turned to me at a department lunch and said, … 'You haven't made clear the difference between passionate and romantic love.' That was the only criticism he ever made of it" (1972: 121).

Perhaps Boas had begun to realize that Margaret Mead was best left to her own devices and initiative. She was the first American female anthropologist to conduct research in such a distant place as Samoa, and was such a prolific writer during her academic career that her name became a household word. Her numerous books and publications, such as *Sex and Temperament in Three Primitive Societies* ([1935] 1963) and *Male and Female: A Study of the Sexes in the Changing World* (1949), established the important role of women in a global perspective.

Margaret Mead's Samoa research has also been the subject of one of the most polemical attacks on another anthropologist in recent memory. One of Mead's main conclusions resulting from her Samoan research was that, unlike America, adolescence in Samoa was relatively free of tension, suggesting that human cultures are remarkably malleable and free from direct biological pressures. Derek Freeman (1983) disagreed with Mead's conclusions quite vociferously, suggesting in fact that a more factual view of Samoan society revealed a world of conflict, strain, and competition. What is evident from this controversy is that both ethnographers were approaching Samoan society from quite different starting points—Mead's from the cultural point of view, and Freeman from socio-biology. In other words, their theoretical perspectives were at odds with each other, a realization that tends to minimize the impact of Freeman's controversial attack.

Photo 4.8: Margaret Mead in Samoan dress, with friends, while she practised the research technique of participant observation during her fieldwork in the village of Vaitogi.

be only "partial" feminist ethnographies that "seem worth the serious moral costs involved" (1988: 27). A main problem, as Strathern (1987) so eloquently articulates, is that the relationship between feminism and ethnography is unavoidably ambivalent and "awkward." The relationship between self and "Other" is problematic because it rests on "incompatible constructions," and an acute sensitivity to power inequalities. What is seen as incompatible is the pretentious anthropological alliance and collaboration between the ethnographer and the Other. The call is for a more egalitarian research process, free from structural inequalities.

Does this mean that males cannot contribute to the feminist project in anthropology? At the University of Guelph, where I have taught a course on anthropological theory for over 20 years, seminar groups are frequently organized. The classes, which were usually comprised of about 70 percent female students, were divided into three or four discussion groups who were asked to consider the question: "Can men make a significant contribution to feminist anthropology?" I used the word "significant" to avoid an automatic *yes* response. Hundreds of students were involved in these discussions over the years and, for the most part, students, females especially, refused to exclude males from the debate on the untenable grounds that female anthropology is all about women. In fact, most suggested that men could be feminists, too, if they promoted the objectives of feminist approaches. The students, while wishing for more male involvement in feminist concerns because this affects the men just as much as the women, thought that men could make a significant contribution if more effort was put into it.

This is not to suggest that there has not been a pronounced male bias in anthropology, as Milton (1979) suggests. During the Boasian period of historical particularism, many prominent women, such as Ruth Benedict and Margaret Mead, made important contributions to anthropology, but this has not always been the case. For most of the history of anthropology, men have controlled the research agenda. As Milton explains (1979: 40): "Male bias in anthropology is often seen as having a dual character; it exists in the theoretical frameworks that have been formulated and used by anthropologists, and in the ethnographic data they analyse. The bias in theory is seen primarily as a product of a scholarly tradition that has been influenced mainly by men, this influence in turn being related to a wider bias in the society of which this tradition is a part."

The current state of dissatisfaction in anthropology regarding the treatment of women is really part of a wider problem pertaining to a male bias in Western industrial societies as a whole (Sanday 1973; Sacks 1979). In ethnography the activities and interests of men have taken precedence over those of women, who have remained relatively invisible. Thus, an attempt to correct the male bias in anthropology, in order to be effective, must be coupled with attempts to do something about the overall sexism in Western society. These issues, then, concern "fundamental principles of social organization on which all cultural products, including male bias in society and anthropology, are assumed to be based" (Milton 1979: 41).

■ Assessment of Theoretical Trends

This chapter began with questions about the nature of the course of anthropological theory. Various approaches were discussed, such as whether or not theory in anthropology was cumulative, if it progressed in a straight line, or if it swung back and forth in a dialectical fashion. There was also the question of anthropological theory as paradigms, and the pervasiveness of such as models of research.

In Kuhn's sense of a paradigm, at any rate, it is safe to say that research in anthropology has never been guided by all pervasive models. Even during periods when there was a strong preference for one type of orientation, such as the Boasian period of historical particularism, there were at least the seeds for alternatives or competing approaches. Anthropology then falls into what Kuhn has referred to as a pre-paradigmatic status, which is to say a number of competing models of research exist, until one finally dominates over the rest.

Whether this will ever eventually happen in anthropology is a questionable concern. Nonetheless, what is evident is that anthropological theory has been pervaded from its early beginning by two alternative perspectives—positivism and phenomenology or relativism. For certain stretches of time, one is quite prominent, then interest in it dissipates, only to have it return to prominence at some future date. In this regard one can safely say that a dialectical shift between positivism and relativism has been the most characteristic theme in anthropology's theoretical history.

Research Design, Strategies, and Methods

World anarchy just around the corner?
Does life seem unfair, corrupt, and bewildering? Do you sometimes wonder if the world has been swept out of control, and
only a drastic overhaul will put it back on an even keel? If so,
somebody wants you: the radical right and the radical left. Both
share the view that Western society is in a state of crisis and that
the revolution is imminent. Each is determined to emerge from
the anticipated anarchy in firm control of the political apparatus.
—Stanley Barrett,
Is God a Racist? (1986: 3)

Research without a point to be made would seem to lack any useful purpose. This is
one of the major areas of criticism with postmodernist anthropology: "prudent thinkers
can rightly question the motives of those who opt for storytelling, rather than applying their intellectual abilities to real theoretical and methodological problems and the
innumerable tangible issues facing human beings around the globe" (Sidky 2004: 412).
The point of research should be that it provides us with new information that we did
not have before. This information may be in a form that allows us to see old facts in
new ways, or it may be an addition to what we already know. Either way, there should
be some point to it all.

In this chapter we set out the main areas of research design and methods used to gather
information. Then examples of anthropological research in Canadian settings are used to
illustrate the ways in which research strategies are conceptualized and carried out.

■ Formulating a Research Design

Step One: Choose an Issue or Problem

Without this there can be no focus or solution. It takes creative thinking to delineate a
research focus, so much depends on how this focus is conceptualized. If we do not have

an issue or problem that has to be solved, or at least understood in some way, then we will never know when we have reached a solution. Putting our research focus in the form of a brief, concise question helps. If we have a body of data, what is it that we want to know about this data? How can this data help us to understand a particular issue in anthropology? Without a focus we never know when to end. Remember that Boas ended up with 5,000 pages of ethnographic notes on the Kwakiutl without informing the reader what the point of it all was. Without a main point, focus, theme, or problem, research can become nothing more than endless data collection.

Box 5.1: The Bamboo Fire: Research among the New Guinea Wape

Anthropological research is conducted in many different parts of the world, under varying social, cultural, and environmental conditions. Even before information can be collected in the field, information on language characteristics, cultural practices, and population demographics must first be gathered from existing ethnographic reports, which in many cases may be non-existent, particularly that pertaining to very remote or isolated people.

William Mitchell describes research among the New Guinea Wape as similar to their lighting of a bamboo fire to drive away the morning's fog: "And so it is with field work. The anthropologist sets a blaze of inquiry to drive away his ignorance and bring the light of understanding to a culture he doesn't know" (1987: 11). He also goes on to indicate that the difficulties of anthropological fieldwork are not just about the practical matters of gathering information; it is that the research process, by necessity, is conducted under conditions so vastly different in almost every respect from one's usual life.

The Wape are citizens of Papua New Guinea, which is an independent nation situated north of Australia that consists of approximately 2.5 million people. The Wape live in a mountainous forest habitat, reside in sedentary villages, and are organized in exogamous patrilineal clans. The indigenous language of Olo is combined with the *lingua franca* of Melanesian Pidgin, which allows for inter-tribal communication over large areas in a land with over 700 mutually distinct languages. Mitchell utilized a variety of research methods, including tape recordings, field notes, photographs, and informant interviews. He also describes, in a highly informative discussion, how the "raw" data of the actual field experience is abstracted through the anthropologist's theoretical stance, creative imagination, and discussion with others.

Mitchell strongly contends that ethnography is not a "fictional invention," despite the abstract route that is employed in an analysis, but a valid and meaningful interpretation "rooted in a corpus of richly detailed field work data. In this sense ... it is an authentic version of what happened and, therefore, *truthful* if not the 'truth'. No ethnographic account can ever be more than that" (1987: 265). In a wider sense, an ethnographic account, he contends, is a product of a "culturally circumscribed theory of knowledge." Mitchell's ethnographic account of the Wape illustrates that a thorough description of the research process itself can be every bit as informative or theoretically significant as the particular details of cultural life that are collected during the process of fieldwork.

Step Two: Choose an Appropriate Theoretical Focus

I am not suggesting that you need to choose a theoretical focus such as historical particularism or cultural materialism, but you need to decide what the general area of your
research falls into. If the area is political organization, then is your focus on local-level
leadership, group decision making, or regional government? Deciding on a general
theme allows you to make a hypothesis or two about what your expectations are with
your research. This general focus can always be refined later as you progress with the data
gathering and at the end of it as well, so it provides a guide or design for what you are
doing. You should have a sense about where you are going.

Step Three: Explore Previous Literature and Knowledge in Your Research Area

Research should have a rationale for what is to be done. You need to spell out in specific
terms what the reasons are that motivate you to do this research. In the social sciences
this process usually involves finding out what other people have done in your area.
Getting to be an expert on the literature in a specific area is an absolutely essential part
of any coherent research project.

An ability to be able to discuss the main ideas previously put forward by scholars who
have worked in your area provides you with the expertise to convincingly put forward
your own ideas. If you do not know what others have done previously, then how can you
expect to convince others that your ideas make a new contribution to knowledge? Making a contribution to the literature is also an essential part of the reason why research
should be published.

You can sort out what your contribution might be by taking either one of two
approaches. The easiest approach is to locate gaps in the literature. Scholars cannot do
everything, and probably there is only a very small fraction done already compared to
what could eventually be accomplished, so find your own niche. Say to yourself: *Here
is a patch of intellectual ground that has not been dug up before. I wonder what I will find?*
Researching a previously uncultivated area allows you to have a built-in rationale for
what you are attempting to do.

The second approach to the literature is somewhat more difficult. This involves seeing
a body of literature in a new sort of way—that is, in providing a new interpretation. This
might involve providing a critique of what has been done previously in order to outline
deficiencies in past research. Here is an example to explain what I mean. It derives from
my study (Hedican 1976, 1986a) conducted in northwestern Ontario regarding local-
level leadership in an Aboriginal community. The general area is political anthropology,
and the more specific sub-area is commonly called "patron–client relationships".

Patrons are leaders who function in informal community settings, who are not usually elected to their position of local influence, but are prominent because they perform
various sorts of favours for their clients and for other people in their communities. The
literature in this patron–client area focuses on Meso-America and the Mediterranean
areas, so I felt that I already had a built-in rationale by discussing this type of political

organization in a northern Aboriginal setting, which had not been done before. So, at a minimum, I had the opportunity to explore one of these gaps in the literature, but I wanted to push matters further into the theoretical domain as well.

As I reviewed the literature, I began to notice several prevailing characteristics of the previous studies. One was that the patron–client relationships seemed to be studies in isolation from a discussion of ecological and cultural settings. Now I knew that I was on to something here that would tie my research together. The ecological setting was an important omission, I argued, because patrons need to use resources to dispense to clients. Where do these resources come from? In the northern Aboriginal community in which I was working, the resources provided by patrons came from government-sponsored work projects. Local leaders were able to tap into these economic resources, and use them to provide jobs for community members, thereby enhancing their status in the rest of the community.

The second area, the cultural setting, was important, I suggested, because norms and values at the local cultural level will affect how local patrons can operate. In northern Ontario among the Aboriginal population, traditional leaders, called *ogima*, were expected to show generosity by sharing the game they hunted. In the modern setting, the Aboriginal patrons were expected to dispense jobs and other economic benefits. This premium on generosity was an important cultural factor determining the success or failure of local patrons, so I made this a crucial point of my study. That is, the suggestion I was making was that the previous literature was deficient in not recognizing the ecological and cultural settings in which patron–client relationships operated. So with this I had my rationale and could discuss my points in the literature of political anthropology.

Step Four: Choose a Method(s) Appropriate to Your Research Topic

Anthropologists use a variety of research methods in their research, depending on what kind of data they wish to gather. The technique of *participant observation* is the *sine qua non* of ethnographic fieldwork. Although it has a somewhat ambiguous label (How do you observe and participate at the same time?), the basic idea is that the researcher remains observant while participating in the lives of the people under study as much as possible. There are times when participating may not be possible, for example, during a religious ritual in which participation is restricted to community members only, but, for the most part, one attempts to attain an involvement in community life, which means living in the same housing conditions as they do, eating their food, and also possibly adopting their styles of dress and learning their language. In other words, one tries to fit in so that the researcher is able to gain some sense of what it is like to "walk a mile in their shoes."

It is also important to remember that the researcher is there for a reason, which is to collect information, so a certain objective distance is required. Usually one does not participate to the extent of marrying into the local population, although some anthropologists have done this. The term "going native" means that the researcher has crossed the line of objective observer and has committed himself or herself to a full participation in the local society, maybe even never returning to his or her own culture.

The point is that maintaining a participant observer role requires discipline and vigilance. You are there to conduct a field study and then return to your own society, not to be assimilated into theirs.

Interviewing is another means of gathering information. Usually one uses *informants* to provide the sorts of specific details that one needs to illustrate a point or to provide the basis for making a case for one particular hypothesis or another. The first thing to remember about interviewing is that this research technique is all about communication in all its different facets. It is also about developing rapport, which is facilitated by putting people at ease. Interviewing is not just about asking questions. Of course one has to decide who to interview, and who might be willing to provide the information one is seeking to gather.

There are also variations in informant reliability to consider, so selecting the right people is an important consideration. There is also the issue of deviant or marginal informants. There are always people in a community who would like to enhance their status in the local community by associating with an important outsider. Watch out for false information that might be provided just to get you interested. In this regard, *cross-checking*, sometimes referred to as *triangulation*, is an important aspect of verifying informant reliability. It is important to double-check all the information that is gathered. It is not necessarily the case that someone is lying or intentionally misleading the researcher, although that happens occasionally. It is just that different people may see or interpret situations in ways that are different from others.

With regard to asking questions, be aware that there are usually cultural norms regarding questioning someone—a proper etiquette, if you will. In our own culture, many people become immediately uncomfortable when someone starts asking about their finances, especially if this person is a stranger. The same goes for certain topics that are usually considered to be a private concern, such as sexual matters or one's religious beliefs. There are also right and wrong ways to ask questions. How direct are you allowed to be in asking for information? Do you have to "beat about the bush" for a while until you get to the point? Obviously a certain amount of sensitivity and tact is required of efficient fieldworkers.

In a *structured interview* one has some rather specific pieces of information that are needed, so the questions are set beforehand and are fairly precise. The advantage of this interview method is that each person interviewed is asked to respond to the same questions, which allows for some consistency and comparability in the responses of each individual.

The more common method employed is the *unstructured interview* method. In this instance the researcher has a general sense of what information needs to be gathered, but is unsure about how the interview will go or about the responses that might be elicited. In this unstructured format, one question leads to another and so forth, in a process of free association down a path of inquiry that could be quite unexpected. The main advantage of this technique is the flexibility that it affords to the researcher in following up on different leads.

At times a *questionnaire* is used in the course of fieldwork, but this method is more frequently used in disciplines such as sociology, where one is apt to be dealing with research participants who speak the same language as the one conducting the research. In some instances the use of a questionnaire involves reading the questions to the subject, and making sure that he or she understands the question. In cultures without a literate tradition, this method can pose added difficulties. In addition, participants may associate questionnaires with government officials whom they might regard as prying into local affairs.

A *case study* approach is another means of gathering information. In this method the researcher wishes to use a particular case, which they would research in some depth, to illustrate the nuances of situations that would not be feasible for one to do for the entire population. This approach is similar to the *life history* method that anthropologists use to focus on the various phases of a person's life to illustrate what it is like to experience the different aspects of the life cycle.

Step Five: Organization and Analysis of Data

After information is gathered, and even during the gathering process itself, the researcher is required to think about isolating certain themes and trends in the information. This allows one to see where more information is required to fill in gaps in the ethnographic record of the research. Are there patterns that are beginning to emerge? Can a certain generalization be supported with the data gathered so far? These are important questions that allow one to tie the data to the original research focus, and eventually to the academic literature. Generalizations need to be supported with a step-by-step presentation of data. Most of the time it is very difficult or impossible, once one has left the field, to go back and collect important missing pieces of data that were originally overlooked, so it is important while in the field to anticipate how the data collected will be used at a future point in time.

Step Six: Draw Conclusions Appropriate to Your Area of Investigation

What is required here is that one follows through with the process developed in step five, which is to draw the trends and themes together in a logical and coherent argument that addresses as precisely as possible one's initial problem or focus. If one puts some creative effort into this process, then one should be in a position to provide a convincing argument or conclusion pertinent to the issues or problems that were initially focused on in step one.

Step Seven: Discuss Wider Trends and Prospects for Future or Further Research

This step requires the researcher to look beyond the specific details of his or her present study to suggest where additional research, if conducted, could lead to further contributions to knowledge. This could be research that one could follow up on in the future as an extension of the present project. It may also involve informing others in this area of study what the extended implications are concerning one's present study. This step acknowledges that research is a continuous process of investigation.

What follows now is a discussion of specific research studies, focusing on methods of research employed, problems encountered, and the general area of anthropological study involved. The first of these case studies focuses on research conducted in northern Ontario among the members of an Aboriginal community who live in an isolated bush region north of Lake Superior.

■ Case Study One: The Anishenabe of Northwestern Ontario

This case study discusses research conducted in a remote area of northwestern Ontario, about 300 km north of Thunder Bay, among the Anishenabe, who are also known as Ojibwa or Chippewa. The focus of the research was a tourist lodge building project at Whitewater Lake, north of the Canadian National Railway line, which is accessible only by float plane or canoe. When I arrived, the lodge was in the early construction phase, so I had the opportunity to study the development of the whole process from its initial conception to the eventual completion. The overall theme of the research was to find out how a successful economic development project could be achieved in a northern Aboriginal community that lacks most resources, except for the members' own skills, initiative, and knowledge (Hedican 2001a, 2001b).

The Research Setting

The Anishenabe live in a rugged country, much of it covered by water, swamps, rivers, and lakes. Dense stands of spruce and birch forests are typical of this area of the Canadian Shield in the eastern Subarctic. Generally the Anishenabe live between the southern areas of the Shield, just north of Lake Superior, up to the Albany River, where there is a gradual cultural merging with the Cree. For the most part, the Anishenabe have subsisted on fishing, trapping, and wild rice harvesting, but all of these activities do not have the income potential to adequately support the growing population. There is an acute lack of jobs at present suited to the remote locations, skills, and lifestyles of the Aboriginal peoples.

The tourist industry, government-sponsored work projects, and commercial fishing provide the main sources of employment. While not readily evident to the passerby, most communities have a hidden economy of subsistence hunting and fishing, firewood collection, and the manufacture of local products, such as snowshoes, sleds, and leather products.

Ethnographic research in this area has not been overly intensive, consisting mostly of various ethnological sketches and surveys in the early part of the twentieth century, and then shifting to more involved, problem-oriented research after the 1950s. Further fieldwork after this time produced more rounded community studies, such as Dunning's (1959) research on the social and economic change in Pekengekum, and Rogers's (1962) study of Weagamow Lake. For the most part, Rogers's (1962: 2) comment that "so little fieldwork has been done in this area [i.e., northern Ontario] that comparison and generalization is impossible" is still largely true today.

Box 5.2: Ruth Landes (1908–1991): Ojibwa Woman

Ruth Landes was born in Manhattan of Russian Jewish immigrants. While working on her master's degree in 1929 on Black Jews in Harlem, Landes sought the advice of Franz Boas, who suggested that she switch her academic interests from social work to anthropology. She received her Ph.D. from Columbia University in 1935 under the supervision of Ruth Benedict. It was Benedict who convinced her to undertake fieldwork with Native Americans. Between 1932 and 1936, Landes conducted research with the Ojibwa (Anishenabe) of Manitou Rapids near Kenora, Ontario, the Santee Dakota of Minnesota, and the Potawatomi in Kansas (*New York Times* 1991).

On the basis of this extensive research, Ruth Landes wrote a series of important ethnographies, such as *Ojibwa Sociology* (1937), *The Ojibwa Woman* (1938), *Ojibwa Religion and the Medewiwin* (1968), and *The Prairie Potawatomi* (1970). Her work is notable for its early emphasis on gender relations. During her research in Kenora, for example, she formed a close working relationship with informant Maggie Wilson, disclosing how Anishenabe women move within different roles in Ojibwa society as a means of asserting their social autonomy. In *The Ojibwa Woman*, Maggie Wilson related the tale of *Man-Hearted Woman*, who led a war party against the attacking Sioux near Warroad, Minnesota.

Later (1938–1939) Landes continued her pioneering fieldwork in Brazil, studying religion and identity among Afro-Brazilian Candomblé practitioners. Her publication on this research, *The City of Women* (1947), discussed how the women-centred sphere of the Candomblé cult was a source of power for disenfranchised Blacks. Landes later returned to Brazil in 1966 during which she focused her research on Rio de Janeiro's problems of urban development (Cole 2003).

Ruth Landes held many academic positions during her professional career, but most were visiting and other short-term appointments. Her longest institutional affiliation was with McMaster University in Hamilton, where she worked from 1965 until 1977, retiring as professor emerita. As a graduate student in Ruth Landes's class on religion at McMaster (1972–1973), I had the opportunity to enjoy her many stories of the founders of American anthropology, such as Ruth Benedict, Franz Boas, and Margaret Mead. Using Ruth Landes as an introduction, I had the privilege of meeting Margaret Mead at the American Anthropological Association meeting at the Royal York Hotel in Toronto in 1972.

Ruth Landes died at Hamilton in 1991 at the age of 82. McMaster University instituted several awards in her honour, such as the Ruth Landes Prize to the student who demonstrated exceptional achievement in anthropology, as well as the Ruth Landes Memorial Research Fund for interdisciplinary scholarship. The Smithsonian Institution in Washington D.C., in the National Anthropological Archives, holds Landes's many papers, artifacts, and related field materials.

Photo 5.1: Ojibwa (Anishenabe) woman at the door of her cabin, between 1923 and 1925, location and photographer unknown. (Source: Archives of Ontario)

The ethnographic experience recounted in this case study describes fieldwork conducted in a remote part of northern Ontario between Lake Nipigon and the Albany River, called Whitewater Lake. It was because of the relatively pristine environment and abundance of pickerel that the Aboriginal residents decided to build a tourist lodge at Whitewater Lake, hoping to establish a tourist industry that could form the basis of a reliable local economy. My fieldwork was focused on studying a successful case of Aboriginal economic development in Canada's North. With this goal in mind, I envisioned that this study would research the economic aspects of the construction phase of the tourist lodge.

Various aspects of the study included the structure of the work crews and their duties, as well as the larger sphere of the social organization of family life in and around the lodge site, as workers were allowed to bring their wives and families with them to White-water Lake. As such, there were other facets of the camp organization not directly tied to the construction activities, as the workers and their families set up camp sites of vary-ing sizes in the vicinity of the construction site. These families also engaged in a certain amount of hunting and fishing to meet their subsistence needs.

My trip to Whitewater Lake involved flying up to Thunder Bay, and from there secur-ing a ride farther north to the village of Armstrong, situated on the CNR rail line. From there I hitched a ride on a float plane that was bringing supplies to the construction site at Whitewater. The overall distance from Thunder Bay was about 400 km. When I first arrived at the construction site, evening was beginning to set in. The plane's motor slowed down after a somewhat monotonous flight over the coniferous forest and lakes below. The construction site was visible below, but at this stage it was only a cleared patch of ground. Since it was starting to get dark, the pilot was anxious to unload his cargo and get airborne again without delay. He motioned to the other side of the bay as he twirled a device to lower the rear flaps. "That's where all the people are camped," he yelled out over the noise of the plane's engine. "Do you see the smoke coming up through the trees? Somebody will see our plane land and come over to get you by boat. You can't walk over there." I was amazed at how quickly he was able to land and take off again.

From the clearing I watched as the roar of the plane's engine became an ever quieter drone, until the plane disappeared into the sunset. There didn't seem to be much here—a partially constructed shed, a few digging tools scattered about, a large stack of logs, and that was about it. But I was soon to realize that there were clouds of mosquitoes and blackflies coming out of the bush in waves. The bugs were already crawling up my sleeves, into my hair, and I was starting to look like I was covered with fur. I started a little fire, and threw on green leaves, creating a large cloud of white smoke around me. It did not take long for a boat to come over from the base camp across the bay from the construction site, and I was finally able to shake off these irksome pests.

Many of the people I had met before during a field trip to this area the previous summer when the tourist lodge was just in its planning stage. I settled into a tent with a young engineering student from New Zealand who had been hired to work on the project. He was curious as to why I would come all this way to conduct fieldwork, but then I asked the same of him. This spot in the northern bush was a long way from home for him. He explained that his brother was working for a Toronto-based engineering firm, and this was a summer job for him. He shoved some stuff about and made room for my sleeping bag and knapsack.

Research Techniques

The next morning after I got out of the tent and began to look around, I noticed that eight or 10 white canvas tents were scattered about, most of which were pitched on plywood platforms. Some were of more elaborate designs, erected over a frame of spruce poles with walls a metre or so high. A small kitchen area was squeezed into the central area of the camp, and I was told that there were quite a few other families camped out along the shore and on the island across from the bay. This base camp was mainly for the single men, who shared sleeping space, two or three to a tent. There was so much going on that interested me, so I pulled out my notebooks and began my fieldwork, which would take me through the summer into the cold weather of October.

My fieldwork techniques involved mainly observing what was going on and asking questions, but trying not to get in the way of the construction work. In the centre of the construction site were four large poles, bound together at the top with a large metal collar, that were to be used as the main frame for the centre tourist lodge. A sort of crow's nest was built on top of this structure, and I would spend many hours perched up there, observing the flow of work activities on the construction site. The various work crews were all visible from above, and no one interfered with my note taking or noticed that I was up there watching.

I also participated to the extent that I was able or allowed to participate in many of the camp's activities, such as eating meals with the men at the base camp, fishing trips after work, or chatting around a campfire in the evening. Conducting interviews was an important part of my research strategy as well, to obtain first-hand information from workers, crew bosses, the construction foreman, and the women and other family members of the workers in the various campsites in the vicinity of the lodge. In other words, I employed primarily the more conventional fieldwork methodology of participant observation, supplemented with additional data-gathering techniques involving questions and answers. These various observations and interviews were then recorded in my field notes, which I kept on a daily basis.

Taking Field Notes

There were numerous bush planes arriving throughout each day, and I was kept busy recording the comings and goings of the people involved. I was particularly interested in the manner in which the camp was forming on an island across the bay from the base camp. It started off occupied by two sisters, their husbands, and their children. Then the extended family of one of the husbands arrived (his mother, single brother, and two sisters). And later, the husband of one of these sisters landed with his own parents. I began to make kinship diagrams of these various relationships, and found an intricate pattern of family ties involved. The emerging formation of this camp seemed to me to be an opportunity to develop a hypothesis about the formation of residential groups under conditions of a wage-work economy, but still in a bush-oriented environment.

My developing interest in the relationships of families around the construction site was an aspect of my study that I had not originally anticipated. I thought that I would be just studying the men on the construction site, but the emerging social environment was an interesting facet in its own right. This sort of thing is typical of anthropological studies; one goes to study one thing, and then finds something else going on that is even more interesting, so the study shifts to take advantage of the new research theme. It's not always possible to predict what anthropologists will find before they get to their fieldwork site, so we have to develop flexibility in our approach.

Over the next several weeks my field notes became filled with comments about various kinship relationships, and what their possible significance could be. The people themselves seemed to feel that they just moved where they felt like it, and I was disappointed with the lack of a more structuralist orientation to their explanations. Other books on the social organization of the Anishenabe, such as Dunning's (1959) Pikangekum study, appeared to have such consistent patterns involved in the explanations of community life, and yet here I struggled with many contradictions and unresolved sociological problems. Whatever patterns there were at Whitewater Lake were evidently hidden from me, at least at first, yet I persevered in my attempts to make sense of it all.

Analyzing Field Data

As it turned out, there was an important lesson for me here, and that was to try and accept the field data as it was—as I properly recorded it. It is the differences that one finds from the work of previous ethnographers, rather than the similarities, that are most significant and are most apt to lead to new insights. These new insights, in the case of my own particular field study, had to do with the way people employed the pre-existing flexible social relationships back in their home communities to adapt to the conditions of the wage-work economy at Whitewater Lake. Here is an example of the way I began to work out these issues, in a preliminary manner, in my actual field notes:

Step 1: Describe the Relationships

27 August

Tommy Quissis returned to Whitewater Lake this morning with his wife Helen and their three girls. They began to set up their camp beside the Kwandibens family as Helma, Helen's sister, is married to Victor Kwandibens. The evolution of the Kwandibens' camp began with Victor, his wife Helma, and widowed mother Charlotte. Victor's brother Morris, a single man, joined them shortly after from the base camp. Next, Victor's sister, Harriette, and her husband Adam Yellowhead set up camp. This camp is further augmented by Harriette's sister, Helen Wynn, and her husband Steve. Steve's parents, Sinclair and Daisy Wynn, then moved close by. The camp is completed when Adam's brother, Elijah, a single man from the base camp, moved in with the group. Sinclair's wife Daisy is a sister of Adam and Elijah Yellowhead.

The following day I attempted a preliminary analysis of the relationships in this camp, trying to account for its formation in light of various historical, cultural, and economic conditions.

Step 2: Account for the Patterns

28 August

An analysis of the structure of this co-residential group demonstrates the significance of the solidarity of brothers in the alignment of residence patterns. There is also a solidarity of sisters, provided their husbands have no close male kinsmen in the area. This is indicated by Tommy Quissis's and Adam Yellowhead's decision to join the Kwandibens group even though Tommy has a brother and father in the area, but both of them are widowed and live in the base camp, and even though Adam's sister lives close by. However, Adam's single brother Elijah moved into the Wynn [section of the] camp. The solidarity of male kinsmen is further indicated by Steve Wynn's decision to take up residence in his father's part of the camp, rather than [live] close by to his wife's family, i.e., the Kwandibens.

An attempt was then made to push this preliminary analysis into a wider sphere of discussion by trying to outline an hypothesis to account for the formation of this particular camp on the basis of more general historical factors.

29 August

Log cabins have a permanency associated with them that inhibits the formation and reorganization of co-residential groups. The Whitewater Lake campgrounds provide an experimental setting for incipient co-residential group formation. There is a paucity of material in the literature on the evolution of these groups. Also, the significance of certain relationships, such as a number of dominant brothers as the core of the co-residential groups, tends to be assumed beforehand.

One may argue that changes in the structure of co-residential groups have resulted from acculturation and an entry into the Euro-Canadian wage economy. In the fur trade economy, a group of brothers who were good hunters and trappers contributed the most to the group. It is assumed that the evolution of these groups began with a group of brothers around whom concentric rings of relatives, through marriage, became attached to these patrilateral kinsmen. The wage economy allows for less dependence upon hunting and fishing for survival as more food can be store-bought than is possible on a trapper's income.

Hypothesis

The evolution of residential groups in the context of a wage-work economic system tends to develop on an *ad hoc* basis, depending on pre-existing relationships with individuals already settled into the work camp.

This, then, was the general pattern of analysis by which I proceeded. First, there was a documentation of particular cases taken as accurately as possible. Two modes of analysis then took place; first, examining the various interrelationships and general patterns of the specific details involved in the internal patterns of the cases; then, second, resorting to more wide-ranging thinking about what these specific instances could possibly mean in the larger context of the literature on Anishenabe (Ojibwa) sociology and cultural practices.

Lessons Learned

From my fieldwork experiences at Whitewater Lake I learned that this documentation of specific details is the most important aspect of any anthropological study. It provides the concrete foundation that one can return to over and over again for subsequent reanalysis and interpretation. The other modes of analysis are also important in their own way, but for different reasons. The analysis taken in the field of specific cases serves more to provide an orientation for what one is doing than to lay out in any specific way the wording of the analysis that will eventually take place at the write-up stage.

What the preliminary analysis does is to force you to think about general patterns and arguments while actually living in the field setting. In turn, this has an effect on what field materials you are apt to collect because you become habituated to the practice of constantly thinking in terms of general patterns and issues. The analysis will probably be changed later, sometimes in a major way, but it does have the side benefit of allowing you to see the way your thinking has changed over the course of the fieldwork, the way ideas get started, and how they relate to the types of issues that one begins to think are important during a very preliminary stage of the data-collection phase.

I also learned that I should probably not take my own life's difficulties so seriously because the Aboriginal peoples living in the remote northern villages struggled much more with life than I probably ever would. In other words, there was also an important personal side to this research that I was mostly unaware of at the time, but that has had the effect of changing me as a person. On the basis of these experiences at Whitewater Lake, I became less likely to take life's trials and tribulations for granted. When I am struggling with some aspect of my life, I think for a moment about how the Native peoples in the bush country of northern Ontario also struggle while having fewer resources at their disposal than I have. They carry on with their struggles with acceptance and dignity, rarely complaining about their lot in life.

The hardships are many for these people: planes crash; people are burned in house fires, freeze in snowbanks, are hit by trains, and live at an economic level that southern Ontario residents would hardly tolerate or be able to cope with. Research in the northern bush country not only allows the fieldworker to appreciate life on life's terms in the northern locale, but also to appreciate the benefits of living in the south as well. Overall one might say that fieldwork engenders a better awareness of life in general because we're able to see our own life's path in a larger, more comparative perspective. These occurrences are the everyday stuff of life—the details, the background, and personalities that fill out our life's experiences, imbue them with meaning, however obscure, and that propel us forward in time.

■ Case Study Two: The Irish of Renfrew County, 1861–1871

Not all anthropological research takes place among contemporary peoples. There are times when a researcher wishes to learn about past peoples, and so has to develop research techniques to uncover this information. This is the field of *ethnohistory*, which involves the reconstruction of the history of societies based on information gathered from oral traditions, written materials from outsiders, linguistic and archaeological data, or any other form of pertinent information. One might also use the accounts of explorers, missionaries, or traders, along with documents such as land titles, birth and death records, and other archival materials.

The techniques of ethnohistory are a valuable means for understanding culture change. One can learn about the various social, economic, and political changes, for example, that occurred among the First Nations peoples of Canada during the fur trade. Such research also has a practical application because it has been utilized as key evidence in legal cases involving First Nations land claims. For the most part, the goals of ethnohistorical research are much the same as ethnographic approaches, which is to say that the goals pertain to understanding the various aspects of people's lives, whether past or present; it is just that the techniques for gathering the information are different.

Research Objectives and Setting

In the following case study the research goal was to understand the various economic and social changes that Irish immigrants to Canada experienced after the Great Famine

Photo 5.2: Early settlers in eastern Canada had the difficult task of clearing heavy forested regions and building houses, barns, and sheds, while attempting to cultivate enough land to plant a meagre crop the first year. Settlers hardly ever knew if their land was suitable for cultivation until the trees had been cleared. Often the chosen land was too rocky or swampy for agriculture, forcing a move to another location. (Source: Public Archives of Canada)

of 1847–1849 (Hedican 2003, 2005a, 2006). The research setting chosen for study was located in Admaston Township in Renfrew County, just east of Ottawa. The reason for choosing this locale was that this part of Renfrew County was one of the last areas of Canada West, as it was called before Confederation, that still had farming land available. Largely for this reason, the Irish moved into this area in large numbers when they immigrated to Canada. Renfrew County as a whole already had a large Irish population, so there was also the opportunity to study the chain migration effect as an aspect of social change.

While various sorts of documents were used in this study, such as church records detailing births, marriages, and deaths, for example, the most valuable source of data was derived from the Canadian census files for 1851–1881. One can uncover a wealth of information in these records pertaining to the names of families, the people's ages, religious affiliation, farm size, acres cultivated, crops planted, and livestock maintained. In other words, it is almost as if one could enter the past, see how the people lived, and record the various statistics of their lives.

One research goal that I thought this information could be used for was to delve into the question of the relationship between the size of families and the size of their land holdings. This question about what determines family size was a way by which I was able to translate the specific sociological details of the census files into a more generalized problem of cultural and social significance. This inductive approach, where one develops a mode of reasoning from a specific case to a larger generalization, is a further example of a typical research methodology in anthropology.

The Research Problem

The literature on the family in historical perspective has had an enduring interest in the determinants of family size, as well as related factors that have been considered to act as causal variables of this phenomenon. Various approaches have been proposed: cultural, economic, sociological, and demographic, to name a few, with no clear decision emerging in favour of one perspective or another. In order to clarify the research problem of what determines family size, a database on an Irish farming community in eastern Ontario during the 1861–1871 time period is utilized. A number of strategies are used, such as comparing family size with the size of land holdings and with the changing structural components of Irish families. It is evident when using this approach that the issue of family size is multifaceted and one that is most advantageously viewed from a cultural relativistic perspective.

The subject of family size and composition has been one of the long-lasting topics in studies concerning human social history. Scholars in various disciplines, such as sociology, anthropology, economics, and demography, for example, have recognized the fundamental importance of the family and household as core institutions in human societies around the world. The socio-economic importance of families and households has resulted in an extensive literature relating to their size, composition, and changing aspects. Even though recent studies from a wide range of disciplines have continued to show a strong interest in the dimension of household size and composition, this body of literature has suffered from several defects.

A number of these studies, for example, attempt to examine a database that is much too varied. Anthropologically speaking, a study that attempts to understand family processes in more than 40 African countries in a single journal article (i.e., Bongaarts 2001) covers far too much social and cultural territory to be of much comparative value. Similarly, a study of family size that extends throughout a 200-year period, such as that which focused on the French Canadian population of early Quebec (Gagnon and Heyer 2001), is apt to generalize too broadly over the temporal landscape. Although it is beneficial to encourage a changing historical perspective, socio-cultural tendencies that are more restricted to specific generations are apt to be missed in such a wide-sweeping approach.

It is a review of literature such as this that provides the rationale for my Irish Canadian study. My attempt in reviewing the existing literature on family size is to suggest that previous studies either cover too much of a time span, as in the Quebec study, or tries to explain the issue of family size across too many diverse cultures, as the African study does. This critique then leads into my Irish study by showing how it offers a different approach than the others in this field of study. First, for example, my study of Irish family size is restricted to a single community—in Renfrew County—and therefore does not attempt unreasonable comparisons or generalizations across too many diverse populations. This restriction allows for a more controlled comparison of changes that are apt to occur in one locale.

Second, attempts to compare factors responsible for variations in family size are aided by the fact that comparable data are available from Ireland itself. This aspect allows for the possibility of determining which factors are more cultural or economic, such as the possibility of examining factors pertinent to family size in the context of population expansion rather than depopulation. And third, the approach taken here extends across a single decade rather than several centuries, thus allowing for a study of variations in family and household size in a more controlled, longitudinal perspective in the same geographical area.

Irish Families in Renfrew County, 1861–1871

Renfrew County is bounded on the east by the Ottawa River and on the west and north by the Pre-Cambrian Shield in which the present Algonquin Park is now situated. As such, soils near the Ottawa River are generally classed as fair to good for agricultural purposes, whereas those closer to the Shield are often thinly distributed over rocky terrain or situated near swamps and forested areas. This region has been mostly settled by Irish and Scottish immigrants, with the Scots arriving earlier, from about 1820 to 1840, and the Irish coming in large numbers during the time of the Great Famine in the late 1840s.

For the Irish, the pattern of settlement was one known as a *chain migration*, whereby an initial settler group provided the focus for the emigration of their relatives and friends from a home community back in Ireland. Although the Irish settlers of Renfrew County came from a diversity of places in Ireland, the majority originated from counties Kerry and Limerick in the western part of Ireland. As Akenson noted, for those attempting to escape the horrors of the Famine,

> The Irish migrant to Ontario arrived in terrible physical condition, but his bodily emaciation should not be equated with cultural impoverishment or with technological ignorance.... In Ontario he passed through the cities on the way to settling successfully in the commercial farm economy of small towns and isolated farmsteads. (1984: 34)

The farming families were often spread out over an extensive territory, yet grouped together in local parishes and contiguous farmlands. These early Irish farmers were faced

Photo 5.3: Large crowd gathered at the memorial erected in 1909 at Grosse-Île, Quebec, in com-memoration of the death of Irish immigrants of 1849. Gross-Île was the site of immigrant pro-cessing into Canada and a quarantine station, where many Irish died of disease and starvation. (Source: Photograph by Jules-Ernest Livernois, Library and Archives Canada)

with the daunting task of clearing fields, planting crops, and erecting buildings for shel-ter and storage of equipment before the onslaught of Canada's relatively harsh winter. Surviving such conditions was no doubt made possible by the help that one family gave to another, referred to as *cooring*, as the Irish called such patterns of co-operation.

In order to understand the social and economic aspects of the Irish farm families of Renfrew County, the Canadian census material of 1861 and 1871 was utilized. The information derived from the Canadian census data was organized in various ways relat-ing to household size and composition, the age of family members, farm size, acreage cultivated, and types of crops grown. The households were then organized in alphabeti-cal order for ease of retrieval, which had the statistical effect of randomizing the sample.

Research Results

The research described in this case study began with an attempt to better under-stand the historical adaptation of Irish immigrants after the Great Famine in eastern

Ontario. A significant part of this adaptation, it was thought, would consist of the role of rural Irish family life in the nineteenth century, especially in terms of the part that family size might play in farm productivity. In other words, a specific empirical question concerning Irish family organization became generalized into a broader issue of the role of family size in social and economic change. Historical studies that were examined presented a diversity of viewpoints on this subject, yet one conclusion on family size tended to predominate, which is to say that family size has generally "declined from between 4 and 6 in the mid-nineteenth century to between 2 and 3 today" (Bongaarts 2001: 278). Concomitant with this general decrease in family size has been a corresponding decline in the frequency of extended families, with the nuclear family now being dominant.

From an economic perspective, family size is seen as largely a function of productive intensity. In farming communities, a large available labour pool within the household is a cost-effective advantage because scarce resources do not need to be expended on hiring outside labour during peak times in the agricultural cycle. The hypothesis would be that family size is positively correlated with the increased size of a farm's landholding. Large farms can produce more food than smaller ones, the reasoning goes, and therefore can effectively support larger families.

In Ireland, on the other hand, large families could be supported on relatively small plots of land, but the balance was a precarious one, especially when there was a lack of diversity in agricultural produce. There were potato blights in other parts of Europe in the late 1840s, but famines did not occur because exports of food products were stopped and other foods were available to feed the population. However, because of Ireland's free-trade policy with Great Britain, about twice as much food was exported out of the country than would have been needed to support Ireland's starving poor.

In the present sample of Irish families in Renfrew County, the results would appear to support this general relationship between family and farm size, yet the results are deceptive in certain ways. One of these issues has to do with the gross size of a farm: many acres might well consist of woodlots, swamps, and rocky ground that are not suitable for agricultural production. A more relevant approach is to examine just the productive areas of a farm, such as the acreage devoted to tillage. In the case of the Renfrew Irish, farmers were able to dramatically increase their productive capacity during the 1861–1871 decade (acreage devoted to crop production increased by nearly five times), but overall population size remained relatively the same. If farm size has such a causal effect on family size, then the question is: Why was there not an equally dramatic population increase corresponding with the very large increase in crop production?

The economic perspective alone does not provide the answer because the presumed spur in population growth was there in terms of an ability to increase productive capacity, but the expected result in population gains did not occur. If we can accept the economic argument that modern families will become more nuclear and less extended as societies urbanize and industrialize, then one wonders why such a trend was already occurring in such a significant fashion in the rural farming community of Admaston Township in Renfrew County during the 1860s in which nuclear families among the

Irish formed 65 percent of the sample size, and in 1971 formed 71 percent of the sample. On the other hand, extended families among the Admaston Irish formed only 13 percent in 1861, and declined even further, to 7 percent in 1871.

Analyzing the Research Results

This case study of the Irish in Renfrew County indicating a dramatic decline in extended families and a corresponding rise in nuclear families is even more interesting because the Irish, in their native country of Ireland, were known for fairly large, extended families but rather quickly dispensed with this family form in their new adopted country of Canada. If family size and composition were strictly a cultural matter, as some researchers would suggest, then we would need to know more about how and why such a rapid change in social organization could occur in the absence of some more identifiable factor that could be reasonably seen to account for this transformation.

The differences between Ireland and eastern Canada in the mid-nineteenth century were rather pronounced. Irish farmers in Ontario were not nearly as constrained as they were in Ireland. A farm size in Renfrew County of several hundred hectares was relatively common, compared with averages in Ireland of fewer than 10 ha. In addition, land in Canada during the 1860s could still be bought from the Crown at reasonable prices or from other farmers who might be moving out of the area. Leasing more land was another alternative to increasing a farmer's landholdings that was not generally available to the farmer of limited means in Ireland. Because the economic circumstances were significantly different between the two countries, we might then conclude that the internal socio-economic circumstances or dynamics as they relate to family size and composition among the Irish are of a more subtle nature.

The extended family in Ireland, for example, can be seen as a survival tactic. Impartible inheritance, passing the family farm intact to one heir only, helped to prevent ruination of the family's landholding by circumventing continued subdivision to the point at which no one could make a living. In Ireland, the family farm was usually inherited by the eldest son, leaving others to emigrate or join the ever growing pool of farm labourers. In the Irish Canadian case, farm size doubled or tripled in Renfrew County during the period of our study, suggesting that fathers were accumulating land, not so much to increase crop production for them or for immediate crop cultivation, but to facilitate inheritance to their sons. In such cases, it might well be the youngest son who eventually inherited the family farm, rather than the eldest as in Ireland, because other sons might already have been given parental assistance in purchasing land of their own.

Summing Up

The point made in this case study of Irish farming households in Renfrew County after the Great Famine is that the subtleties of social organization are not likely to be uncovered in the large-scale comparisons that transcend nations, regions, and cultures. Rather, such factors as farm size and fertility patterns are probably more important than many might think as a determinant of family size. Human beings have the ability to make their own decisions, within certain parameters, but they are not ruled by social and economic forces, nor are they entirely powerless over the cultural materialist transformations at work in any given time period.

What we can therefore conclude is that what determines family size is not to be found in the large-scale statistical generalizations of political economy. The determinants of family size are embedded in the specific social and economic aspects of each individual society. As far as the Irish families of Renfrew County are concerned, even they did not exhibit any degree of uniformity to a set pattern or norm that a researcher could confidently assert was the result of one particular causal determinant or another.

This case study also illustrates that the goals or objectives of ethnohistorical research in anthropology have the ability to deal with important social and cultural questions. Even though the research is conducted in the context of people who lived many decades ago, the goals of the research—to understand various aspects of social and cultural organization—are essentially the same as anthropological research conducted among contemporary peoples. The research methods involving archival materials, such as the Canadian census data, may be different from the usual methods of participant observation and interviewing, but the overall objectives remain much the same despite the large separation in time between the two modes of research.

■ Case Study Three: The Radical Right in Canada

It is hard to imagine a more difficult or dangerous research project than that conducted by anthropologist Stanley Barrett, which focused on White-supremacist groups in Canada (Barrett 1984a, 1987). Those people belonging to such groups espouse a philosophy of racial hatred. They believe that interracial breeding is dangerous, that Blacks are an inferior species, and that Jews are engaged in an international conspiracy to gain control of the world. The methodology by which an anthropologist is able to study people belonging to the radical right differs rather dramatically from the two case studies previously discussed because of the potential danger to the researcher. How does one conduct research in such a potentially explosive situation?

The Research Problem

Many Canadians probably believe that their country is much more racially tolerant than most other areas of the world, such as South Africa or the southern United States. Yet many people of colour, Aboriginal peoples, or those of Jewish descent will say that they have been subjected to racial discrimination on a frequent basis. Jewish cemeteries and synagogues, for example, are often vandalized. In some cases the discrimination is more subtle than the outward forms of violent attacks, such as refusing to rent to a person of colour, or not hiring them in your business or factory. Barrett's research suggests

Figure 5.1: Cartoon depicting the arrival of Mennonites in Canada in derogatory terms. Prejudicial treatment of certain minority groups, such as Asian, Irish, or Aboriginal people, has been a common occurrence in Canadian history. (Source: The Canadian Eye Opener, 21 September 1918, Glenbow Museum, Calgary, Alberta)

that "No matter whether the dimension is time, place, or social class, racism has been endemic in Canada" (1987: 307).

When discrimination against ethnic minorities appears on a persistent basis, it is referred to as *structural or institutional racism*. Institutional racism means racism that is intrinsic to the structures of society. It may be expressed in a formal sense in the laws of the land, such as prohibiting Aboriginal peoples to vote in federal Canadian elections until the 1960s, or less visibly in patterns of employment or in the context of school textbooks. Institutional racism has a tendency to reproduce itself because it is embedded in society itself. Regardless of the individuals involved in racist acts, the institutional framework continues because the structure that disadvantages certain groups and gives advantages to others perpetuates itself due to the ingrained patterns of discrimination in the society itself. From the perspective of anthropology, how does one research people with such racist beliefs?

Photo 5.4: A certificate issued by Canada's Immigration Branch, Department of the Interior, indicating that "the sum of five hundred dollars being the head tax due under provisions of the Chinese Immigration Act," dated Vancouver, 2 August 1918. (Source: Vancouver Public Library)

Researching White-Supremacist Groups

Barrett identifies two main research methods by which he was able to gather information on White-supremacist groups in Canada—archival research and unstructured interviewing. He found that there was an enormous amount of archival material on the right wing. Some of this material was in the form of newspaper articles, found in university libraries and provincial archives. The most important materials were publications produced by the right-wing organizations themselves, such as the Ku Klux Klan and the Western Guard. Anti-racist organizations were another source of publications.

As important as these sources of information were to Barrett's study, most of the research consisted of face-to-face interviews with right-wing members. In order to gain entry into the right-wing groups, he employed a technique that he referred to as *deceptive candour*. Many right-wing people associated anthropology with a belief that Blacks were savages and Whites were civilized, mirroring the outmoded evolutionary thinking of 100 years ago. In this context anthropology was seen in a positive light by the White supremacists because they believed anthropology has vindicated their right-wing views.

There are ethical issues here to be sure, and Barrett (1984a) has published on ethics and subversive research in anthropology. However, for the most part, he did not argue against the supremacists' mistaken view of anthropology, nor did he confirm their beliefs. An ethical dilemma arises here. To what extent do we look the other way and not denounce racist attitudes in order to conduct research among the perpetrators of racism? If the researcher immediately confronted them on their beliefs and began to denounce them, most assuredly they would not participate in the research and the opportunity to gain valuable knowledge would be lost. This research technique of deceptive candour could be seen as a rationalization that allowed the research to continue without at the same time validating racist attitudes. In any event the racists believed that his book would ultimately confirm and validate their miscreant beliefs. "My implicit assumption," Barrett explained, "was that a different ethics operates when studying racists compared with studying the victims of racism" (1996: 137).

The bulk of the information gathered in Barrett's study was gained through extended unstructured interviews. He would begin, for example, with a statement such as "There is widespread racism in Canada." The White supremacists would see this situation in a positive light because it proved in their minds that races should not mix together. They would then begin to expound on their views, with Barrett commenting at various points as a way of changing the direction of the interview. The unstructured nature of the interviews allows for a more conversational format, and he did not take notes during this time. As Barrett explains, he followed a system of memorization:

> Immediately after the interviews, which lasted on an average of three to five hours, I would write down what I had memorized. Usually this was about 20–25 pages of notes; occasionally over 50 pages were produced from a single interview. Sometimes a member of the extreme right would ask whether I had a tape recorder concealed in my jacket or briefcase. I would always invite them to check me thoroughly. (Barrett 1984a: 11)

After such an interview he explains that he felt so sickened by what he had heard that he would intentionally eat in a Jewish restaurant as a way of centring himself and restoring a sense of moral balance.

Research Implications

A research project such as this one conducted among White supremacists and radical right-wing groups is apt to tell us as much about the techniques of research as it does about the particular research findings themselves. Barrett's view that there are two different sets or codes of research ethics—one for the victims and another for the victimizers—would no doubt be seen as unprofessional by some. This type of

Photo 5.5: Knights of the Ku Klux Klan standing in front of a cross in Kingston, Ontario, 31 August 1927. (Source: Archives of Ontario)

Box 5.3: Irish Travellers: Same-Race Racism

Brock University anthropologist Jane Helleiner (2000) has conducted a significant body of research into the discrimination against Irish Travellers. The Travelling People constitute a Gypsy-like minority within Ireland that has been subjected to state policy of assimilative settlement. The Travellers, sometimes also known as Irish Tinkers, are an itinerant population that has been a long-standing target of racism within Ireland. Helleiner's research analyzes the history of local and national anti-Traveller discourse in government records, newspapers, and in the Irish Parliament (Hedican 2005b).

Helleiner's research was conducted during the course of long-term residence in a Traveller camp near Galway City in the west of Ireland so that she could support her findings with concrete, factual material. As she (2000: 101) asserts, "I argue that Traveller culture and identity have been and continue to be produced out of sets of unequal social relations that simultaneously link travellers to the wider political economy and create the more intimate ties of family and community." As such, Helleiner makes her case that discrimination against Irish Travellers is an instance of "same race racism," or "racism without race," which is to say that anti-Travellerism is a form of inferiorized difference that does not invoke biological inferiority, but rather notions of undesirable cultural difference. Unfortunately, her conclusion on the subject of racism in Ireland is not particularly encouraging: "As anthropological work continues to demonstrate, despite predictions of an increasingly globalized world where social inequality and cultural differences are erased, these phenomenon are not disappearing but rather being created and/or reproduced in the course of economic and political change" (2000: 6).

situation brings into question the ideology of a value-neutral social science. Indeed, Barrett not only was interested in better understanding the beliefs of the White supremacists, he was also determined to undermine the beliefs and activities of the anti-Semites and racists.

When it comes to research in anthropology, do not the racists have rights too? In one sense the racists themselves are also victims of a hated-filled ideology that might have been inculcated into their consciousness when they were only children and were unable to sort out the right and wrong of it all. In any event, is there any hope at all that social scientific research on racism would have any chance of changing the beliefs of the White supremacists? One doubts if such ingrained beliefs can ever be changed by science.

There are many researchers today who believe that a purely objective social science, if it ever existed in the first place, is now a thing of the past. They would also espouse the view that such social scientists as anthropologists should stop trying to sit on the moral or ethical fence and begin to choose sides. This would probably be a matter of speaking out against injustices in the world, against hunger, poverty, authoritarian regimes, genital mutilation, and the like. Some would go further and suggest that social scientific research should be utilized in an advocacy role, promoting the political goals and objective of suppressed minorities. Of course there are others who believe that this sort of advocacy stance is taking the social sciences in an entirely wrong direction. They believe that the goal of social science should be to understand social situations, but not participate in them, because by doing so it changes the outcomes of the very situations they are studying. There is no correct position here. Both sides have their valid points and their deficiencies as well.

■ Comparing the Case Studies

The three studies discussed in this chapter—an Aboriginal construction camp in northern Ontario, Irish farmers in eastern Ontario in the 1860s, and Canadian White supremacists—would appear to be so diverse as to defy comparison. In fact, one of the reasons for choosing these three projects is to illustrate the diversity of anthropological research across space and time. Yet, ultimately, the three projects all have the same goal, which is to better understand the human condition. It is only the research settings themselves that are different.

The three projects do illustrate as well that different projects involve different research techniques. The Aboriginal construction site did not allow for much participation since that could upset the work schedule, but observational methods were of great benefit. The Irish study also did not allow for participant observation, unless one had a time machine, but the archival material, especially the detailed Canadian census data, provided a wealth of information on farm families and their agricultural production. In Barrett's study of racist groups, the unstructured interview provided the best research results.

The lesson here is that one has to decide what kinds of questions need to be asked to obtain what kinds of answers. When research goals have been firmly established, then appropriate techniques are chosen in an attempt to obtain the information that will provide answers to the questions originally set out. There is a proper sequence to the whole process of the research investigation that has been set out as outlined in the initial part of this chapter. It all begins with a sense of curiosity about why people behave the way they do, and all the rest follows from this simple question.

6 Marriage and the Family

Hi, Dad ... I mean son ... I think
LONDON (Reuter) Former Rolling Stone Bill Wyman's son is to marry his ex-wife's mother, a British newspaper said today.

Wyman's 30-year-old son from a previous marriage, Stephen, has announced his engagement to Patsy Smith, 46, the Sun newspaper said. Smith is the mother of Wyman's former wife Mandy, 22.

Neither Wyman nor the couple were available to confirm the report.

—The Toronto Sun (date unknown)

There is an old song about love and marriage going together like a horse and carriage. This sentiment, that marriage is based on love, may reflect the sentiments of many in modern society, but there are more practical considerations involved as well. The problem is that love is a fleeting emotion at times—we fall in and out of it for reasons that are not well understood. If love was an easily definable entity, then there would be no need for most of our songs and poetry.

My parents were married for 55 years. There is no doubt that they felt a deep affection for one another, yet when they were young, divorces were almost impossible to obtain. Until relatively recent times, divorce was considered unacceptable for both social and religious reasons. In addition, divorce was not available as a legal option in all parts of Canada. A woman striking out on her own with children in tow would have had a very difficult time of it, finding suitable employment, daycare, or social assistance, so people learned to put up with more than they seem to be willing to tolerate in a relationship today. According to the latest statistics, many more marriages end in divorce today than in the past (45.8 percent of marriages in the United States ended in divorce in 2002). In Sweden, according to a recent newscast, three-quarters of the adult population are single and living alone. Certainly times are changing over the last generation or so, and one wonders if marriage is on the way out, or becoming vastly transformed in some manner, especially with the recent legislation allowing same-sex marriage.

■ The Concept of Marriage

For most of recent human history, in most cultures, finding love is the least of people's worries when choosing a marriage partner. Other practicalities enter into the equation, such as the ability of a husband to support his wife and children, status considerations of rank and prestige, and other matters not directly tied to marriage itself. For much of the history of anthropology, there has been a preoccupation with recording all the possible permutations of marriage relationships, such as how many women are married to a particular man (*polygyny*), how many men are married to one women (*polyandry*), or the marriage of one woman to one man (*monogamy*). Later a French anthropologist, Claude Levi-Strauss, suggested that we are missing the whole point about marriage. Marriage is not so much about ties between particular individuals, which is a very typical Western way of looking at it, but is all about the alliances that are formed through marriage between family groups.

Thus, research in anthropology shifted to an emphasis on what came to be called the *alliance theory* of marriage. As Edmund Leach (1968: 545) explains, "Marriage, for Levi-Strauss, is not simply a matter of establishing a legal basis for the domestic family; it is an *alliance* resulting from a contractual exchange between two groups—the group of the husband and the group of the bride." This exchange can take several different forms. One of these may involve a *direct reciprocity*, such as exchange of sisters between two men, or there may be a *delayed reciprocity*. If we give you a woman now, you give us back one of her daughters. Or within a larger system referred to as *generalized reciprocity*: We will give you a woman now if you give us some cattle; then later we will use the cattle to obtain another woman from elsewhere.

The standard definition of marriage found in many anthropology texts—that marriage is a socially approved sexual and economic union between a man and a woman—has all sorts of problems inherent in it, especially in today's society of same-sex marriage. A previous focus (Box 5.2) has been on Ruth Landes's discussion in *The Ojibwa Woman* (1938), referring to the Kenora region of northwestern Ontario, of a historical person called Man-Hearted Woman. Man-Hearted Woman led war parties against the Sioux (Sioux Lookout is not far away), hunted as well as any man, and even married a woman and raised a family. Her wife was no doubt impregnated by a surrogate male, a stand-in as it were, but the children were regarded as her own. So here we have a more or less "normal" Ojibwa family, except that both parents are female.

What we can say about such marriages is that the biology of either spouse is entirely beside the point—it is their social roles that count. You do not need to be a male to be a husband nor, one presumes, to be a female to be a "wife." Some societies distinguished between the role of *pater*, who is the father with legal rights over a child, and the *genitor*, who is the actual biological father but who does not have legal rights. The child is entitled to bear the name of his or her pater and inherits his property. The two roles of pater and genitor may be combined in one person, but they are each in themselves sufficiently important to separate them.

The male who fathered the children of Man-Hearted Woman, or the genitor in the case of an ancient Roman family may be called a *proxy father*. In many societies it is

---

Box 6.1: The Polyandrous Toda Family of India

The Todas are a pastoral polyandrous society living in small villages scattered across the plateau of the Nilgiri Hills in southern India. They have become famous in anthropology for their relatively rare marriage pattern in which a woman marries two or more men at one time. Often the husbands are brothers, a marriage pattern that is termed fraternal polyandry, although there are also monogamous marriages as well. The origin of the Toda is obscure. They have lived for centuries in relative geographical and social isolation from other nearby hill tribes, resulting in social and cultural traits remarkably different from their neighbours. Their distinctive physical appearance, manner of dress, and other customs have made them the subject of anthropological curiosity for over a century.

Toda subsistence is based on the herding and maintenance of a large number of buffalo, which involves elaborate dairying rituals. The dairies are located apart from the villages and are situated on sacred ground. The rituals associated with the dairying rituals are administered by an all-male order of priests who perform the sacred tasks of churning and clarifying the butter, or *ghi*. *Ghi* is the only form of the sacred buffalo's milk that can be touched in any manner by those in Toda society who are not priests.

Social organization among the Toda is a complex blend of endogamous moieties or major divisions. Each of these divisions is further divided into a number of exogamous clans characterized by distinctive rules of descent and residence. For example, six of the clans follow a rule of patrilineal descent, and five are matrilineal. Technically, then, the Toda kinship system could be termed one of dual descent. A village consists of several small huts, a dairy where buffalo milk is processed, and a shed for buffalo calves. As the seasons change, the buffalo are moved to the best pastures, and a whole Toda village may be relocated to another part of the plateau.

During the colonial era the British authorities respected Toda territory and kept their grazing lands intact. Unfortunately, since the Second World War, the Toda population has gone into decline because of disease that has threatened to decimate the tribe, leading to intervention by Indian government officials who have introduced medical help from the outside. Some Toda have also begun to engage in agriculture, and dairying has since suffered a decline along with the practice of polyandrous marriages (Emeneau 1937; Mandelbaum 1941; Queen and Habenstein 1974: 18–47).

---

considered so important for every man to have legitimate progeny that various arrangements are entered into whereby the children sired by one man are actually counted as the children of another. This is especially the case when there is a transfer of property, called *bridewealth*, from the groom's family to the bride's family at the time of marriage so that any children a woman may have are considered to be legally those of the male on whose behalf the bridewealth was actually paid. A *dowry* is a related term meaning the property a bride brings with her into her husband's household at the time of marriage. A woman's dowry is usually considered her personal property and not the property of her husband.

The term "bridewealth" has the unfortunate connotation of implying that the groom and his family are buying or purchasing a wife. Because of this largely inaccurate implication, the term *progeny price* has gained a wider acceptance in social anthropology because it implies that the groom and his family are compensating the wife's family for the progeny or children who are now lost to the wife's family as a result of her marriage. In some societies in which the people do not have many material possessions to exchange at marriage, such as in hunting and gathering societies, services may be performed by the groom for the bride's family. This *bride service* usually lasts for a short period of time, often until the first child is born, at which time the married couple move permanently near the groom's family.

The bridewealth or progeny price payment is considered so binding that even the death of a husband does not invalidate the marriage. In such a case the deceased husband is replaced by another male member of his family, usually a young brother, thus the term *levirate* (from the latin *levir*, meaning a husband's brother) is used to describe such occurrences. Any children subsequently born between the existing wife and the new husband are nonetheless considered the children of the deceased husband. In the Book of Deuteronomy, for example, ancient Jews were instructed that:

> the wife of the dead shall not marry without unto a stranger; her husband's brother shall go in to her, and take her to him as a wife, and perform the duty of a husband's brother unto her. And it shall be that the first-born which she beareth shall succeed in the name of his brother which is dead. (quoted in Lienhardt 1978: 110)

Alternatively, some societies practise the *sororate* under which a woman is obliged to marry her deceased sister's husband, in other words, a dead wife is replaced by her sister. The primary function of such practices is that both the sororate and the levirate preserve the stability of existing relations between families whose members have married.

A much less common arrangement of proxy fatherhood also operates in another way as practised among the Nuer, an East African cattle-herding society, called a *ghost marriage* (Evans-Pritchard 1951: 108). This marriage arrangement is predicated on the idea that every man has a right to bear male offspring in order to continue his own line of descent. If a man happens to die before his marriage arrangements are complete, or if he has only daughters and dies before producing any sons, then it is the duty of another of the husband's kinsmen to marry the widow. Any children born of this marriage will be counted as the dead man's children. Evans-Pritchard reckoned that there were probably as many ghost marriages as there were more conventional ones.

■ Marriage Restrictions and Preferences

There are no societies that anthropologists have ever heard of whose members allow a person to marry anyone they please. There are always some sort of restrictions or rules that govern who one may marry and, conversely, who one may not marry. These rules are sometimes vaguely or precisely defined, depending on various circumstances, in terms of how much members of a society wish to prevent or encourage various sorts of relationships. There is a vast degree of cultural variability in these matters, although there are also some general principles that would appear to be common for most societies.

Marriage rules, with regard to the selection of a spouse, generally fall into two categories. *Endogamy* means that for a marriage to be legally recognized, the husband and wife must belong to the *same* social group—for example, in orthodox Judaism a Jewish man must always marry a Jewish woman and vice versa, unless the non-Jew converted to Judaism (Kallen 1977: 24). *Exogamy* is a law of marriage specifying that the husband and wife must come from *different* social groups. Following Levi-Strauss's view of marriage as primarily a form of alliance and exchange, the rule of exogamy could be formulated as "marry out or die out".

■ The Incest Problem

The *incest taboo* is sometimes considered a form of exogamy, but this is not correct since the incest taboo is a rule that prohibits sexual relations between close family members, whereas exogamy is a marriage rule. As such, incest refers to sexual behaviour and exogamy to marriage. The incest taboo, which prohibits sexual relations between parents and children or between brothers and sisters, is usually considered a cultural universal, but the theories put forward to explain it are varied and, on the whole, not very conclusive.

Take, for example, the so called *inbreeding theory* of incest, which suggests that sex is prohibited among family members because of the fear of harmful physical effects that could be manifested in the resulting progeny. Such a theory presupposes a knowledge of Mendelian genetic principles involving dominant and recessive genes, knowledge that is not likely to be possessed by most people even in a modern society. In any event, deleterious genetic repercussions depend on the incidences of such harmful genes in the gene pool of particular breeding populations—genes, for example, of hemophilia among the royal families of Europe, or congenital hip displacement among Aboriginal Americans, cannot emerge in a breeding population that does not have these genes in the first place. Also, many deleterious genes are recessive ones, which can become masked by less harmful dominant ones. Inbreeding does not always lead to deleterious consequences as it can go the other way, promoting or enhancing desirable qualities, leading to an improvement in a population, which is the reason for breeding horses, livestock, plants, and so on.

Sigmund Freud's *psychoanalytic theory*, as formulated in his *Totem and Taboo* (1913), accounts for the incest taboo by suggesting that it is a reaction against unconscious incestuous desires. It is sometimes also referred to as the *Oedipus complex*, which is to say, the unconscious desire of the human male to kill his father and mate with his mother. It is not altogether clear how Freud's theory works in society. However, "I would not be as prepared as most of my colleagues to ridicule Freud. He was probably wrong about the details, but he asked the right questions" (Fox 1967: 61).

Box 6.2: The Barabaig: East African Cattle-Herders

Studies of East African cattle-herders have played a prominent role in the development of social anthropology, especially during the period of British colonialism. The Nuer of the Sudan are probably the best known ethnographically because of the prominent publications of Evans-Pritchard (1940, 1951), although other societies, such as the Barabaig of Tanzania, are similar in many respects, especially their association with the "cattle complex" (Klima 1970). The description that follows uses the convention of the "ethnographic present," which is to say, it uses the cultural details originally recorded by the anthropologist at the time of study.

The so-called "cattle complex" refers to a widespread and classic cultural type in Africa in which the herding of cattle and the use of cattle products influences practically every aspect of such societies. This includes, for example, property relations, sorcery, social status, initiation ceremonies, marriage, clan and lineage relations, and settlement patterns. Among such societies there is a near constant movement of cattle in search of pasture and the use of water holes, such that the seasonal alternations of wet and dry seasons shape the rhythm of life.

Every person born in Barabaig society automatically becomes a member of a number of different groups. He or she is a member of a family and at the same time a member of a clan. Among the Barabaig, the clan is the largest social grouping and is composed of male and female members who claim common descent from a founding ancestor in the distant past whose family constituted the original group. Descent is mainly concerned with defining social relationships among people who share a common ancestor, such that clans among the Barabaig are patrilineal. This is another way of saying that clan membership is determined by tracing descent through a long line of male connecting links, starting with the father and up to the father's father and so on until the founding father is reached. In actual practice clan membership traced in this manner becomes somewhat imprecise the further back the genealogy is followed.

Clan membership has an especially important role in marriage practices, which is particularly evident in determining the potential spouses for any one person in the descent system. Barabaig men strive for an ideal situation in which they acquire many cows, many wives, and many children. A series of livestock transactions is an integral part of the marriage system and forms the legal basis upon which the marriage rests. In the past marriages were arranged by the parents. However, in later times the young man takes the initiative, starting with an investigation conducted into the kinship and economic background of the girl's family.

The primary consideration is that a Barabaig man is prohibited from marrying any woman who is also a member of his clan. Secondly, he cannot marry any woman from his mother's or grandmother's clan. Some Barabaig men have married outside their tribe, since there are advantages and disadvantages to marriage of this kind, but most men eventually decide to marry a woman in his own village or nearby community. A primary consideration concerns calculations about the number of cattle that will have to be given in bridewealth to the girl's family. Children born of the marriage belong to the kinship group of their father; however, if a woman is barren, some cattle may have to be returned to the husband's family. The transfer and exchange of cattle between individuals and groups is therefore a complex and elaborate aspect of Barabaig society, never more so than on the occasion of marriage.

A theory with a stronger sociological orientation was presented by Edward Wester-marck ([1891] 1921) in what could be called the *childhood familiarity theory* of incest. His theory is a version of the old idea that familiarity breeds contempt or, in this version, sexual attraction is blunted among people, even though they might not be related, who grow up as children in the same familial setting, such as a Jewish kibbutz. There is not really enough ethnographic evidence to assess this theory one way or another. In any event, even if it could be shown that unrelated children who grew up in the same household together avoided each other as sexual partners, it does not disprove many other possible explanations for this phenomenon, such as economic or religious factors, aside from sociological ones.

A functionalist version is the *family disruption theory*, presented by Malinowski (1924). As the argument goes, families would be destroyed, or at least sufficiently preoccupied so that their very survival would be at stake, if brothers competed sexually for sisters, or fathers with sons over available females in the household. There are several difficulties with this theory. One is the problem of how the incest taboo came into being in the first place—functional theories fare poorly in explaining the origins of just about every sociological issue. The other is that there is so much assumed in the explanation that has never been actually tested. We can assume that fighting in the nuclear family could threaten group survival, but what is the empirical evidence?

There is also the problem of explaining the exceptions to the incest prohibition. Among well-recorded cases, the Hawaiian and Egyptian royal families encouraged brother–sister marriage and, therefore, mating. In the Polynesian case the concept of *mana*, or spiritual power, is thought of as a reason for this practice since there were apparently attempts to prevent *mana*'s dilution through marriage of royals with commoners. As far as the Egyptians were concerned, Cleopatra was the product of generations of incestuous relationships and did not appear too defective, mentally or physically, at least to Marc Anthony.

It is evident, then, that no satisfactory explanation exists for explaining the incest issue. One wonders, however, if all of these intellectual ruminations over the last century have missed the point, which is to say that explanations should probably not be sought to explain why human societies avoid it, but why incest still persists unabated as a major social problem. The old explanations are small comfort to the many young girls and boys molested by parents, siblings, grandparents, or other relatives. One hears daily on the news about sexual assaults on young victims within their own households, which are supposed to be safe, nurturing havens for child rearing, rather than sites of horrific abuse. Should not the explanations then try to account for the persistence of these unspeakable crimes, rather than place the focus on why they supposedly do not occur in the first place?

■ Cousin Marriage

There are many places in the world where a cousin is a preferred marriage partner. Although the reasons why this practice might take place tend to vary from society to society, anthropologists have found it useful to distinguish between two types of cousins.

Box 6.3: The Kariera Kinship-Marriage System of Australia

The kinship-marriage system of most of the Aboriginal Australians has been described by one authority in this field of study as "the most difficult and complex kinship system in the world; and the great paradox is that it occurs in such a simple stone-age economy" (Fox 1967: 183–184). If we use the Kariera system (Romney and Epling 1958) as an example, the basic underlying principle concerns the exchange of women between groups, which is another way of describing a pattern of "reciprocal exogamy." Faced with the fundamental challenge of all small-scale societies that face possible extinction, the rule of survival is "marry out, or die out."

The Kariera system involves two patri-moieties, such that two clusters of kinship groups based on patrilineal descent exchange marriage partners. It is based on the rule that a man marries a woman who is a bilateral cross-cousin, which is to say, children of siblings of the opposite sex, on either the man's father's side (patrilateral) or mother's side (matrilateral) of the man's kinship group (i.e., bilateral). What follows from this pattern is that a man marries either his mother's brother's daughter, or his father's sister's daughter, as a preferential pattern.

If this pattern is maintained from one generation to the next, it is apparent, then, that the system is one of sister exchange such that a man's father's sister has married his mother's brother. It then follows that the child of such a union would be the man's wife again by sister exchange, who is both his mother's brother's daughter and father's sister's daughter. It is very helpful to work these relationships out on a sheet of paper, in which case it becomes evident that such a system is the logical outcome of the exchange of "sisters" over the generations.

It is also important to indicate that it is not necessary that men actually exchange their true or biological sisters as we would understand sisters in a European sense of female siblings in a nuclear family, but only those classified as "sisters." This wider classification would include an extension of the term "sister" to include, for example, one's mother's sister's daughters, as well as one's father's brother's daughters, i.e., female parallel cousins. While such a pattern may appear complex to those not familiar with such a marriage system, the basic rule is that reciprocal alliances be maintained between the two halves of the moiety, which are comprised of patrilineal clans in the Kariera case. This system of "sister exchange" therefore means that the two patriclans that have exchanged women at one time in the past continue to do so in subsequent generations. As Fox (1967: 186) explains, "Thus, if there is an exchange arrangement between patriclan A, and patriclan B, all a man of A has to do is make sure he marries a woman of B. There is no need for this woman to be genealogically his *actual* MBD/FZD [mother's brother's daughter/father's sister's daughter]. Now, it is true that in Australia the actual exchange of sisters does take place, so sometimes [a man's] wife will indeed be in this category, but there is no necessity for it."

The reason for this is that a man is only likely to marry an actual first cousin when the exchanging units are quite small, but in most cases of larger marrying units, it is simply a woman of a reciprocal clan that he marries. In anthropology these are referred to as "classificatory" (as opposed to "real") cross-cousins because they are "classified" with the real ones. From the Kariera point of view, they are not necessarily pursuing a "rule" of cross-cousin marriage, but simply exchanging women between two descent groups.

Parallel cousins are the children of siblings of the same sex, such as the children of one's mother's sister, or father's brother, hence the term "parallel," indicating that the gender of the linking siblings is the same. Children of siblings of the opposite sex are called *cross-cousins*, meaning that there is a cross or opposite-sex relationship of the linking siblings. Since cousins can be either male or female, and related to someone on either their father's side (*patrilateral*) or mother's side (*matrilateral*) of the family, then it is possible to distinguish four different types of cousins.

Patrilateral parallel cousin marriage is relatively rare, yet it is found in ancient Greece and China, where the inheritance of property is an important consideration. This form of marriage functions to maintain property and status in the male line of descent. However, most cousin marriages tend to be of the cross-cousin variety, which is especially the case of marriage with a male's *matrilateral cross-cousin*. One reason for this form of marriage is that many people reckon kinship through the male line only so that people on their mother's side of their family are not considered relatives at all. Thus, a cousin on a man's mother's side—a matrilateral cross-cousin—is considered a non-relative and therefore an available marriage partner. Such marriages are a way of marrying someone close to you because a man is taking his wife from his mother's kinship group without it constituting an incestuous relationship.

Cousin marriage is a way of establishing close ties between different kinship groups, thus promoting alliances and encouraging the opportunities for various types of exchanges to occur. Some kinship groups will exchange wives only with one other kinship group, such that they receive wives from one group, and give wives to the other. In terms of this wife-giving and wife-receiving relationship is concerned, the two groups could be said to form one half of a larger whole, thus the term *moieties* (from the French word *moitie*) is applied to this sort of marriage relationship. More generally with moieties, a number of kinship groups comprise each half of the overall whole.

■ Marriage in Canada

The federal government of Canada has exclusive authority governing marriage and divorce in Canada under section 91 (26) of the Canadian Constitution. However, the Constitution also gives provinces the power to pass laws regulating the solemnization of marriage. As far as marriage rates are concerned, in 2001 there were 146,618 marriages in Canada, down 6.8 percent from 157,395 in 2000. Prince Edward Island has the highest crude marriage rate of 6.5 per 1,000 people, and Quebec has the lowest rate at 3.0 per 1,000.

Marriages in Canada can be either religious or civil, and can be performed by clergy, marriage commissioners, judges, justices of the peace, or clerks of the court. The majority of marriages in 2001 (76.4 percent) were religious, with the remainder performed by non-clergy.

There are a number of marriage restrictions in Canada preventing the following people from becoming married under the federal Marriage (Prohibited Degrees) Act:

2. (1)   persons related by consanguinity, affinity or adoption is prohibited from marrying each other by reason only of their relationship.

2. (2)   No person shall marry another person if they are related
   (a) lineally by consanguinity or adoption;
   (b) as brother and sister by consanguinity, whether by the whole blood or by the half-blood; or
   (c) as brother and sister by adoption.

Additional rules governing marriage have also been set by various provinces. These rules generally relate to the age at which one may marry, usually anyone over 18 or 19 years of age, or between 16 and 18 with parental consent. British Columbia allows the marriage of people less than 16 years of age with the consent of the Supreme or County Court.

■ Same-Sex Marriage

If one surveys the anthropological literature on marriage, it becomes evident that *same-sex marriages* are not necessarily a new phenomenon, even though in most societies where the spouses are of the same sex, they occupy different roles, one husband and the other wife. In Canada, Bill C-23 was passed in 2000, which extended the rights of common-law partnerships to same-sex couples under the Modernization of Benefits and Obligations Act. On 20 July 2005, Canada became the fourth country in the world, after the Netherlands (2001), Belgium (2003), and Spain (2005), to legalize same-sex marriage across the country with the passing of the Civil Marriage Act. Before the passage of this act, court decisions starting in 2003 had already legalized same-sex marriage in eight of 10 provinces and one of the three territories. By this time more than 3,000 same-sex couples had already married in these areas.

The Civil Marriage Act was introduced by the Liberal government of Paul Martin on 1 February 2005 in the House of Commons. In December 2006 the House of Commons reaffirmed this legislation by defeating a Conservative motion to re-examine the matter. Passage of the Civil Marriage Act also made same-sex marriage legal in the provinces of Alberta and Prince Edward Island, along with Nunavut and the Northwest Territories, where challenges to the passage of this act had previously taken place. With the passage of this act, gay and lesbian couples were able to obtain marriage licences in the same manner as opposite-sex partners.

According to the Constitution of Canada, the definition of marriage is the sole responsibility of the federal government, even though some provinces, such as Alberta, had previously passed their own laws, which repudiated any federal reference to same-sex marriage. Alberta initially opposed the new legislation and had threatened to contest cases of same-sex marriage under the notwithstanding clause of the Canadian Charter of Rights and Freedoms. The former premier of Alberta, Ralph Klein, later recanted his province's opposition under the proviso that no one, such as a marriage commissioner who was personally opposed to such marriages, should be forced to perform them. A Supreme Court ruling on 9 December 2004 indicated that the Charter's protection of freedom of religion granted religious bodies the right to refuse to perform same-sex marriages if the performance of such marriages conflicted with their beliefs.

From June 2003, which is the date of the first legal same-sex marriage in Ontario, to October 2006, there were 12,438 same-sex marriages contracted in Canada (Larocque 2006). Since this time, South Africa (2006) and California (2008) have subsequently allowed the performance of same-sex marriages. In addition, the Department of Citizenship and Immigration in Canada acknowledges same-sex marriages contracted between immigration applicants and Canadian citizens or permanent residents.

■ Divorce Rates in Canada

In 1900 less than 15 divorces were granted in all of Canada. Prior to 1968, adultery was the only legal ground for divorce. The Canadian Divorce Act came into effect in 1968 and allowed for a divorce on the grounds of marriage breakdown; the couple had to have been separated for a period of at least three years. During the years 1968–1970, the number of divorces jumped by almost 200 percent as a result of this legislative change. The Divorce Act was amended in 1986, which shortened the length of time a separated couple had to wait to be divorced from a three-year separation period to only 12 months. With this legislation the number of divorces in Canada took another large jump as 96,000 new divorces were granted in 1987.

In Canada, under the federal Divorce Act, a divorce may be granted for one of the following reasons:

a. the marriage has irretrievably broken down, and the two parties have been living apart for a year,
b. one party has committed adultery,
c. one party has treated the other party with physical or mental cruelty of such a kind as to render intolerable the continued cohabitation of the spouses. (s. 8 (2) (b) (ii) of the Divorce Act)

On a global perceptive, the world divorce rate for 2002 indicates that Sweden had the largest percentage of marriages ending in divorce (54.9 percent), followed by the United States (45.8 percent). The divorce rate in Canada is 37.9 percent, and India has the least divorces (1.1 percent). Figures available from Statistics Canada reveal that the number of divorces during the years 2000–2002 fell slightly by 1.4 percent with 70,150 divorces at the end of this period. The divorce rate by the thirtieth anniversary of marriage in Canada for the 20002 period was 37.7 percent, a figure that has remained steady for a number of years.

As a general rule, the longer a marriage lasts, the less likely it is to end in divorce. About 60 percent of the divorces in 2001 and 2002 had not reached their fifteenth anniversary. Couples with marriages between four and five years old were the most likely to divorce. After five years, the risk of divorce decreases. As far as the nation-wide statistics are concerned, marriages in Newfoundland and Labrador had the lowest divorce rate over 30 years, as not quite 22 percent of marriages there ended in divorce in 2002. Quebec, however, had a divorce rate of 47.6 percent, the highest in the country. This means that Quebec, if it were a separate country, would have the second-highest divorce rate in the world, only behind Sweden in marriage breakups.

One relatively neglected aspect of the same-sex marriage legislation of 2005 concerns the issue of same-sex divorce. On 13 September 2004, a lesbian couple in Ontario was granted Canada's first same-sex divorce. The initial divorce application was denied because the federal Divorce Act defines a spouse as "either of a man or a woman who are married to each other." However, the Ontario Superior Court of Justice eventually ruled that the definition of "spouse" in the Divorce Act was unconstitutional. A similar ruling in June 2005 granted a divorce to another lesbian couple in British Columbia. Subsequent amendments to the Civil Marriage Act and the Divorce Act now permit same-sex divorce.

Divorce in other cultures differs from the Canadian situation in several significant ways. In the first place there is less emphasis on a married couple separating because a rupture in group relationships is more important than what happens to the people in a marriage. For example, Leach explains that "the phrase 'their marriage has broken up' refers to the disintegration of the domestic group rather than to the termination of contractual relations through divorce" (1982: 182). Among the Nuer, a marriage can never be terminated unless the initial cattle given as bridewealth are returned (Evans-Pritchard 1951). In other words, the "ties that bind" in marriage are more difficult to break than in Canada today. As Robert Murphy has observed, "There is in the modern conjugal family a great contradiction between the decrease in its utilitarian functions and the intensification of its emotional climate; both are root sources of the rising divorce rate" (1979: 81).

■ The Family

If marriage functions to regulate mating among humans and to provide a socially approved environment for the procreation of children, then the family can be seen as the important context for the transmission of culture and the socialization of the young. The family prepares children for adult roles in a society, instilling values, ideas, and techniques of a culture. There is a significant economic aspect pertaining to the division of labour between spouses, and the transmission of property and status. The reproductive aspects provide for the nurturing of the young by the provision of food and shelter, and links with a wider network of kinsmen. There is a replacement function as well, in that new community members are produced to replace the ones already departed.

One grows up in a *natal family* or *family of orientation*. Later, when married, the individual produces his or her own *family of procreation* or *conjugal family* in which children are raised. The *nuclear family* is the most elemental unit, comprising a married couple

Photo 6.1: Bobbie Crump family posing in an automobile in Edmonton, Alberta, c. 1918. Mr. Crump came to Canada from Oklahoma, c. 1911–1912. He first settled in Calgary, then Edmonton, and finally in Breton, Alberta. (Source: Glenbow Museum Archives, Calgary, Alberta)

and their children. *Extended families* are common in many parts of the world. The extension can be vertical, comprising three or more generations in a *lineal* fashion such that grandparents and grandchildren are attached to the nuclear unit. These extensions can also extend out horizontally or *laterally*, including one's aunts, uncles, and their children. In some societies a *patrilateral extension* is preferred—that is, including relatives on the father's side—whereas in others there is a preference for a *matrilateral extension*, which would include the mother's relatives.

Such large extended families are valued in some societies because they provide important economic and social advantages, such as providing more workers, or increased protection and support. We should also distinguish between a family and a domestic group. A family is comprised of individuals related to one another, but not necessarily resident in the same location. Members of the same *domestic group* live in the same household and usually eat their meals together, but this arrangement may include unrelated people. Another complex family form is the *polygynous family*, which consists of a number of separate families, often living in different households or domestic groups, linked by their relationship to a common father.

■ Residence Patterns

A newly married couple usually moves out of their parents' household to a new location to start their family. The term *residence patterns* refers to the location that a married couple moves to after marriage. *Patrilocal* or (*virilocal*) residence is a pattern in which the married couple lives in close proximity to the husband's male relatives. Usually there is a co-operative reason that brings related males together that has to do with their subsistence activities, such as hunting, fishing, or animal husbandry. Warfare may be another factor providing an advantage that brings males together for mutual protection. Patrilocal residence comprises over 60 percent of known cases recorded by ethnographers, and in Canada it is a common practice among the Algonquian-speaking Cree and Ojibwa of northern Ontario and Quebec.

In *matrilocal* or (*uxorilocal*) residence, the husband leaves his family and moves in close proximity with his wife's parents' household. The Huron and Iroquois of southern Ontario practised this form of residence. It is commonly associated with small-scale agricultural or horticultural societies in which the women play a significant role in subsistence production. The society also usually traces its kinship ties down through the female line, so those women play a central organization role in the society as a whole. Women are also likely to own the house sites and make important political decisions in leadership selection.

Avunculocal residence is also associated with descent through the female line. However, in this case, the newly married couple move near the groom's mother's brother (i.e., the husband's maternal uncle). In kinship systems where descent is traced through the female line, a male's biological father actually belongs to a different descent group than he does, so the most important male figure in his life—as far as training and other acculturative factors or the inheritance of property are concerned—is apt to be his maternal uncle. This residence pattern illustrates the strong bonds between males that can occur even in societies in which descent is reckoned through females.

In *neolocal residence* the married couple establish their household without much consideration given to where the parents of the wife or groom live. This system provides for a maximum amount of flexibility and is common in industrial societies in which geographical mobility is needed in the pursuit of education and employment.

Ambilocal or (*bilocal*) residence allows the married couple to choose between living with the husband's relatives (patrilocal) or those of the wife (matrilocal). This residence pattern, like neolocal residence, allows for flexibility so that couples can move to locals where labour requirements are highest. In the case of societies engaged in a foraging economy, it allows couples to move to areas with the greatest availability of food, the location of which may vary because of seasonal fluctuations in subsistence resources.

■ Profiles of Canadian Families

Canada is a country characterized by a great diversity in climatic conditions, physical environments, and cultural variability. The country's residents are situated primarily in urban settings clustered along the southern border with the United States. About 30 percent of the population live in rural areas, many engaged in the resource-extraction industries of mining and forestry, while others live on farms and in fishing communities in the coastal regions.

Social and cultural diversity was evident when the first European settlers arrived in the 1600s as the Aboriginal First Nations spoke about 50 separate languages. The Aboriginal populations had made successful adaptations to all of Canada's major geographical regions from the high Arctic, to the eastern woodlands, the Prairies, and both coastal environments.

Fur trading settlements along the St. Lawrence River and the Hudson and James Bay coastlines were the site of cultural mixing, leading to the formation of Métis populations. Later, yet still prior to Confederation, large numbers of French, English, and Irish populations migrated into Canada, seeking the rich farmland of southern Quebec and Ontario. With the completion of the Canadian Pacific Railway in the late 1880s and the opening of the Prairies for grain farming, immigrants from eastern Europe moved west in increasingly large numbers, establishing small communities in Manitoba, Saskatchewan, and Alberta. The railway also provided a new access to resource-rich British Columbia, which began to grow substantially with immigrants from the British Isles, joining the relatively large and diverse Aboriginal First Nations.

As one would expect, given these historical factors, the family life of Canadians reflects this demographic and social differentiation. Canada has had a tendency to preserve its diversity with its official policy of multiculturalism, resulting in accommodative rather than assimilative social processes. Processes that would encourage a more assimilative tendency have been partly forestalled in Canada because of the relative isolation of the existing populations in many areas of the country, especially before the advent of television and adequate roads. It is therefore difficult to say what might be called the

Photo 6.2: Mi'kmaq family camp, Nova Scotia, c. 1890. (Source: Nova Scotia Archives)

typical Canadian family. As one sociologist commented, "There is no one Canadian family. With its distinctive geography and history, Canada is much too heterogeneous to have one or ten or twenty distinctive family types. As the geographical setting, and as the social class, religion, ethnic, occupational, and other groupings vary, so too do our families" (Elkin 1970: 31). In keeping with this theme of social and cultural diversity, the approach taken here is to provide brief profiles of four varieties of Canadian families—Inuit, Hutterite, Quebec agricultural, and steelworker—in order to illustrate their internal composition, characteristics, and challenges.

■ The Netsilik of the Central Arctic

The Netsilik, or *Netsilingmiut*, are an Inuit society sometimes referred to as "the People of the Seal" because of their reliance on seal hunting as a main subsistence activity. However, they also hunted caribou from kayaks with light spears, and fished for salmon in the rivers and narrow lakes of their territory. The following account is based on fieldwork by Asen Balikci (1970), conducted in the 1960s in the Pelly Bay region prior to the Netsilik's movement into permanent settlements. His research, therefore, reflects a traditional style of life on the land rather than the settled living conditions that exist today.

Photo 6.3: Inuit woman drying fish. Some of the fish are hanging on a line while the rest are spread out on the rocks, Taloyoak (formerly Spence Bay), Nunavut, 1951. (Source: Photograph by Richard Harrington, Library and Archives Canada)

The diversified subsistence activities of the Netsilik kept them moving about their territory in an annual cycle of hunting and fishing. In the winter they travelled about on sleds made of wood and sealskin, pulled by two or three dogs, and lived in snow houses heated by soapstone lamps. The Netsilik social organization was characterized by relatively simple and flexible aspects. They had bilateral families, meaning that they traced their relatives through both the husband's and wife's families, which was a common characteristic of the Inuit. One functional explanation is that in times of need, such a social organization provides the maximum number of relatives that one could rely on for food and shelter. In addition, numerous partnerships of a more or less formal nature provided strong links to non-relatives.

One such partnership was the *name-sake system*. As Balikci (1970: 199) explains, "Personal names were thought among the Netsilik to possess a personality of their own characterized by great power and a distinct ability to protect the name bearer from any misfortune." According to the name-sake system people with the same names are therefore thought to have similar souls or personalities. In a different settlement one could always count on someone with the same name as you to provide food, shelter and other necessities of life. Such support mechanisms were an important aspect of survival under the rigorous conditions of the Canadian Arctic.

The Netsilik have a strong preference for marrying cousins, which has the effect of leading to a considerable overlapping of kinship categories. Such practices also result in relatives being connected in various ways, such that two different kinship terms might apply to the same individual, and certain individuals related to a person by both blood (*consanguinity*) and marriage (*affinity*). Needless to say, such kinship relationships could be a complicated matter for the ethnographic fieldworker sorting out the various parties involved. Kinship terms are also divided in certain cases by age, such as terms for elder and younger brother. In addition, men and women each have their own set of kinship terms, although there is some duplication as, for example, in the same terms for (same-sex) cousins, which are used by both males and females. Cousins of the opposite sex are called by the same terms one uses for one's own siblings, i.e., the terms one uses for brothers and sisters are also extended to include cousins who are of the opposite sex to the speaker, such that girls call their male cousins "brother" and boys call their female cousins "sister."

The Netsilik, according to Balikci (1970: 94–101), have a tendency to marry cousins, even first cousins, even though all cousins are considered relatives. He points out that among most Inuit groups, cousin marriage was forbidden as incestuous, so the Netsilik are relatively unique in this regard, leading to the curious situation in which a man could call his spouse either "wife" or "sister" since the sibling term "sister" was extended to include same-sex cousins as well. However, Balikci does not give any empirical data on how many actual marriages there were of this sort, only indicating that this was a preference in the choice of one's spouse.

The Netsilik have a preference for patrilocal residence, although in reality the residence pattern is a fairly flexible one. For various reasons, such as the necessity of hunting, a young man may establish residence with his maternal uncle or stay

Photo 6.4: Inuit men dancing and drumming, Alaska, c. 1903–1915. (Source: Glenbow Museum Archives, Calgary, Alberta)

with any one of his aunts. These were close relatives of his and a young man could expect help from them, reflecting the *bilateral* kinship system of the Netsilik, which includes relatives from both the father's and mother's side of the family. Given that a hunter and his family often had to take long, dangerous trips and risk meeting strange people in different settlements, "under such circumstances, kinship extensions were invaluable, for in a hostile land they widened the area of social security of the individual" (Balikci 1970: 101).

The nuclear family, consisting of the father, mother, and children, was the most significant social unit among the Netsilik. While there were no rules restricting the number of wives a husband may marry, polygynous marriages were relatively rare, probably because it would be very difficult for a Netsilik hunter to support more than one wife and their children. There was no particular marriage ceremony as the girl simply moved her belongings to her husband's household. It was common for girls to marry at about 14 or 15 years of age, and for boys usually around the age of 20 when they were able to support a wife. This pattern of patrilocal residence was motivated by the hunting way of life. It was essential for the young man to hunt in the areas that he was familiar with, and to be associated with other males who were his hunting companions. The nuclear family was also the basis for the division of labour in the family. The husband hunted and fished, made all his own weapons and tools, fed the dogs, and made the snow house. His wife scraped the caribou skins, butchered seals, cleaned fish, cared for the fire in the soapstone lamps, and generally was responsible for all of

Photo 6.5: Akulack and wife, Bathhurst Inlet, Nunavet, c. 1915. (Source: Photograph by G. Moodie, Glenbow Museum Archives, Calgary, Alberta.)

the kitchen activities. She also made all of the clothing and boots for the family, sewed tents and skin containers, and covered kayaks.

The Netsilik nuclear family was linked to a wider circle of social relationships through the extended family, related through consanguineal ties. This extended family network comprised a number of nuclear families living in close proximity to the husband's patrilateral kinsmen. Such extended families were necessary for survival as the men of these families hunted together and shared their catch with other members of the extended group. The Netsilik use the term *ilagiit* to refer to this circle of relatives, which formed a close-knit group of personal kindred.

From the viewpoint, then, of any Netsilik individual, his or her kinship universe is packed rather closely around the nuclear family through which the closest bonds of intimacy and support are developed. Outside of the nuclear family is a ring of other relatives, usually related through kinship ties to the husband, forming the extended family, which is also necessary for survival. In an even wider circle of relatives are those to whom one is related through their mother, or matrilateral kinsmen, who may also act as a supporting mechanism, but less often than the male relatives. It is possible, then, to view the Netsilik kinship universe somewhat like the concentric rings formed when a pebble is tossed into a pond—tight at the centre, but dissipating in strength as the rings extend farther out.

■ The Hutterites of Southern Alberta

The Hutterites are a communal religious sect, similar in some ways to the Amish and Mennonites, except that they have embraced modern technology in their farming techniques while maintaining their traditional social organization. Various Hutterite colonies are scattered throughout the United States in North and South Dakota, and in Montana. In Canada they are concentrated primarily in southern Alberta, but are also located in smaller numbers in Saskatchewan and Manitoba. The research reported here was conducted by John Hostetler, born of Amish parentage, and Gertrude Huntington, comprising 280 individuals in 38 nuclear families during the 1960s (Hostetler and Huntington 1967).

The Hutterites originated during the Protestant Reformation in the sixteenth century and are one of three surviving Anabaptist groups, with the other two being the Mennonites and Old Order Amish. The Anabaptists were nonconformist groups who rejected infant baptism and membership in a state church. As a result of their nonconformist stance, the Hutterites were the subject of prosecution in Europe—Jacob Hutter, their founder, was burned at the stake in 1536—leading to their eventual migration to North America in 1874. Three colonies, or *Bruderhof*, were founded in South Dakota in 1874–1877, with a subsequent migration to the southern Prairie provinces of Canada in 1918 after persecution in the United States over the conscription issue for military service during the First World War. Eventually new colonies were formed in Saskatchewan in 1952 and Manitoba in 1954. The 60 or so colonies in Alberta own or lease about 2,900 ha of land per colony, or about 23.5 ha per person, compared to about 49 ha per person for other farm families in areas of Alberta where Hutterites live.

The basic principles of Hutterite life are based on utopian-like principles, such as the elimination of extremely poor or wealthy members, motivation without the incentive of private gain, a high degree of security for the individual, all within a communal society. The Hutterites believe that living communally is the divine order of God. The communal will, not the individual will, becomes important as the good of the majority governs the various stages of life for the Hutterite person. The basic layout of a Hutterite colony consists of a kitchen complex, the longhouses or living houses with their associated sheds, and a kindergarten.

Each longhouse has four separate apartments, each with its own entrance, typically comprising three rooms. The apartments are sparse, comprising a large table with straight chairs, a cupboard with a few dishes, and several bedrooms with double beds and a crib. Meals are prepared for the colony members by the women in the communal kitchen three times a day. A family's laundry is also washed in this building, and the colonists come to bathe or shower here as well. The Hutterite do not have church buildings, which they associate with state religions and persecution, so religious services are held in the schoolhouse.

Courtship among the Hutterite is usually long, lasting from about two to six years. The average age at marriage is 22 years for women and 23 years for men. A couple may have as many children as they wish as birth-control practices are not allowed. Few people

Photo 6.6: Elias and Jacob Walter and their families, members of the Stand Off Hutterite Colony, Alberta, 1963. (Source: Glenbow Museum Archives, Calgary, Alberta)

remain unmarried; fewer than 5 percent of the population remained unmarried over the age of 30. Divorce is rare as only one case has been reported since 1875. It is common for the bride and groom to come from different colonies as they have an opportunity to meet during social gatherings, which bring together members of several nearby colonies. The colony's permission is required before a couple may marry. After a brief ceremony, which lasts about 15 minutes and is mainly comprised of instructions by the preacher, the couple returns to the bride's family's apartment. The husband serves up small glasses of wine to her parents, after which the couple proceeds to every house, serving the people and receiving good wishes for their married life.

After several days of singing and social activities, the couple eventually leaves for the young man's colony. Before they leave, colony members give small presents to the bride, such as a bedspread, several lamps, towels, soap, a laundry basket, and so on. The colony itself gives the bride several larger gifts, such as extra bedding or an electric sewing machine. Such items are not regarded as gifts because it is believed that the woman has earned these as a working member of the colony. All of these goods are then loaded up into several trucks and taken to the groom's colony, where further singing and celebrations take place.

The wedding service usually takes place on a Sunday morning. Members of a colony look forward to a wedding as it is the happiest gathering of friends and relatives. Since weddings can be expensive affairs, double or even triple wedding ceremonies are encouraged. Weddings formalize a marriage, but they also strengthen inter-colony ties. Since the couple live in the husband's colony and in his parents' household, his adjustment is minimal compared to his wife as all of his primary ties are maintained. She is now under the direction of her mother-in-law, which places the wife in a vulnerable position as she has only her husband for support and information and knows few other people in the colony. Her only secure niche is her bedroom, which is considered hers alone. The saying is that the bedroom belongs to the wife, the colony to the husband. However, marriage functions to support a husband's dominant position and to stress his wife's dependence. Biological brothers also tend to co-operate closely among themselves and with their father in many areas of life. The wives, on the other hand, are not likely to see their mothers again until after their children are born.

Socialization of children within the family is one of the most important reasons for the stability and success of Hutterite colonies. The goal of the society to live communally is achieved by successfully preparing individuals for communal life and by increasing their dependence upon human support and contact. From early childhood to adulthood there is no weakening of the enculturation process, which emphasizes individuals' subservience to the colony. In return, the colony provides protection and support for its members throughout their lives.

■ St. Denis: A Rural Quebec Parish

St. Denis: A French-Canadian Parish, written by Horace Miner ([1939] 1967) on the basis of fieldwork conducted in the 1930s, is considered by many to be a classic in Canadian anthropology. During the time period the research was conducted (1936–1937), many rural communities in Quebec were quite isolated and dominated by the Catholic Church. This was a period before the Quiet Revolution, during which highways were constructed into the rural areas, television served to break down the parochial isolation, and the influence of the Catholic Church was considerably diminished. For example, divorce during the period of Miner's research was unthinkable, yet today Quebec has one of the highest divorce rates in the world.

■ The Redfield-Lewis Controversy

St. Denis is associated in anthropology with a period of community studies, influenced most prominently by Robert Redfield and his anthropology colleagues at the University of Chicago; indeed, Redfield wrote the introduction to Miner's ethnography. Redfield's approach, epitomized by his fieldwork in the Mexican village of Tepoztlan (Redfield 1930), emphasized the internal consistency of rural village life, its cohesion and harmonious social relationships. These conclusions were severely criticized in a later study of the same village by Oscar Lewis (1951), who found rampant factionalism, homicides,

---

Box 6.4: Oscar Lewis (1914–1970): The Culture of Poverty Debate

Contemporary articles in the *New York Times* (2008, 2010) attest to the continuing interest in the controversial theory concerning the "Culture of Poverty." First proposed nearly a half-century ago by America anthropologist Oscar Lewis (1966a, 1966b), the basic principle behind the theory is that the culture of poverty is an adaptation to the marginalization experienced by the poor in a class-stratified, capitalistic society. Lewis contended that the lives of slum-dwellers in urban centres transcended national boundaries, and that there were cultural similarities in the reactions of the poor to their impoverished conditions of life.

Lewis based his conclusions on research into the urban poor of Mexico, San Juan, Puerto Rico, and New York City, finding that families were characterized by high divorce rates, a fatalistic view of life, and common feelings of helplessness and inferiority. Mothers and children are often abandoned by their husbands and fathers, leading to matrifocal families headed by women. People enmeshed in the culture of poverty tend not to participate in community life, and make little use of hospitals, banks, and other institutions. In other words, according to Lewis, the culture of poverty perpetuates poverty from generation to generation because of its effects on children. Children grow up learning the basic values and attitudes of this subculture and have difficulty later in life in breaking free of these conditions in order to take advantage of new opportunities that may present themselves in their lifetimes.

Several sociological studies echo Lewis's findings, such as Elliot Liebow's (1967) *Tally's Corner*, which finds a sympathetic audience in the hopelessness and despair of urban life. In addition, anthropologist Ulf Hannerz's ([1969] 2004) *Soulside*, a study of an African American Ghetto in Washington, D.C., suggests that even if the situational forces were removed, there would still be a cultural lag, making the poor resistant to changes in adaptation and behaviour.

The culture of poverty approach has nonetheless been the subject of considerable criticism. Kenneth Little's (1957) study of West African urban communities shows that the poor do participate in many voluntary associations. In the *New York Times* (2010) article "'Culture of Poverty' Makes a Comeback," it is indicated even as far back as the Johnson administration that there was widespread support for the idea of the urban Black family caught in an inescapable "tangle of pathology," which conservative thinkers regarded as "attributing self-perpetuating moral deficiencies to black people, as if blaming them for their own misfortune." Ironically, Oscar Lewis grew up on a farm in upstate New York, far removed from the sorts of urban situations that became a research focus in his later life (*New York Times* 1970).

---

and a rising crime rate, among other social problems. This quarrel among anthropologists became known as the *Redfield-Lewis controversy*.

This controversy illustrates, in one of the very few cases in which anthropological fieldwork was replicated at a later date, how an ethnographer's different perspectives can lead to sometimes dramatic differences in interpretations of social systems. Anthropologists have now reached the conclusion that both Redfield and Lewis were actually correct in their conclusions because they each emphasized a different aspect of the Tepoztlan community. Redfield portrayed the ideal or formal belief system (the way the people themselves saw their community), while Lewis depicted the actual or informal system (the way it actually was). Both versions of the village were therefore valid, yet each was also incomplete. In a way each version of Tepoztlan complemented the other, filling in the neglected areas that the other overlooked. Yet, one wonders how so radically different interpretations of the same community are possible, given the scientific, objective aspirations of the disciple.

In a similar manner, Miner's account of St. Denis was also the subject of criticism, but on different grounds than the Redfield-Lewis controversy. Philippe Garigue, for example, questioned the accuracy of Miner's account of rural Quebec, especially the conceptualization of the old rural lifeways as resembling those of Redfield's folk or peasant societies, which focused on the relatively isolated, family-oriented, and self-sufficient community. By contrast, from Garigue's (1956, 1960) perspective, he sees the traditional culture of Quebec as having been that of a mainly commercial and urban society. Miner countered by denying that his description of the St. Denis community had "been distorted to fit a preconceived concept," and that he did "not exclude relevant data because they do not conform to the scheme" (1967: vi). Nonetheless, whatever interpretations or theoretical positions may serve as the vantage point for the St. Denis community study, one still has to rely on the basis ethnographic facts of St. Denis community life that Miner gathered at the time of his fieldwork.

■ The Traditional French Canadian Family

French Canada began in 1584 with the establishment of the colony of New France. Growth of this colony was relatively slow for the next century or so, consisting mainly of small rural farms strung out along the St. Lawrence River. The term *habitant* came to identify the person of the countryside, living in a kinship-oriented community, and dominated by an agricultural way of life. Work in the woods clearing farmland was also an essential activity. Others left their families during the summer to work as *voyageurs*, rowing the boats and paddling canoes for the fur trading companies in Montreal. It would have been a lonely life for those left behind on the rural farm if it were not for the companionship of the members of their parish church, friends, and extended family.

Farmsteads usually consisted of a narrow strip, about 244 m wide and 2.5 km long, extending from the river's shore up to an elevated portion of wooded area in the back of the property. The homestead began at the waterfront and the settlers worked their way uphill, clearing land for their vegetable gardens, buildings, and hayfields. When population increased, a church was eventually built and a parish developed, often in conjunction with a small village, which supplied goods such as cloth and implements for the farms in the area.

Marriage was not so much a matter of the individual choosing a spouse, but was more of a family matter. Potential marriage partners were not located randomly in the existing rural population, but within groups of families or through membership in local church groups. Marriage of cousins was common in St. Denis as Miner ([1939] 1967: 78) records that 14.5 percent of marriages were between third or closer cousins, reflecting an endogamous mode of mate selection. The Church did not condone marriage to a second or closer cousin, but such marriages were possible if one was willing to spend a certain amount of money to secure a dispensation from the *curé*—the closer the cousin, the higher the fee.

Courtship usually lasted only a few months, often in the context of parties or other social activities. Marriage was by contract with dowries, and with the consent of parents a necessary condition. The father of the groom made a formal request, on his son's behalf, of the bride's parents for her hand in marriage. After the details of the marriage contract were worked out to the satisfaction of both family groups, the marriage banns were read during the ensuing church services, asking the attending congregation if anyone knew of an impediment to the marriage of the engaged couple, otherwise "forever hold your peace." The wedding was usually held in the bride's parish, with her *curé* conducting the service. The wedding parties often began at the groom's home, then moved from house to house on different nights. A short honeymoon to Quebec or another nearby centre was common.

Photo 6.7: Woman checking mail in front of rural farmhouse, Bolton Glen, Quebec, 1912. (Source: Photographer William James Topley, Library and Archives Canada)

A close identification with one's kinship group is a common sentiment among the *habitants*. "The main characteristics of the French-Canadian family," Garigue (1960: 197) suggests, "can be said to be an extensive kinship recognition only partially weakened by geographical scattering, and extensive exchange of services among recognized kin, a strong sense of household, unity, and a large sibling group." By most standards, family size as large as 10 or more children was a preferred pattern. While the Church would encourage early and fertile marriages, there is no doubt a productive advantage in having a large number of family members to share in the prodigious workload of the agricultural economy, especially given a low level of farming technology.

An expanding population requires a corresponding increase in amounts of arable land, a situation made problematic by the resistance of farm owners to divide farms among their offspring. This preference for *impartible inheritance*, whereby only one son inherits the farm intact, a practice also utilized by the Irish to prevent further fragmentation of their already small farms, put pressure on the non-inheriting offspring to continually develop new farm acreage. In the Irish case, discussed previously in the section on ethnohistorical research, the sons who did not inherit the family farm were forced to either emigrate or turn to wage labour. In the rural Quebec case, there was, until recent times, still sufficient new land available that sons could purchase, probably with the financial help of their parents, existing woodlots that could be cleared, or small farms that could be expanded later with additional purchases of land. In any event, given a rapidly expanding local population, and the elder generation's existing sentiments regarding the inheritance of farms, there was continual pressure on agricultural resources in rural Quebec. This pressure would not be relieved until the 1950s with the expansion of road building and the eventual urban migration and industrialization of Quebec.

These various trends, such as a tendency toward impartible inheritance, also had similar kinship repercussions as those prevailing in Ireland. With the reluctance of the aging parents to leave the family farm, their duties were usually taken over by the oldest son, who waited in abeyance in anticipation of his eventual inheritance. This situation had the effect of delaying the marriage of the inheriting son. When he eventually married, his wife would be subjected to the controlling influences of her mother-in-law, causing potential conflicts. This family arrangement, consisting of a married couple, their children, and aging parents, is called the *stem family*. It is an inherently unstable unit for various reasons since it ceases to exist with the death of the son's parents, or does not come into being until he has children of his own.

Most farms in rural Quebec, however, would not have the stem family pattern because only one son of many inherits the family property. This would suggest that nuclear families living on their own farms would be the most prominent form, with ties of support to extended family members beyond the nuclear household. In many cases the eldest son does not want to wait the several decades, at least, for his parents to relinquish their hold on the farm, so older brothers often leave the community, seeking help from other relatives in nearby communities. A middle son is therefore the most likely to inherit the farm, with the expectation that he will take responsibility for helping to establish the younger brothers who will not inherit. Daughters may be sent to convents if they are not able to establish substantial dowries, which is an important factor in finding marriage partners. Other daughters may migrate to urban settings or end up as maiden aunts in their brothers' families. As Miner ([1939] 1967: 77) explains, "the same lack of opportunity which makes the men leave the parish keeps other men from coming in from a distance to establish and take wives in St. Denis."

■ Hamilton's Steelworker Families

Steelworker families in Hamilton, Ontario, are subject to economic pressures external to their own community, and even to their own country (Leach 2005). Stelco is Hamilton's major employer, so when it applied for bankruptcy protection in January 2004, over 20,000 families were directly affected. With a decline in the global demand for steel, the previous 20-year period of relative prosperity came to an end. Stelco reported a loss of $168 million for the third quarter of 2003, with a massive pension deficit and company debt. Leach's informants reported that the large-scale layoffs also coincided with increased family troubles, both social and economic.

The traditional single-income breadwinner-type of family could no longer survive. Unemployed husbands scrambled to find other employment, which became increasingly scarce. Wives, who up to this point had been able to be stay-at-home moms, now sought part-time work wherever they could find it. Child care became a major problem, the expense of which could severely curtail any economic gains of the wife's new job. Grandparents took up some of the slack in child care, but they understandably did not want to be tied down all day with their grandchildren.

The worsening economic situation placed many families in a precarious position. Steelworker families became subject to mortgage foreclosures, termination of leases on rental accommodation, and disruption in household services because of unpaid bills. Many couples were working on their second marriage, so a slackening in the support payments from unemployed former partners further decreased incomes available for household budgets. Women also reported a corresponding increase in violence within the home. Family strife began to proliferate. As Leach (2005: 2) reports: "This corporate bankruptcy is the latest chapter in the unravelling of livelihood security in Hamilton steelworker households. But the consequences are inscribed in the lives, memories, and bodies of steelworkers and their families."

The steelworker families of Hamilton illustrate how households in industrial societies are directly tied to structural shifts in the global economy. Of course, northern Canadian communities have been the subject of boom-bust cycles for many decades as mines, pulp mills, and other extractive industries expand and contract, leaving single-industry towns with few economic options when the source of a town's livelihood goes into decline. Now, on a much larger global scale, even large cities such as Hamilton in Ontario's so-called "Golden Horseshoe" are becoming subject to similar economic and social consequences as their northern counterparts.

Photo 6.8: Workmen operate ladle to pour molten steel into ingot moulds at the Stelco Steel Company of Canada plant, Hamilton, Ontario, 1944. (Source: Ronny Jaques, National Film Board of Canada, Library and Archives Canada)

The transformation of Hamilton's working class has been dramatic in the space of only a couple of decades. During the post-1950s period, there was a high global demand for steel, and lifestyles were supported by good jobs, with the expectation that this way of life would last forever. Now there is insecurity on a day-to-day basis. It becomes increasingly evident to the members of Hamilton's working-class families that they suffer from an unequal access to wealth and power. Steelworker families also illustrate gendered forms of inequality. Males tend to control household budgets, with the result that valuable household funds are often devoted to the husband's entertainment, to the neglect of essential needs at home. Even in the face of these economic difficulties, women are encouraged by their male partners to remain at home, thus reinforcing the illusion of normalcy within the household.

Economic and political decisions made many thousands of miles away from Hamilton can have disastrous local results. Stelco's economic plight was due in large part to a slumping global demand for steel products, but these were in turn due to decisions that were as much political as economic. The United States, for example, lifted its protective tariffs against the European Union and other steel exporters, thus providing stiffer competition for Stelco products. One would think that Stelco's proximity to American markets, which is closer than European sources of steel, would offer a competitive edge. Yet decades of strikes and strong unions in Hamilton led to relatively high wages in the steel industry, which, in conjunction with increasingly uncompetitive factory facilities, are all factors in reducing demand for Stelco steel products.

Massive job cuts in the 1990s was a major part of Stelco's survival strategy, following the corporate restructuring of the 1980s. Women's participation rates rose to unprecedented levels when men could no longer rely on the expectation of secure employment in the steel industry. This struggle with economic uncertainty led to dramatic transformations in Hamilton's working-class culture. Women struggled with attempting to manage low-paying employment outside of the home, while still burdened with most of the household chores of cleaning, child rearing, cooking, and budget management. In addition, as one female informant related during an interview, her husband's "volatile temper and history of violence dominated this relationship and was threaded through our conversations" (Leach 2005: 2). Women bear the scars of men's brutality, while the men themselves bear the scars of decades of manual work in the steel mills.

Anthropologists have a role to serve in documenting the social and cultural processes of industrial societies, as well as those of agrarian and hunting cultures. There is critical work to be done by today's anthropologists in investigating the class and gendered process of globalization. Anthropologists have a ground-level view of the everyday activities through which people live their lives. There is therefore a unique opportunity to link the apparently mundane activities of so-called ordinary people with the broader shifts of unequal access to wealth and power, as illustrated by the study of Hamilton's steelworker families.

▪ Challenges All Families Face

The four family profiles discussed in this chapter—the Inuit, Hutterite, French Canadian, and Hamilton steelworkers—illustrate that despite varied environmental and cultural backgrounds, families everywhere face similar challenges. Perhaps the most important of these challenges is how to successfully adapt to the ecological conditions that support life for family members. Whether one makes a living by hunting and fishing, agricultural production, or industrial employment, families adapt to their economic circumstance by a division of labour, by incorporating successful adaptive techniques passed down through the generations into their daily affairs, and by relying on the knowledge and support of extended kinship networks.

In most cases such terms as *nuclear family* perhaps draw too much of an arbitrary social division since no family is truly isolated from the social and economic environment in which they are situated. As families are initially established by marriage, with the birth of children bonds of dependency develop. Over time the family matures as the children grow to adulthood. In turn, these children become the parents, aunts, and uncles of a later generation. Bonds of support extend outward through time, adding one to another, like the growth rings of a tree. In this regard the modern North American family probably sees itself as more independent than is actually the case.

Families suffer from the pangs of dislocation that are part of the job mobility cycle and a division of labour that removes adult members of the household for long periods of time during the day. Many children today return home to an empty household and are left to their own devices, an unfortunate circumstance brought on by high divorce rates, single-parent households, shift work, and the lack of nearby kin who are free enough to provide support. The challenge facing all families is how to maintain the internal bonds of support within the family unit while also providing for the necessary economic means for the survival for its members.

7 Kinship, Descent, and Affinity

An Americo-Liberian family ... a full house
Woodrow wasn't exactly sure, but he thought that altogether he
had forty-two brothers and sisters. Maybe more.

—Russell Banks,
The Darling (2005: 109)

An old saying reminds us that we can choose our friends, but not our relatives. Like it or not, we are stuck with the family of relatives that we are born into. What is amazing, though, is the truly inspirational manner in which human beings manipulate these relationships in various ways, and the extent to which they have explored just about every option or variation that is possible. Kinship relationships have been reckoned laterally or horizontally on both the father's and mother's sides of families, vertically, through fathers and their male kin, through mothers and their female kin, through both sides vertically at once, or even switching sides to suit certain opportunities. This variability is also evident in the ways in which we label our relatives as we group and separate them into all sorts of patterns. We tend to regard our kinship system as "natural" and the one another tribe uses as incomprehensible to us.

For the anthropologist, kinship is therefore only partly about biology and more about social relationships. For this reason the terms "kinship," "descent," and "affinity" need further explanation. *Kinship* refers to the relationships we have with people who are related to us by blood (*consanguineal*) and by marriage (*affinal*). *Descent* pertains to the tracing of kinship relationships through one's parents, usually through the mother or father, but not both. Members of a *descent group* share a sense of identity based on the belief that they are all descended from a common ancestor. We may therefore recognize kinship links with certain people, such as our mother, but not a descent link if she belongs to a different descent group from us, which is the case if descent is traced through the male line. Your mother, in this instance, would then belong to the same descent group as her father and brothers, but not to yours since you would belong to the same descent group as your father. However, as Mair (1968: 63) reminds us, "Nobody recognizes kinship with all the people to whom he is linked by common descent." The reason for this is that as a common ancestor recedes into the past, he or she tends to become forgotten and the descendants no longer think of themselves as kin.

■ Tracing Descent

In different societies people recognize a variety of ways of tracing kinship relationships and, as a result, in the groups that are formed by these differing principles of descent recognition. There are basically two ways to trace descent: laterally, which is to say, in a horizontal manner out through the relatives of one's own generation, or in a lineal manner, which is up and down through the generations.

In a *bilateral descent system* one traces relatives through both the father's and mother's sides of the family. This version is sometimes referred to as *cognatic descent*, meaning tracing descent through *both* male and female links. This descent principle is common in Western industrialized societies, and in hunting-and-foraging groups. The emphasis in this type of system is to pack one's kinship universe with close relatives, in concentric circles if we can use this analogy, such that our recognition and familiarity recedes as the circle widens into distant relatives. Sometimes all that binds people together in such a system is a common surname, but then they will have to root around to find out if they have common linkages with known relatives. The boundaries of such a system are usually diffuse and imprecise.

A bilateral system also places little emphasis on genealogical depth since usually only grandparents, or maybe in rare cases great-grandparents, are remembered and recognized. Another characteristic of this system is that we share only certain links with particular relatives with only our siblings and no one else. Our uncles or aunts are only the same uncles and aunts to our own brothers and sisters. This means that the kinship universe in bilateral systems is idiosyncratic or situationally specific, depending upon one's vantage point in such a system.

A far more common method of tracing descent is through *either* one's father's *or* mother's relatives. These are referred to as *unilineal descent systems*. In a *patrilineal (or agnatic) descent* system, one traces relatives up to one's father, grandfather, and so on. This means that one would share the same descent links with one's siblings (both male and female), father, and his brothers and sisters, and so on, up through the grandparental and great-grandparental generations. In terms of one's own children, your sons and daughters are both included if you are a male. If you are a female, then your children would be included in the descent group of your husband. Also included in this group of relatives would be the children of your father's brother (paternal uncle), who are your *parallel cousins*, but not the children of your father's sister (paternal aunt), who are your *cross-cousins*.

We can see then that such a system operates differently from a bilateral system, in that the unilineal system has the effect of dividing the cousin category into two separate groups (i.e., cross and parallel). In many societies using a unilineal principle, cross-cousins, especially *matrilateral cross-cousins* if the system is a patrilineal one, are considered ideal marriage partners, while the category of parallel cousins are usually included in an extension of *sibling terminology* and therefore called "brother" and "sister." As such, they are usually not considered potential marriage partners as marrying such a person would be considered an act of incest, as if one were marrying one's biological brother or sister.

Box 7.1: Scottish Crofters: The Problem with Scottish "Clans"

Geall is a Gaelic-speaking island community of crofters in the Scottish Outer Hebrides (Parman 1990). The Scottish crofter is the tenant of a *croft*, or a small unit of agricultural land, usually comprising .5–2 ha. The croft is a strip of land adjoining a main road consisting also of a croft house (owned by the crofter) with a small garden patch behind it. The crofter rents his croft from a landlord, the rent of which includes a share of the common grazing land held by the crofting township. Croft members also share in the responsibility of maintaining land and fencing, organizing communal sheep roundups, and generally promoting the agricultural viability of the township.

The term "clan" (actually, the term *clann* simply means "children"), as used by the Scots, refers to a group of people who share a common surname or who can link themselves, through male *or* female linkages, to an ancestor with this name (McDonald 1986). Thus, in the strict sense of the word, the Scottish term is at odds with conventional anthropological usage because, for example, a clan in anthropology refers to people belonging to the same unilineal descent group whereby descent is traced consistently through either male (patrilineal) or female (matrilineal) lines. The Scottish usage of "clan" cannot also be equated to the anthropological term "kindred," which refers to all the descendants through *all* links (male and female) from a common ancestor; thus, kindred consists of a person's bilateral relatives.

Since the Scottish use of "clan" refers to relatives who can link themselves through *either* male *or* female relatives but not *both*, as in the case of bilateral descent, then the proper term for the Scottish kinship system is *ambilineal descent*—that is, tracing relatives through either male and female linkages. In an ambilineal descent system there is some switching back and forth between the connecting male or female relatives, either done consistently or at random, depending on the situation, which is not the case with either patrilineal or matrilineal descent. In conventional anthropological usage, then, ambilineal descent is a form of cognatic descent in which individuals have a choice of reckoning kinship along either maternal or paternal links (Parman 1990: 107–109).

Perhaps one could say more correctly that Scottish "clans" are ambilineal with a "patrilineal bias" because of the practice by which children take the name of their father. As an example, a person could consider himself or herself linked to the Ferguson clan because his or her father's mother's father was a Ferguson (meaning that Ferguson was the person's grandmother's maiden name). In other words, anyone can claim membership in a clan group if he or she can demonstrate descent, through male or female linkages in any combination, from someone whose name is the clan name. In practical terms, demonstrating such "proof" is not usually necessary, since in the history of highland clans, non-relatives often took the name of a person to whom they gave allegiance or expected protection. In this sense Scottish clans hardly seem to be a kinship group at all, but more of a common-interest association.

Patrilineal descent systems, usually coupled with patrilocal residence patterns, are commonly found in societies practising pastoralism, or in more advanced, intensive agricultural systems. For the most part, anthropologists think that there is a close relationship between the descent system and a society's economy. In other words, there are probably certain functional relationships that would promote the use of one particular descent system over another, depending upon the ways in which societies adapt to their environment, make a living, and feed themselves. In pastoral societies, it is an economic advantage to have male kinsmen located in the same area so that they can look after their herds of horses, cattle, goats, or camels in common, thereby reducing the threat to such herds and reducing the workload. In intensive agricultural systems, men related by common lines of descent probably held land in common, thus taking advantage of an economy of scale, helping each other out during times of peak labour requirements, such as crop planting and harvesting.

In a *matrilineal (or uterine)* descent system, one traces kinship links through one's mother. Your brothers and sisters are part of your kinship group, but not your brother's children as they are part of his wife's group. If you are male, then your children belong to your wife's kin group; if female, then both sexes of your children are in your group, but only your daughter's children (your grandchildren) are part of your group. Also included are your mother's brothers, but not their children, and your mother's sisters and their children. Maternal grandmothers and their brothers are included as well, but not the latter's children.

In almost all known cases, matrilineal descent is associated with an agricultural base in which relatively few crops are grown, known as *horticulture*. In societies practising matrilineal descent, there is often a strong association with fertility, with Mother Earth as the giver of life. Women usually plant the crops, although men do the heavy clearing of the land, and women are regarded as the owners of the fields, houses, and village sites. While men may be leaders in such societies, women often play a prominent role in the political process. *Matrilocality (matrilocal residence)* is the most common form of post-marital residence, so villages are composed of women who are born in the location of their mothers and grandmothers, while men must move to their wives' villages. Typically, then, women in the villages have very strong bonds built up over a long period of time, while men are dissociated from their own villages and are often not known to other men in the village.

Patrilineal (about 45 percent) and matrilineal (15 percent) comprise 60 percent of the world's societies studied by anthropologists. Two other systems are much less common. In *double descent* (or *double unilineal descent*), an individual is affiliated with a group of matrilineal kin for some purposes and with groups of patrilineal kin for other purposes. Most often double descent is tied to inheritance rules, such that a person will inherit some property from his or her mother's kin group, such as movable property in the form of cattle or household goods, and other property from his or her father's group, such as fixed property in the form of land and house sites.

In *ambilineal descent*, an individual is affiliated with groups of kin related through men *or* women. This descent system resembles bilateral descent except that ambilineal descent maintains a narrow rather than a broadening grouping of kin on each ascending generation. Both bilateral and ambilineal descent are called *cognatic descent* systems because both male and female links are used, even though one (bilateral) stresses a horizontal grouping of relatives, while the other (ambilineal) stresses a narrow, vertical grouping of kin. In some cases of ambilineal descent, one has the option of choosing between *either* the father's *or* the mother's descent group, but not both. In some other cases, there is a switching back and forth through the generations, alternating between maternal and paternal connecting links. Because of this twisting pattern, sometimes ambilineal descent is called a *rope system*. In these cases, *bilocal* (not to be confused with *neolocal*) residence, which is sometimes referred to as *ambilocality*, is commonly practised as the preferred post-marital residence pattern.

■ Descent Groups

Descent groups are comprised of people who can trace their kinship links through a line of males (patrilineal) or females (matrilineal) back to a common ancestor. Thus, descent groups are comprised of people recruited automatically by birth, descended in a single line, using a unilineal principle. A *lineage* is a unilineal descent group in which its members trace membership to a common, known individual, usually tracing back about four to six generations. When lineage members live in close, everyday contact with each other, we call this a *local descent group*.

Lineages function in several important ways. They regulate marriage by forcing members to seek their spouses outside their own group (lineage exogamy), therefore strengthening bonds with other lineages, and simultaneously reducing the potential for conflict within the groups over access to possible marriage partners. There are often economic functions as lineage members frequently hold property in common, such as herds of cattle, or the land upon which their domesticated animals graze. Lineages also engender a sense of common identity and foster a feeling of mutual aid, security, and protection.

Corporate groups are lineages or possibly some other form of unilineal descent group whose members hold property in common, meaning that since membership is clearly defined, one has a claim to the productive resources of the lineage. This is an important consideration when it comes to marriage payments, such as bridewealth, that would require resources beyond what any one individual could raise on his own. Sometime the groom must pay the resources used in marriage payments back to the corporate group, or sometimes only a nominal payment is made in the form of interest on the loan.

As membership becomes larger, *lineage fission* frequently occurs as lineage groups break apart and their members move to new locations. The cause of such fissioning could have to do with factional disputes among prominent leaders, or because available resources cannot support the growing population. In time members of the same lineage, because of the fissioning process, may forget about their common links and see themselves as separate groups among whom marriage relationships are possible.

It is also possible that lineages that have fissioned off from a parent lineage maintain connections with the old lineage. In other words, the fissioning process leads to the

---

Box 7.2: The Grand Valley Dani: Muddled Models

Papua New Guinea has always held an enduring interest for anthropologists because of its cultural variability and complexity. There are more separate languages in New Guinea than in any other comparable area of the world. Geography is at least partly responsible because of the numerous valleys, swamps, jungles, great meandering rivers, coastal lowlands, and the highest mountainous regions between the Himalayas and the Andes. These features tend to encourage social isolation and inhibit widespread communication. In such a microcosm, certain cultural traits develop and flourish, hardly influenced by the diffusion of other such traits from outside any one particular area.

New Guinea is especially known for its unconventional kinship systems. Just when British social anthropologists thought they had the kinship world covered with their neat delineation of patrilineal, matrilineal, and bilateral, anthropologists beginning fieldwork in New Guinea after the Second World War had difficulty making sense of highland kinship and descent rules following the African models commonly in use up until this time. Barnes (1962: 5) called this problem "the African mirage in New Guinea," and then went on to explain: "It has been easy to make the mistake of comparing the *de facto* situation in a Highland community ... with a non-existent and idealized set of conditions among the Nuer."

As evidence of this difficulty, Margaret Mead, during her fieldwork in the 1930s among the Mundugumor, encountered a confusing (to her) descent system that local residents called a *rope*. Mead explained that the Mundugumor are not organized into clans: "A rope is composed of a man, his daughters, his daughters' sons, his daughters' sons' daughters; or if the count is begun from a woman, of a woman, her sons, her sons' daughters, her sons' daughters' sons, and so on. All property ... passes down the rope" ([1935] 1963: 172). In other words, the Mundugumor descent system is unilineal, but alternates each generation from a person of one sex to the next. A man and his son therefore do not belong to the same rope; neither do brothers and sisters. Because of this tendency of local residents to switch descent links back and forth between connecting relatives of different sex through the generations, anthropologists have since called such a system ambilineal descent, although there could be many different types or variations of this sort of system. Mead is to be given credit for sorting out a system for which there was no previous precedent in the anthropological literature, and for not allowing pre-existing kinship models to muddle her analysis.

Karl Heider's (1997) study of the Dani of Papua New Guinea's central highlands also delves into the intricacies of kinship and social organization. The Dani are a horticultural society whose members subsist mainly on sweet potatoes, but also to a lesser degree on pork, which they eat only on ceremonial occasions. The diet is supplemented with a variety of other crops, such as taro, yam, bananas, and cucumber. Among the Dani there are two named exogamous patrilineal moieties, Wida and Waija. Each Dani, then, is a member of the same moiety as his or her father and marries only people of the other moiety. Given that such a system automatically rules out half the members of the opposite sex as marriage partners, and given other limiting factors such as age differences and already-married status, there is a fairly limited choice of mates for any young Dani.

Even though the Dani moieties are patrilineal, they have what Heider (1997: 69) calls "a complicated twist" in the process of reckoning descent, which he explains thusly: "all children are born into the Wida moiety, regardless of their father's affiliation. But later, at a Pig Feast, before they are to be married, those boys whose fathers are Waija go through an initiation or induction which makes them Waija ... so there is a kind of delayed-action patrilineal principle at work. I can suggest no reasonable explanation for this arrangement ... maybe there is no 'explanation' ... at all" (1991: 69–70). In anthropological fieldwork, it is best to be honest.

---

formation of new segments, which, in turn, grow in size until they too, in turn, fission into another segment. This process is called *segmentation*, and the combination of lineages that results from a more or less equality of size as a result of this fissioning is commonly referred to as *segmentary lineages*. In a segmentary lineage system, lineages are commonly organized in a hierarchical order, such that a *maximal lineage* A may encompass segments A1 and A2, which in turn encompass further segments A1a, A1b, A2a, A2b, and so on. In turn, all members of lineage A may have a feeling of solidarity among themselves, but also a feeling of opposition to a comparable aggregate, say lineage B, with its various subgroups or segments. The opposition is usually balanced, referred to as *complementary opposition*, such that lineage A1a will only oppose one of equal size in the opposite side, such as lineage B1a, but not higher up or lower down on the scale of segments (see Leach 1982: 142–144, 236–237; Fox 1967: 123–131).

A second type of unilineal descent group is the *clan*. Lineages and clans cannot be precisely separated into different types because lineages can even be incorporated into clans. Nonetheless, clans are composed in the same way as lineages, as descent is traced in only one connecting link. However, clans are often quite large in membership compared to lineages because for the latter, common membership is not usually traced to a known *apical* ancestor but to some mythological figure. Clan membership, then, can frequently be traced back 20 or 30 generations, linking one person to another in either the male or female line. Eventually the connecting links become obscure and connections are finally made to animals, plants, or creatures of spiritual origin.

Clans are usually identified with a symbol or *totem*, which could be an animal, plant, or other phenomenon. As a historical note, the term "totem" entered the English language through a fur trader named John Long ([1791] 1971), who was traversing the north shore of Lake Superior in Ontario by canoe in the 1790s. He entered an Anishenabe (Ojibwa) village near Pays Plat and asked through an interpreter where the people were from, meaning "Who are you related to?" The Anishenabe thought that he meant "Where is your village?"; *odanah* being the word for "town" or "village" in their language. Eventually *odanah* became transformed into the word "totem," symbolizing a clan symbol rather than a place of origin.

In some cases, members of the same clan are thought to embody the qualities of their totemic ancestor, such as members of a bear clan showing prowess and endurance, or members of the deer clan showing speed and agility. As with lineages, clans can perform certain economic functions, such as a common ownership of resources, or have political organization in the form of clan councils. However, clans, because they are larger than lineages, are often not localized. Members of the same clan could be spread out over a large territory with only a vague sense of common membership, such that clans regulate marriage only to the extent that there could be a common understanding that one does not marry someone with the same clan symbol, even though direct links to a common linking ancestor cannot be specifically identified.

Anthropologists identify several other types of descent groupings. One of these is a *phratry*, which is a unilineal descent group composed of a number of (supposedly) related clans. Members of a phratry cannot accurately trace their descent links back to a founding ancestor, but they believe that such an ancestor once existed. When an entire society is divided into two halves, these divisions are called *moieties*, from the French word *moitie*. Often these two divisions are composed of various lineages or clans in a more or less roughly equal balance. Often these divisions regulate marriage, such that the members of exogamous moieties exchange marriage partners back and forth. Among the Seneca Iroquois, for example, Bear, Wolf, Turtle, and Beaver clans form one half of a moiety, while Deer, Snipe, Heron, and Hawk form the other half. There is often a form of *institutionalized reciprocity* that emerges in villages divided into two such divisions. One moiety will make the funeral arrangements for their counterpart, which will be reciprocated for the other half when the need arises.

Societies using a bilateral form of kinship are not able to define their kinship group with the same precision as people with a unilineal descent system. Usually with a bilateral descent group, membership becomes fuzzy on the outer edges and it becomes difficult to identify people other than to say that they are distant cousins. The term *kindred* is used to refer to a bilateral kinship group in which a person traces his or her relationships in an ever-widening circle of relatives through both maternal and paternal kin, in addition to his or her sons and daughters. In this sense, kindreds could also be called *ego-centred* or *personal* kin groups because any one person's terms of reference in such groups will be different from any other, except for one's own siblings.

In industrialized societies such as Canada, kindreds are a common form of kinship organization. Most Canadians can identify their relatives up to their grandparents, but not usually beyond this generation. They can also identify relatives laterally out to their first cousins, but not usually out to second or third cousins, except if special genealogical records are kept. There is bound to be some ambiguity involved in tracing relatives using bilateral descent, especially if one assumes some degree of relationship with a person who has the same surname as you. At some point it is hardly practical to call certain people relatives when no discernible connection can be made. Take, for example, the so-called Scottish clan, which was really a form of a cognatic descent group, *clann* in Gaelic meaning "children" or "descendants." In the Scottish case, there was a certain patrilineal tinge to such groups because of their practice of patrilocal residence and the inheritance of surnames. However, a true Highland Scot bears two names: his father's and his mother's. Robert McAlpine McKinnon is a McKinnon through his father and a McAlpine through his mother (see Fox 1967: 158–159).

A bilateral kinship system is a form of *cognatic descent* because both male and female links are used to determine membership. Societies that use an ambilineal system also use a form of cognatic descent because the reckoning of descent is through a combination of male and female ancestors. The main difference between bilateral and ambilineal descent is that the former is characterized by a broadening span of kin on each ascending generation, while the latter maintains a narrow line of kin. As such, a group of relatives employing ambilineal descent is referred to as a *cognatic lineage*, meaning a group whose members trace their descent genealogically from a common ancestor. In the older literature in anthropology, cognatic lineages were referred as *ramages* or *septs*.

■ Kinship Terminology

All societies employ linguistic labels, which we may call *kinship terms*, to refer to people's relatives. A society's corpus of such terms is that society's *kinship terminology*. As a general rule, there is considerable variability among the world's cultures when it comes to kinship terminology as there are no universal patterns. It is important, however, when discussing kinship terms to distinguish clearly between the linguistic *form* of a kinship term and its *content* or *meaning*; the two do not always go together. The terms *brother*, *bruder*, and *frere* all mean the same, i.e., a male sibling of mine, but the linguistic form in each case is different. On the other hand, we may use the same term "brother" in different ways, for example, to refer to a male sibling or just a comrade or friend without really any kinship content implied, except in symbolic terms. Kinship terminology is therefore primarily a method of *kinship classification*.

Some kinship terms have a very restricted *content*, such as "father," meaning the male kinsman from whom I am directly descended. In Canada, "father" means only one person and in this sense such terms are called *descriptive* kinship terms because a different term is used for each relative. On the other hand, a kin term such as "cousin" is a wide-ranging one. In this case, "cousin" could be called a *classificatory* kinship term because many people could be included under this label. Cousin is also a very imprecise term because we do not know if such a person is male or female, or is on our father's or mother's side of the family. Many societies would find such kin term usage as involving an intolerable lack of precision. *Classificatory terms* are ones that merge or equate relatives who are genealogically distinct from one another in that the same term is used for a number of different kin. We can characterize a society's kinship terminology as relatively descriptive or classificatory, depending on the propensity to use specific kinship terms to describe particular individuals or classify groups of relatives together under relatively few kinship terms. A kinship terminology is therefore also a system of contrasts and similarities. There are behavioural implications here as well because when we call two or more people by the same kinship term, then we also tend to treat them in a similar manner.

Kinship terms can also be understood as to their content or meaning along three primary dimensions—age, sex of referent, and sex of speaker. If we use the Anishenabe or Ojibwa-speaking people of northern Ontario as an example, we can see some rather pronounced differences in kinship usage than many readers may be used to (Dunning 1959; Rogers 1962). One of the characteristics of the Ojibwa kinship system is to employ a separate set of kinship terms for men and a separate set for women. We call this *a male-female speaking system*. In this regard, when referring to siblings, men and women use the same terms to refer to siblings of the same sex and a separate term for siblings of the opposite sex. This is called the *cross-parallel sex distinction* of sibling terminology.

The Ojibwa also employ an age distinction in their sibling terminology, such that elder siblings and younger siblings (to the speaker) are differentiated. In turn, elder siblings are distinguished by sex into male and female terms, but younger siblings are not so differentiated.

The differences between English and Ojibwa sibling terminology are therefore quite apparent. English speakers simply refer to "brothers" or "sisters" using no other distinguishing feature other than that of the sex of the sibling to which one refers. Among the Ojibwa, siblings are distinguished by a variety of terms—siblings of the opposite sex of the speaker, siblings of the same sex as the speaker, elder male siblings, elder female siblings, and younger siblings. In addition, while English speakers distinguish "aunts" and "uncles" from "father" and "mother," in the Ojibwa kinship system the term "father" is extended to include also one's father's brother, and "mother" is correspondingly extended to include one's mother's sister. Separate terms are also then used for cross-sexed individuals of the parental generation, such as terms for one's father's sister and mother's brother. As we might expect from the Ojibwa system, the term "brother" is also extended to include one's father's brother's sons and mother's sister's sons. The same is applied to a similar extension of "sister." These siblings are, of course, one's *parallel cousins* who are distinguished from one's father's sister's children, and mother's brother's children, who are classed as *cross-cousins*.

Among the Ojibwa, cross-cousins are called by a term meaning *"sweethearts"* and, as such, are potential marriage partners. As the Ojibwa case illustrates, kinship terminology can also offer clues to behavioural patterns such as marriage. Any reference to sexual matters among parallel cousins, who are called your brother and sister, is strictly forbidden, a pattern referred to as an *avoidance relationship*, implying respect and formal courtesy. A man would also have an avoidance relationship with his mother-in-law and a woman with her father-in-law. Among cross-cousins, a degree of sexual freedom prevails, something anthropologists refer to as a *joking relationship*, implying the bawdiest sorts of language, horseplay, and allusions.

The distinction between English and Ojibwa kinship terms also illustrates the differences between *lineal* and *collateral* relatives. *Lineal* relatives are ones to which a direct line of descent can be established, such as father, mother, son, or grandson, in English. *Collateral relatives* are a sort of second line of kin, such as aunts, uncles, and cousins. In the Ojibwa kinship system, which groups fathers and father's brothers together, along with mothers and mother's sisters, there is a pattern called *collateral merging*. On the other hand, some societies distinguish the parental generation even further, distinguishing between father, father's brother, and mother's brother, which is referred to as *bifurcate collateral*.

Altogether, anthropologists have grouped societies together in terms of the ways in which they classify cousins and siblings on the one hand, and those of the parental generation on the other. Here is an example of such a classification system using terms in one's own generation:

Hawaiian	x cos = //cos = siblings
Eskimo	[x cos = //cos] ≠ siblings
Iroquois	x cos ≠ [// cos = siblings]
Sudanese	x cos ≠ // cos ≠ siblings

Or in terms of the parental generation:

Generational	Fa = FaBr = MoBr
Lineal	Fa ≠ [FaBr = MoBr]
Bifurcate merging	[Fa = FaBr] ≠ MoBr
Bifurcate collateral	Fa ≠ FaBr ≠ MoBr

Therefore, in terms of our distinction between English and Ojibwa kinship terminology, we can now say that English speakers use an Eskimo-type cousin terminology with a lineal terminology for the parental generation. The Ojibwa, on the other hand, use an Iroquois-type cousin terminology and a bifurcate merging terminology for the parental generation.

We will now examine three specific examples of kinship in a Canadian context: the Huron matrilineal system, Algonquian kinship terminology, and Afro-Canadian families in Nova Scotia.

■ The Huron and Matrilineal Descent

The Huron (also known as Wendat or Wyandot, which was the name for their confederacy) were members of the Iroquoian language family who, in 1649–1650, were defeated by the Iroquois and subsequently dispersed (Tooker 1964; Trigger 1969). Along with their neighbours and linguistic relatives, the Petun, the Huron numbered about 20,000 people and lived in southern Ontario in villages between Lake Simcoe, Georgian Bay, and Lake Huron, called Huronia. They were agriculturalists or horticultural people, as anthropologists would refer to their economy, who grew such crops as corn, beans, squash, and sunflower seeds. They also ate the meat of deer, rabbits, and turtles, along with forest products such as wild rice, berries, nuts, and various leafy vegetables.

The villages of the Huron were composed of an outer palisade of vertical poles and longhouses, called *ganonchia*, which varied in size according to the number of occupants, but were generally about 12 m wide, 12 m high, and 25 m long. A village might have as many as 50 to 100 of these houses and contain 300 to 400 families. Four or five hearths for cooking and heat were set along a central passageway, usually two or three paces apart. The families around each hearth were nuclear, and the people slept in bunks or platforms, called *andichons*, along the inside walls of the longhouse, comprising about 5 m in length. The bunks were set on pole frames about 1 m from a bark-covered floor, high enough to avoid the chill of the ground, but not so high as to catch the smoke from the fireplaces. Storage areas were placed at each end of the longhouse, as well as along the rafters. Large baskets contained corn, beans, and squash. Snowshoes, fishnets, firewood, and clothing were hung in other available spaces. Fish hung from the rafters to dry. There were holes in the top of the longhouses that permitted smoke to escape, yet the Jesuits complained in their journals about the density of smoke inside the houses. The villages were moved and rebuilt every eight to 12 years as the cornfields became exhausted of nutrients and firewood became scarcer.

Every longhouse in the Huron village belonged to a matrilineage headed by a prominent older woman. The longhouses, in terms of their social composition, were comprised of elderly matrons, their husbands, unmarried sons, daughters, and their daughters' husbands. It might also include the older woman's sisters and their families. All of the

Photo 7.1: Four generations of the Gros-Louis family on the Huron reserve of Lorette, near Quebec City, Quebec, c. 1880. With the defeat of the Wendat (Native name for Huron) of Huronia, Ontario, in 1649, reserves were established in Quebec, such as Lorette in 1697. (Source: Photographer Jules-Ernest Livernois, Library and Archives Canada)

women in a longhouse, along with their children, belonged to the same matrilineage, which formed a matriclan with other lineages related to each other through the female line. Each longhouse had the totemic insignia of its clan painted in red outside, such as a beaver, bear, hawk, or deer. When men married, they moved into the villages of their wives (matrilocal residence) and, in the event of a divorce, were required to leave the longhouse and return to the longhouse of their own matrilineage.

The Huron were monogamous, but apparently divorce was frequent. The Jesuits reported that a woman might have 12 or 15 husbands at different times in her life. The Jesuits also noted that marriage was "nothing more than a conditional promise to live together so long as each shall continue to render the services that they mutually expect from each other" (in Tooker 1964: 125). However, if the couple had children, they rarely separated. One suspects that divorce, when it occurred, was usually instigated by the wife because, as far as the man is concerned, "we are reduced to a wretched life, seeing that it is the women in our country who sow, plant, and cultivate the land, and prepare food for their husbands" (in Tooker 1964: 126). The Huron did not marry any relative in either the direct or collateral line, however distant the relationship, and practised clan exogamy. A potential husband usually asked the girl's parents for permission to marry, but she did not always follow their advice.

Every Huron was a member of one of four tribes and one of eight clans (Trigger 1969: 54–57). Each of the Huron tribes was a distinct political unit and made up of one or more villages that had its own territory. Members of the same clan, or members of a clan with the same name, claimed descent from a common female ancestor. However, *fictive kinship* was commonly employed to determine clan membership. Fictive kinship is claimed kinship without evidence of biological descent. Such claims are frequently made to facilitate interaction in societies where kinship is of great social importance. There was no territorial basis to clan membership, and members of the same clan apparently were found living in many villages and in all the Huron tribes. One was a member of the same clan to which his or her mother belonged, with the father belonging to a different clan.

As far as kinship terminology was concerned, Huron kin terms were similar to that used by other Iroquoian peoples in that the term for "mother" also included one's mother's sister, and the term for "father" also included one's father's brother. The term for "mother" was also used for one's father's sister, but a special term was used for one's mother's brother. Parallel cousins were called "brother" and "sister," and the word for "cousin" was reserved for cross-cousins only, with no attention paid to whether they were on the father's or the mother's side. This distinction between cross- and parallel cousins suggests that at one time they might have practised cross-cousin marriage, which was a common marriage practice among their Algonquian (Ojibwa and Ottawa) neighbours who lived around the shores of Georgian Bay and on Manitoulin Island. All consanguineal relatives of the second ascending generation were called "grandfather" and "grandmother" and those of the second descending generation called "grandson" and "granddaughter." There were separate sibling terms for "older brother" and "younger brother," and for "older sister" and "younger sister."

After the Huron–Iroquois war, by the 1650s only weeds were growing in the corn-fields of Huronia. Its people abandoned their villages and moved to Wisconsin, Michigan, and other northern states, while others relocated to Loretteville near Quebec City. All that remained of the villages containing 20,000 people were the charred remains of hearths and poles and the rotting bark of their longhouses. Eventually, in the 1700s, bands of Algonquian-speaking people, called the Mississauga, began to move into southern Ontario from their northern territory around Sault Ste. Marie, and the Wyandot confederacy of the Huron was all but forgotten.

■ Algonquian Kinship Terminology

Studies in kinship sometimes describe a particular form of descent or marriage pattern. At other times anthropologists seek to answer certain questions about society by using kinship data. In this section on Algonquian kinship, the question is: Is there a relation-ship between the complexity of a society and its kinship terminology? In other words, are there functional interrelationships that can be identified between kinship and the wider area of social organization (Hedican 1990b)?

This question about kinship has stymied anthropologists for decades. The early evo-lutionists thought that there were "primitive" and "civilized" forms of kinship and mar-riage. However, an evolutionary link between kinship and social organization has never been proven. To make matters complicated, as we have noted previously, some of the less complex societies in a technological sense have very complex kinship and marriage patterns, as evidenced by the Australian Aborigines. One of the problems, then, has to do with how we define social complexity. A purely economic and technological bias, as is often the case when people in Western societies view those regarded as "primitive," really does not help us to understand the issue of complexity. Social complexity is almost an invisible matter—you cannot just take out a marriage and kinship system and view it as a concrete object.

The relationship between kinship and social organization is further complicated by the fact that people in Western industrialized societies such as Canada have among the least complex kinship system of any of the world's societies. The bilateral descent system used is, for the most part, fairly minimal; there are not usually many members in this kinship universe; nuclear families are rudimentary; and the neolocal residence pattern seems to defy any rational explanation. So, given these apparent difficulties, a different approach is required. In this section, rather than compare societies over a wide, cross-cultural basis, our investigation is restricted to the members of a single-language family, in this case the Algonquians. The hope is that by using this restriction, developments within the same language family will highlight trends that would be otherwise obscured by comparisons that are like comparing apples with oranges. In these cases we are com-paring apples—just different varieties—such as Delicious, Mackintosh, and so on.

Before we proceed further with this discussion, a word of caution is necessary. Read-ers will need to concentrate and follow the discussion step by step, not skipping over

Photo 7.2: Wabunosa, Ojibwa, Garden River, Ontario, n.d. (Source: Photographer Philip H. Godsell, Glenbow Museum Archives, Calgary, Alberta)

anything they do not understand. It's not really rocket science, but some attention is important to get the gist of the argument. The idea is to put into action the kinship concepts and terminology discussed thus far, and then to apply them to a specific problem or situation.

Aboriginal peoples of the Algonquian linguistic family (note that Algonqu*ian or* Algonk*ian* refers to the language family, while Algonqu*in* or Algonk*in* is a specific tribe living near the Ottawa River) inhabit a vast area of eastern North America, stretching from the Subarctic areas of northern Canada to the eastern seaboard and Great Lakes areas. In historic times, branches of the Algonquian family moved out onto the Prairies grasslands, while another group, the Yurok-Wiyot people, migrated to California at some unknown time in the past. As could be expected from people spread over such a wide geographical area, there is a corresponding diversity in subsistence economy and settlement patterns.

Hunting-and-gathering bands inhabited the northern areas from Hudson Bay and Labrador to the southern Great Lakes region, horticulturalists lived in various locations around Lake Michigan, and pastoralists lived in the western plains. Community patterns ranged from the sedentary villages of southern climates to the widely scattered bands of northern hunters. Ties of kinship were an important integrative mechanism in Algonquian social organization, but the particular characteristics of these ties is a matter of some variation. Clans and lineages, mainly of the patrilineal variety, tend to characterize the more permanently settled peoples of the south, while people of the northern and western areas have a bilateral emphasis with less genealogical depth in tracing descent.

Ethnographers and linguists' research on Algonquian kinship terminology has also been quite extensive, such that Algonquian kinship is probably one of the most intensely studied of all the world's societies. In historical terms, the research extends back well over a century, to Morgan's monumental work, *Systems of Consanguinity and Affinity of the Human Family* (1870). There is also in-depth coverage of all the various branches and geographical areas inhabited by Algonquian peoples. Most of the studies are based on data collected during the course of ethnographic fieldwork, so for the most part they can be regarded as primary sources.

So extensive is the fieldwork on some Algonquian groups that one could have as many as a dozen different research reports from which to choose. There is usually a considerable degree of consistency in such studies, but where there are differences, this allows for discussion of functional relationships and historical processes of change. This is especially true for groups that have spread out over a large geographical area, such as the northern and Plains Cree, or the Ojibwa (Anishenabe), who seem to have so many divisions and appellations (Saulteaux, Bungi, Chippewa, Mississauga, and so on). In such cases, one cannot be entirely certain of the degree to which there is mutual intelligibility or deeper linguistic differences.

There is also the problem of what is actually being organized. Is this a linguistic grouping, or are we also including other cultural phenomenon as well? Without broaching the more general, troublesome problem at this point as to whether we should refer to language *and* culture, or language *in* culture, it is nonetheless clear that kinship terminology has two important aspects. As we discussed earlier in this chapter, kinship terms are both linguistic labels and bundles of features or components. We have the problem here, then, of trying to decide on the interrelationships, if any, between the linguistic form on the one hand, and the cultural content of this form on the other. The question then becomes one of what we are classifying—form or content, or both? One might proceed, for example, to study such linguistic cognates as "sister," *soeur*, and so on, but it would be a mistake to assume that such terms have the same meaning, or refer to the same bundle of components.

The study of Algonquian kinship terminology can therefore be looked at as an opportunity to examine a wide range of problems that are important to the study of kinship as a whole. The first of these problems has to do with the historical development of Algonquian kinship terminology that anthropologists have identified during the course of their fieldwork. In other words, did one set of kinship terms evolve into another, or were there ancient prototypes, long since disappeared from use, that were the ancestors of the terms used today? The second problem that interests us pertains to the interrelationships between Algonquian kinship terminology and the interaction of various social and cultural features of the terminology. "Father" in English, for example, is a kinship term, but this term also implies a certain social status as an authority figure, breadwinner in the family, and so on.

In order to reduce our discussion of these historical and functional issues to some manageable form, the following discussion will be restricted to *sibling terminology*. Sibling terminology is a set of kinship terms that are used for what English speakers know as words for "brother" and "sister," but in many other societies the usage of these terms differs greatly from this usage in English. The reason for restricting the discussion in this way is that the terms that one applies to siblings are frequently the most varied and complex in a culture's kinship terminology, but not always so as in English, which has only a rudimentary kinship terminology overall. However, in many societies sibling terminologies are a complex set of terms. Some of these aspects of sibling terminology were discussed previously with regard to the Ojibwa of northern Ontario, so part of the foregoing discussion serves to refresh the reader's memory as well introduce a wider discussion and analysis.

Taken as a whole, Algonquian sibling terminology reveals some rather interesting characteristics. These peculiarities, or distinguishing characteristics, revolve around two features. One of these features is the basic uniformity throughout the various Algonquian societies in the use of a three-term system specifying relative age (elder and younger sibling) as the primary component or division, with the elder category further divided by a secondary component of relative sex (male and female). This yields, therefore, a sibling terminology comprising three terms meaning "elder male sibling," "elder female sibling," and "younger sibling."

A second feature is that about half of the Algonquian societies have additional sibling terms specifying "same-sex sibling" as speaker, and "opposite-sex sibling." But in the same/opposite-sex system, there is considerable variation. Among the Ojibwa, Potawatomi, and Menomini, the same-sex category is further divided into male and female parts, yielding an additional three-term system meaning "male same-sex sibling," "female same-sex sibling," and "opposite-sex sibling." However, among the Fox and Kickapoo, it is the opposite-sex sibling category that is divided by sex, yielding three terms meaning "male opposite-sex sibling," "female opposite-sex sibling," and "same-sex sibling." The most complex pattern is found among the eastern Algonquians, namely the Delaware, Penobscot, Abenaki, and Malecite, who divide *both* the same-sex and opposite-sex categories by sex, yielding four terms. In addition, as mentioned above, all of the societies that use the same/opposite-sex distinction also use the three-term relative age system.

For members of societies that have a relatively simple sibling terminology, just distinguishing between terms for "brother" and "sister," the complexity of the Algonquian sibling terminologies must seem beyond comprehension—why would a society go to such lengths to divide the sibling category into so many different parts? What purpose would such a complex system serve, if any?

While I do not believe that there are any readily available answers to these sorts of questions, one might consider two possible approaches to unravelling the issue. One approach would be to assume that kinship terminologies serve some useful function in human societies—that under certain circumstances, it is important to divide people into various categories. The reason for this could be that by categorizing people into various slots, we then can treat people with the same label in the same way without having to consider their various personal quirks and characteristics.

A second reason is that kinship terminologies just evolve on their own for not much of a reason or purpose that we can detect, and that is beyond any particular member of a society to control, in the same way that certain ancient dinosaurs have various bumps, boney protrusions, and other oddities that just seemed to have emerged for no particular reason other than that they just did. This second possibility pretty much goes against the grain of most social scientists, who may feel that everything has a reason for the way it evolved the way it did, and that we have an obligation to provide an analysis and explanation. Possibly some things just cannot be explained; they just are, and that is all there is to it.

■ Afro-Canadian Communities of Nova Scotia

Frances Henry (1973) has called the Blacks of Nova Scotia the forgotten Canadians. As the Foreword to Henry's ethnography indicates, her "study lays bare the appalling conditions of Blacks in Nova Scotia, a people trapped in the wasteland of economic deprivation and social neglect; locked out of the resources of the country by White racism and the isolation of a subculture of poverty" (1973: vii). As an example of the discriminatory policies that have harmed Blacks in Nova Scotia, Henry discusses the destruction of Africville. Africville, a Black community founded in 1848, was bulldozed in the 1960s in the name of urban development. At the time of its destruction, Africville was a settlement of about 400 people and 80 families, and consisted of many dilapidated houses

Photo 7.3: Africville house, with two children on the doorstep and laundry on the line, 1965. (Source: Photographer Bob Brooks, Nova Scotia Archives)

near the Halifax city dump. Africville's residents were forced to relocate when their community was destroyed, yet they continued to suffer social and economic hardships after their move to public housing projects.

Henry's research on Black Nova Scotians was conducted during 1969 in two communities. One was a semi-urban community located near a major city and appeared somewhat more prosperous than other communities. The other was a small, rural community situated in the southern part of the province. As such, these two communities provided for a discussion of contrasts and similarities because of their different social and economic characteristics. The methodology of the study used two data-gathering techniques. One was an initial ethnographic study of the two communities, complemented by a survey of a large number of respondents from other areas of the province.

The history of Blacks in Nova Scotia began as far back as 1606 with their presence in Port Royal of Acadia. Then, during the 1780s, about 3,000 American Blacks arrived in Nova Scotia after the American Revolution. These were not slaves, but mostly freemen who were veterans of the Loyalist forces of the revolution. Another influx of migrants came as a result of the War of 1812 when approximately 2,000 Blacks, who were veterans of the British military, settled in Nova Scotia. The Annapolis Valley was the site of about a dozen Black communities, while others settled near Halifax and northern Nova Scotia. Many of these communities suffered from marginal social and economic situations because of discrimination and poor agricultural conditions. A large contingent of 1,200 Blacks left Nova Scotia in 1791 for Sierra Leone in Africa because of the unfavourable agricultural conditions and long, cold winters.

It is evident that historically, Nova Scotia's economic basis has not kept pace with that of the Canadian economy as a whole. Per capita income, for example, is considerably lower than the Canadian average, and unemployment rates are relatively high. These are both factors contributing to an outward migration from the province, and the prognosis is that the economic future of the province is not very bright. These are all important factors affecting the local Black populations of the province. Rural settlements in Nova Scotia were often poverty stricken, and urban slums existed in the larger population centres.

At the time of Henry's research there were some 45 Black communities in Nova Scotia, ranging in size from a few families to larger populations of 1,500–2,000 people. According to the 1961 census, there were 11,900 Black people living in Nova Scotia. However, Henry suggests that these estimates are largely inaccurate and that a more realistic estimate of the Black population would be between 20,000 and 25,000 people. In Nova Scotia three types of communities were identified: (1) rural-based communities that were essentially non-agricultural; (2) those that were semi-urban but located some distance from urban centres; and (3) communities that were urban, existing either within the city as urban ghettos or as small enclaves on the fringes of smaller cities. In rural and semi-urban areas, substandard housing was evident. Many houses, consisting of only two or three rooms, housed a family of six to eight people. In the urban areas, row housing was common, often split into apartments and rooms for multiple dwellings. The urban dwellings often had more furnishings, appliances, and possessions than in rural homes. Welfare subsidies in the rural areas accounted for as much as 50 percent of the annual income of many households.

The two communities selected for more in-depth ethnographic study included a rural economically depressed one, while the second was a somewhat more prosperous semi-urban community. The first, Vale Haven, is a small rural community in southeastern Nova Scotia, about 400 km from Halifax. It is one of three other Black communities in the area, all within about 20 km of each other. In 1970 the community contained 53 households and a total population of 295 people. Over 53 percent of the residents were under 15 years of age. There are 23 more men than women. Out-migration is said to account for the relatively large number of children left behind by migrating parents. The economic strain of caring for so many dependent children is a great burden on the community. Nine of the households are headed by women, but an equal number of men, usually older widowers, are also living alone. Local work, as Henry (1973: 43) describes it, is "unstable, transitory and seasonal in nature."

The household composition of Vale Haven is a complex mix. "Although the majority of households contain nuclear families, extended families—including grandparents, collateral relatives, grandchildren, welfare children, and occasionally non-relatives 'boarding in'—are also found" (Henry 1973: 46). Grandchildren are often cared for by their grandparents as their parents migrate out of the community for work. In other instances, when the mother has temporarily migrated, young female relatives, such as nieces and

Photo 7.4: Family discussion at the dining room table, Africville, 1965. (Source: Photographer Bob Brooks, Nova Scotia Archives, from a collection entitled "Gone but Never Forgotten")

cousins, live in as "house minders" to care for the children. There are also instances of married women who have taken in common-law partners as their husbands have permanently migrated out of the community. Sometimes illegitimate children will be brought up by relatives of the mother, particularly when the mother leaves the community.

There is a substantial amount of intermarriage between families in the community of Vale Haven. Marriages between cousins take place frequently. Intermarriage with Whites in the area rarely takes place, thus limiting the pool of marriage partners available to Blacks and encouraging a more endogamous marriage pattern.

The other, more prosperous Black community of Far Town consists of a string of houses and landholdings of various sizes, strung out along both sides of an unpaved country road about 1 km from Halifax. In Far Town, houses are modest in size, but kept in good repair and adequately painted. Severe overcrowding, common in many other Black households in other areas, was not evident in this community. Far Town's population of about 700 people is contained in 52 households. The vast majority of households contain nuclear families, but a sizable number of families are extended by the inclusion of grandparents. In the nuclear family, authority seems to be fairly equally distributed between husband and wife, especially when both are working.

The community consists of 12 major groups, five of which are known as "old families." Intermarriage among these 12 groups is common; similarity of surnames is frequent. There are also a large number of out-marriages, usually involving women who have come from nearby communities or elsewhere in the province. Both endogamous and exogamous marriages are found in the community, and there does not appear to be a preference for one or the other. Overall, families are relatively stable and there are few instances of separation or divorce. Five or more children per household is common as most couples desire large numbers of children. Unlike Vale Haven, there are no welfare children in Far Town.

The more prosperous position of Far Town and, one would suspect, the greater stability of family life, is a result of greater opportunities for employment. Both men and women in Far Town have opportunities for employment, so that combined household incomes are high. Men work at jobs in a nearby city or in woodlots. Women are employed as domestic help or hospital workers. This is not to suggest that high incomes in Far Town versus those in Vale Haven are the sole determinant of family composition and stability, but it certainly plays a prominent role. This is especially the case for Vale Haven, where a lack of available jobs locally forces men and women to leave their homes in search of employment outside the area. This out-migration, even if temporary, puts additional economic stress on those left behind, resulting in single-parent households and a combination of people grouped together for economic survival.

The ethnographies of Far Town and Vale Haven in Nova Scotia illustrate the flexibility of bilateral descent systems and their ability to respond to changing economic circumstances. Vale Haven suffers from greater economic difficulties than Far Town. In Vale Haven, the household situated on the nuclear family extends vertically to incorporate grandparents, and laterally to include aunts, uncles, nieces, and nephews. Such households may even include non-relatives as a means to consolidate living arrangements and thereby reduce the costs of maintaining the family. At times children live with their grandparents because parents are employed out of town, which is also a strategy to maintain the family while being flexible enough to take advantage of employment opportunities even though they are outside the community. In Far Town, there is more stability in family cohesion because employment is higher than in Vale Haven and in closer proximity to the family's home. Thus, in Far Town out-migration is less prevalent and households are less apt to incorporate other kin in the household as a mechanism to reduce costs. Bilateral kinship, coupled with an emphasis on the nuclear family and neolocal residence, provides the same sort of flexibility in industrialized countries as it does for the opportunistic requirements of hunting-and-gathering societies as well.

■ Summing Up

Kinship systems among human societies represent an extremely varied pattern of groupings and separations into people's blood (consanguines) and marriage (affines) relatives. Anthropologists have not understood very well the reasons for all this variability in marriage and kinship patterns. The early evolutionists, as one might expect, thought that there was a line of change from primitive systems, such as group marriage, to more civilized patterns, such as monogamy and the nuclear family. Such suggestions have never been proven, and probably never will be. In any event, the whole notion of primitive versus civilized kinship is not considered a fruitful avenue of research, according to most anthropologists. There is a curious fact in all of this, and that is that the most (so-called) civilized peoples have the most simple or rudimentary kinship patterns, and the people with simpler technologies, such as the Australian Aborigines, have the most complex marriage and kinship patterns imaginable.

What we do know is that there is a very close relationship between the behavioural patterns in a society, in terms of the ways in which people are classified, and the ways in which people are treated. In examining kinship terminology, for example, the ways in which relatives are grouped together and separated are often a reflection of existing marriage patterns or expressions of common identity. Kinship bonds people together in economic ways as well, as in the corporate structure of landholdings, marriage payments, and inheritance patterns. Kinship therefore reflects the wide variations in human behavioural patterns, and humans' imaginative creativity in conceptualizing their social, material, and biological universes.

The three specific profiles discussed in this chapter—the Huron, Algonquian, and Afro-Canadian—although widely separated in space and time, illustrate the importance of economic factors in kinship and family characteristics. Although it is a truism that everyone needs to make a living to survive—whether hunter, agriculturalist, or wage earner—the manner in which a society organizes its economic pursuits has undeniable effects on the organization of family life and the manner in which kin are organized in humans' often complex conceptual universe. There may be great variability in terms of how humans organize their social life while feeding themselves and their dependants. However, the basic facts of life are pretty much the same across these vast temporal and spatial dimensions.

8 Political Economy

Making sense of Thunder Bay
Common sense and anti-intellectualism are important themes in working-class culture. The negative attitudes towards women and Natives which refracts the Boy's understanding of their role in the social relations of production are firmly embedded in common sense. As a mode of thought, common sense forms the substratum of the Boy's analysis of society.

—Thomas Dunk,
It's a Working Man's Town (2007: 132)

Political economy refers to the role of leadership, political authority, and power in production, distribution, and consumption of goods and services. In Western industrialized societies, modes of production and political leadership are relatively discrete or separate areas of society. However, in most other societies, there is an intimate interrelationship between the political and economic spheres, with multiple ties joining them together. It makes sense in social anthropology, then, to discuss the two areas together, rather than separate them analytically, because of this intermingling of the two aspects in most societies.

The ethnographic record in social anthropology comprises many hundreds of societies, both past and present, such that the study of political economy in a cross-cultural perspective becomes a daunting task. First, there is anthropologists' attempt to develop meaningful characteristics that could be compared across cultural boundaries. What, for example, are the essential characteristics that distinguish hunters and gatherers from other types of societies? Second, there is the drawing out in each cultural situation of the essential nature of political and economic processes. Under such circumstances, any cross-cultural generalizations become meaningless unless a variety of types are isolated, such that these types allow for the grouping of societies with similar, but probably not all, characteristics. If one desires to reduce the inherent complexity of the many hundreds of disparate societies that anthropologists have studied, then there is no other choice but to develop such a topology, mindful of the fact that there is the probability that certain cultural nuances will be lost in the process.

The convention in anthropology with regard to the discussion of political economy is to reduce the many societies of the world into four relatively distinct types: Bands, Tribes, Chiefdoms, and States. At one time—say, about 10,000 years ago—all of the world's societies were at the band level of complexity, and through time various states emerged so that it is inevitable that we regard these four types not just as a topology but as also indicating a possible progression in social evolution. It is necessary to keep in mind, though, that a society does not necessarily have to change at all toward these more complex types, or even to go through the various stages from one to another. The aspect of inevitability associated with the earlier unilinear evolutionary modes of thought characteristic of the so-called "armchair" period in anthropology has made anthropologists today more cautious in their pronouncements of social progress. There is always the possibility of ethnocentric ideas becoming associated with the use of terms such as "primitive," or "less developed." In other words, social progress, however that may be conceived, is not always inevitable as some societies may become less complex over time while others become more "developed" in term of their social, economic, or political dimensions. All societies do change, however, and it is necessary to account for these changes in a coherent, systematic manner.

■ Band Societies

A *band society* can be regarded as a fairly small, usually nomadic local group, consisting of hunter-gatherer families, occupying a specifiable territory, and that is politically autonomous. Roles in the society are based on *achieved status*, which is to say that individuals attain their position in the society through their own abilities. Political leadership, then, is based on these achieved qualities. The *headman*, a person who holds a leadership position in the band society who leads primarily by example, may provide a symbolically unifying position in a community, but exercises influence by persuasion rather than by imposing sanctions or acting in a coercive manner.

Community decisions are usually made by a process of group *consensus*, which is to say that lengthy discussions among the adults of the society are held, which allows people to present their views before decisions affecting the group as a whole are made. Similarly, religious specialists, such as *shamans*, hold their power in the community by the effectiveness of their divination or curing skills, but do not hold a specific role beyond their personal abilities and do not have coercive powers.

A band is often referred to as an *egalitarian society* because every person in the community of a given age/sex category has an equal access to economic resources, power, and prestige. The *mode of production* is primarily one of *food collection*, which is to say that all forms of subsistence technology in which food-getting occurs is dependent upon naturally occurring resources, such as wild plants and animals. An *optimal foraging strategy* is often employed by the hunters, such that an attempt is made to maximize the returns of their labour in deciding which animals to go after. Hunters will generally pursue large game, such as moose, deer, or caribou, rather than smaller game, such as rabbits, because

Box 8.1: The Dobe Ju/'hoansi of Botswana, Southern Africa

The Ju/'hoansi, formerly known in the ethnographic literature as the !Kung bushmen, live in a sparsely populated area of the Kalahari Desert of northwestern Botswana, near the border of Namibia (Lee 1979, 1993). The relative isolation of the Kalahari environment has tended to insulate the Ju/'hoansi foraging culture from heavy influences from the outside world and allowed its members to maintain a relatively intact way of life, although significant changes have taken place in recent decades.

The ethnographic studies of the Ju/'hoansi by University of Toronto anthropologist Richard Lee and his associates extended over nearly three decades, from 1963 to 1991. Lee initially encountered the Ju/'hoansi at the Dobe waterhole when they were living almost entirely by hunting and foraging. This fortunate circumstance allowed him to study the Ju/'hoansi's foraging adaptation, an important aspect of human evolution, as a reasonably intact way of life. The ethnographic study of the Ju/'hoansi was a very broad-based analysis of environmental resources, subsistence techniques, kinship, marriage, ritual, and belief systems.

The profile that emerged from this case study of the Ju/'hoansi has done much to change existing views of "primitive" society. Far from leading a hand-to-mouth existence in which band members are continually existing on the brink of starvation, the Ju/'hoansi needed to work only a few hours a day to meet their caloric needs and lead vigorous lives. This leaves much time for the people to participate in ritual and dance, as well as other leisurely activities involving other various forms of social interaction.

Another important aspect of this study involves a change in anthropologists' conception of hunting-and-gathering societies. Much of the literature in this area had previously focused on men's activities, while the role of women was neglected. Among the Ju/'hoansi, a careful analysis of time spent in subsistence production indicates that women, through their everyday gathering of roots, tubers, berries, and nuts, actually contribute more calories of food to the group than does the relatively sporadic hunting of men. This suggests that in future studies of foraging societies, the role of women in the local food-getting economy needs more attention than has been given in the past if more accurate analyses are to be conducted.

The independence of neighbouring Namibia in 1990 brought significant changes to the Ju/'hoansi of the Kalahari in the Dobe area of Botswana. Although many groups have been able to maintain a traditional way of life, the advent of Western medicine and material culture has brought about change in certain areas of life, which justifies some optimism for the future. The people of the Dobe have experienced the arrival of clinics, stores, schools, and airstrips. They have gone from a way of life almost exclusively devoted to hunting and gathering to one involving mixed farming, herding, and wage work. Yet even in the face of these contemporary developments, the Ju/'hoansi have been able to maintain their resilience and adaptability.

the expectation of a return on their productive efforts is greater than if it was fragmented by hunting smaller prey. The *division of labour* is mainly along lines of sex, age, and ability, with men hunting and women specializing in gathering and processing plants.

Kinship, especially in the form of bilateral descent, plays an important integrative role in band societies. Not only do most people in the band consider themselves related to one another, either by ties of blood or marriage, but kinship ties are important in food distribution. *Sharing* among group members is an important survival tactic. Some hunters have greater skills or opportunity for success than others, and

Figure 8.1: The attire adopted by a successful anthropologist may not be understood by former classmates.

so food distribution along kinship lines allows for an equitable food supply for all members and prevents some people from starving. This is the principle of *generalized reciprocity*, which is to say, giving without any immediate or planned return.

Hunters of the Boreal Forest

In Canada, band societies were found in a large arc extending from Labrador, across northern Quebec, south of James Bay into northern Ontario and Manitoba, and over to the Northwest Territories. This is a vast ecological zone of *boreal forest* of the Subarctic, consisting of many lakes and rivers with a vegetation cover of spruce and pine forests. Algonquian-speaking people, such as the Naskapi (Innu), Cree, and Ojibwa (Anishenabe), live in the eastern Subarctic, while Dene (or Athapaskan) peoples, such as the Chipewyan, Dogrib, and Kutchin, live in the western boreal forest region. The main game animals hunted are the moose, deer, caribou, beaver, and musk oxen. Birchbark was used extensively in the eastern Subarctic for making canoes and covers for wigwams (*wigwas* means "birchbark" in Ojibwa). Birch was also used for the frames of snowshoes and the ribs of canoes. In the western Subarctic area, skin houses were more common. Ethnographic sources used in this section on band societies of the boreal forest include Robert Dunning's *Social and Economic Change among the Northern Ojibwa* (1959), June Helm's *The Lynx Point People: The Dynamics of a Northern Athapascan Band* (1961), and my own study, *The Ogoki River Guides: Emergent Leadership among the Northern Ojibwa* (1986a).

Photo 8.1: A large Cree hunting party travelling by canoe on the Kaniapiskau River, Quebec, c. 1924–1936. (Source: Glenbow Museum Archives, Calgary, Alberta)

Hunting strategies varied from region to region. In the Barren Grounds of Labrador, large caribou herds migrated from area to area in search of food. Often they were hunted at narrow river crossings, where young caribou could get separated from the herd or were more vulnerable when swimming. In northern Ontario and Quebec, moose are more solitary animals, but during certain times of the year, such as the fall rutting or breeding season, they congregate in larger numbers. Moose are also more vulnerable to attack during the late winter, when they tend to break through the snow crust in an attempt to run. Mostly they do not run as far as caribou when startled, and hunters working as a team can backtrack along the moose's trail in the snow to find the animal hiding behind a clump of bushes.

The beaver is another important source of food and fur. Like the moose, beaver live in an aquatic environment, and Aboriginal hunters are skilled at setting traps at the entrance to beaver lodges. Deadfall traps are also sometimes used to hunt beaver as they forage for popular trees for their dams and lodges. Larger versions of deadfalls are used for bear hunting. Nets are used for fishing trout and whitefish in the larger lakes, while occasionally larger fish, such as sturgeon, will be speared in more shallow water. When fish are spawning in the spring, a small river or creek will be diverted into shallow pools, where fish such as pickerel and smelts can be speared or gathered up in baskets.

Religious beliefs are often closely allied with the hunting way of life. In *Bringing Home Animals*, Tanner (1979) describes the relationship between religious ideology and mode of production among the Cree hunters of Mistassini in northern Quebec. Great care is taken to show respect for the animals hunted by the Cree. Their belief is that all animals are guided by a master of the animal, who allows animals to be given to humans so that they can survive. Animal bones are placed on platforms in the trees or wrapped in birchbark, so that dogs cannot chew on them. The Cree believe that if respect is not shown to the animals, then their hunting will not be successful.

Among the Naskapi, who call themselves the Innu, a religious specialist attempts to communicate with the master of the caribou through a special divination ceremony. In this ceremony, called *scapulamancy*, the scapula bone (shoulder blade) of the caribou is heated over a campfire. During the heating process, the caribou bone begins to crack and show round burn spots. The Innu shaman then reads these bones as one would read a map of various geographical features, such as mountains, lakes, and rivers. On the basis of the various crack and burn marks, the Innu shaman then directs hunters to parts of their territory where they expect to find caribou. One suggestion or interpretation of this divination ceremony is that it encourages hunting success because the heating of caribou bones often leads to randomized cracks and burns. Since the hunters are directed to particular areas of their territory on the basis of these burn marks and cracks, the divination process thus leads hunters to hunt in areas in a more random fashion than would otherwise be the case if hunters kept returning to areas where they previously had success.

Among the Ojibwa (or Anishenabe) of northern Ontario, the *shaking tent ceremony* is an important method of communicating with spirits of both humans and animals. A small conical tent is constructed of four poles, which is covered by skins and open at the top. Loops made from saplings are hooped around the inside of the tent to give it some rigidity, and various noise makers, such as caribou hooves, are tied to these hoops. The shaman, or *djasakid*, enters the tent through a small flap at the bottom. The shaman says some prayers and then begins to call in the spirits, who enter through a small opening in the top of the tent. Before long the tent begins to shake violently, causing the rattles to make a considerable noise. After a while the shaking subsides and a variety of voices, along with that of the shaman, can be heard inside the tent in a confused cacophony of noise. Some of the voices are the spirits of dead animals instructing hunters where to conduct their hunt; in other cases the voices are those of deceased ancestors who had come to communicate with their living relatives. People who have been standing around the tent might then approach the small flap at the bottom, ask questions of their departed love ones, and receive answers to their questions in return.

In terms of social organization, bilateral descent was common throughout the boreal forest, yet there were regional variations. The Ojibwa, for example, originally migrated from east of Lake Superior in the Sault Ste. Marie area and south of the Great Lakes, where they had a patrilineal descent system with exogamous clans. As they migrated northward into Ontario, the Ojibwa began to develop more of a bilateral emphasis to their kinship system, but one with a patrilateral tinge such that an elder male headed a group of his sons, their wives, and children. This became known in the literature as the *patrilateral extended* family, thought to have emerged as a result of the fur trapping economy, which developed in the late 1600s (Dunning 1959). On the other hand, the western area of the Subarctic was partly matrilineal. The Kutchin, Tuchone, and Kaska had matrilineal exogamous clans. Post-marital residence in the west was mostly bilocal, with some neolocal, while in the east patrilocal residence was more prominent.

Treaties were signed with the British government prior to Confederation. The Robinson Superior Treaty of 1850 was signed with the Ojibwa (Anishenabe) north of Lake Superior up to the height of land around Lake Nipigon. Later, in 1905, the Ojibwa and Cree ceded the rest of northern Ontario with Treaty No. 9. In the Northwest Territories the Dene signed treaties between 1899 (No. 8) and 1921 (No. 11). The Cree, Innu, and Inuit of northern Quebec signed the James Bay Agreement in 1975.

The treaty negotiation process did not lead to any mass influx of settlers into the boreal forest, and even today the northern Algonquians and Dene are the largest populations in their traditional territories. A sharp economic decline occurred in the 1950s with the virtual demise of the fur trapping economy. Later, after the James Bay Agreement in 1975, there was massive flooding in northern Quebec, and the Cree had to move their villages. In northern Ontario, the pulp and paper industry caused large areas of deforestation, resulting in a decline in animal populations. In addition, pulp mills near Dryden in northwestern Ontario were responsible for mercury pollution of the Wabagoon River system, causing hardship for the Aboriginal communities of White Dog and Grassy Narrows. In the Mackenzie Valley corridor of the Northwest Territories, pipeline construction was averted with the Berger Inquiry of 1974, but the Tar Sands project around Great Slave Lake has led to widespread water pollution. Environmental degradation and the consequent negative impacts on Algonquian and Dene traditional subsistence practices threaten to undermine their traditional ways of life in the boreal forest. These are the same sorts of challenges to survival that band societies in other parts of the world also face as industrial societies push hunters out of their forest habitats in the search for mineral, forest, and petroleum development.

■ Tribes

Band societies are dependent upon hunting, fishing, and gathering to support their subsistence economies. *Tribes* are involved in either food production, rather than food collection, or pastoralism. *Food production* is a form of subsistence technology in which food-getting is dependent upon the cultivation and domestication of plants and animals. In cultures at the tribal level, such as the Huron, *horticulture* is the mainstay of the food production process. *Horticulture* is plant cultivation carried out with relatively simple tools and methods with periodic cultivation of new fields as soil fertility drops due to the lack of fertilization. *Swidden* horticulture, or *slash and burn*, is a form of shifting cultivation in which the natural vegetation, usually forests, is cut down and burned off, which adds nutrients to the soil. The cleared ground is used for a short time until crop yields decline, and then the soil is left to regenerate, allowing nature to replace nutrients in the soil. Sometimes attempts are made to sustain soil fertility by using composted plant material or, in the case of the Iroquois, by growing a combination of crops, such as beans (a nitrogen-fixating plant) and corn.

Pastoralism is the other main economic activity of tribes. *Pastoralism* is a form of subsistence technology in which food-getting is based directly or indirectly on the maintenance of domesticated animals. *Transhumance* refers to pastoral nomads' movement from one territory to another to provide pasture for their animals. Some hunting or minor crop production may take place in pastoral societies, but these activities are subsidiary to the raising and care of their domesticated animals. The type of animals that pastoralists raise varies widely depending on suitable ecological conditions, such that camels and goats are raised in arid areas, or horses and cattle in grasslands.

Horticulture and pastoralism raised the quantity and reliability of available food from that found in band societies, which in turn allows for larger local populations and different forms of social organization in tribes. While bands typically have bilateral descent, in tribes matrilineal descent is common among horticulturalists and patrilineal descent among pastoral societies, usually involving exogamous clans. Besides kinship ties, tribes also have organizations that cut across descent boundaries, which creates different forms of group loyalties. One such organization common in tribes is the *age-grade system*, which is a category of people who happen to fall within a particular, culturally distinguished age range. An *age set* is a group of people of similar age and the same sex who move together through some or all of life's stages. Most often there are three such age grades involving young initiates who go through a *rite of passage*, which is a communally celebrated ritual that marks the transition of an individual from one institutionalized status to another. An adult role might be another stage, allowing a man to marry, own cattle, and act as a warrior. An older age set might be composed of those in the elder

---

Box 8.2: The Pastoral Nomads of Baluchistan

Pastoral nomads differ from one another in major ways. Some live in harsh desert environments, while others inhabit lush plains and mountainous regions. The range of animals raised is also quite extensive, such as horses, camels, goats, cows, sheep, or other herbivores. In the Middle East, Baluchistan, meaning "land of the Baluch," is a vast area divided by the national boundaries of Iran, Pakistan, and southwestern Afghanistan. It consists generally of harsh desert conditions with a sparse population situated, for the most part, in small agricultural oases, herding camps, and small trading centres. The pastoralists living in this region are dependent upon the camel, the ship of the desert, for transportation, hides, and milk.

Baluchi camping groups consist of several dozen households whose members live in black goat-hair tents. They repeatedly break camp, folding up their heavy tents, packing their belongings on reluctant and protesting camels, and then migrating toward a destination in a fairly circumscribed home territory. These migrations are not random expeditions but involve deliberate practical strategies that are usually related to economic production and the welfare of their livestock of camels, sheep, and goats. The relocation of Baluchi camps is usually intended to move the livestock closer to good pasturage and good water, or away from animals thought to suffer from disease. Migration among pastoral nomads is therefore an adaptive response to desert conditions in which edible grasses and water are unevenly distributed over the landscape.

There are times when these nomadic expeditions bring different pastoral groups into conflict with one another, especially when there is competition over the available resources necessary to feed livestock because of drought or infrequent rainfall. Conflict can also occur within groups, such as when the camels eat dates from a palm tree not belonging to the camels' owner, resulting in feuds between different kinship lineages. In such conflicts, lineages tend to oppose one another according to genealogical opposition, which could result in the feuding parties splitting apart and moving to different territories (Salzman 1999).

---

generations who are important leaders or political members of village councils. *Sodalities*, which are various forms of associations or clubs, are another group based on non-kinship principles found in tribes.

Leadership in tribes is not usually based on one individual, such as a headman, but on a community council, which is composed of the leading members of the various lineages. Decisions such as when and where to move a village are made by *consensus*, which is to say that everyone on the council is allowed to express his or her opinion, the pros and cons of various courses of action are debated, and then the majority decision that emerges is the one that people are bound to follow. At times factions could develop, leading to the splintering off of a particular group who might form their own local society, but such actions are relatively rare because it is safer to be in a larger group than a smaller one.

The Blackfoot: Warriors of the Western Plains

The Blackfoot were originally hunters in the forested region near the western Plains, but with their acquisition of the horse in the early 1700s, their culture became vastly transformed. The horse allowed for freedom of movement and great ease in hunting the buffalo, the mainstay of their food supply. While their subsistence economy is primarily a hunting one, their reliance on a domesticated animal, such as the horse, and their need to move from one pasture area to another, have led anthropologists to classify tribes such as the Blackfoot as pastoralists rather than as band societies of hunters and gatherers. Ethnographic sources on the Blackfoot used in this chapter include John Ewers's *The Blackfoot: Raiders of the Northwestern Plains* (1958), Malcolm McFee's *Modern Blackfoot: Montanans on a Reservation* (1972), and Clark Wissler's *Societies and Dance Associations of the Blackfoot Indians* (1913).

The Blackfoot of southern Alberta and northern Montana are an Algonquian-speaking people, related to the Ojibwa, Cree, and Mi'kmaq. It is possible that the Blackfoot lived in the forested region of northern Alberta and Saskatchewan for many thousands

Photo 8.2: Blackfoot warriors on horseback, Alberta, 1907. (Source: Library and Archives Canada)

of years, while the other Algonquians moved eastward in prehistoric times, eventually reaching the Atlantic coast. There is much archaeological evidence that cultures surrounding the Plains used this area on a seasonal basis for hunting and religious rites. The Head-Smashed-in site, north of Calgary, is a good example of the hunting techniques of the pre-horse hunting strategies of running buffalo over cliffs or driving them into dead-end canyons. Stone alignments of circles and other configurations, commonly called "teepee rings," are probably signs of a developed interest in the cosmology of planets, stars, and seasonal changes, which would have been necessary to track the migrating herds of animals.

Once the Blackfoot acquired horses, which moved northward from the Spanish in the 1500s to the Navajo and so on from tribe to tribe, their newfound mobility brought them into contact with various other Plains cultures. The Sioux of the Dakotas are linguistic relatives of the Iroquois, who continued a hunting lifestyle rather than take up horticulture, as did the Mohawk, Seneca, Oneida, and other Iroquoian peoples. The Assiniboine (meaning in Ojibwa, *ahsin*—stone, and *eboine*—to cook with) are a branch of the Dakota Sioux, who originally lived in Manitoba and northern Minnesota. The Cheyenne are another Algonquian society whose members migrated westward from their home territory south of Lake Superior. The Navajo and other Apache tribes, such as the Kiowa, had originally lived in the Northwest Territories, but migrated southward along the Pacific coast about 800 years ago. They were one of the first peoples to trade for horses from the Spanish, which allowed them to move northward onto the Plains. Other migrants to the Plains were settled horticulturalists, such as the Mandan, Crow, Pawnee, and Arapahoe. The Shoshoni and Comanche came eastward over the Rocky Mountains onto the Plains, where they had previously engaged in a plant-gathering subsistence economy of the Great Basin.

All of these various tribes, with their diverse cultural and linguistic origins, intermingled on the Plains, borrowing traits from each other until a somewhat homogeneous Plains culture emerged that had many common traits. They all lived in skin teepees, and the men wore breechcloths, leggings, and buffalo robes. Religious beliefs centred on the *vision quest* for young males, belief in a *guardian spirit*, and performance of communally based rituals, such as the Sun Dance. Warfare was also common among the Plains tribes, usually involving raids for horses and *counting coup* in order to demonstrate personal bravery. Men's associations, based on raiding and warfare, were also a common feature of Plains social organization. Horses made all of this lifestyle possible, and there was great pride in their ownership. The horse was an integral part of the Plains culture, providing the mobility for buffalo hunting, warfare, travel, and the transportation of their material goods using a *travois*.

The Blackfoot culture also became transformed from its small, hunting-gathering base in the north to a more complex society featuring age-grade societies, Sun Dance rituals, horse pastoralism, and a life in teepees placed in a circular formation for their summer camps. There were three large tribes of Blackfoot—the Piegan are the largest band, the Blood (or Kainai, meaning "many chiefs"), and the Siksika. The Blackfoot men were hunters and warriors, gambled for entertainment, planned raids, and held feasts and ceremonies. The women did much of the butchering of meat, drying of skins, and making of clothes for their families.

Each teepee was occupied by a single household, comprising a husband, wife, and children. A prosperous warrior might have several wives if his hunting skill was good enough to support a larger family. Most often the additional wives were sisters (*sororal polygyny*) since they would all stand in the same kinship relationship to the husband as did the original wife, and would all live in the same teepee. It was a custom of the Blackfoot that the first wife was the manager of the household and owner of the teepee. Kinship terminology was *bifurcate merging*, which is to say that the same kinship term is used for "father" and "father's brother," and a separate term from these for "father's sister." This form of kinship terminology is commonly associated with a lineal descent system; however, the Blackfoot also used bilateral descent. Post-marital residence was of the patrilocal variety since women moved to their husband's band upon marriage. The basic unit of Blackfoot social organization was a band of about a dozen households, which stayed together during their winter camp, but assembled with other such bands in the larger summer camps. Households were apt to move between these local bands, depending upon kinship alliances, friendship ties, or the wealth and prestige of particular leaders.

Kinship ties were not as important in Blackfoot social organization as in many societies because of the cross-cutting memberships in clubs, associations, and other organizations, which tended to reduce the significance of kinship ties and loyalties. The age-grade system forged lifelong bonds of friendship among people who went through the same ceremonies and stages of life together. One was able to rely on these age-mates for support and protection, possibly even to a greater degree than one could count on actual kinsmen. Warrior societies had names such as All-Crazy Dogs, Pigeons, or Mosquitoes, and were corporate groups, meaning that they survived through time despite changes in individual membership. There were also medicine men's societies, comprised of males who owned important medicine bundles and powers. These men were responsible for the presentation and organization of the Sun Dance, while a women's society, called Matoki, built the ceremonial lodge for the dance. All of these non-kin organizations created bonds of friendship and loyalty that contributed to tribal solidarity.

Near the end of the 1700s, fur trading companies began to build posts in Alberta and Saskatchewan on the northern fringes of the Blackfoot territory. There was some trade in buffalo hides between the Blackfoot and the newcomers, but this trade was much more limited than was the case with Aboriginal societies farther north and east of the Plains. Eventually the buffalo became depleted in the Plains, and the Blackfoot's numbers were drastically reduced by smallpox epidemics in 1869–1870, and by starvation in subsequent years. In 1874 the North-West Mounted Police moved into the Blackfoot's territory to control the liquor trade on the Canadian side of the border and established Fort Macleod. In 1877 the Blackfoot and Assiniboine signed a treaty ceding their lands, and the Canadian Pacific Railway was built through Blackfoot territory in 1883. Shortly after, they were settled on reserves and the Blackfoot were pressured into stopping the performance of the

Sun Dance as part of the Canadian government's general program of assimilation. Other social and religious customs, such as the burial of the dead on tree platforms and polygynous marriages, were also stopped under coercion. Young Aboriginal children were often taken away from their families and placed in residential schools, where they suffered abuse. The suffering caused by the residential school system has only recently been recognized and apologized for by Prime Minister Stephen Harper in June 2008.

Today there has been a revival of Plains First Nation heritage with powwows, dance competitions, rodeos, and a revival of the Sun Dance. The Blackfoot still own horses. Some also farm wheat, barley, and hay, or raise sheep and cattle. In Alberta, many work in the petroleum industry and on the Kainai reserve, one of the largest in Canada, where employment is provided by a prefabricated housing plant. The Blackfoot are no longer buffalo hunters and Plains warriors as in days gone by, but they have nonetheless survived and today maintain their heritage within the larger Canadian society.

■ Chiefdoms

Chiefdoms differ from bands and tribes because of their centralized political and social institutions. Chiefdoms can also be considered *rank societies* in that there is an unequal access in the society to status positions and prestige, yet an equal access to economic resources, resulting in a ranking of families in a class system. This means that most people in the chiefdom have about the same standard of living, as those with the most prestige do not garner more economic resources than those of lower status. Descent groups are also ranked as some are considered more prestigious, or higher on the status scale, than others. Overall, societies of the chiefdom type have a hierarchical or pyramidal structure. This means that social groups are ranked one on top of the other as one ascends the social scale, with fewer and fewer positions of prestige as one nears the top of the socio-political structure.

The main economic mode of exchange characteristic of chiefdoms is *redistribution*, which involves the accumulation of goods, and sometimes labour as well, by a particular person at a centralized location, with a subsequent distribution of these goods back to other members of the society. The purpose of the redistribution mode of exchange is to gain prestige for the person distributing the goods as a means of demonstrating generosity and thereby laying claim to a position of status in the society. The redistribution can take place at different levels, depending upon the status position sought, such that some redistribution are relatively minor ones involving portions of a village, while others may extend out so that members of other villages are invited to receive goods.

Leadership positions tend to be held on a hereditary basis, such that leaders do not hold their positions necessarily because of their own personal qualities, but according to their role and status in the political structure. *Status* refers to a position or standing in a society that is socially recognized, while a *role* is the pattern of behaviour associated with a particular status. Hereditary political positions are an example of *ascribed status*, which is a position in society determined for a person at birth, as opposed to *achieved status*, which a person acquires during his or her lifetime. For chiefdoms, ascribed status is usually based on a person's sex and his or her position in particular descent groups, which allow the person access to positions of prestige in the society. In some chiefdoms, *ambilineal descent* is common such that people can use *either* their father's *or* their mother's family kinship lines, depending upon which line is most useful in attempts to attain particular status positions.

Another characteristic of chiefdoms is that they are composed of communities of large *sedentary* populations. The people live in one village all year round (except those moving because of marriage) and have a reliable food source, which is usually based on food production on a larger scale than horticulture. There may be combinations of crop production and fishing, which was common in Melanesia and Polynesia, but the growth of a variety of crops to provide an abundant food supply, even a surplus, was the prevalent pattern of chiefdoms. Only on the West coast of North America were chiefdoms able to exist based on a hunting, fishing, and gathering economy.

Northwest Pacific Coast Cultures

The Aboriginal societies of Canada's Northwest coast were unique among the world's societies because of the complexity of their social organization, the development of sophisticated wood carvings, and a varied ceremonial life on the basis of what is considered a rudimentary economy. The available resources from the sea, inland rivers, and mountain ranges were so abundant that nowhere else in the world was there a hunting-gathering economy with such a varied and plentiful food supply. Basic anthropological sources for the Northwest coast societies include Franz Boas's *Kwakiutl Ethnography* (1966), Helen Codere's *Fighting with Property* (1950), James Spradley's *Guests Never Leave Hungry* (1972), and M. Anderson's (2004) article on the Tsimshian potlatch.

In Aboriginal times, the Northwest coast must have been an immense drawing force for the hunting societies of North America as nowhere else in Canada was there such a large population density. There was also considerable cultural and linguistic complexity, suggesting that the original migrants to the coast came from a variety of different cultural and geographical backgrounds. In the southern portions lived members of the Salish language family, comprising about nine languages distributed on the coast (Bella Coola, Squamish, Songish) and an almost equal number in the interior plateau region (Shuswap, Okanagan, Lillooet). Farther up the coast are members of the Wakashan language family, such as the Nootka of Vancouver Island, the Kwakiutl on the Douglas Channel to Bute Inlet, and the Bella Bella, who live on the coast along Queen Charlotte Sound. The Tsimshian family, consisting of the Niska of the Nass Valley, Gitskan on the Upper Skeena River, and Tsimshian of the Lower Skeena, are also members of the Penutian language phylum (the level larger than the language family), of which the Mayans of the Yucatan Peninsula are distant relatives. The Haida of the Queen Charlotte Islands and the Tlingit of the Alaskan panhandle are thought to be members of the Dene language family, but there is some dispute about this matter among linguists.

Photo 8.3: A Clayoquot carries out a ceremonial purification, in order to render himself pleasing to the spirit whale, 1916. The Clayoquot is a Central Nootka First Nation of British Columbia. (Source: Photographer Edward S. Curtis, Library and Archives Canada)

Geographically the Northwest coast consists of a rugged terrain, comprising numerous inlets and fiords, making communication from one region to another difficult without the aid of large boats or dugout canoes. The climate is generally mild, with snow occurring only on rare occasions and usually in the mountainous regions. The winter months consist of rainy days most of the time because of the ascent of moisture-laden air coming off the ocean, which precipitates as it makes contact with the cooler air of the mountain slopes. The result of this moist, relatively mild climate is a proliferation of plant life and a subsequent rich biotic environment. Hunters on the coast had available numerous salmon, especially in the summer spawning runs, which they caught with spears and weirs. One variety of fish weirs channelled the salmon through a funnel into a large trap made of poles and basketry material. At other times, part of a river was diverted into shallow pools, where the fish could be netted or speared. The catch would then be dried for later consumption.

Candlefish, or *olachen*, was another important food source. It has very high oil content and was taken in prodigious quantities by dip nets on its runs up the Fraser River. Seals were hunted with harpoons along the shoreline or sometimes in rivers, as were sea otters. Land mammals, such as deer and mountain goats, were hunted for meat and skins. Along the shore, various kinds of seafood could be collected, such as clams, crabs, and mussels. Women gathered roots and berries for food and medicinal purposes when they were seasonally available.

The villages on the Pacific coast tended to resemble one another, despite the linguistic diversity in the area, suggesting that cultural borrowing was prevalent among the different cultural groups. The houses consisted of large, rectangular multi-family dwellings constructed from cedar logs and planks made by splitting the wood with wedges and stone mauls. In front of each house was a large carved pole, which represented the heraldic crest and history of the family members. Mounds of earth were piled up along the inside walls of the houses, providing a platform for cooking, sleeping, and storing goods. Above the fireplaces were fish-drying racks strung out in rows from the ceiling. The houses had a board floor and a central smoke hole in the roof. Overall the houses were built as a single room, measuring about 15 m wide by 40 m long. Platforms were constructed in front of the houses, with rows of steps leading down to the beach. Villages ranged in size from relatively small ones, comprising just a few houses, to those with over 30 dwellings and an overall population range of from 200 to 700 people.

The basic building blocks of Pacific coast social life were the lineages comprising groups of kin living in the same village. In the northern areas of the West coast, matrilineal descent was common—among the Tsimshian and Haida, for example—while in the southern areas, such as among the Kwakiutl and Salish, patrilineal descent was more prevalent. Lineages were ranked in a rough order in terms of status, wealth, and prestige. Lineages sponsored various ceremonial events, such as births, marriages, and, most importantly, a great feast called the *potlatch*. Societies were divided socially into different classes, based on the ranking of individual lineages, in a hierarchical structure. At the top of the social hierarchy were the noble families, headed by a chief, down through the commoners and slaves, which comprised about 10 or 20 percent of a village's population. Marriages usually took place within a person's own rank or status, thus marital endogamy was a factor preserving the system of inherited status and social class. People could shift their allegiances using ambilineal kinship linkages—for example, if a man was dissatisfied with members of his father's lineage, he might take his wife and family and live with his mother's lineage or even that of his wife.

The *potlatch* was the most important feast held by Aboriginal First Nations of the Northwest coast at which great quantities of food and material goods were given to the attending guests in order to gain status and prestige for the host. The potlatch is a prime example of a *redistributive* mode of exchange in which goods are brought together in a central location and then given away to those attending the ceremony as a means of attaining status for those sponsoring the feast. While food was usually given away in great quantities during a potlatch, the main focus was on valued items, such as blankets, canoes, slaves, and especially large sheets of copper. Various dances and dramas were performed. Long speeches were made, extolling the virtues of the potlatch hosts.

Contact with Europeans changed the potlatches dramatically. First, there was a proliferation of goods available because of the sale of furs, especially sea otter pelts, to the Hudson's Bay Company. Second, smallpox and other epidemic diseases swept through the Northwest coast populations, decimating the local Aboriginal populations and consequently leaving many high-status positions vacant. A flurry of potlatching began to take place in the late 1800s, spurred on by new wealth introduced into the economic system and the vacancy of so

Photo 8.4: Elders potlatch at Capilano College for the opening of the David Neel photograph exhibit, August 1990. (Source: UBC Historical Photographs)

many status positions. The Canadian government, thinking that these giveaway feasts were impoverishing Northwest coast societies, banned the potlatch in 1884 until 1951. There were not only economic motives involved for this suppression of Aboriginal practices. Missionaries believed that Aboriginal ceremonies, such as the potlatch and Sun Dance, were heathen practices that prevented the First Nations peoples' conversion to Christianity.

Today the Northwest coast Aboriginal population is probably still a fraction of what it was before the epidemics that depleted the local villages. When British Columbia entered Confederation in 1871, the province refused to negotiate land claims with the Aboriginal peoples, arguing that this was the federal government's responsibility. As a result, there have never been any treaties signed with B.C., aside from three minor land transfers on Vancouver Island. Aboriginal populations and land issues remain, for the most part, unresolved. The Niska, of the Nass Valley, took their case to the Supreme Court of Canada in 1973, where they lost in a split decision. The land claims and other resources issues, such as fishing rights, in British Columbia have spurred the emergence of a number of Aboriginal political organizations in the province. The Kwakiutl formed the Pacific Coast Native Fisherman's Association in 1936, and eventually merged with the Native Brotherhood of British Columbia in 1942 (LaViolette 1973; Patterson 1972).

The Pacific coast cultures were the largest and most complex of all Aboriginal societies in Canada. They had relatively large populations, despite the dramatic decline; were well organized because of their chiefdom heritage; and had significant issues, such as land claims and fishing rights, which provided a focus for their organizational efforts. Eventually these organizational efforts provided some of the stimulus for national-level Aboriginal political organizations in Canada, such as the National Indian Brotherhood in 1968, and the Assembly of First Nations, with its inaugural meeting held in Penticton, British Columbia, in 1982 (Frideres 1998: 257–274).

■ States

States are a political organization characterized by centralized decision-making units influencing a large population size. Most states are comprised of cities with many full-time occupational roles involving a sophisticated division of labour; public structures such as libraries, schools, and government offices; full-time religious specialists; and a hierarchical social structure divided into various classes. There is also a government monopoly on the use of power, force, and legitimate authority, which controls such aspects as military forces, taxation, and bureaucracy. The large populations of the state are supported by a developed food-production system, usually involving intensive agriculture, irrigation systems, crop rotation, and a market economy that distributes agrarian production. In pre-European times in North America, state-level societies were found in Central and South America among such peoples as the Mayans, Incas, and Aztecs. There were no Aboriginal states in Canada prior to European settlement. In discussing aspects of the Canadian state, we will use ethnographic examples from grain farmers in Saskatchewan, and working-class culture in Thunder Bay, situated in northwestern Ontario.

Box 8.3: The Aztec Empire of Central Mexico

When the Aztec empire of Mesoamerica reached its greatest power around AD 1500, the capital city of Tenochtitlan and surrounding suburbs had an estimated population of over 2 million residents (Berdan 1982: 14). At about the same time, the capital cities of Europe were considerably smaller (Paris 300,000, London 50,000, and Seville 60,000). The entire population of central Mexico, roughly corresponding to the area of the Aztec empire, had an estimated indigenous population of over 25 million. This large population was supported by a sophisticated mode of food production in which an abundance of maize (corn), beans, chiles, squash, and various fruits were grown.

Maize, comparable in size and overall characteristics to some varieties cultivated in parts of rural Mexico today, was grown successfully from the tropical lowlands to the high plateaus throughout Mesoamerica. On relatively flat lands and in some shallow lake beds, irrigation agriculture was the rule. Floodwater irrigation systems were constructed over large areas. The soils were fortified and replenished by nutrients carried in the water such that the need for fallowing was not necessary. Crop rotation, as well as the rich organic material dredged up from the canal bottoms, was also used to further increase yields. Surplus agricultural production must have been an extremely important factor in the urban development of Tenochtitlan because it would have supplied subsistence goods to the numerous urban specialists, such as artisans, merchants, priests, military officers, and bureaucratic officials.

The Aztecs, or "Mexica" as they called themselves, were skilled engineers who were responsible for constructing magnificent cities, impressive temples to the gods, and other administrative buildings still standing after many centuries. They were also ferocious in battle and able to subjugate the peoples in a vast territory, bringing into the capital large quantities of tribute and slaves. Captured warriors were often sacrificed to the gods in elaborate rituals and cannibalistic feasts.

After the arrival of the Spanish in 1519, the Aztec population went into drastic decline, decreasing by as much as 90 percent in some areas because of disease and warfare. The death of their great ruler Moctezuma, famine, the religious zeal of Catholic missionaries, the many massacres perpetrated by Cortés's army, and the general decline in influence of the Aztec nobility were demoralizing factors for the surviving population. Despite these catastrophes of the Spanish conquest, many indigenous groups retained their ethnic identities, although the Mexican population plunged to just over 1 million people at the beginning of the seventeenth century.

Under Spanish rule, the Mexican society, which had been highly stratified in pre-conquest times, became increasingly homogeneous. As greater numbers of male immigrants began to arrive, they acquired Indian wives or mistresses, and the creation of a mestizo population began to develop. Over the course of the following 450 years, the Aztec culture became blended with the Spanish to produce the unique way of life that is characteristic of much of Mexico in the twenty-first century. Mexico City today remains one of the most densely populated urban environments on the planet.

Farm Management in Saskatchewan

The Prairie provinces of Saskatchewan, Alberta, and Manitoba are known as "Canada's breadbasket." Canada is one of the largest grain producers in the world, with exports out of facilities in Vancouver, Churchill, and Thunder Bay carried by its national railway system. Prior to the settlement of the Prairies, most of Canada's wheat was grown in southern Ontario, from about 1820 to 1860, prior to Confederation, when this region was called Canada West. This was a time of family farms in which mixed farming was practised. Farmers grew wheat for their own consumption and export to the United States and Britain, along with barley, oats, and potatoes. Livestock was also raised, especially horses for ploughing and transportation, sheep for wool, cows for milk and butter, and hogs for a winter meat supply. Most of these family farms were about 20–81 ha in size, and depended on large families to share in the labour requirements (McCallum 1980: 9–24).

By the end of the 1850s, most of the available agricultural land in Canada West was already settled, reducing the availability of land. Wheat production in eastern Canada also went into sharp decline at this time because of soil exhaustion, barriers to trade with the United States, and falling grain prices. At about the same time, in the western Prairies, the buffalo were dying out and the Aboriginal tribes of Blackfoot, Assiniboine, and Plains Cree were experiencing severe food shortages. Desperate for food, Aboriginal families pleaded with managers of trading posts for handouts. Between 1871 and 1877, six different treaties were signed with the Aboriginal First Nations of the southern Prairie region, and were subsequently settled on various reserves established in this region.

The demise of the buffalo and the settlement of Aboriginal tribes on reserves left an open range for livestock production. This period was a relatively short-lived one, from the 1880s to about 1905, when the Canadian Pacific Railway began to bring in a large influx of immigrants, who began an era of intensive homesteading (Bennett 1982: 35–55). The railway established towns and villages at regular intervals, usually about a day's drive by horse and carriage from each other, or about 10–20 km apart. Free-range ranching began to go into decline when land, surveys, titles, and fences restricted livestock pasture feeding areas. The homesteading period of mixed farming, combining grain crops and subsistence agriculture on 65 ha plots, grew rapidly. Soon farms began to enlarge to 129.5 ha units, especially in the drier areas. At times crop yields were low and unpredictable, leading some homesteaders to become discouraged and to sell off their landholdings.

For the first several decades of the twentieth century, moisture conditions in the West were adequate for grain crops until the Great Depression and drought of the 1930s created a halt to the pattern of rapid agricultural development (Ervin 1985). Prices fell and markets retracted; survival, not growth, became the management strategy. During the Second World War prices improved, and after the war the economy began to move again. Economic recovery brought about agricultural changes, such as increased farm mechanization and a necessity to increase landholdings in order to remain agriculturally competitive.

Population size reached a peak about 1920 and steadily declined thereafter until the early 1970s. By the mid-1970s, a population plateau had been reached as government assistance programs helped allocate more water and land to homestead farms that were still, for the most part, undersized as economically viable agricultural units.

Box 8.4: The Peasant Household Economy in the Peruvian Andes

The peasant economy is generally considered to be positioned between a strictly subsistence-based economy in which all goods produced are consumed almost entirely by household members, and a market economy in which goods are produced for cash or exchange outside the household. The intermediate peasant household aims to produce a surplus beyond its immediate consumptive needs, and to acquire goods that its members cannot produce themselves through exchange at local markets. The issue of whether peasant economies are a transitional economic form between subsistence and market economies, or if they are a separate type or category unto themselves, is a matter much debated in the socio-economic literature (Wolf 1955, 1966; Hedican 2003, 2009).

In the Andes, small-scale peasant household-based units are a ubiquitous economic form. Such households may be the foundation of the local economic system, but they do not stand alone because of the relationships between the household economy and the ties that bind it to the wider community. As Mayer (2002: xiii) suggests, "The household is also affected by the kinds of links it establishes to commodity markets and to the money introduced to the Andes during the period of Spanish colonial domination—money that increased in importance as the markets expanded and became more inclusive." In this sense, Mayer uses the term "articulated" to describe Andean peasant households because they are interrelated with other households, their communities, and the commodity markets.

One of the central features of the Andean household-based peasant economy is that it is closely linked to the household's kinship organization of production, which, in turn, reinforces relationships with communal village-based institutions. In this light, the Andean rural economy is as much a social network of exchange as it is a purely economic one, and these cannot be separated from one another. Thus, the household has remained the basic institution of production, distribution, and consumption in Andean economies for at least the last 4,000 years.

A central characteristic of the Andean household pertains to the kinship system, which is a bilateral one. This means that a person traces descent through both parents, and household membership is transmitted to both male and female children. Such a system thus creates overlapping memberships such that the bilateral descent group, or kindred, cannot form corporate groups that persist over time. Married couples, as heads of household in the Andes, are therefore surrounded by kin of various kinds of diminishing degrees of relatedness, which can have an effect on obligations that may be claimed, but also allows for a greater degree of flexibility than is allowed by other kinship systems, such as those based on unilineal descent, in which there may be a greater number of predetermined, fixed roles.

Andean households attempt to produce enough food from agriculture to feed their members, but many are not able to extend much beyond this. If there is surplus labour available to the household, it is dedicated to cash pursuits, which are likely to involve migration out of the village, although a few cattle-breeding families can generate income from this activity alone. This means that most households are divided into two sectors, one comprised of members who stay at home to manage agricultural production, and another consisting of those who migrate out to obtain cash. These many interesting aspects of the peasant household economy, which is still an important unit of production in many parts of the world, continue to offer research opportunities for anthropologists, economists, and historians.

Many villages disappeared over this 50-year period. Horses and buggies gave way to trucks and automobiles, reducing the need for villages to be 16 km apart along the rail line. Regional service centres emerged as significant distribution points for goods, services, and as retirement communities. Many left the region for jobs elsewhere—in the mines of British Columbia or on ranches in Montana—but about a quarter of these returned to take over farms from their fathers. The wages saved while working elsewhere allowed for a fresh start.

The farming communities of Saskatchewan were differentiated by religion and ethnicity. The first wave of ranchers, mainly from the U.S., were former cowpunchers from the Dakotas and Montana. The so-called "town ranchers" were mostly British Isles settlers. The farmers, on the other hand, were a polyglot group representing almost every European nationality. The two groups began to merge in the 1960s, when farm homesteaders started to move into livestock production on a large scale, and ranchers began to find it necessary to develop intensive methods of forage production as their access to free range disappeared. It was also during this period of the 1960s that the Hutterites began to settle the region, buying out small farmers and consolidating their purchases into larger, communal landholdings.

As time went on, farm families faced mounting difficulties as one generation took over from the previous one. The main source of conflicts among household members revolved around the problem of farm succession, as it did in our previous discussions of French Canadian farmers in St. Denis or the Irish of Renfrew County a century before. The father is inclined to look to only one of his sons as the successor, yet the son viewed as the most suitable by the father may reject this role. There

Photo 8.5: Farmers with wheat lined up at an elevator, Piapot, Saskatchewan, 1912. (Source: Glenbow Museum Archives, Calgary, Alberta)

are also conflicts among the sons over the succession issue, especially if the father delays making a choice or handles the issue badly by seeming to favour one son over another, causing further resentments in the household.

The son who eventually takes over the family enterprise is not free of difficulties. The costs of production are always rising, making it difficult to maintain a certain standard of living. People today are also less willing to continually delay gratification by reinvesting in the farm enterprise to meet these rising costs. When the young man takes over from his father, he will be expected to refinance the farm enterprise in order to invest in new technology to maintain a competitive edge in the business, and to contribute to his parents' retirement income. All of these various factors have led to a drop in the number of small family farms.

The small family farm in Canada's Prairies is under severe stress because of the rising expectation of those in the farming business. Young people now wish to go to college or university, increasing expenditures further, and many may not wish to return to the farm with its demanding hours of work and great financial investment. For many farm families, life in the surrounding towns and cities, with its more relaxed workload, has a strong appeal. In addition, large-scale agribusinesses, with their access to virtually unlimited investment capital and land, provide severe competition to the small farming family. The relatively low return on one's labour on the farm may breed dissatisfaction among some household members as they view possible higher rates of return in other occupations, tempting many young people to leave agriculture altogether.

In social anthropology we are apt to see the family farm not only as a business enterprise, but also as a residential kin group. The North American farm household is primarily composed of a nuclear family, and the relatively small size of such social units poses constraints on growth and development, thereby hindering competition with other farm enterprises. Within such nuclear families there is an emphasis on individual goal fulfillment, which may also inhibit a sharing ethic of pooling materials and labour. In many other societies, whether in peasant societies of Asia or Latin America, or even in industrial societies, such as those in Europe and Japan, the operation and financing of the farm are in the hands of a larger, extended kin group. Such larger kin networks provide an adaptive advantage over the nuclear family because tasks and finances can be shared out on an extensive basis.

This larger available workforce of the extended family household provides opportunities for expansion that are more difficult to accomplish in the smaller nuclear units as limited labour resources provide a significant restraint on the size of the nuclear farm enterprise. Nuclear families must meet their labour requirements, not from within the household, but by purchasing it during the peak times of the agricultural cycle, thus incurring additional costs that a larger kin network might not need to expend. These sorts of economies of scale (by which farm costs are reduced by increasing landholding and mechanization, thereby reducing labour requirements), as they affect household size and composition, is especially evident in the Hutterite colony. While Hutterite colonies are composed of nuclear families, like ranchers and farmers, the contrast between their communal co-operative farm system and the more individualistic farm enterprise is particularly evident. Even when there are adjoining farms operated by brothers among farmers, there is less co-operative interaction among them than in Hutterite colonies. The labour shortages suffered by nuclear families could have been alleviated by the more co-operative patterns utilized by Hutterite farms.

We are therefore led to think of the family farm in terms of residential kin groups as much as we think of them as a business enterprise. The contribution that anthropology makes to the study of agrarian societies lies in its more comprehensive approach, in which economic and social aspects are combined in an overall analysis. Economic decisions are not based on aspects of resource use and distribution alone, but are part of a family's larger social needs and requirements, of which economics is only one, albeit important, part. As family farms attempt to adapt to new, changing conditions, the social strains in households that result from these changes are just as important to individual family members as the larger economic ones with which they must also cope. Conflicts among family household members are partly structural, which is to say that they are built into any farm, such as the issue of succession, and partly individualistic as changing norms and values lead to new aspirations not experienced in previous generations. One of the lessons that anthropology brings to the study of agrarian social institutions is that there is a need to examine ways to harmonize or synthesize the various economic and social roles of different family members.

Women's Roles in Economic Development

There is a major flaw in Bennett's otherwise admirable study of Saskatchewan farm management—women are virtually invisible. His study purports to study farm families, yet much of the discussion is about the activities of men, leaving the impression that everyone else in the farm family, except men, are some sort of backdrop to the males' plans, actions, and decisions. The implication is that women (and children) are there in a supporting role to the main cast of characters, who are men.

If one examines the fairly detailed index to Bennett's *Of Time and the Enterprise*, under the "Agrifamily system," there are 65 lines devoted to this topic, with only one entry for women. There are entries under "Women"; however, these are scattered across dozens of pages without a continuous discussion of the role of women in agricultural farm life. One might suggest that the book was written in the 1980s when the role of women was not given the due consideration that it does today, but this is still hardly an adequate reason for leaving the impression that the roles of wives and daughters is not nearly as important in farm life as those of fathers and sons.

Women's roles in economic development have been an important area of discussion in anthropology, at least since Ester Boserup's (1970) critique of development studies, which tended to undermine women's economic contributions. Several recent studies—such as Hoodfar's (1997) research on women's roles in the markets of Cairo, and Bossen's (2002) ethnography of Chinese women and rural development—have contributed to anthropologists' understanding of women's work and gender in economic and techno-logical development in other cultures. Such studies have illustrated women's access to markets and property outside of their own households, and the manner in which divisions of labour have changed in recent times. Anthropological studies of women's role in economic development show that in different cultures, gender is an important aspect of consumption and production.

Similarly, on the Saskatchewan family farm, a gendered perspective places women's economic activities in a more ethnographically accurate position. However, as Bennett (1982: 133) indicates, there is a problem of perspective, such that "The underlying cultural conception is that women are the dependents [*sic*] of men." Hence, in farming, any contribution that women might make to production is viewed as an informal, personal service—an acceptable exchange for the support given them by men. Such concepts are reinforced by the legal sanctions that surround marriage and inheritance. At the time of Bennett's ethnography, laws pertaining to Saskatchewan matrimonial property guaranteed a widow's right to the house of the matrimonial home, but there was no guarantee that a woman would be entitled to half the assets of the enterprise upon divorce. Thus, even though Saskatchewan's laws have probably changed in the interim since Bennett's ethnography, at that time there was hardly an equitable division of property between spouses at the time of a divorce, based on the opinion that a woman's contributions to the farm enterprise were less than those of her husband.

This legal environment also helps to explain Bennett's position with regard to the role of women in the farm enterprise, at least to the extent that women's roles would appear to be undervalued. In fact, Bennett offers a candid statement regarding the anthropological perspective of his studies. As he outlines: "our protocols of data collection originally were based on the idea of a single male operator as the manager and director of 'his' enterprise and household" (Bennett 1982: 133). Even though he acknowledges that the idea of a single-enterprise manager who acted independently was probably rare not only in Saskatchewan but in North American agricultural society as a whole, Bennett justified his focus on male activities to the neglect of women's contributions because of conventional ideas that were prevalent in his area of study. In other words, if the people in an anthropologist's study devalue women's work, then the ethnographer, who is supposedly bound to adhere to the norms of the population under study, is therefore similarly justified in the same sort of devaluation on the grounds that he or she is following local conventional norms and values.

If this all begins to start to sound like a self-fulfilling prophecy or a justification of injustice, then one is probably correct. In fact, I would suggest that the whole context of the discussion regarding whose role is more important—that of the husband or the wife—is misplaced. The roles of both are complementary entities, neither of whom could fulfill his or her own role without the corresponding help of the other. On these grounds alone, the roles of husband and wife are both equal. In many ways it is like a discussion of which role is more important in procreation, when in fact the ultimate goal is not achievable without the participation of both sexes (discounting, of course, recent developments in *in vitro* fertilization, uterine implanting, and so on).

For the most part, the household manager/wife has the responsibility of translating the needs of the farm enterprise with the more specific needs of the household members.

These two sets of needs are not always in congruence with one another, and so there are trade-offs, negotiations, and even heated arguments over the allocation of scarce farm resources. The availability of these resources fluctuates through time, such as in the severe periods of restraint during the "Dirty Thirties," or more prosperous times when grain prices are high and weather conditions are optimal. In either situation, there are always decisions concerning investment—buy a new combine or build a larger house—that involve opportunity costs since a decision in one area is apt to preclude economic action in another. The family is at time like a court, where particular causes are debated, before decisions are reached. Given that family members have to live with each other on a day-to-day basis, there are good reasons for reconciliation, compromise, and appeasement. The success of the farm enterprise, seen in this light, is as much a social phenomenon as it is an economic one.

Aboriginal Women and Development Issues

I should probably not be too harsh on Bennett's ethnographic approach regarding the role of farm women in rural Saskatchewan, given my own ethnographic experiences. Early on in my academic career, I was conducting a study of a northern Anishenabe (Ojibwa) community, eventually entitled *The Ogoki River Guides* (Hedican 1986a). When the manuscript was sent in for possible publication, the editor of Wilfrid Laurier University Press, at the time a woman, had an important question. She wanted to know if the Aboriginal women in the community had not made a greater economic contribution to community viability than I had indicated in my various charts and tables. The question had caught me off guard, and I said I would check through my field notes to see if any amendments were needed in the ethnographic write-up. I then proceeded to look through the reports in my possession of workers and their incomes for various community projects, based on the information supplied to me by community leaders.

The reports that were given to me were based on summaries of community members' job participation, which were subsequently sent to the various granting agencies that provided the funds. In other words, my idea of employment was narrowly interpreted to mean the people who earned income, and income that was reported to the government for tax purposes. On this basis, the role of women in the cash economy appeared rather minimal compared to men. However, the editor's inquiry made me realize that the economic activities of women in the community were largely invisible to me. First of all, I did not hang out with the women as I did with the men. I was afraid that associating with the women might be misinterpreted in a sexual way rather than an academic one, which most people hardly understood anyway. So my practice was not to spend much time with women, who usually averted their eyes in any event when they saw me approaching them on the trails, in the store, or in other areas of the community.

What I did not see because of this one-sided nature of my investigation was that women spent quite a bit of time at home, ostensibly looking after their children, but also making things as well. The women not only cooked meals, made clothes, and tended their cabins, but they also made handicrafts, such as mittens, moose-hide jackets, beaded necklaces, and a host of other items, which were sold either by themselves to missionaries or schoolteachers, or by a local store to tourists. I asked the storekeeper about the sale of these handicrafts. "Did you sell them for the women?" "Did you buy them yourself, and then attach a mark-up?" "What was the monetary value, per year, of this work?" "How many women gave you handicrafts to sell?" So many questions, so few answers. The storekeeper said that he didn't keep records of this sort of thing. I believe he didn't want to have tax issues if records were kept. He could give me rough estimates, and that was about it.

I tried to incorporate the storekeeper's vague information into my table on earned income, vague as it was. I was sure that there was a gross underestimate in the procedure, as many of the woman's handicrafts could have been traded among themselves for other items or labour. I also realized that women were major participants in the unearned, or transfer payment, part of the local economy. There were women collecting widow's pensions, social assistance, old-age pensions, and so on. For all of these items I had to use the educated guess method, which is hardly a method at all.

What was evident to me was that my inexperience as an ethnographic fieldworker had major flaws when it came to the economic role of women. Looking back, I realize that I rationalized the situation by telling myself that I was doing the best job that I could do under the circumstances. In reality, though, I had hardly made any attempt to approach the women and ask them questions. There were things that I could have done. For example, I could have approached their husbands and explained what I was doing with my research, and asked if it was all right if I were to ask their wives or daughters a few questions relating to my investigation. That would have brought the questioning out in the open, and publicly credited the women with activities that were of sufficient importance that an outsider was interested in what they were doing. At the same time, it would have alleviated the possibility of suspicion. Alternatively, I could have hired another woman in the community to ask the questions for me. Such a person would know far better than I would as to what questions to ask, what answers to expect, and the women questioned would feel more comfortable about such an interview process.

There are cultural issues when men talk with women or, I suppose, when women ethnographers discuss research issues with men. However, men in other cultures might be apt to regard North American women as having a right to ask questions because they are in positions of power in their own country. I am not saying that women fieldworkers have an easier time of it than men, but there are certainly advantages and disadvantages that researchers of both sexes have to contend with.

The issue at hand in this section concerns the role of Aboriginal women in economic development. What is evident is that a researcher has to do some digging, but the results of this search are certainly revealing. A report prepared by Cam Mackie (1986: 211), who was a coordinator of a federal government task force on Native economic development, indicated with regard to the role of Aboriginal women that:

A recent conference on native women and economic development was the first conference for almost half of the women there. Most of them were successful businesswomen whose companies included construction, restaurants, fine arts stores, clothing manufacturing, consulting services, fishing lodge operations, and so on. The majority of the successful businesses have never received any financial support from government. They did it the hard way, on their own initiative.

Most of the businesses reported for this conference were in the service sector economy, possibly the fastest-growing economic area in Canada. The conference report also conveys a positive image of Aboriginal women's role in local economic development, one that is not simply an adjunct to men's economic activities.

Among the Carrier people of central British Columbia, Fiske (1988: 186) has investigated the role of women in the fishing business:

> State intervention, combined with capital inflows and development, left salmon, the most valued resource, in the hands of women, and at the same time reduced the resources exploited primarily by men.... Appreciation of women who provide well for their families and communities has implications for women as political actors and community leaders. Today, women and men often rationalize female political actions by reference to their abilities as fisherwomen.

While these reports provide a positive portrayal of Aboriginal women in economic change, more recent studies continue to indicate significant economic disparities between Aboriginal and non-Aboriginal communities in Canada, as well as between men and women within these communities. Some Aboriginal groups see these disparities as symptomatic of the structure of Canadian society itself. For example, the Métis Women's Association of Manitoba sees Aboriginal problems as a symptom of larger social and cultural problems. As far as they are concerned, as long as development initiatives are handled solely by outsiders and men, the structural problems will remain (Frideres 1998: 430–439). Finding solutions to these structural, embedded issues is a problematic matter since deep, ingrained discriminatory attitudes toward Canada's Aboriginal populations make positive changes on the economic front very difficult to achieve.

In general socio-economic terms, Aboriginal women tend to fare less well than their male counterparts, reflecting a similar trend in the larger society. As far as male–female differences in labour force participation and income levels in Canada are concerned, there is considerable evidence that Aboriginal women are less active in economic activities than men. Aboriginal peoples are participating more in the labour force over time. However, this participation is still marginal and not representative of the sorts of jobs that many other Canadians enjoy. In all, Aboriginal participation in the labour force of this country is about 20 percent lower than the national rate. Among status Indians living on reserves, more than 40 percent of the men and only 25 percent of the women are employed. Among the non-status Aboriginal population, nearly two-thirds of men and 40 percent of the women have jobs (Blaser, Feit, and McRae 2004; DIAND 2004; Hedican 2008).

The greater economic problems experienced by Aboriginal women than men could be a product of sexual and gender discrimination, something that Gerber has referred to as "multiple jeopardy." As she explains (1990: 69), "Canadian women appear to be at a distinct disadvantage whenever their incomes and educational or occupational achievements are compared with those of men, and women with combined minority statuses seem to suffer multiple jeopardy." One conclusion that has become increasingly evident is that Aboriginal women in Canadian society are doubly disadvantaged as females of ethnic minorities. Such women also carry an additional handicap because of the dependent status of Aboriginal peoples on the reserve-based communities within Canadian society. As a general conclusion with regard to state societies is concerned, many groups are incorporated within this structure, but not all groups so incorporated have access to the same advantages. In Canada, the Aboriginal populations have been divested of their lands, and remain at a seemingly permanent economic disadvantage because of the lack of meaningful resources, educational skills, and investment opportunities that are available to other, advantaged sectors of the population.

Working-Class Culture in Thunder Bay

Thunder Bay has the largest grain elevators in the world, and therefore is a primary destination of the grain grown in the Prairies provinces. Thunder Bay, and the region around it, is also based on primary resource-extraction industries, such as forestry and mining. The service sector economy also plays an important economic role in the region, especially in terms of tourism and the associated businesses, which provide accommodations, food, and fuel. Labour force requirements in Thunder Bay are therefore based on these extractive and service-oriented economic activities, thus, in Thomas Dunk's terms, *It's a Working Man's Town* (2007).

Thunder Bay has its origins in the Aboriginal First Nations who, since the retreat of the last ice age about 10,000 years ago, hunted and fished around the rivers and lakes emptying into Lake Superior. Fur traders and explorers were attracted by the rich trade in beaver pelts and a search for routes to the Northwest, initially establishing posts at Sault Ste. Marie (1668), Nipigon (1679), and Kaministikwia (1679). Later, a band of Scottish traders working out of Montreal founded the North West Company and built a post called Fort William in 1807 on the route to the Lake of the Woods.

By the 1840s, prospectors had discovered veins of silver not far from Sault Ste. Marie, causing a clash with the local Ojibwa population, who burned down their tents and rigs in protest over the lack of a land settlement with the British Crown. Not long after, in 1850, the Robinson Superior Treaty was signed at Fort William with the Aboriginal bands in the area, which led to further developments. The Silver Islet mine near Thunder Bay was discovered in 1869, followed by other mines of the ore-rich Precambrian shield at Sudbury (1883) and Kirkland Lake (1911).

Forestry began in northern Ontario with the lumbering of white pine in the Ottawa Valley, starting in 1870. Pulp and paper mills, based on the extensive tracts of northern Ontario's spruce forests, were situated in Thunder Bay (1911), Dryden (1911), Nipigon (1921), and other locations along the shore of Lake Superior. Transportation was initially based on canoe routes, but in 1885 construction of the Canadian Pacific Railway

Photo 8.6: Shanty gang, Arnprior, Ontario, January 1903. Loggers in northern Ontario would spend all winter living in log cabins, or shanties, coming out of the woods only after the snow melted and the logs could be driven downriver. (Source: Photographer Charles Macnamara, Archives of Ontario)

blasted through the rock cliffs of Lake Superior's north shore. The establishment of highways was relatively late in the area, with Highway No. 11 constructed from Matheson to Cochrane in 1927, and Cochrane to Thunder Bay in 1944. Highway No. 17, which links Nipigon with Sault Ste. Marie, was officially opened in 1960. Trans-Canada Airlines began commercial flights out of Thunder Bay in 1947. Prince Arthur's Landing became Port Arthur in 1882, later to be amalgamated with Fort William in 1970 to become Thunder Bay, locally referred to as Lakehead.

Presently Thunder Bay is the largest grain-handling port in the world, and the third busiest harbour in Canada. Raw materials produced by local inhabitants are shipped out for processing, and finished products are imported. As Dunk (2007: 52) indicates, "Large corporations whose principal responsibilities lie with investors who live outside the region determine the economic future of the region and the lives of the local inhabitants." To give an example of this hinterland–metropolis dependency, the forest products industry alone employs 60–70 percent of northwestern Ontario's labour force, which, in Thunder Bay, pays about 85 percent of the total wages in the manufacturing sector.

Photo 8.7: Thunder Bay grain elevators, the largest in the world, June 1980. (Source: Ministry of Agriculture, Food, and Rural Affairs, Archives of Ontario)

Economic disparities within the Thunder Bay area itself, between local Euro-Canadians and Aboriginal peoples, are startling. Annual male incomes, for example, as reported by Dunk (2007: 59), are about $25,000 for Thunder Bay as a whole, while only $12,600 for the nearby Fort William Reserve. The unemployment rate for people 15–24 years old was 15 percent for Thunder Bay, and 56 percent for the reserve. For those over 24 years old, unemployment in Thunder Bay was 10 percent, compared to 29 percent on the First Nations reserve. Even more tragic is the plight of the Aboriginal women within Thunder Bay: 61 percent of the women surveyed were single mothers, 63 percent were on social assistance, 77 percent were unemployed, and the mean annual income was

$8,900, which is $9,000 below the National Council of Welfare's poverty line. Evidently the Aboriginal First Nations of northern Ontario have not shared in the mineral and forestry wealth generated from their ancestral lands.

Not only are Aboriginal peoples economically deprived, living for the most part well below the acceptable poverty line established for the rest of Canadians, they are also subject to intense racist attitudes from the local White population. As Dunk (2007: 103) explains, "The white's understanding of their own subordinate position in the broader society is refracted into a racist perspective against native people." Similarly, in a pamphlet called *Bended Elbow*, a deplorable piece of racist literature written by a Kenora nurse, the view is expressed that "They shoot each other, stab each other; they get so **god-damned** [emphasis in the original] drunk they lay on the railroad tracks to sleep and are cut in half or they drown" (Jacobson 1975: 5). In his study of Crow Lake (Sioux Lookout), north of Kenora on the Canadian National Railway line, David Stymeist (1975: 93–94) comments in his ethnography *Ethnics and Indians* that "The most tragic fact in the Crow Lake situation is that the town is able to benefit significantly from the poverty of Native people—For a Native person locked into this system, the hypocrisy of bureaucratic agencies and the violence and prejudice of the local white society become two omnipresent and inescapable forces against which only direct action may seem reasonable."

An important question, then, is: To what extent are the Whites' racist attitudes toward Aboriginal peoples in northwestern Ontario explainable as part of working-class culture? Dunk suggests that working-class people in Thunder Bay nurture resentments for many others besides Aboriginal peoples, although probably not to the same virulent degree as that experienced by members of First Nations. Just as working-class males in Thunder Bay use the term "Indian" to "express symbolically their alienation from the southern-based power bloc [which] reverberates with racist overtones" (Dunk 2007: 160), their "common sense" mode of thought leads to anti-intellectualism and gender stereotyping. They see a dichotomy between words and things as expressed in the opposition of talkers and doers—"women talk too much ... men know when to keep quiet" (2007: 149). Other "talkers," such as teachers, lawyers, salesmen, and politicians, are seen as people who do not produce anything that is useful. They live off the labour of the workers who "produce useful things," and who "possess practical skills. The male workers are contemptuous of the mild-mannered parasites and soft-spoken vultures who live off our daily sweat" (Dunk 2007: 142).

Dunk's theoretical explanation for the behaviour and attitudes of Thunder Bay's working-class culture is founded on the interplay between resistance and hegemony. Hegemony is an all-suppressive force that keeps the working class from rising in the economic and social scale. "Hegemony," Dunk suggests (2007: 35), "is a process which has continually to be renewed and which is continually resisted and altered by the subordinate classes in society." The labour of the working class is devalued by not being fairly rewarded, and by an inadequate return for one's contribution to the production of goods. In turn, it is the "parasites" that "do nothing but talk," who are rewarded with fine clothes, houses and cars. It is a matter of social injustice as the workers see the situation that causes them to lash out

Photo 8.8: Logjam on White River, near Englehart, Ontario, c. 1925. In the logging days of northern Ontario, logjams were a frequent occurrence, often requiring dynamite to break them apart. (Source: Photographer E.J. Zavitz, Archives of Ontario)

against southern bureaucrats, women, and Aboriginals. They also are fond of sabotaging the work environment, such as "killing time" by hiding out in washrooms, or by causing equipment to malfunction and thereby necessitating "down time."

These are all examples, according to Dunk's interpretation, of "resistance" to an unfair socio-economic structure that rewards talk but not action. Sabotaging the work environment is a way of "getting even," and of ultimately decreasing the profits of those who control the workers by controlling the means of production. In other words, the behaviour of Thunder Bay's working class is seen in terms of a Marxian analysis of class struggle. Thunder Bay is therefore a space where the theme of a culture of resistance is played out, where the web of domination and subordination in contemporary Western capitalist society is laid bare. Acts of resistance are a "cathartic mechanism, a way of releasing pent-up frustrations for both society and individuals" (2007: 86). As Marx's famous statement indicates, "Men make their own history, but they do not make it just as they please; they do not make it under circumstances chosen by themselves, but under given circumstances directly encountered and inherited from the past" ([1852] 1978: 9). It is this lack of control over historical circumstances chosen by others, involving means of production, one's labour power, and investment, that leads to frustration and alienation of working-class people in modern capitalist society.

■ Looking Back, Looking Forward

At one time—say, about 10,000 years ago—all of the world's people lived in band societies. Life, for the most part, was good for these people. The overall world population was relatively small compared to later centuries, when food gathering shifted to food production, so there was a lot of room on the planet to roam around. People in band societies had the time to enjoy their friends and family, and, as far as we know, their workload was not great. It was only when hunting and gathering societies were pushed into the more marginal areas of the world by large, agricultural societies that the hunting-gathering way of life was devalued. People began to think of hunting societies as living a desperate hand-to-mouth existence, with starvation and food shortages common. These things did occur, but only because the hunters, after their dislocation from benign environments, were forced to live in ecological circumstances where the available biomass was far less than before.

Band societies and their hunting-and-gathering economies survived because of an egalitarian ideology in which sharing and giving without expectation of return was a dominant social and economic characteristic. As societies became larger because of increased food production, social differentiation began to take hold, such that different classes emerged. As in the case of chiefdoms, while this was a hierarchical type of society, resource distribution was still on a more or less equitable basis. There were those in the society with higher class standing than others, but the standard of living was much the same for commoners and those of noble birth. States involve a more mechanized mode of food production, allowing for greater concentrations of people, but also creating significant class and wealth differences. Class was now welded to an inequitable distribution of resources in society, thereby exacerbating the problem of social differentiation and conflict.

Where the world's population goes from here, where it is today as this new millennium unfolds, is a matter of some speculation. However, if we view historical trends over the last several thousand years, there is every reason to expect that these trends of population density, and an unequal distribution of the world's resources, will continue into the near future, barring a major world catastrophe. The main lesson that this transition from bands to states tells us is that humans have a propensity for complex organizational forms. We seem to have a built-in drive to produce more than what we need, leading to the inevitability of ever-increasing resource exhaustion of the planet. We are already seeing this process take effect with the escalating price of petroleum production, and the frenzied response to find alternatives before it is too late. The lesson that seems to have been missed along the way is that progress, in whatever form, seems to entail significant costs that, in turn, seem to create even larger problems to solve.

And so we try to organize our way out of the dilemma. The European Union is rapidly making individual states an obsolete concept, while attempting a sharing mode to reduce costs and duplication of efforts. Free traders have the same idea in mind by reducing tariffs and the cost of trade, but few remember that Ireland's Great Famine of 1847–1850 was largely caused by a free trade policy. More than twice as much food was exported out of Ireland during the late 1840s than was needed to keep the Irish population fed and healthy. So is it only a matter of resource distribution? The answer is "only partly." There always seem to be those who want more than their fair share, even at the expense of others. The Rwandan genocide of 1994 and its horrific social aftermath are essentially no different from the Ireland of 160 years ago, as far as the people who were displaced and starving are concerned.

9 Ethnicity and Identity

Don't I know you?
I cannot experience your experience. You cannot experience my experience.
We are both invisible men. All men are invisible to one another.
Experience is man's invisibility to man.

—R.D. Laing,
The Politics of Experience (1967: 16)

■ The Nature of Experience and Identity

How do we really know what other people think and feel? How do we know what their experience of this world is like? Is it possible to find out if our own experiences of life are in any way similar to what other people experience? We may talk about our experiences with others as a way of relating or setting into context our own experiences. But in the end, all we can do is experience others in terms of how we experience ourselves—it's all an inside job.

The phenomenon of culture and identity—or how it is that we come to see ourselves in particular ways that are somehow similar to some people, but different from others—is an interesting philosophical question. It is a question about phenomenology, about the subjective nature of experience. As social scientists, we find philosophy interesting, yet we are guided by what people tell us about how they see the world. We have some faith that there is, at a minimal level, a shared, concrete reality that we all experience in broadly similar ways. There has to be some agreement on this point, otherwise our investigation becomes meaningless. We have to assume that everyone, despite differences in social and cultural backgrounds, will experience getting hit on the side of the head with a baseball bat as a painful, negative experience.

Even with some commonalities of experience, which we may assume because we are all mammals with essentially the same biological makeup, the nature of identity—that is, how we see ourselves—is a vastly complicated matter. First, there is the combination of factors that comprise identity. There are the families that we are born into, and the norms, values, and perspectives that we learn as a result of the enculturative process.

Box 9.1: The Ainu of Japan: Identity Conflict in East Asia

The Ainu are an enigma. They occupy the Japanese island of Sakhalin and are sometimes referred to as "the Caucasoid race of the Far East" (Sugiura and Befu 1962; Ohnuki-Tierney 1984). The origins of the Ainu are shrouded in mystery, and the abundant body hair of the men is in striking contrast to the Chinese, Koreans, and Japanese, who are the major populations of the Far East. Their appearance and their language, which is completely unintelligible to outsiders and seemingly unrelated to any other known language, are unusual. The Ainu were also a hunting-and-gathering people living in small scattered settlements, which is in sharp contrast to the neighbouring agricultural populations.

The Ainu thus became a society of considerable interest to ethnographers, physical anthropologists, linguists, archaeologists, and scholars from other disciplines due in part to their puzzling identity. The Ainu homeland at one time consisted of a territory that was much larger than it is today, extending from the Russian Kamchatka peninsula down through the northern part of the main Japanese island of Honshu. Over time the agricultural populations on the main island formed denser settlements, then states, and finally the Japanese nation. The Ainu groups in the north continued their hunting-and-gathering way of life, but population expansion from the south diminished their territory.

The impact of the Japanese government on the Ainu also intensified with the exploitation of natural resources in the northern islands. To facilitate the process of resource exploitation, many Japanese immigrants were brought into the Ainu habitation area. Ainu labour was also needed, so Japanese officials assumed direct administrative control over the Ainu. A new government policy of assimilating the Ainu was also instituted, and they were encouraged to speak the Japanese language. In some areas, attendance in Japanese schools was compulsory.

Today the traditional Ainu way of life has almost disappeared, remembered only by a diminishing group of elders. Dancing and religious ceremonies are often conducted for tourists. In terms of overt behaviour, there is little to distinguish the younger generation of Ainu from their Japanese counterparts. However, today many Ainu are asserting their cultural identity. In 1972, "radical" Ainu bombed an exhibition containing Ainu artifacts because of a perceived insult to the Ainu people. Many Ainu also oppose the excavation of Ainu gravesites, and there are even those who propose the establishment of an Ainu republic. It is also evident that there are many parallels linking the Ainu colonial experience with that of the First Nations of North America.

The enculturation function of the family is a crucially important factor in forming one's personal identity. In our families we learn survival skills and how to behave in relation to other people. In families children receive the training that they will need to participate properly as members of their society (Aceves 1974: 124–126).

People's identities are also based on who their relatives are and, as such, on kinship status in relation to others. One's kinship title is an important sign of identity. We learn that people close to us are related to us as fathers, brothers, or aunts and, in turn, we are known to others by our own kinship roles as sisters, uncles, or mothers. Of course there is a wide variation in these kinship roles from culture to culture, so that in some societies one's father's brother might also be called "father," and have the same sort of authority over a child as the biological father has in Euro-Canadian society.

Personal names are another symbol of identity. In Euro-Canadian society the child takes the surname of his or her father, but this is not a universal pattern. In my research among the Anishenabe (Ojibwa) of northern Ontario, when I was constructing people's genealogies I discovered that some families used at least two surnames, one English and the other Aboriginal. For example, one family was known among the local residents as "Shawahamish," but used the name "Slipperjack" for treaty and other outside purposes. When treaties were signed, most Anishenabe did not use a surname, perhaps thinking that a surname was the same as the name of their clan. When asked for their name when signing the treaty, they might have said "Peter Wolf," and that surname stuck. Others, unsure of what to do when asked for a surname, gave the name of their local Hudson's Bay Company factor. Another form of identification was the Aboriginal person's trapping territory, so one might have identified himself or herself with this location when asked for a surname. Once these names were written down, and outsiders asked on repeated occasions for a surname, it became a routine matter to use the same one over and over, thus making such names more or less permanent.

Surname patterns in other cultures can take on a variety of forms. As noted earlier in our discussion of kinship terminology, a Highland Scot bears two names, that of his father and mother. James McDaid McDougal is a McDougal through his father and a McDaid through his mother. In some Scandinavian countries, boys took the first name of their father and used it as a surname, and girls did the same with the names of their mothers, so that sons and daughters would have different surnames, even though they lived in the same family. This is a form of parallel descent, such that males traced descent through the male line, and women through related females (Fox 1967). In a somewhat similar pattern, in Islamic Arabic cultures a person may be known as the son or daughter of a certain person, such that Mohammed ben Yusef is called Mohammed son of Yusef (Aceves 1974: 126). In other societies a child may receive one name at birth that would change several times through life as his or her status in that society changed.

Russians use a naming system called *patronymics* whereby they use both their Christian first name and the patronymic "son of" (-yevitch) or "daughter of" (-yevna), combined with the father's first name. For Russians of the aristocracy, the polite form of address would be the first name and the patronymic. Among close friends and family members, the first name, or a diminutive form, would be used alone. In Leo Tolstoy's novel *Anna Karenina*, for example, her brother's full name is Prince Stephan Arkadyevitch Oblonsky, or simply "Stiva" among friends and those in his family. Anna is called Anna Arkadyevna Karenina. Tolstoy's full name is Count Leo Nikolayevich Tolstoy, meaning the son of Nikola Tolstoy. In addition, according to the old tradition, Russians do not celebrate birthdays, but name days—that is, the feast day of the patron saint after whom one is named. These are all examples of the ways in which names are used as symbols of identity.

Kinship terms are also a means of social identification comprising both a linguistic label for a person, as well as conferring a particular status. In a broader sense, language has a role in identity because it serves as a common symbolic system that fosters feelings of group or cultural solidarity. On the other hand, linguistic diversity may be at the root of serious political and social problems, as is evidenced in Canada by French-speaking and English-speaking citizens. The First Nations of Canada also have their own languages, which numbered over 50 separate languages when Europeans first arrived in this country. It may not be a particular language people use *per se* that is the problem, but that language is used as a rallying focal point for supporters of particular causes. The squabble in Montreal over the use of English versus French street signs is an example of this sort of problem. The signs themselves were not the problem because everyone knew, for example, what "stop" and *arrêt* mean; the issue was over their symbolic political nature.

■ Ethnic Identity in Canada

Before the European settlement of Canada, among the First Nations peoples identity was based on kinship relationships, such as clan membership, language use, and geographical location. Hunters knew intimately the various rivers, lakes, and landmarks in their territory since they would constantly travel throughout their own area in search of game and fish. Identity, then, stemmed from an association with the land, and with the members of one's kin group. Hunters depended upon the land and the sharing of food with their close relatives for survival under often harsh ecological conditions.

Early European settlers learned from Canada's Aboriginal peoples how to survive in the bush, or which crops grew best along the St. Lawrence River system. Europeans were also dependent upon the Aboriginal population as military allies in defending the southern border. This need to defend military positions was probably a major reason for granting the Iroquois extensive tracts of land along the Grand River near Brantford in the late 1770s. During the War of 1812 Aboriginal leaders, such as Tecumseh and Pontiac, played as significant a role as Isaac Brock. However, with the quelling of hostilities between the British and the United States, the identification of Aboriginal populations with the military defence of Canada was diminished. Canada's legal obligations toward Aboriginal peoples were established with the Indian Act of 1876, specifying a category of "registered" or "status Indians," who were deemed to be a federal responsibility.

The Indian Act, in one sense, has also fractured the Aboriginal population of Canada into various categories, such as status, non-status, and Métis, thereby creating various subgroups who are forced to identify with one particular status or another. To confuse matters further, as far as the legal and personal identity of Aboriginal peoples is concerned, status Indians could lose their status, a process called enfranchisement, and as such fall into the non-status category. Before the passage of Bill C-31 in 1985, for example, a status woman who married a non-status man would lose her status, and her children, who were born with status, would lose theirs as well. Bill C-31 was meant to correct this inequity or sexual discrimination against Aboriginal women, but it has caused further problems because only some of the Bill C-31 people who had their status restored could pass their status on to their children. Legislation such as the Indian Act and Bill C-31 have fractured Aboriginal identity in Canada into a myriad of competing interest groups.

When the Aboriginal peoples' role as military allies diminished, Canada had other needs. From about 1825 to 1870, the Irish came to Canada in large numbers, eventually becoming the third largest ethnic group in Canada. This was partly the result of conditions back in Ireland, such as the Great Famine of 1847–1850, but also because of the availability of farmland in Canada West, as Ontario was called before Confederation. With Confederation in 1867, English and French were deemed the official languages of Canada, a legal position to which the First Nations peoples felt discounted in their role as founding members of Canadian society.

Later, Canada needed the labour of Chinese immigrants to help build the Canadian Pacific Railway, especially for work in the Rocky Mountains. When the railway was completed, eastern European peoples were needed to populate the Prairies, so people such as Ukrainians were sought after. With the emergence of the logging and forest industry of northern Ontario, Finns and other Scandinavians were encouraged to migrate to Canada to work in the bush camps. The result is that today Thunder Bay has a Finnish consulate and the largest Finnish population outside of Finland. Large cities, such as Montreal and Toronto, also experienced a surge of immigration, with enclaves of Italians, Greeks, and Jewish people. In British Columbia Japanese immigrants were important in developing the Pacific coast fisheries and in establishing export connections with Japan. More recently, immigrants of East Asian descent have made important contributions to Canadian life, especially in the economic business sector.

The identity of Canadians is based on recognition of a common national territory with its geographical and cultural diversity. Canadians celebrate their diversity, along with the commonalities of a shared political and economic system. When Prime Minister Trudeau tabled his statement on multiculturalism in the House of Commons in October 1971, Canada clearly began a process of recognizing the inherent worth of cultural diversity, as opposed to the melting pot process of the United States. New immigrants can choose to become absorbed into the larger fabric of Canadian socio-political life, or can maintain a cultural identity of their country of origin. Most newcomers to Canada eventually find themselves somewhere between these two poles, possibly participating in the economic sphere of the country, while maintaining religious and other cultural practices of dress and social interaction particular to their own heritage.

In some cases the boundaries of ethnic identity are strictly maintained, such as among Hutterite or Jewish populations, while for others, such as Italians or Ukrainians, there is a slow process of integration that takes place step by step with each successive generation. For others, discrimination, as experienced by Blacks or Aboriginal peoples, may restrict their fuller participation in Canadian social, economic, and political affairs. Aboriginal peoples, for example, were allowed to vote in federal elections only in the 1960s as they were not actually considered to be Canadian citizens up to that point.

What we can learn from this historical discussion is that identity in Canada is a complex phenomenon involving acculturative experiences, kinship and other social relationships, linguistic symbolism, and political activism. In further examples discussed in this chapter, we will also explore the religious implications of identity in a Toronto Jewish community, the political basis of Métis identity, the Mi'kmaqs' attempt to negotiate Aboriginal identity, and the emergence of Nunavut among the Inuit as a form of cultural revival.

■ Jewish Identity in Toronto

The manner in which ethnic identity is formulated can take many forms. Sometimes it is social, sometimes political, and, in the case of the Jewish community of Toronto, religious as well. In the Jewish case, religion functions as a boundary-maintenance mechanism, defining the sometimes ambiguous edges of the ethnic minority, especially in cases of marriage to non-Jews. Religion, then, plays all-pervasive roles in supporting the integrity of an ethnic minority and also acts as a symbol of social identity. Religion reinforces the commonalities of the Jewish experience, and differentiates this experience from those of non-Jews (Kallen 1977).

Kallen's study focuses on the Jewish community in Toronto. She finds that historical factors are an important aspect of Jewish identity. This is especially the case from the time of the Diaspora, which is the dispersion of the Jewish people from their homeland in Palestine about AD 70, to the formation of the state of Israel in 1948. Throughout this nearly 2,000-year time period, Jews were ethnic minorities in the host nations in which they resided, suffering from many forms of discrimination. Problems of Jewish ethnic identity stemmed from their lack of acceptance in these home countries, which placed them between cultures, unable to find a secure position within either. The national hosts' treatment of Jews also influenced how Jewish people came to view themselves.

A discriminatory historical background has also been responsible for how contemporary Jews in Canada define themselves—as victims of collective discrimination—so their identity is seen as inherently problematic. Discrimination against Jews is still prevalent in Canada today, from the anti-Semitic slogans and swastikas spray-painted on synagogues, to the ranting of the Western Guard in Toronto and the vandalism of Jewish cemeteries. It is small wonder if many Jews feel that Canadians do not accept them, and that they live and work in a hostile environment. From a social and cultural perspective, "Jewishness" as a form of ethnic identity is highly responsive to changes in social and environmental conditions.

Ethnic identity at any one point in time is a complex synthesis of existing historical and social elements that undergo a process of evaluation by individuals themselves, by other members of an ethnic group, and by members of the outside society. As such, Jewish identities in Toronto involve a process of feedback or interplay between internal and external factors, each playing on one another, as the various factors or components of the ethnic identity are evaluated. In the case of Jewish identity, it is founded on three core elements. Religion is probably the most important of these factors. Before the time

---

Box 9.2: Frances Henry: Challenging Racism and Anti-Semitism

Frances Henry is professor emerita of anthropology at York University, Toronto, and is one of Canada's leading experts in the study of racism. She has spent most of her academic career combating racism and anti-Semitism, which has also been an important facet of her personal life as well. Her books include *The Colour of Democracy: Racism in Canadian Society*, 4th ed. (2009), co-authored with Carol Tator, which has been widely used as a university text and has been published in multiple editions. This work demonstrates the authors' pioneering research in this field, such as how the "new racism" is identified with the concept of "democratic racism," manifested within Canadian institutions. She has also written *Racial Profiling: Challenging the Myth of a "Few Bad Apples"* (2006), also co-authored with Carol Tator. As part of her specialization in Caribbean anthropology, she has published the only book on Caribbean communities in Canada, entitled *The Caribbean Diaspora in Toronto: Learning to Live with Racism* (1994).

Until the age of eight, Frances Henry lived in a small town in Germany and was a victim of the Nazi regime. She has experienced anti-Semitism and is no stranger to racism. Frances Henry has participated in the Black culture in Canada and Trinidad as a wife, mother, scholar, and activist. Her choices have located her at times at the margins of Jewish and Black culture. As Henry indicates: "I have felt it personally as a Jewish refugee from Hitler's Germany where much of my family was wiped out. I have since experienced it as the mother of two Black children growing up and going to school in Canada" (1994: xi).

Frances Henry has been a member of the Royal Society of Canada since 1989. She has appeared as an expert witness on the subject of racism, racial discrimination, and prejudice in Canadian society. She has also testified on aspects of Caribbean culture, such as religion and family organization, on behalf of migrants to Canada.

---

of Abraham, Jewish identity was fragmented along various tribal lines. The followers of Abraham were the first of the tribal groups to identify themselves as a specific religious group called the Hebrews. A central aspect of this Judaic religion of the Hebrews was the idea of an ancestral homeland, known as the Land of Israel, which had been promised to Abraham and his followers. Jewish identity, then, became focused on these three aspects: religion (of the Hebrews), ancestry (from Abraham), and an ancestral homeland (the Land of Israel).

For the nearly 2,000 years of the Diaspora, however, these three components of Jewish identity tended to vary through time and place and by individuals and communities. Some Jews, for example, viewed the return to the "Promised Land" with utmost importance. The idea of a territorial point of reference became central in political Zionism, which had the goal of returning Jews to their ancestral homeland. Among other Jews, ethnic identity was more firmly ensconced in an adherence to Judaic law and an observance of the various commandments of this code, such that Jewish identity has a prominent religious focus. Some other Jews rejected their Jewish heritage altogether and

Photo 9.1: Hebrew school picnic at Bowness Park, Calgary, Alberta, 1912. (Source: Glenbow Museum Archives)

became Christians, becoming absorbed into the general population of the host nations in which they lived. One can see from this Jewish example that ethnic identity can involve arbitrary labels and definitions, dependent to a large extent on the fluidity of historical change and shifting social conditions both within and outside the group itself.

In order to protect itself as a distinct ethnic group in Canada, the Jewish community has been engaged in boundary-preservation strategies. These strategies involve rules by which members of the Jewish community guide themselves. These are essentially screening devices that are meant to insulate the community and thereby preserve the core set of principles (Judaic law and customs) and practices (religious observances) of the community in the face of long-term contact with the outside world. One important boundary-maintenance mechanism involves a religious prohibition against intermarriage between Jews and non-Jews unless the non-Jew converted to Judaism. The marriage of a Jewish person to a non-Jewish person was considered the ultimate sin; such individuals were considered to have left their faith, were regarded as dead, and funeral rites were carried out for them. However, from about 1880 to 1920, the mass migration to Canada of Jews who were fleeing anti-Jewish violence in eastern Europe altered the nature of the Jewish community and the interrelationships between Jews and Anglo-Canadians.

The new Jewish immigrants to Canada, who came mostly from segregated ghettos of European cities, favoured a more pluralistic strategy of integration, rather than the more assimilationist orientation of their predecessors. Prior to the 1880s, the Jewish population of Canada was relatively small and there was a reduced social distance between European Jews and their Canadian hosts. The result was a high rate of intermarriage between Anglo-Jews and Anglo-Christians, leading to a high degree of absorption of Jews into the Anglo-Christian community. After 1880, the trend in intermarriage was reversed and the Jewish community adopted stricter rules of interaction with those outside the Jewish community.

For those among the second generation of the Canadian Jewish community—that is, mostly those born in Canada after 1920, there is somewhat of a dichotomy between the Orthodox Jews, who are those committed to a more or less strict adherence to Judaic law, and Conservative Jews, who are more secular and pragmatic in their outlook. Among Conservative Jews, the more isolationist orientation of their Orthodox counterparts is giving way to placing increasing importance on university education and professional occupations. Conservative Jews tend to reside within a predominantly Jewish suburban area close to a Conservative synagogue, but residence patterns are more spread out than is the case with the Orthodox Jewish community.

A third group is the Reform Jewish adults, who tend to identify themselves with both Jewish and Anglo-Canadian reference groups. Members of the Reform Jewish community are even more pragmatic than their Conservative neighbours, and tend to accept only those beliefs and practices that are meaningful in the context of Anglo-Canadian society. Many traditional Judaic observances, such as dietary and Sabbath laws, are rejected as archaic remnants of the past. Unlike the Orthodox and Conservative Jews, Reform-oriented Jews must simultaneously satisfy the demands of two primary reference groups—Jewish and Anglo-Canadian. Their attempt to gain prestige in both groups involves playing the role of middlemen between Jews and members of the Anglo-Canadian society. For example, Reform Jews feel that it is important to sponsor interfaith programs to promote mutual understanding and goodwill between Jews and non-Jews. Orthodox populations disapprove of such interfaith forums because they could lead to intermarriage.

Reform Jews, unlike their Orthodox counterparts, seek to reduce the social distance between themselves and those in the Anglo-Canadian society. The strategy of the Reform Jews is to increase, rather than minimize, contact with the larger society, and they accomplish this by moving to the neighbourhoods of Anglo-Canadians, and seeking membership in their clubs and social groups. Their efforts to gain membership in Anglo-Canadian institutions have not always been successful because of discriminatory barriers and anti-Semitic beliefs. They have adopted a defensive strategy to counteract the effects of these barriers by creating parallel institutions within the Jewish community, based on the Anglo-Christian Canadian model.

The Jewish community in Toronto illustrates the different aspects of ethnic identity among the first (immigrant) and second generation of Jews. It also illustrates differences in contemporary expressions of ethnic identity among the second-generation

Photo 9.2: Calgary Hebrew school graduation ceremonies at a Jewish community centre, Calgary, Alberta, 18 June 1959. (Source: Glenbow Museum Archives)

Orthodox, Conservative, and Reform Jews as these relate to the degree of distinctive ethnic socialization within the immigrant families. Jewish identity tends to be strongest among the Orthodox second-generation families, whose social and religious contacts are more restricted, than among Conservative and Reform families. Orthodox Jews also place a stronger emphasis on a commitment and transmission of Judaic traditions than the other two groups. These three Jewish groups show us that the nature of ethnic socialization, of boundary-maintaining mechanisms, and the degree of social distance are related aspects of an ethnic group's struggles to sustain a distinctive religious and social group in the face of external pressures from the larger Canadian society. However, as Kallen (1977: 116) concludes, "Torontonian Jewish parents and youth alike take pride in identifying with Canada, in nationally defined terms, as their country of birth and/or citizenship."

In a more recent study of Canada's Jews, Tulchinsky (2008) echoes Kallen's conclusion. Tulchinsky suggests that the history of Canada's Jewish community has as much to say about the development of Canada as a nation as it does about the Jewish people themselves. At the time of Jewish emigration to Canada in the late nineteenth to early twentieth century, Canada was firmly under British control. At the same time as Jewish identity was being forged over the ensuing decades, Canada itself was undergoing a transformation in its attempts to establish an identity separate from Britain, while at the same time attempting to prevent the Dominion from being absorbed by American expansion. Tulchinsky's study therefore proposes that the formulation of Jewish identity in Canada emerges as a process concurrent with the emergence of a national Canadian personality.

◼ The Politics of Métis Identity

As far as ethnic groups in Canada are concerned, the Métis find themselves in an ambiguous position. Not really Aboriginal nor Euro-Canadian, but a mix of both, they nonetheless lay claim to a distinctive identity. The Métis originated during the fur trade era, when Scottish and French traders took Aboriginal women as wives. Through time such unions laid the foundation for a burgeoning population in the Canadian North, which began to regard itself as a distinct community. This identity resulted partly from a rejection by their mothers' Indian communities, who called such offspring "burnt sticks," and by their European fathers, who seldom took such children back to their home country when they eventually retired from the fur trade. Nonetheless the Métis regard themselves as Canada's only true indigenous population, and they regard others—including the Indians and Inuit, as well as the Europeans—as immigrants (Purich 1988; Redbird 1980).

With time the Métis population became sufficiently large so that during the time of Louis Riel and Gabriel Dumont, they began to regard themselves as a separate nation with its own laws and political institutions. The so-called "Riel Rebellion" was not so much a revolt as a suppression of a large, organized, and armed population who posed a threat to the new country's sovereignty on the Prairies.

Today the Canadian Constitution makes specific mention of the Métis people of Canada, so one would presume that they have special rights in this country that are distinct from those of other ethnic groups. The Métis also have their own political organizations at both the federal and provincial levels, which means that Métis identity has become a political issue, as well as a social and cultural one. The Métis National Council represents the Métis at the federal level, after breaking away from the Native Council of Canada during the constitutional talks of 1982 (Sawchuk 1982). For many years the Métis and the non-status Indian population formed a loose political amalgamation with common organizations in most provinces, in addition to the Native Council. Over time, however, it became apparent to the Métis that their interests diverged significantly from those of the non-status Indian population.

The political agenda of the non-status Indian people, for example, was to have status restored for those who had lost it as result of enfranchisement, which was mainly due to the marriage of status Indian women to non-status males. With the passage of Bill C-31 in 1985, many people who had lost their status regained it, thus depleting the non-status Indian population of the Native Council and its provincial affiliates. On the other hand, the Métis political agenda is different from that of the non-status Indian

Photo 9.3: Louis Riel (1844–1885), centre of second row, and the councillors of the provisional government of the Métis nation in 1870. Riel was a leader of the Métis people of the Canadian Prairies and a founder of the province of Manitoba. He sought to preserve Métis rights and culture as their homelands in the Northwest came progressively under the Canadian sphere of influence. The Battle of Batoche (9–12 May 1885), Saskatchewan, was the decisive battle in the North-West Rebellion, resulting in the defeat of the Métis provisional government. Riel was hanged for treason in Regina on 16 November 1885, although today he is regarded by many as a Canadian folk hero. (Source: Library and Archives Canada)

population. The Métis are not concerned with a restoration of Indian status since their political agenda is focused on recognition of the Métis as a distinct indigenous society in Canada. The Métis needed their own political organizations to express their concerns, one that was not tied to the objectives of those in the non-status Indian population. Both groups—the Métis and non-status Indians—originally formed a political alliance because they were left out of the distribution of resources, which went mainly to the status Indian population, but with time just the fact that both the Métis and non-status Indian group were sidelined was not sufficient motivation to continue this shared alliance. These divergent political agendas were rooted in differences in the identities that each group wished to present to the larger public in the political arena.

The above discussion of alliances and changing political agendas illustrates the problem of what could be called ethno-status distinctions in Canadian society (Hedican 1991). Today there are dozens of Aboriginal political groups competing among themselves for recognition, legitimacy, and scarce economic resources. The status Indian population—that is, those Aboriginal peoples who are legally recognized as Indians under the Indian Act—are represented by the Assembly of First Nations. The Native Council of Canada continues to represent a diminished non-status Indian population, while the Métis Council of Canada has representatives in most provinces, especially in western Canada. The Inuit Tapiriit Kanatami of Canada is the national-level organization representing Inuit interests across the Canadian North, with various subgroups stretching from the Mackenzie Delta to northern Quebec and Labrador. The Native Women's Association of Canada has a focus on Aboriginal gender issues. In addition, there are many provincial and regional groups with their own interests in land claims, health, economic development, and so on. With so many Aboriginal organizations, there is apt to be considerable confusion over who represents Aboriginal interests in Canada, raising the question as to why so many special interest groups are necessary.

The answer to this question is that Aboriginal identity in Canada is extremely fragmented by such important pieces of legislation as the Indian Act, which officially recognizes some Aboriginal peoples, but not others. Then there are the changes to the Indian Act, such as Bill C-31, which was supposed to eliminate sexual discrimination in the Indian Act, but resulted instead in further fragmenting the status population. Now, while a status Indian can no longer lose status or gain it through marriage, there are nonetheless some status Indians who can pass on their status to future generations, while there are others who cannot. It is all a very confusing and complicated matter that practically needs a constitutional lawyer to sort out, but the issue of Aboriginal social and political fragmentation in Canada seems to get progressively worse with each passing year. In sum, the Indian Act fragments the indigenous population of Canada by dividing this population into those with "status," which is to say those whom the federal government legally recognizes as "Indians," and those indigenous peoples who are "non-status" and, therefore, non-Indians, and who lack the official legitimacy of those in the status category. Thus, the status and non-status indigenous groups tend to compete with each other over scarce resources from various levels of government, both provincial and federal.

It is evident, then, that in Canada an Aboriginal person's ethnic identity is partly a matter of self-identification and partly a matter of government edict. Even if one goes back to the 1920s in Saskatchewan, for example, an individual with mixed Indian-White ancestry was given the option of registering as an Indian with the federal government, thereby acquiring access to band membership, as well as legal status. The membership question at that time was "based upon socio-cultural considerations and the choice of people of aboriginal ancestry either to be treated or not be treated as Indians" (Dyck 1980: 30). In the rest of Canada, band membership was not a matter of choice. As more and more status Indian women lost their status through marriage to those without status, there was an increasing community on the outskirts of reserves of Aboriginal peoples without status. Many of these people, because they were cut off from the reserves' sources of housing and employment, lived in shacks without running water and had few jobs. When commenting on the Métis of the Mackenzie District in the Northwest Territories, Richard Slobodin suggests that these are situations of ethnic segregation: "A partial segregation may be developing at present, however, here, as in some other settlements, for [the] Indian Affairs Branch is assisting Treaty families in the construction of new housing which is being erected on

---

Box 9.3: Personas Mexicanas: Chicano Students in Los Angeles

James Vigil makes a highly pertinent point about ethnicity in his study of Chicano high school students in Los Angeles. It is indicated that "there is much more diversity among the Mexican-American population than ordinarily thought" (1997: vi). The implication is that many people think of "ethnics" in stereotypical terms, seeing such things as language, food, dress, and other cultural characteristics as the defining features held in common by members of one particular ethnic group, and which distinguishes its members from other groups.

In Vigil's ethnography, he posits that in the minds of many Anglo-Americans, the Chicano student population is characterized by exceptionally high dropout rates and poor school performance. The fact that the students are Mexican seems to provide a sufficient explanation for this performance without delving deeper into the issue. Vigil researches the autobiographies of Chicano students and uncovers significant internal differentiation, such that they fall into three identifiable groups: (1) Mexican-oriented, (2) intermediate, and (3) Anglo-oriented. Personal adaptation varies not only with each category, but also *within* each category. After reading this case study, it becomes difficult to make generalizations about students of Mexican descent without identifying which category is used as a reference point of discussion.

This research does, however, mirror to a degree the experience of members of other ethnic groups. For example, for young people, being Mexican is losing its stigma because of greater acceptance by the larger society and an increasing Mexican-American population, which represents a very large voting bloc in many states and is almost 10 percent of today's total American population. Although there are still many families living in poverty, there is also a rising middle class whose members have become increasingly suburban and anglicized. Thus, there is a general move away from the inner city poor and into the larger mass of the working-class population. These trends further reflect a move into the mainstream of the larger society, which has historically been a phenomenon of many ethnic minorities in the United States.

---

two new streets at the back or landward side of the settlement. Non-Treaty Métis families receive no direct assistance in house-building" (1966: 20).

When Desmond Tutu, the famous Black South African leader was taken on a tour to such a community in northern Manitoba, he was appalled, and indicated that nowhere in even the worst conditions in South Africa had he seen such deplorable living conditions. All of these locations are mostly hidden from the public eye, in the isolation of the Canadian North, in one of the richest countries in the world. Similarly, in his study of northern Manitoba Métis settlements, Joe Sawchuk comments on the manner in which housing represents a noticeable boundary between different segments of an Aboriginal community. A visitor, he notes, is taken "to a reserve near his home [and] shows them the relatively new and well-built houses in which the Indians are living. The reserve has no fence or boundary to mark it off, but when driving out of the reserve he points out the dilapidated shacks along the road and says, 'We are now leaving the reserve and entering the Métis community'" (1978: 42). Thus, as far as the Métis of the Canadian North are concerned, ethnic identity is based on deep-seated social, political, and economic issues.

■ The Mi'kmaq of Nova Scotia: Negotiating Identity

The Mi'kmaq are an Algonquian-speaking people, related linguistically to the Ojibwa (Anishenabe) and Cree, who inhabit the East coast of Canada in the provinces of Nova Scotia, New Brunswick, and several surrounding areas. Archaeological research, at the Debert site in Nova Scotia, indicates that Aboriginal peoples have inhabited this area for about 10,000 years. For the most part, their subsistence activities depended upon seasonal hunting and fishing. During the summer months the Mi'kmaq gathered in large social groups comprising several hundred individuals along the Atlantic coastal region. In the fall and winter months they divided into smaller groups comprised of extended family members, and headed inland to the more sheltered areas, where they hunted game such as moose and caribou (Robinson 2005).

The Mi'kmaq encountered Europeans earlier than many other Aboriginal groups in Canada. They were visited by Jesuit missionaries, such as Father Pierre Biard in 1616, who described their subsistence patterns: "In January they have the seal hunting.... If the weather is then favourable, they live in great abundance, and are as haughty as Princes and Kings. From the month of May up to the middle of September, they are free from all anxiety about their food; for the cod are upon the coast, and all kinds of fish and shellfish" (in Robinson 2005: 20–21). Although they depended on a variety of food resources for their daily subsistence, the Mi'kmaq gathered most of their food from the ocean.

The early period of European contact began in the seventeenth and late eighteenth centuries with missionaries' attempts to convert the Mi'kmaq to Christianity. The missionaries attempted to undermine their traditional belief system by calling the religious shamans "devil worshipers" and their religious ceremonies as "diabolical ceremonies." Even today, the Mi'kmaq concept of the "great power" (*kji-manitou*) is equated with the Christian notion of the devil. French trappers and traders influenced Mi'kmaq subsistence patterns with the Europeans' demand for furs, seal, oil, and fish.

The arrival of the British initiated a period of colonization, which led to the Mi'kmaq's loss of control over their traditional lands and the resources in them. Halifax was founded in 1749 and in the following year, 2,500 new settlers arrived, which further restricted the Mi'kmaq's access to their subsistence resources. By the end of the 1700s, the Mi'kmaq were relocated, through the signing of several treaties with the British, to wilderness areas that European settlers considered unsuitable for development. Patterns of deprivation and poverty were already becoming evident among the Mi'kmaq by the first half of the nineteenth century.

Christian missionaries were successful in converting many Mi'kmaq to Catholicism. From the Mi'kmaq's perspective, however, baptism was seen in the context of establishing a political alliance rather than strictly as a religious matter. Language barriers

Photo 9.4: Mi'kmaq women with baskets, possibly three generations of one family. (Source: Notman Studio, Halifax, Nova Scotia Archives)

between the European clergy and the Mi'kmaq led to misunderstandings and ideological difficulties. Even today it is unclear to what extent pre-contact beliefs and religious expressions have been supplanted by Christian religious concepts as in recent years, there has been a steady resurgence of Aboriginal religious traditions. Over the last three decades, the Mi'kmaq have become increasingly involved in a general cultural revival of powwows, sweats, and sacred circles (Robinson 2005: 28–29).

As far as modern Mi'kmaq identity is concerned, the religious situation points to a mixture of traditional and Christian beliefs, but without one clearly dominant over the other. Mi'kmaq identity issues are concerned with accommodating the older, traditional forms of life, with newer ones coming from outside their culture. The Mi'kmaq are not entirely powerless, politically or economically, in this culture contact situation. They are not, as some would presume, passive victims of uncontrollable circumstances. In fact, the Mi'kmaq are attempting to establish a new basis or premise of Aboriginal–White relations in the context of a renewed phase of cultural creativity. In this context, the Mi'kmaq's activities are instructive in drawing our attention to the negotiative aspects of ethno-political behaviour (Larsen 1983).

For the modern Mi'kmaq, political and livelihood issues are intertwined. It is not so much a matter of the Mi'kmaq negotiating a new basis of Aboriginal ethnic identity that is important but of negotiating more directly for the resources that would enhance their livelihood. Since the available resources are severely limited, making an adequate living requires an increase in ethnic awareness, Larsen suggests. Economic assets, such as social assistance and other forms of transfer payments, are scarce, and people compete with each other for them. "Welfare is part of an ethnic estate.... Conflicts are transported to the level of ethnic identity through welfare.... The welfare economy creates a competitive strategic situation" (Larsen 1983: 127). Thus, interpersonal conflicts can ultimately end up becoming an issue of ethnic identity because welfare is seen as a commodity that must be competed for in the local economy.

The Mi'kmaq community has been fragmented to such an extent that the unequivocal identification of "Indians as Indians" has become an almost impossible task. Location of residence is a divisive issue as some Mi'kmaq live on a reserve, while others do not. Some Mi'kmaq are well off economically because they have good jobs, while others dwell in poverty because of unemployment. In addition, many Mi'kmaq have lost their legal status for various reasons, and are therefore not even considered legally as "Indians."

These various divisions in the Mi'kmaq population point to the fact that there is a clear absence of definable criteria of ethnic identity (such as status versus non-status, reserve versus non-reserve), and these discordant variables have detrimentally affected the Mi'kmaq's ability to negotiate effectively with government agencies over resource issues. Larsen's ethnography of the Mi'kmaq's dilemma is put in succinct terms: "The absence of clear criteria also implies that ethnic identity has become a bone of contention among Indians themselves" (1983: 132). It is these sorts of situations involving uncertainty over a concretely definable ethnic identity that increase the difficulty of Aboriginal socio-political life.

Photo 9.5: Birchbark summer camp, Henry Sack and his wife Susan, near Hubbards, Lun. Co.,
1935. (Source: Photographer Constance Fairbanks Piers, Nova Scotia Archives)

What the Mi'kmaq case illustrates is a state of disorientation brought about by conflicting expectations: Do we turn to the past for inspiration, or to the future? A sense of harmony in the Mi'kmaq community is disrupted when there are incongruous expectations. There is a question about who the people should rely on for help—the missionaries, government officials, or their own leaders? This confusion leads also to a sense of ambivalence about how to proceed in the future and about the coping strategies that could be effective in surmounting local problems. Today the Mi'kmaq are struggling with questions of self-identification: Who are we, vis-à-vis others? Are we part of Canadian society, or a separate entity altogether? The Mi'kmaq have a right to ask such questions because they do not seem to be sharing equitably in the rich resources of their country. The issue for many Mi'kmaq is how to get back what has been lost in the past—what has given their life meaning—and, in turn, how to reclaim their Aboriginal identity and feelings of self-worth.

Mi'kmaq identity is not based any single criterion, and even those criteria that are used are at times ambiguous. In terms of language use, for example, many Mi'kmaq still continue to use their Aboriginal language. Language functions as a way of signalling identity, but Mi'kmaq can be used only on reserves, where the people are familiar with the language, which is not always the case with each reserve. On reserves close to large urban centres, fluency in Mi'kmaq is less extensive than in rural areas, where greater use of the language has been retained.

Surnames and place of residence are also modes of identification. However, many surnames that are typically seen as Mi'kmaq (such as Doucette, Paul, Bernard) have a French origin, although there have been Aboriginal names that have been retained. Physical appearance is also not a good indicator of Mi'kmaq identity as there have been three centuries of French (and other European) intermarriage, so there are Mi'kmaq with red hair and blue eyes, who nonetheless see themselves as having a Mi'kmaq heritage. At one time a hunting-and-fishing subsistence economy was an indicator of Mi'kmaq identity, but now these activities are carried out mainly for recreational purposes, whereas wage labour is the most common mode of making a living. Even residence on a reserve does not necessarily "make you an Indian" (Larsen 1983: 60–61).

Even though the criteria signalling Mi'kmaq identity are not always clear, they do have a sense of their own heritage, especially as opposed to Euro-Canadians. The Mi'kmaq take pride in exhibiting their handicrafts, displaying their cultural skills, and re-enacting Aboriginal customs. There is also a sense that they were here first, which justifies the Mi'kmaq's claim to an Aboriginal identity. This sense of ethnic priority in the settlement of North America sets up a situation of delayed exchange, in the sense that First Nations peoples gave up their land or had it taken away, depending on how you view the issue, so that land claims is an important factor in the negotiation process between Aboriginal peoples and Euro-Canadians. It also implies that the settlers and colonizers owe a debt that has not been fully repaid.

This is the sense in which Larsen (1983) uses the term "negotiating identity," and LaRusic (1979) employs it in a study of the Cree, entitled *Negotiating a Way of Life*, which is as a form of exchange between Aboriginals and colonizers. There is a sense among the Mi'kmaq that now is the time to collect the rent for the unbalanced history of colonization. Taken a step further, the Mi'kmaq consider themselves the Aboriginal inhabitants of the country, so compensation is due in the same manner as a thief would be made to compensate the victim of a theft. According to this view, ethnic identity has a negotiative component as an aspect of exchange, in which compensatory principles are bartered back and forth in a legal-governmental framework. Although the Mi'kmaq do not have unequivocal distinguishing markers of ethnic identity that apply to everyone, such as surnames, physical appearance, or place of residence, they do see themselves as Aboriginal people who have suffered from a common experience of oppression in Canadian society. These commonalities of experience "have become the basis of negotiation between Indians and government agencies with which they have to deal" (Larsen 1983: 132).

■ Nunavut: Canada's New Land

The map of Canada changed for the first time in 50 years—since Newfoundland joined Confederation in 1949—when Nunavut became the third territory in the far North on 1 April 1999. Nunavut is comprised of a vast arctic landscape whose residents, in a 1995 referendum, chose Iqaluit to be the capital of the new region carved out of the Northwest Territories. Iqaluit is a government, transportation, and business centre of 4,500 people, situated on the southern tip of Baffin Island. The new premier is Paul Okalik, a 34-year-old lawyer who governs a territorial government of 15,000 residents, of whom about 84 percent claim to have some Inuit ancestry. The residents of Nunavut are scattered in settlements over an area the size of Atlantic Canada and Quebec (Purich 1992; Stout 1997).

Jean Chrétien, the prime minister of Canada at the time of Nunavut's inauguration, was evidently proud of the Inuit's achievement since he was, at one time, the minister of Indian Affairs in the Trudeau government of the 1960s. "It is personally very important to me," said Chrétien in a *National Post* article, "because when I started as minister of Indian and Northern Affairs in 1968, we were discussing at that time to establish responsible government in the Yukon and Northwest Territories. For me to be associated with this great step for the Eastern Arctic is extremely important" (Ohler 1999).

The creation of Nunavut was not the result of a short-term process. The Inuit have been striving for independence and self-sufficiency for many decades (Legere 1998; Mahoney 1999). Despite the initial euphoria of Nunavut's inauguration, the region has nonetheless many challenges to overcome in an attempt to become truly economically independent. Average incomes in Nunavut, compared to those of other Canadians, are very low; unemployment is comparatively high; and drug and alcohol abuse are significant social issues in many Inuit communities. Because of these mounting social and economic ills, some observers have suggested, as Anderssen (1998) has in a *Globe and Mail* article, that Nunavut is destined to become just another Aboriginal welfare case.

Although the problems facing Nunavut residents are far from minor, Premier Okalik appears optimistic about the future. In delivering his oath of office, Okalik pronounced that "Today the people of Nunavut formally join Canada. Today we stand strong and we welcome the changes Nunavut brings" (Ohler 1999). However, it cannot be an easy matter to govern a new territory of several million square kilometres of tundra, ice caps, and rocky, frozen coastline. As other Aboriginal leaders in Canada view the inauguration of Nunavut from their own vantage point, some must be puzzled about how quickly the Inuit have arrived at this rather startling success when they themselves have been grappling with self-government issues for many more decades than the Inuit. The Inuit are still newcomers on the Aboriginal political scene, but they have brought about their proud achievement by using an effective strategy.

The Inuit's success in Nunavut can be summed up in one word—organization. First, the Inuit formed an umbrella political organization in 1971 called the Inuit Tapirisat of Canada (ITC), which was designed to negotiate with outside government officials, land claims, and economic development. The ITC also created several subgroups to deal with such issues as housing in the North and communications with the Inuit Broadcasting Corporation. The Inuit created their own local television shows, which were meaningful to northern residents. The programs circumvented the influx of southern-based television, which disseminated values not consistent with the image that Inuit leaders were attempting to instill in Nunavut's residents. The ITC also articulated its efforts with six regional associations stretching across the Canadian Arctic, such as the Committee for Original People's Entitlement (COPE), founded in 1970 in the Mackenzie Delta community of Inuvik, or the Labrador Inuit Association, established in 1974 at Nain. The Inuit also sent their young people to outside educational institutions so that they could understand Euro-Canadian society and deal with complicated constitutional legal issues. Thus, the social and political movement that culminated in Nunavut must be understood as a complex organizational effort that had specific goals in mind.

Compared to other Aboriginal groups in Canada, the success of the Inuit must appear as a rather sudden success story. It must be mentioned, though, that the Inuit, because of their isolation, have been spared the catastrophic consequences of contact with European societies. Although the Inuit have suffered their share of problems over the last several decades as a result of this contact, the Inuit population was not decimated by smallpox and cholera epidemics, as was the case with other First Nations in Canada. The Inuit territory was also not pillaged by mining, deforestation, and pollution, which destroyed the subsistence base of many other Aboriginal societies.

The isolation of the Inuit has spared them the dubious benefits of the older model of reserves, treaties, and outmoded colonial practices. What is different for the Inuit is that they have been spared the 300 or so years of constant social, economic, and political turmoil that other Aboriginal groups in Canada have experienced. In addition, European settlers preferred the American border region, so that the depletion of game and forests that affected other First Nations peoples did not occur in the Arctic, at least not to the same extent as it did farther south. As a general rule, those Aboriginal groups that were situated the farthest from large-scale European influences suffered less dramatic deleterious consequences of contact. Social distance from colonizing powers acts as a buffer zone, allowing for a measure of cultural continuity among minority indigenous populations.

Photo 9.6: Kenojuak, Inuit Artist, Cape Dorset, N.W.T., 1961. (Source: Library and Archives Canada)

Social and geographical distance has played an important role in the preservation of ethnic identity. The Inuit no longer exhibit the ostensible features of Inuit identity, such as igloos, dogsleds, or hunting whales with bone-tipped harpoons, but the organizational principles that made their adaptation in the Arctic a successful one are still in place. This organization involved the coordination of hunters, manning, for example, different seal breathing holes, or the distribution of game through kinship or other social mechanisms. The Inuit Tapirisat was built on these same principles of group effort in which survival, in an environment where hunting success for any one individual was unpredictable, depended on a social ethic of sharing and co-operation. The overt symbols of Inuit identity have changed, but the more important, deep-seated ones remain intact.

This is not to suggest that sharing and co-operation were not also important cultural characteristics among other Aboriginal groups, it is just that colonial practices more severely disrupted the cultural and social organization of non-Inuit First Nations peoples to a greater degree. Government practices and legislation, such as the Indian Act (which was not applied to the Inuit until 1939), also played a role in dividing non-Inuit Aboriginal societies into many competing subgroups, which inhibited wider organizational efforts. The older model of colonial practices, based on reserves, treaties, and Indian agents, has not proven to be very practical or effective. It has tended to stifle rather than promote local initiative. The new model of interaction upon which Nunavut was founded is based on the concept of indigenous self-determination.

The achievement of this goal is not simply a matter of redefining Aboriginal identity so that it is compatible with new objectives. This goal of self-determination is also contingent upon a striving toward economic self-sufficiency through the control of material resources. At present, the Inuit have little control over the resource base of the Canadian Arctic. It is evident that this fact opens an immense gap between the vision of Nunavut and the practical realities of its implementation. While the people of Nunavut express a desire to break out of the older colonial bonds, over 90 percent of Nunavut's funding is underwritten by the federal government. Part of the problem is that Nunavut, with its present population of 25,000 people, does not have the needed population mass to form a stable tax base, nor is there a sufficiently viable employment base to generate additional consumer spending. When one adds the rising cost of living and the markup of consumer goods due to transportation costs, there is definitely an economic stumbling block to the political initiative of Nunavut self-sufficiency.

Granted, Nunavut's problems are not all economic, nor are they fundamentally any worse than those in many other Aboriginal areas of Canada, yet the Inuit have distinct advantages. One is that they use the same language, *Inuktitut*, which greatly facilitates communication across the vast expanse of the Arctic. They also have a common political structure in Nunavut's government and the Inuit Tapiriit Kanatami (formerly the Inuit Tapirisat), which facilitates decision making. The Inuit are goal-oriented. They decide on what they want to do, then implement a program of action. Although the Inuit people today still live in many scattered settlements across the Arctic, satellite communication has brought the people closer together and has brought about a common sense of destiny and purpose.

■ Ethnic Identity: Summary of Issues

The people of Nunavut may lack a strong economic base at present, but they have begun to overcome the lack of a shared sense of who they are as Aboriginal people. Fleras and Elliot refer to this as a shared "sense of peoplehood." As they explain, prior to Nunavut, "This inability to foster pan-Inuit identity and aboriginality undermined efforts to exert control on central authorities to negotiate territorial self-determination" (Fleras and Elliot 1999: 165). We might therefore conclude that the emergence of this pan-Inuit identity was the most crucial factor in the resurgence of the Arctic

---

Box 9.4: The Irish of Inis Beag: Sex, Repression, and National Identity

Inis Beag (in Gaelic, meaning "Little Island") is a pseudonym for a remote island off the coast of Connemara, in western Ireland. It contains a small, isolated, Gaelic-speaking Irish Catholic community that supports a population of about 350, mostly living by subsistence farming and fishing. The average age at marriage is 36 for men and 25 for women. A man is considered a "boy" until the age of 40.

Messenger's (1983) ethnography of Inis Beag is fairly conventional as he describes subsistence activities, family, community, religious beliefs, and emigration. However, his (1971) discussion of sex and repression has attracted widespread attention. On the basis of his fieldwork (1958–1966), Messenger arrives at the conclusion that the Irish of Inis Beag suffer from extreme sexual repression. He cites the following examples: sexual intercourse is regarded by both sexes as a necessary evil that must be endured; married couples conduct intercourse in the dark and fully clothed; breastfeeding is avoided; dogs are whipped for licking their genitals; and parents will not discuss sexual issues with their children because everyone is so embarrassed by the topic. Drinking and alcohol-fuelled fights result from these repressive attitudes and behaviour.

Messenger presents Inis Beag attitudes concerning sexual issues as a form of deviant behaviour, or even as a pathological perversion, and the blame is clearly placed on the Catholic Church because of the "techniques of social control exercised by the priests and an over-whelming fear of damnation," yet "the islanders know little of church dogma" (1983: 88–89). "The basic personality structure of Inis Beag islanders," Messenger (1983: 107) states, is characterized by "such traits as sexual puritanism, hypochondria, depression, masochism, conformism, and ambivalence towards authority." He also extrapolates, stating that these traits are furthermore a "major component of Irish national character" (1983: 103).

There is no evidence presented to suggest the extent to which the Irish of Inis Beag agree or disagree with Messenger's description of their sexual attitudes or behaviour assessment. Messenger notes that "the islanders still express considerable bitterness over the conditions of poverty and servitude experienced by their ancestors during the 300 years that they lived under alien landlords" (1983: 14), a situation that could make the Irish sensitive about how they are depicted by outsiders, especially if this depiction is considered derogatory. Messenger also notes that a well-known Dublin newspaper feature writer was denounced in the 1960s and not allowed to return to the island after writing a series of articles describing the people of Inis Beag as living in poverty (1983: 24–25).

There is also the widely publicized anthropological study of mental illness and schizophrenia in rural Ireland by Nancy Scheper-Hughes (1979), which was thoroughly denounced in the Irish press and resulted in her prohibition from carrying on further research in Ireland. Her study prompted an outrage almost as strong as that provoked by Frank McCourt's (1996) Pulitzer Prize-winning novel, *Angela's Ashes*, because of his stark depiction of Limerick's appalling poverty. Scheper-Hughes's study, in part, has also sparked a debate about what anthropology's role could be in the rhetoric concerning Irish national identity.

Other anthropologists have entered the fray, with Silverman and Gulliver, for example, arguing that a heavy concentration of anthropological studies focusing on the west of Ireland was, in their opinion, "unacceptable," leading to "a general view of rural Ireland as poor, 'peasant,' and demoralized" (1992: 8). In addition, Brody's (1973) ethnography, *Inishkillane: Change and Decline in the West of Ireland*, would also appear to be a focal point for the sort of criticism evoked by Messenger's study, with Peace (1989: 106) noting that Brody fails "to recognize the diversely creative and innovation processes through which people currently constitute their economic and political lives." Anthropology has served as a mirror with which the Irish might reflect upon themselves, and therefore plays a role in discussion of Irish identity, however that role might be conceived.

---

peoples in shaping their vision of Nunavut. The collective political action that led to the inauguration of Nunavut was preceded by a shared communal awareness that inspired the Inuit to redefine themselves from victims of colonial practices to active promoters of constitutional reform.

The Inuit case study concerning the emergence of Nunavut provides an instructive study of the importance of identity issues in the modern world. Identity links thought and action. It also links culture with political empowerment by providing a vehicle for bringing about a shared vision. It is also evident that ethnicity and identity have become significant socio-political issues in today's world. Many social movements today have resulted from a re-evaluation of ethnic identity. The reason for the formation of such movements is that identity is associated with powerful symbols around which political and social forces coalesce.

In Canadian society, the multicultural ideal as a matter of state policy comes face to face with social, economic, and political realities (Fleras and Elliot 2002). Canada is not free from rigid racial and ethnic sentiments that have led to increased social tension in society. In this regard, Jewish identity in Toronto is based as much on the discriminatory practices of those in the larger society, which has led some Jews to isolate and socially withdraw, as much as it is on a common heritage. The Métis in Canada also struggle with identity issues, but in their case it has more to do with their attempt to present themselves to the large society as a distinct group that deserves special recognition because of their indigenous heritage. Their concern with identity is mainly a problem of reformulating, and then presenting an image that the wider society can recognize. In the Mi'kmaq case, their problem is negotiating the terms of their identity so that they can be beneficiaries of their distinct Aboriginal and legal status.

The Jewish population of Toronto, the Mi'kmaq of Nova Scotia, the Inuit of Nunavut, and the Canadian Métis are quite diverse in terms of ethnic background, cultural traditions, and social composition. Despite these differences, they all struggle with similar identity issues. In all of these groups, the people are attempting to reaffirm a sense of cultural identity that is imbued with positive attributes. The members of all of these groups are attempting to maintain a sense of common social integrity, so that they are not absorbed by the large society. They resist the assimilative pressures that would dissolve their group boundaries, yet must still participate in the larger society to the extent that they are not excluded from the benefits of living in a modern nation-state. Canada's vision of multiculturalism is a work in progress, allowing for cultural diversity in the face of forces promoting integration and unity.

10 Anthropology in the Future

All the great empires of the future will be empires of the mind.

Winston Churchill, 1953

I'm not interested in the future. I'm interested in the future of the future.

Robert Doniger, 1999

—quotes from Michael Crichton, *Timeline* (1999: vi)

Life would become boring in a hurry if we could see into the future, yet terrifying as well, so it's probably best that we cannot do it. Who would want to know the exact time of their death, or that of all their loved ones? It is the unexpected that makes life interesting. Not knowing what to expect keeps us on our toes, but we still like consistency and predictability as well. Even though, as the Doris Day song "Que sera sera" goes, the future is not ours to see, it does not stop us from constantly trying to see ahead of where we are. Remember, today's the tomorrow that some of us dreaded yesterday.

■ Probabilities, Science, and Rituals

People want predictability in their lives. The weather report is an important part of every newscast. If a high-pressure area is forecast for our area, we expect nice weather. Of course it might rain anyway, so all that would happen is a cancellation of our planned trip to the beach. In many societies, though, determining the weather is a crucial aspect of survival. Farmers need to know when to plant their crops, when to harvest, and the rituals to perform in order to prevent catastrophic events such as floods, locust infestations, or any other occurrence that could lead to starvation.

We all assume the sun will rise tomorrow, so we take this for granted because if it does not, then not much matters anyway. For all other situations, since we do not know precisely what will occur tomorrow, we deal with predictability based on the probability of any particular event happening. There are people in our society, such as statisticians, who can tell you that there is a greater probability of being run over by a car as you step off the curb than there is of dying in a plane crash. Even so, when a passenger plane takes off, we might be anxious, half expecting the whole plane to blow up. Off course such things do occur, and frequently enough that we have reason to be apprehensive. There are probabilities worked out for practically every situation that one could think about. And, of course, statistics, the dread of many an undergraduate student, is a fine art in itself with its magical, esoteric formulae.

The expectation or probability of any event occurring leads us to make certain assumptions, but there are situations so serious that we do not want to leave things to chance. Modern politicians have their opinion polls, and it would be unthinkable for them to act without consulting them. Similarly, the ancient Romans consulted the entrails of chickens as a form of *augury* or *divination* before going into battle. The Naskapi or Innu of Labrador, as was discussed earlier, heat up scapula bones before embarking on a caribou hunt. Practically all societies known to anthropologists perform certain rituals to put the odds more in the people's favour. All societies have their *taboos*. Breaking certain rules is seen to bring hardship, bad luck, or even death. Professional baseball players are notorious for their rituals. Many will not change certain articles of clothing if they are on a winning streak. Some will hop over a line on the field, believing that stepping on it will bring misfortune. It would appear that there is some correlation with the likelihood of getting a hit—a .300 hitting percentage is considered excellent—and the degree of uncertainty involved (Gmelch 1982). As uncertainty increases, so does our need for ritual and magic.

Anthropologists and sociologists have had a long-term, enduring interest in ritual, magic, and religion. Emile Durkheim, in *The Elementary Forms of Religious Life* ([1912] 1968), suggested that the functional aspects of religious rituals were most important because they increased social solidarity. When members of a particular society come together to perform rituals, they create common bonds that lead to greater social cohesion. Earlier, Edward Tylor, in *Primitive Culture* (1871), put forward the idea that magic, religion, and science were similar in that they were all attempts to explain what happens in the physical world. However, he also saw these three systems as separate from one another. Magic, according to Tylor, was an attempt to manipulate supernatural forces and beings to act in particular ways. Alternatively, he saw religion as an attempt to appease supernatural forces.

Tylor's theory of religion was based on the idea of *animism*, which was a term that he used to describe a belief in a dual existence for all things—a physical, visible body, and an invisible soul. In animism there is a belief in personalized spiritual beings, such as ghosts, souls, spirits, or gods. Tylor also based his concepts on an evolutionary perspective common at the time. Religion, for example, was seen to have evolved from animism to polytheism (the belief in many deities) to monotheism (the belief in one supreme being).

Today anthropologists do not see religion, magic, and even science in such mutually exclusive ways as many societies have forms of all three aspects in use at various times. In one way or another, all three systems are based on certain assumptions that if ritual acts are performed in an acceptable manner, positive results will occur. We may not be able to explain in all cases why these positive occurrences happen, so in some ways magic and science are not too far apart. They both involve rituals—the scientific method is as good an example of a ritual process as one might find—that, if performed correctly, lead to predictable results.

■ The Future in Fiction

Authors of literary fiction have a free rein to explore any number of social possibilities in the past, present, or future. They are not constrained by the usual laws of science— utilizing time travel, for example, to reach their desired destination. What is interesting about literary fiction from an anthropological point of view is the extent to which concepts of future societies emanate from the social or cultural context in which they are ultimately imbedded. The author's task is to break out of these bonds to some extent— to present a world to the reader's imagination that never existed before as a means of exploring social possibilities.

Take, as an example, H.G. Wells's *The Time Machine* (1895). Published at a time when many people in English society had an overly optimistic view of society's progress, based on the nineteenth-century notion of evolutionary advancement, Wells's dystopic vision of humanity is set nearly a million years in the future. London, at this futuristic time, has seen the evolution of two disparate human forms (races or species?). On the surface, above ground, live the Eloi, who are gentle, childlike creatures living a care-free existence. Living underground are the Morlocks, who were at one time subservient to the Eloi, but now prey on them.

Wells's story is a parable about what happens in the Darwinian model of evolution by natural selection. By setting the novel nearly a million years in the future, we have the opportunity to speculate on what happens when the "lower orders" degenerate, a sort of evolution in reverse. It is also a critique of the nineteenth-century view that human society will inevitably progress into ever more capable beings, ultimately leading to a utopian existence. From Wells's perspective, the Darwinian model as applied to human beings, with its overly optimistic view of human capabilities, is one of inevitable failure. The problem with Wells's portrayal of social evolution is that it appears too directly linked with human physical evolution. Social and cultural change can occur quite rapidly, over a very large scale of humanity, and these changes are in no way dependent upon changes in our physical forms. Just look how much the world has changed over the last 100 years, with its great leap in technological development. If humans are still around in a million years, there is absolutely no way of predicting what human society will be like as the time span is just too great.

Aldous Huxley's *Brave New World* (1932) is another non-utopian view of human society at some indeterminate point in the future. In this world, state power has become so insidiously imbedded in the human consciousness that the boundary between exploitation and happiness has practically disappeared. Sophisticated technologies and mass

Box 10.1: An African Utopia in Nigeria

Nigeria is the most populated country in Africa, with over 150 million residents. It is also known for its oil wells and diverse ethnic mixture of various cultures. One of the interesting ethnographic aspects of Nigeria involves the study of a wealthy theocracy of about 1,200 people situated on the west Pacific coast (Barrett 1977, 1996: 118–128). A community of members with utopian religious ideals was located in an isolated part of the Niger delta, accessible only by canoes and boats. The houses and other buildings were built entirely on stilts or large poles, and an extensive network of boardwalks formed streets, which were so sturdy that cars could even drive upon them. The village was founded in 1947 by a group of fishermen who had been inspired by God. The basis of the community's religious beliefs is a combination of Christianity and indigenous Yoruba beliefs and rituals.

The residents of this utopian community also believe that God has blessed them with immortality on Earth as a reward for their beliefs. As such, they do not have a burial ground because they believe that no member of their community would ever die. They call them-selves the Holy Apostles, and hold to the belief that God wishes them to live a completely communal lifestyle. All private money and financial transactions within the village are com-pletely banned, and all goods, such as food, housing, and clothing, belong to the community as a whole. A community treasury holds the community profits from fishing and other eco-nomic activities, which are reinvested by the *oba* (king) and other members of a ruling elite.

The social organization of the community is also affected by the religious ideals. The family is banned, males and females are divided into different sectors of the village, and mar-riage at various periods of time was also prohibited. The community also became a remark-able success story in economic terms, far greater than any of the dozens of other surrounding villages; however, its political structure is based on the authoritarian rule of an elite class that dominates the rest of the population.

For 20 years the community's success was remarkable, becoming one of the most pros-perous villages in west Africa. After this period, though, the community began a sudden decline and the economy faltered. Community bonds began to disintegrate, possibly because of the authoritarian regime's oppressive control, and residents began to defect to the outside world. In all, this west African utopian community suffered the fate of many other similar communal religious ventures, with a spurt of zealous energy in the beginning, but declining after a generation or so. Few such utopian communities have escaped this fate, but a few groups, such as the Hutterite Bretheran of western Canada, are a notable exception.

consumption have produced a version of social stability in which even human beings are manufactured by a state monopoly. There are five different classes in this society, arranged in a hierarchical order. Social mobility, however, is practically impossible to achieve, allowing the upper class to maintain monopoly on power.

As a commentary on contemporary (for the 1930s and the near future) society, the world state in Huxley's novel is successful in foreseeing a world in which sex and reproduction are uncoupled from emotional experience. This all-out quest for the consumption of goods and services by a population who sees little value in any other pursuit should make readers today squirm in their seats. Is Western humanity really any different today from what Huxley predicted 75 years ago?

As university students in the 1970s we, of course, had all read George Orwell's *Nineteen Eighty-Four* (1949) and wondered, as the fatal year approached, how true his predictions would be. The 1970s was a period of widespread dissent in the university community against state military intervention such as the Vietnam War, and there was the killing at Kent State of students who were involved in peaceful demonstrations. Heroes—John Kennedy, Robert Kennedy, and Martin Luther King—were gunned down. The separation of the youth in America from the older generation was never more evident, as was the state's use of force to subdue dissent. Then we had Watergate, and the Nixon fiasco played out on television day by day, deepening our cynicism.

There was no doubt in many young people's minds that Orwell was a remarkable visionary, and that the apocalyptic insights of *Nineteen Eighty-Four* was upon us with all its stark reality. All of the dangers of totalitarian society are played out for us in our telescreen-monitored world. Big Brother is watching our every move. Citizens are inundated with "Newspeak," and "Thoughtcrime" (rebellious thoughts) is illegal. The protagonist, Winston Smith, works at the Ministry of Truth, altering historical records for the ruling party's benefit. In this novel we are forewarned about the abuses of authority. Television was only in its infancy in Orwell's time, but today we can see how evident its role is in moulding contemporary people's opinions and modes of thought—we might shudder in recognition. Have you ever wondered how many times a day you might appear on a closed-circuit camera? They are just about everywhere—in people's homes, banks, shopping malls, on many street corners, to name a few locations. Police claim that such surveillance reduces crime. Civil liberty groups claim that the public use of such observation posts curtails one's freedom, and usurps the presumption of innocence. Orwell would not have been surprised by such debate.

Isaac Asimov may not have been the greatest of novelists in a literary sense, but his insightful combination of scientific fact and fiction has produced some stunning insights. This is especially the case with *I, Robot* (1950), in which Asimov coined the term "robotics." He also set out the general principles of robotic behaviour, known as the Three Laws of Robotics: (1) robots may not injure human beings, (2) a robot must obey the orders of humans, and (3) a robot must protect its own existence, as long as such protection does not conflict with the first two laws. In a masterful discussion of the topic of robotic "thinking," or robotic psychology, we are led to wonder why it is that we know so little about the artificial intelligence that humans create. Computing was only in its early infancy when Asimov wrote this story in the 1940s, yet his vision of the importance of computer software and our increasing reliance on robotics is amazingly accurate for its time.

Robert Heinlein's *Stranger in a Strange Land* (1961) became even more of a symbol of the 1960s' counterculture than Orwell's oppressive yet quite believable futuristic vision of society. In Heinlein's novel, Valentine Smith, the orphaned son of the first Mars explorer, returns to

Earth. Since he was not socialized in an Earth social environment, Smith must learn to be human. Smith begins to preach his version of spirituality based on free love, and is successful in converting a large following. In one sense we can identify with Smith and his alienation from society as so many young people did in the 1960s, yet we might also reflect on the harm caused by someone with such misanthropic intentions—such as Charles Manson, Branch Davidian leader David Koresh, or Jim Jones of the Peoples Temple—to be distrustful of people's incomprehensible need to follow prophets and ill-fated causes.

Michael Crichton has a knack for turning controversial scientific topics into highly successful novels and movies, such as *The Andromeda Strain* (1969) and *Jurassic Park* (1990). Crichton received an M.D. from Harvard Medical School and has taught anthropology courses at Cambridge University, England, so we would expect that he would have some developed understanding of the influence of science on the human social world. In *The Terminal Man* (1972), for example, we are presented with humanity's predicament with our machines. The main character is a computer scientist who has become obsessed with the notion that machines conspire to take over the world. Neurosurgeons implant a tiny computer in his brain in an attempt to treat his disorder, but the patient eventually goes berserk and wrecks the main computer in the hospital's basement. The issue at hand has to do with societies that are dependent upon complex technologies, especially to the extent that our very survival is based on a reliance on machines and an artificial environment.

In a later novel, *Timeline* (1999), we are introduced to the notion of historical research involving the enduring science fiction theme of time travel. In this case, a group of scientists, using the method of "quantum teleportation," travels to the year 1357 in the Dordogne River region of France. The plot centres on two warring factions of renegade knights, defrocked monks, and several intriguing women. The historians are thrown into this mix and, as one might expect, are barely able to return to their present time after many life-threatening experiences. Ethical issues relating to this variety of research, such as not manipulating past events, are dealt with in a somewhat cavalier manner so as not to get in the way of an interesting story. However, an impassioned plea is made that we accept the novel's premise—that time travel is possible, based on the idea of parallel universes and quantum technology. The reader should consult David Deutsch's *The Fabric of Reality* (1997) and an earlier article in *Scientific American* on "The Quantum Physics of Time Travel" (Deutsch and Lockwood 1994) before one spends a lot of money buying tickets for travel to the great beyond (or behind?).

Perhaps Crichton's most interesting literary endeavour, *Next* (2006), explores the controversial (what else?) topic of genetic engineering and recombinant DNA. Ever since the cloning of Dolly the sheep in 1996, the public and scientific community have become intrigued with the notion of creating new and possibly useful life forms. Of course there are many ethical issues involved, especially when it comes to cloning humans, or even stem-cell research. However, Crichton's novel tends to avoid these messy concerns when we are introduced to the story's main protagonist, who has produced a chimp comprising some of his own DNA. The chimp is capable of speech, and has a relatively large brain, all packed into a typical primate body.

When the scientist is informed by his boss that he must terminate this experiment, he scuttles the chimp out of the laboratory and attempts to pass him off as a member of his family, telling everyone that this is his child who suffers from a hirsute condition. Of course, not everyone falls for this story, especially, as one might expect, the ape's school-teacher, leading to the scientist and his ape son being forced to flee town. Here again the scientific premise is a valid basis for discussion of such important contemporary issues. Unfortunately, Crichton's story tends to degenerate into a sort of scientific Keystone Cops chase around the United States.

The true horrors of our modern age may be much closer than we might expect. In Vincent Lam's Giller Prize–winning novel for Canadian fiction, entitled *Bloodletting & Miraculous Cures* (2006), we are faced with the everyday events of a large Toronto hospital. Lam, a medical doctor as well as author, offers an insider's view of the SARS (Severe Acute Respiratory Syndrome) epidemic, the possible effectiveness (and deficiencies) of Chinese medicine, and tense evac flights to China, where a doctor brings home the SARS virus. But it is in the hospital emergency room, where there are frenzied and febrile attempts to save patients on the brink of death, that we see modern technology stretched to the limits of its capabilities. There is always the human factor as well, as doctors, nurses, and technicians make life-and-death decisions while often suffering from severe fatigue and other incapacitating factors.

There is a scene near the end of Lam's book in which several ambulances arrive at once, leading to a mixup of the diagnoses of two patients. The attending doctor frantically attempts to save the lives of both patients simultaneously, although treating each of them for the wrong symptoms:

> The charge nurse waves the second stretcher into the next bay. The battle extends, now a voice overhead asks for more combatants, for float nurses. I give the orders to each bay. I think I am being clear but maybe I am not. I say, "No, not that one, give it to the other guy." I pull back the curtain between the two stretchers, to see them both. I am floating, moonwalking.... Start CPR on the second guy. Gravity is diluted, and it is too slow ... it all happens drifting sideways. I say, "Push Amio three hundred." It's as if it's compressed into a single moment of rushing, shouting, wrappers on the floor, blood on the arm, foot poking out from under the sheets.... On and on, five minutes, ten minutes. The second guy is getting cold. The second guy dead. (Lam 2006: 328)

The emergency room of a modern city hospital should be the site of an ethnography that details the confusion, drama, and breakneck pace of the everyday battles to save human lives. As if Lam's novel is not scary enough, msn.com news (1 July 2008) reported that a New York City hospital agreed in court to implement reforms at a psychiatric ward, where surveillance footage showed a woman had fallen from her chair, writhing in pain and eventually dying as hospital workers failed to help for more than an hour. Esmin Green, 49, had been waiting for nearly 24 hours in the emergency room when she toppled from her seat, falling face down on the floor. Other patients seated nearby did not react at all. Eventually someone on the medical staff approached, nudging Green with her foot, as if to wake her. The camera footage showed that security guards appeared to notice the prone body at least three times, but made no attempt to see if she needed help. The New York City Health and Hospitals Corporation, which runs the hospital, said six people had been fired as a result, including security personnel and members of the medical staff. Green was born in Jamaica, and the hospital had agreed to fly her body home for burial.

How does a news story such as this make you feel about your society?

■ The Disappearing World

As a general rule, anthropologists have not shown a great deal of interest either in the future directions of their discipline, or in the possible future of human societies. This is a curious matter because one would think that forward-looking viewpoints would be an essential part of trying to determine the direction anthropology is taking. Possibly anthropologists might regard such forward-looking ideas as unfounded speculation, and therefore not worthy of serious intellectual thought. It could also be that a sound theory of social change in the discipline underlies the problem because a lack of a sense of direction is not likely to lead to sound thought on the future directions that human societies should take.

The issue of forward-looking viewpoints in anthropology really comprises two separate areas. First, there is the issue concerning the future direction of anthropology and, second, what anthropologists think the future of human societies will be. A case in point regarding the first issue concerns an article that Levi-Strauss wrote for the journal *Current Anthropology* in the 1960s. We should keep in mind that Claude Levi-Strauss is one of the most creative and imaginative anthropologists that the discipline has ever produced, so his opinions should be held in special regard. In his article entitled "Anthropology: Its Achievements and Future," Levi-Strauss (1966) points to the value of basic ethnography on the vanishing cultures of the world, and in particular to the publications of the Bureau of American Ethnology, founded in 1879. He then warns us that "The day will come when the last primitive culture will have disappeared from the earth, compelling us to realize only too late that the fundamentals of mankind are irretrievably lost.... It is precisely because the so-called primitive peoples are becoming extinct that their study should now be given absolute priority" (1966: 124–125).

So the question that can be asked now, nearly a half-century after Levi-Strauss's plea, is: Has anthropology taken his advice? For the most part, the answer to this question is an unequivocal *no*. Even by the standards of the 1960s, Levi-Strauss's call for a widespread study of so-called dying primitive cultures was largely outmoded. This was the call that an earlier generation of anthropologists were making in the late 1900s, when Aboriginal tribes in the American West, such as the Sioux, Blackfoot, and Comanche, were undergoing rapid cultural disintegration as a result of warfare and slaughter of the buffalo. By the 1960s, anthropologists were becoming far more interested in studying

Box 10.2: Globalization of a Brazilian Fishing Village

Conrad Kottak's (2006) ethnography, *Assault on Paradise*, documents the effects of globalization on the small fishing village of Arembepe in Brazil over a 40-year period. When Kottak's fieldwork first began in the 1960s, Arembepe could be reached by travelling on dirt and sand roads with a four-wheel–drive vehicle. The village population comprised about 750 people, and most men fished for subsistence and cash using an unmotorized fleet of boats. The village had a small market economy, which supported little social differentiation. Besides fishing, villagers grew and sold coconuts, ran small stores, and sold small items from their homes. For women, there were few opportunities to make money.

Over the following decades, Kottak noticed that Arembepe was in a state of flux, as major and dramatic transformations were taking place. One of the most prominent changes was that Arembepe had developed social stratification, with growing wealth disparities becoming increasingly evident. These disparities were most noticeable in the fishing industry. Most fishermen were catching fewer fish per day than in the earlier fieldwork period of the 1960s, but boat owners were drawing 10 times their previous profits. These increases in profits coincided with the motorizing of fishing boats with the help of government loans. However, these loans generally were given to older, more successful captains, who began to prosper more than younger fishermen, who were less successful in securing loans because they lacked sufficient collateral. Younger fishermen were also less able to accumulate enough capital to buy a motorboat through their own fishing efforts.

Profits earned from motorized fishing boats were then reinvested in more costly fishing technology, such as larger and more expensive boats, which, in turn, increased the owner's share of the catch. As the value of property increased, local wealth disparities increased as well. As time went on, a swell of immigrants also became important stakeholders in the local fishing industry, further increasing social distance. Eventually many of Arembepe's young men gave up fishing altogether and sought jobs outside the community, especially in a new titanium factory built by a multinational corporation. On the other hand, new economic opportunities were created for women by developments in the summertime tourist trade, thereby reducing gender stratification.

Globalization is a contemporary phenomenon that refers to the accelerating interdependence of nations, regions, and communities into a world system (Appadurai 1990). This process is primarily an economic one whose spread is facilitated by mass communication media and modern transpirations systems. Television is also an especially important factor in the spread of the globalization process as a moulder of opinion and socialization agent in today's world. Technology and the media have increased a craving for new commodities, opening up a global culture of consumption.

Arembepe has completed a transformation from a basic subsistence-oriented economy to a cash-based market economy. The people of Arembepe now produce goods for exchange in a worldwide capitalist system rather than for local consumption and village markets. In this case study of a Brazilian community's introduction to globalization, it is also evident that global processes are not just economic in nature, but social as well. Social change in Arembepe illustrates the means by which an egalitarian society is transformed into a stratified one through a structural transformation due in large part to the pressure of global forces.

---

the impact of modern society on Aboriginal peoples, especially in the areas of economic development, colonialism, and resource deterioration.

Partly the problem of developing a forward-looking anthropology is a matter also of not having a sufficient number of anthropologists to study all of the interesting possibilities for research. Remember that anthropology is still a relatively small discipline, especially compared with sociology and economics, so that funding for anthropological projects is severely restricted compared to these other larger fields of study. Another issue is that even if anthropologists showed a strong desire to conduct the sort of research that Levi-Strauss was calling for, this type of research is not entirely possible because the subjects of this research are becoming resistant to being studied.

Some of this resistance stems from the less-than-flattering idea that if anthropologists are interested in your culture, then it must be "primitive." There is also the association of anthropology with colonialism (Asad 1973; Lewis 1973). In some people's eyes, anthropologists are associated with missionaries and government agents as oppressors of Aboriginal peoples. Anthropologists may object to this type of label, but then again they have not done a great deal to dispel this misconception, if it could be called one.

The issue of control over research is another problem area, leading to resistance to anthropological research. Aboriginal peoples in Canada, for example, often want to control the research agenda so that they benefit from research, rather than allowing anthropologists to come into their community, conduct research on arcane academic pursuits, then leave without ever making any lasting use of local knowledge. An excellent case in point concerns the research of anthropologist John Cove of Carleton University in Ottawa. In *Shattered Images: Dialogues and Meditations on Tsimshian Narratives*, Cove (1987) relates how he was initially interested in traditional Northwest coast salmon fishing in order to test certain ecological theories about the potlatch. He was awarded a research grant from the National Museum of Man (now the Canadian Museum of Civilization) to conduct fieldwork among the Gitksan, a branch of the Tsimshian.

When Cove arrived in Gitksan territory, he was shocked to find that the Gitksan-Carrier tribal council had refused to give him permission to conduct the research as proposed in his application to the council. "Their grounds," he explained, "were the irrelevancy of my topic to the needs of the people" (1987: 3). Eventually a compromise was reached, but in a radically different form than what Cove had originally planned. The tribal council then requested that he cancel his museum sponsorship on the grounds that they did not want the museum to control Cove's research results, and that he sign a contract with the tribal council. The project was changed so that it focused on traditional land use, the results of which could be used in a court case involving Gitksan land claims. Overall Cove conducted eight fruitful years of research. The people were co-operative because they felt that his research had a direct benefit for them in their land claims dispute.

From today's perspective, it is not a matter of anthropologists rejecting Levi-Strauss's plea for anthropology to focus on a sort of ethnographic salvage operation of dying cultures. It is a matter of Aboriginal peoples becoming more empowered to the extent that they can control aspects of anthropological research, so that both parties—the anthropologists and the local people—benefit from the research. The Gitksan, Cove (1987: 3) explains, "wanted to prepare for both litigation and negotiation of their claim, and consequently needed a systematic analysis of pre-contact society," which was an area of expertise that anthropologists knew about and whose knowledge would benefit the band while at the same time contributing to basis ethnographic research.

■ Beyond Civilization

Paul Bohannan, former president of the American Anthropological Association, presents some intriguing ideas about the future of human society in article entitled "Beyond Civilization." His main point is that every time humans set out to solve a problem, the solution does not fit very well because by the time the future arrives, the conditions have changed so much. He explains his position this way:

> When we reach solutions to today's problems, the society and culture that we will have built for the purpose will be of a sort the world has never seen before. It may be more, or less, civilized than what we have, but it will not be civilization as we know it. (1971: 54–55)

This is certainly not good news. The implication is that our solutions will always be of the stop-gap variety, which are not really solutions at all.

Perhaps Bohannan's prognosis rings a familiar bell with the reader anyway. How are we dealing with such pressing problems today, such as pollution, global warming, the global financial crisis, and genocide in Africa, AIDS, or our dependence on petroleum products? There is a very long list of such issues. Our solutions tend to be makeshift, and we hope someone else will come up with a way to fix the problem. Meanwhile, time marches on.

One of our difficulties, as social scientists, is that we do not have a very firm grasp on how we got to where we are. Since the future tends to be a trajectory of past trends, it is virtually impossible to look forward with any degree of confidence. "Look back in order to see ahead" should be our motto. As far as humans are concerned, the big revolution happened about 10,000 years ago with the development of agriculture. We have always seen this phenomenon as an immense benefit. Living in small-scale societies, chasing animals around, can be a precarious existence. With agriculture, there was a larger, more dependable food source. Population grew rapidly. So also did social hierarchy, the spread of disease, warfare, and the potential for starvation in the event of crop failure on a scale that hunters would never have imagined.

Looking back, have the benefits of agriculture been worth the potential calamity? There are those who think agriculture was a big mistake, and now, having chosen this path, we cannot go back and are destined to total ruination. Jared Diamond (2008), for example, states that agriculture, according to the title of his article, was "The Worst Mistake in the History of the Human Race." He grants that there are advantages to agriculture, although he does not see it as a major advance in culture evolution. First of all, he points out that the hunting-and-gathering way of life has always been given a bum rap, something that University of Toronto anthropologist Richard Lee (1979), on the basis of his research among the !Kung San bushmen (Ju/'hoansi) of the Kalahari Desert, has been suggesting for years.

The !Kung are not necessarily the best example of hunting and gathering because they live in one of the most inhospitable environments on Earth, and are therefore not typical of this way of life. However, as Lee demonstrates, the !Kung probably work less than agriculturalists—possibly less than three or four hours a day are devoted to basic subsistence activities. The rest of the time they devote to ceremonial activities, visiting kin, telling stories, or just resting. It is the women who contribute most of the caloric intake of the group, based on their foraging activities. Men contribute needed protein through hunting, but the group could not live on this activity alone. The !Kung are generally in good health, do not suffer from disease or starvation, despite the ecological limitations of the Kalahari. Population densities are relatively low, and are adjusted to the availability of resources.

Diamond thinks that agriculture was a terrible mistake—"a catastrophe," he suggests, "from which we have never recovered" (2008: 105–106)—and that the "costs" of agriculture have been too high. In agricultural societies, those at the top of the social hierarchy—the elites—have generally enjoyed sufficient food, good health, and a long life. However, those lower down on the scale, such as the landless poor and labouring classes, have not seen the same improvements in life as those in the upper echelons of the socio-economic ladder. Aside from social inequality, we can also add the deleterious effects of agriculture, such as water pollution, soil exhaustion, and disease. Modern agriculture exacerbates the problems even further, with the pollution of our air by tractors and processing plants, chemical poisoning from herbicides, and river diversions associated with dam constructions. As Bohannan observes, "today we know that civilization itself is threatened—threatened by itself" (1971: 50).

We are living in a naive, childish mental state if we think that we will get away with the destruction of our planet. Anthropologists know all too well—and maybe they should be more aggressive in reminding the public of this fact—that there have been hundreds of civilizations that at one time existed on this planet but that are now extinct because they could not adapt. Sometimes the problem is that the societies were not diversified enough, that they were too limited in scope, so that when ecological conditions changed, the people were not capable of adapting to something else. It is evident that our own modern age is like this, and we are likely to suffer the same fate. We have come to rely far too much on petroleum production and the internal combustion engine. As many people say, we are addicted to oil.

Panic is almost setting in as these words are written. The price of running the family auto increases exponentially, day by day, even hour by hour. Yet people lumber around in the suburbs in their SUVs and pickup trucks, many of which are larger than any of the 1950s' Cadillacs. Our Coupe de Ville life is based on a sad illusion of economic prosperity and self-sufficiency.

■ Anthropology's Lessons

Anthropology has compiled a record of many hundreds of cultures, both past and present. Most of these cultures no longer exist. Some died out completely, leaving hardly a trace of their existence, except for a few artifacts and bones. In other cases the people were absorbed into a usually larger society, where, after a few generations, the assimilation process left little of their cultural past. There are also cases where some cultures have managed to survive into the modern age, hardly altered in any fundamental degree from what they were hundreds or even thousands of years ago. The question, in the form of a lesson from anthropology, is this: Can we identify aspects of cultures that have survived for long periods of time, as opposed to those that have died out?

If we examine the cultures that have survived for very long periods of time, there is one fundamental characteristic that tends to stand out—they have not made a significant impact on the environment. They have been sustainable for long periods of time because the people in these cultures do not alter their ecological settings in harmful ways that could threaten their existence. In other words, they are what we would call low-impact cultures.

There are other characteristics as well. Population densities are relatively low, and the people maintain a somewhat equitable balance between the biomass available for food in their environment and their consumption patterns. They also tend to spread out over a large area, thereby also minimizing environmental impacts. The surviving cultures tend to have relatively low energy needs, and are not involved in large-scale projects that result in deforestation, water-diversion activities, or pollution.

In terms of the peoples of North America, the cultures that have survived the longest have tended to live in the more secluded northern areas of the boreal forest. The Cree, northern Ojibwa (Anishenabe), and western Dene (Athapaskan) provide excellent examples of cultures that have survived largely intact for many thousands of years. On the surface, their cultures look different than what they might have been several hundred years ago, but the changes are deceiving as they are more superficial manifestations of change rather than those that are fundamental, or of a core nature to a culture. For example, the Aboriginal peoples no longer wear animal skins as they have adopted many items of Western clothing. Yet many people in these northern areas still wear mittens, moccasins, and even jackets of local manufacture because their durability and warmth are superior to those items made outside.

The northern Aboriginal peoples of Canada may have traded rifles for bows, arrows, and spears. They may have adopted steel traps for wooden ones; they live in log cabins or ones constructed from manufactured lumber rather than in skin or birchbark huts; they use metal pots instead of clay ones, or canvas canoes instead of bark ones. All of these items, however, have been adopted because they make the

"These are humans. Normally they are quite harmless, but if you touch their food or make fun of their beliefs they can become VERY aggressive."

Figure 10.1: One of the lessons of anthropology is that there has never been a culture, or biological species, known to last forever. In the future, what do you think the Homo sapiens *species will be known for?*

Aboriginal person's life easier in the northern bush. The new cultural items merely replace an existing earlier item because it is either more efficient or more durable. These new items have not been used to radically alter their environment, or to deplete the game or other natural resources.

What is being replaced are aspects of material culture. The more fundamental cultural aspects—such as community organization, family and kinship ties, world view, or belief in the supernatural world—remain largely the same as what it was prior to the advent of Europeans. In my own fieldwork in northern Ontario among the Anishenabe, I had an opportunity to experience their culture on a first-hand basis over a relatively long period of time.

My fieldwork was conducted in an Aboriginal village comprising about 150 people, approximately 300 km north of Thunder Bay. Everyone lived in small log cabins. There were no cars, trucks, or roads in this village, nor was there electricity (except for a small generator for the use of the school). The people lived mostly by subsistence hunting, fishing, and berry picking. As far as the economic structure of the community was concerned, there was some cashflow from part-time employment, mostly as guides for tourists. Other money was derived from old-age pensions, widow's allowance, unemployment insurance, and some relief payments. My estimates were that the food derived from the bush was of a much greater quantity and monetary value than store-bought items.

Archaeologists estimate that Aboriginal populations moved into the northern areas of Canada soon after the last ice age some 10,000 years ago (MacDonald 1968; Wright 1976; Dawson 2004). Over this period of time the people have adapted to the warming trend of the post-glacial period and the arrival of Europeans with their goods and ideas. They are also attempting to adjust to the recent threats to their livelihood in northern Ontario caused by the deforestation brought about by the pulp and paper industry, and in northern Quebec by the large-scale flooding brought on by the James Bay Hydroelectric Project.

One wonders what chance our modern industrial society has of lasting 10,000 years compared with the low-impact Aboriginal societies of northern Canada. In all likelihood it will have trouble making it past the next century, given the present rate of environmental damage, population growth, and the ideology of mass consumption. This is not to say that one should advocate returning to the pioneers' way of life because that would hardly be a practical solution to our present problems. But what would be possible is a radically different ideology of consumption, developing less environmentally destructive patterns, and forming modes of living that use economies of space rather than mass urban sprawl. If we wish to avail ourselves of the lessons of anthropology, we must get with an environmentally friendly program, or face the inevitable rubbish heap of failed cultural experiments. At present our future prospects, based on what we know about other cultures, does not appear very bright.

■ The Future of Anthropology in Canada

The fastest-growing field of anthropology at the present time is applied anthropology, and its associated field of medical anthropology (Ervin 2005; Hedican 2008).

Anthropology has changed dramatically over the last century. At one time it used to be sufficient, as a disciplinary goal, to document the disappearing so-called primitive cultures. Today anthropologists have sought to make their discipline more practical, to make it more in tune with the needs of contemporary society in its search for solutions to pressing problems. Anthropologists have begun to jump out of the ivory tower and into the practicalities of everyday life.

Anthropology, or at least the social or cultural version of it, has as its main contribution the study of local-level communities. Anthropologists see social life at the ground level, which usually involves relatively long periods of study. It is these characteristics of a local-level viewpoint, in conjunction with an extended period of study, that make social anthropology unique among the academic disciplines. What this means is that any forward view of anthropology should recognize its strengths and build on them.

For the most part, in the history of anthropology in Canada there has been a focus on Aboriginal peoples. Anthropologists working in Canada have made major contributions to the discipline as a whole with their descriptions of the potlatch and Pacific coast chiefdoms. Anthropologists in Canada have also made unique ethnographic contributions to the study of the Arctic Inuit and their adaptations, as well as to the study of the northern Algonquians and Athapaskans of the Subarctic forests. Furthermore, anthropologists have contributed to the understanding of Canada's multicultural policy through their research on the Jewish community of Toronto, Hutterite colonies in Alberta, the Black settlers of Nova Scotia, working-class culture in Thunder Bay, farmers in rural Quebec, and steelworker families in Hamilton. Certainly this does not exhaust the lengthy list of ethnographic research that demonstrates Canada's ethnic vitality.

As applied anthropology gains strength in Canada, it will begin to assume a greater focus for research in the future. This focus will involve a search for solutions to various economic, social, and political problems facing the Canadian people. One of the major future issues is the problem of mutual coexistence within the multicultural framework. Francophones in Quebec have voiced a concern over their perceived inequities, which need to be addressed if Canada is to remain one country. Anthropologists can contribute to a better understanding of the needs and aspirations of ethnic minorities such as the French-speaking people of Quebec, of the disadvantaged maritime populations, as well as the long-standing difficulties that Aboriginal peoples have suffered almost from the beginning of European settlement.

There are also important resource issues that need to be addressed because these impact significantly on local populations. Canada has built its wealth through resource-extraction industries in the areas of mining, fishing, and forestry. Fish stocks are diminishing in our coastal waters, and the pulp and paper industry in Canada has declined dramatically because of deforestation. In the local communities that depend on these resources, there is a pressing need to find alternative means of employment. Anthropologists can aid in this search by assessing the skill levels of local people to determine possibilities for developing new local employment opportunities that make use of local resources.

Employment is also a pressing need among Aboriginal populations who have some of the highest unemployment levels in all of Canada. Since many Aboriginal communities are situated in rural and remote areas, there is a pressing need for creative thinking about ways to provide local employment that is compatible with these distances from markets and does not negatively impact the surrounding environment. Anthropology students of the future will, hopefully, lend their expertise to the expanding areas of research opportunities in Canada, and thereby contribute to a vibrant and unique intellectual tradition extending into the decades of this new millennium. Humans' capacity for creative thought and their curiosity in the world around them will be pushed to the limit if they are to survive in the future. Above all, as anthropological studies amply indicate, the lessons of the past cannot be forgotten if species-threatening mistakes are to be avoided in the future.

Appendix: Internet Resources

■ Aboriginal Organizations

Assembly of First Nations (AFN)
www.afn.ca
The Assembly of First Nations is the representative organization of the First Nations in Canada, comprising over 630 communities. It is designated to present the views of the various First Nations (Aboriginal peoples with status under the Indian Act) through their leaders in such areas as Aboriginal and treaty rights, economic development, education, and justice issues. National Chief is Shawn Atleo, hereditary chief of the Ahousaht nation, Vancouver Island, British Columbia.

Inuit Tapiriit Kanatami (ITK)
www.itk.ca
The Inuit Tapiriit Kanatami, formerly the Inuit Tapirisat of Canada, was founded in 1971 and is the national Inuit organization of Canada. It represents the four Inuit regions— Nunatsiavut (Labrador), Nunavik (northern Quebec), Nunavut, and the Inuvialuit Settlement Region in the Northwest Territories, comprising 55,000 Inuit living in 53 communities. The ITK president is Mary Simon, who was born in northern Quebec on the Ungava coast.

Métis National Council (MNC)
www.metisnation.ca
The Métis National Council is a national-level political and cultural organization founded in 1983 with the goal of promoting Métis self-government. Its activities also include the establishment of a Métis National Registry and it works toward ensuring the harvesting rights of Métis nation citizens. The president of the MNC is Clement Chartier.

National Association of Friendship Centres (NAFC)
www.nafc.ca
The National Association of Friendship Centres is dedicated to the improvement of the quality of life of Aboriginal peoples in urban environments by supporting activities that encourage access to, and participation in, Canadian society. The NAFC is a network of 117 friendship centres and seven provincial/territorial associations nationwide. The NAFC president is Vera Pawis Tabobondung.

■ Academic Associations and Societies

Canadian Anthropology Society (CASCA)
www.cas-sca.ca
CASCA was originally founded in 1974 as the Canadian Ethnology Society (CESCE). Today CASCA has over 500 members from across Canada and around the world. Its aims are to ensure continuing financial support for anthropological research, and to commit to excellence in Canadian anthropology graduate programs and in the teaching of undergraduate anthropology.

Canadian Association for Physical Anthropology (CAPA)
www.capa.fenali.net
CAPA is an association of about 100 members whose aim is to increase awareness and understanding of physical (biological) anthropology. Physical anthropologists study adaptation, variability, and evolution in a biocultural context. The discipline is multidisciplinary, crossing the boundaries between the natural and social sciences in order to provide an understanding of human diversity and complexity. A journal, the *Canadian Review of Physical Anthropology*, was published in the years 1979–1988, and back issues are available online. Today CAPA publishes a newsletter in place of the journal.

Canadian Ethnic Studies Association (CESA)
www.confmanager.com
The CESA was founded in 1971 with goals to stimulate scholarly debate about current theoretical and practical issues in the area of ethnic studies. It also seeks to encourage understanding among Canadians of diverse cultural heritages by fostering equal participation in Canadian society.

Society of Applied Anthropology (SFAA)
www.sfaa.net
SFAA aspires to promote the integration of anthropological perspectives and methods in solving human problems throughout the world, and to advocate for fair and just public policy based on sound research.

■ Careers in Anthropology

JobRapido
www.job-rapido.ca/anthropology
Lists everything from student assistants, field archaeology, forensic anthropology, and college positions across Canada.

◾ Government Departments and Agencies

Indian and Northern Affairs Canada (INAC)
www.ainc-inac.gc.ca
INAC is one of the federal government departments responsible for meeting Canada's obligations to First Nations, Inuit, and Métis, and for fulfilling the federal government's constitutional responsibilities in the North. INAC is one of 34 federal departments and agencies involved in Aboriginal and northern programs and services. Hon. John Duncan, minister of INAC.

Ontario Ministry of Aboriginal Affairs (OMAA)
www.aboriginalaffairs.gov.on.ca
The Ontario Ministry of Aboriginal Affairs was established in 2007 as a stand-alone ministry that replaced the Ontario Secretariat of Aboriginal Affairs. OMAA's mandate is to promote collaboration and coordination across ministries on Aboriginal policy and programs. The OMAA minister is the Hon. Chris Bentley.

Status of Women Canada
www.swc-cfc.gc.ca
Status of Women Canada is a federal government organization that promotes equality for women and their full participation in the economic and democratic life of Canada. Hon. Rona Ambrose, minister of Status of Women.

◾ Journals

Anthropologica
www.anthropologica.ca
Anthropologica is the official publication of the Canadian Anthropology Society (CASCA). It publishes peer-reviewed articles in both French and English that are devoted to social and cultural issues, whether they are prehistoric, biological, linguistic, applied, or theoretical in orientation.

Canadian Ethnic Studies (CES)
www.umanitoba.ca/publications/ces
Canadian Ethnic Studies is a peer-reviewed, interdisciplinary journal founded in 1969 and devoted to the study of ethnicity, migration, inter-group relations, and the history and cultural life of ethnic groups in Canada.

Canadian Journal of Native Studies (CJNS)
www2.brandonu.ca/library/cjns
The CJNS is the official publication of the Canadian Indian/Native Studies Association. The journal publishes original research in the field of Native studies and, although the majority

of articles deal with indigenous peoples of Canada, it also publishes articles dealing with indigenous peoples worldwide.

Current Anthropology (CA)
www.journals.uchicago.edu/CA
Current Anthropology is a peer-reviewed academic journal sponsored by the Wenner-Gren Foundation for Anthropological Research. CA publishes across all subdisciplines of anthropology, encompassing the full range of anthropological scholarship on human cultures. It is especially noted for its topical articles, which usually include added commentaries from noted anthropologists in the field.

Ethnology: An International Journal of Cultural and Social Anthropology
www.pitt.educ/~ethnolog/
Ethnology was founded in 1962 with the goal of offering the broadest range of general cultural and social anthropology. The journal provides its readers with an opportunity to stay rooted in traditional anthropology, while keeping current with new directions in the field.

Human Organization
www.sfaa.metapress.com
Human Organization is the journal of the Society of Applied Anthropology. The journal regularly includes sections on government and industry, health and medical care, and international affairs. A special emphasis is given to the practical aspects of anthropological research and the possible roles that anthropologists could play in non-academic settings.

International Indigenous Policy Journal (IIPJ)
www.iipj.org
The IIPJ is a peer-reviewed journal led by an advisory board made up of distinguished people from Australia, Canada, the U.S., and the Russian Federation. Among the journal's goals is to promote evidence-based policy-making, and to encourage equality-based research on partnerships with indigenous peoples.

■ Museums and Archives

Canadian Museum of Civilization
www.civilization.ca
The history of the Canadian Museum of Civilization began in 1856 with its establishment by the Geological Survey of Canada. Today the museum, located in Gatineau, Quebec, directly opposite Parliament Hill, is divided into a Research and Collections Branch. Research is conducted in the fields of archaeology, ethnology (particularly First Nations of northern North America), folklore, and Canadian history.

Glenbow Museum
www.glenbow.org

Calgary's Glenbow Museum was established in 1954 based on an extensive collection of western Canadian and international artifacts donated by oil magnate, Eric Harvey. Today the museum has a particularly large collection of unpublished documents, photographs, and material culture relating to Aboriginal peoples, frontier exploration, and the development of western life.

Hudson's Bay Company Archives (HBCA)
www.gov.man.ca/chc/archives/hbca

The Hudson's Bay Company was founded in 1670 by a Royal charter and given access to a vast territory in Canada's North, called Rupert's Land. The HBC archives are a treasure trove of documents and related material relating to the fur trade and the later development of a retail empire. A microfilm service is available, as well as opportunities for family history research, which can be accessed through your local library.

Museum of Anthropology, University of British Columbia
www.moa.ubc.ca

Vancouver's Museum of Anthropology was founded in 1949 and is renowned for its spectacular architecture and unique setting overlooking the surrounding mountains and Pacific Ocean. The museum's collections and exhibitions give access and insight into the cultures of indigenous peoples around the world. Visitors are greeted by massive totem poles and other Northwest coast artifacts in the museum's Great Hall.

Provincial Museum of Newfoundland and Labrador
www.thecanadianencyclopedia.com

The Provincial Museum of Newfoundland and Labrador, located in St. John's, contains permanent exhibits on the history of Newfoundland and Labrador fishing, industry, archaeology, and ethnology of the province. The museum also contains an extensive collection of Aboriginal material culture from the Innu, Mi'kmaq, and Inuit, as well as archaeological material associated with the Beothuk, Thule, and Maritime Archaic cultures.

Royal Ontario Museum (ROM)
www.rom.on.ca

The Royal Ontario Museum's diverse collections of world cultures and natural history make the ROM one of the largest museums in North America. The ROM is also the largest field-research institution in Canada with research and conservation activities that span the globe. It also participates in an active publication program, as well as an online image collection of ROM artifacts and specimens.

■ Research and References

Aboriginal Canada Portal (ACP)
www.aboriginalcanada.gc.ca

The ACP contains links to research on various topics, such as governance, education, housing, and social development. It has links to census results and analysis pertaining to Aboriginal populations in Canada and historical maps of First Nations, Inuit, and Métis.

Anthropological Index Online (AIO)
www.aio.anthropology.org.uk

Anthropological Index Online provides a searchable index to the contents of over 770 journals and publishers in more than 40 languages, and from all academic institutions around the world. Publications can be searched by year (beginning in the early 1950s), title, author, journal, or subject area.

Anthropology.net
www.anthropology.net

The mission of anthropology.net is to create a cohesive online community of individuals in anthropology. It provides extensive links and references for all areas of anthropology, reviews websites, and provides interesting articles and commentary on topical issues.

Anthropology Tech
www.anthrotech.com

"Making anthropology matter to people" is the motto of this website. Anthro Tech, founded in 1998, provides cost-effective technological services for start-up ventures, non-profit organizations, government agencies, and small businesses specifically in the areas of ethnography and rapid needs assessment.

Human Relations Area Files (HRAF)
www.yale.edu/hraf/

The Human Relations Area Files, founded in 1949 at Yale University, is a global compilation of cultural material ranging from kinship, religion, political organization, and most other related aspects of social and economic organization. The mission of HRAF is to encourage and facilitate worldwide comparative studies of human behaviour, society, and culture.

■ Related Subjects

Black Settlement in Nova Scotia
www.museum.gov.ns.ca

This website provides a number of links to information on Black Loyalists who settled in Nova Scotia between 1783 and 1785 as a result of slavery and persecution during the American Revolution. There is also a description of an archaeological excavation of Birchtown (1784), a Black Loyalist community in southern Nova Scotia.

Centre for Refugee Studies (CRS), York University
www.crs.yorku.ca
The CRS is engaged in providing information for public discussion and policy development, and supports teaching and refugee and migration studies. Refugee studies are conceived in broad terms as being concerned with the displacement of populations for reasons of persecution, expulsion, and violation of human rights.

Hutterian Brethren
www.ualberta.ca/~german/PAA/Hutterites
Provides research and historical material on the Hutterite Brethren of Alberta from their emigration from eastern Europe in the nineteenth century, the social organization of Hutterite colonies, education, work, and religious beliefs.

Glossary

Aboriginal:	The indigenous or original inhabitants of a particular territory.
acculturation:	The process of interaction between two societies in which the culture of the society in the subordinate position is drastically modified to conform to the culture of the dominant society.
achieved status:	A position in society that is earned rather than inherited; contrasts with ascribed status.
action anthropology:	See "applied anthropology."
adaptation:	A process whereby populations adjust either biologically or behaviourally to social or physical environments in such a way as to enhance their survival.
affinity:	Related by marriage; see "consanguinity."
age-grade system:	See "rite of passage."
Algonquian (Algonkian):	The largest language family in Canada, including such groups as the Cree, Blackfoot, and Mi'kmaq.
ambilineal descent:	A form of cognatic descent in which individuals have a choice of reckoning their descent links either through maternal or paternal lines.
ambilocal residence:	A post-marital residence pattern in which a couple reside after marriage with either the husband's or the wife's relatives.
animism:	The belief in the existence of spiritual beings, or the "theory of souls," as posited by Edward Tylor, a nineteenth-century anthropologist.
Anishenabe:	The Ojibwa's term for themselves, usually translated as meaning "original people."
anthropology:	A term derived from two Greek words, *anthropos* for "human" and *logos* for the "study of"; the scientific study of humankind from social and biological perspectives.
apical ancestor:	The founding ancestor of a unilineal descent group through which all subsequent members are descended.
Apollonian:	A configuration of culture that emphasizes restraint and moderation in human conduct. A term used

	by Ruth Benedict (1887–1948) in reference to the psychological characteristics of the Zuni; contrasts with Dionysian.
applied anthropology:	The study of the practical applications of anthropological knowledge, especially in terms of solving social problems.
archaeology:	The scientific study of extinct cultures through the examination of material artifacts and remains, although some recent archaeology, termed "salvage archaeology," studies the material remains of still surviving societies.
armchair anthropology:	A somewhat derogatory term for a period of anthropology in which research was based on the reports of travellers, missionaries, traders, or other secondary sources; research not based on first-hand ethnographic research.
ascribed status:	A position in society that is based on one's birth or inheritance, rather than one earned through individual effort, such as those based on sex or descent; see "achieved status."
assimilation:	An ethnic group's loss of identity because of its absorption into the society of a dominant group.
australopithecines:	One of any of the varieties of fossil hominids who lived in southern Africa about 2.4–3 million years ago, believed to be the ancestors of modern humans. They had relatively small brains, but had upright posture and were able to walk on two legs, referred to as bipedalism.
avoidance relationship:	The inhibition of social interaction, especially between affinal relatives.
avunculate:	The complex of special relations between a mother's brother and his sister's child.
avunculocal:	A post-marital residence pattern in which the married couple reside with the husband's mother's brother.
band:	A territorial-based social group, usually of relatively small-scale, who live by hunting and gathering; one of four cultural types, such as tribe, chiefdom, and state.
bilateral descent:	The system of kinship structure in which an individual belongs equally to the kindred of both parents.
bilocal:	A post-marital residence pattern in which the married couple live with either the parents of the bride or groom.

Boasian:	Refers to the research perspective characteristic of Franz Boas (1858–1942).
bride service:	See "suitor service."
bridewealth:	See "progeny price."
case studies:	A research technique in which specific instances or cases are utilized to illustrate general points of discussion.
chain migration:	A migratory pattern based on a flow of individuals in a linked sequence from one location to another; usually based on commonalities of kinship and location of origin.
chiefdom:	A type of socio-political organization characterized by a centralized political structure, a redistributive economy, and a large sedentary population; intermediate between tribal and state-level societies.
childhood familiarity theory:	An explanation of the incest taboo promoted by Edward Westermarck; see also "natural aversion theory."
clan (sib):	A unilineal kin group in which its members regard themselves as descended from a common ancestor, usually legendary or mythological.
classificatory kinship terminology:	A system of kin reckoning in which members of a nuclear family are classified along with distant relatives in each generation. For example, in the Iroquois system, a person refers to one's father's brother with the same term that is used for one's "father" and, correspondingly, one's mother's sister is called by the same term that is used for one's "mother." Also, in accordance with this system, the terms "brother" and "sister" are further extended to include one's parallel cousins, which is to say, the children of one's mother's sister and father's brother.
cognates:	Words that sound alike, have a similar meaning, and are ultimately derived from the same source, e.g., father and *pater*, or horn and cornu.
cognatic descent:	A form of kin reckoning in which relationships are traced through both males and females.
collaterals:	People who trace descent from a common ancestor and are consanguineal kin, but in different lines of descent, such as cousins.
colonialism:	A policy whereby a nation seeks to establish a long-term socio-political and economic domination over another people, usually by the installation of an administrative structure using members of the dominant society to facilitate control.

complementary opposition:	See "segmentary lineages."
configurationalism:	The theoretical orientation holding that the distinctive and characteristic quality of a culture derives from the special relationship of its parts to one another, especially in terms of the unconscious psychological patterns or configurations that are seen to account for cultural patterns; primarily associated with Ruth Benedict (1887–1948).
consanguinity:	Literally means "blood relationships," which is to say, descent based on kinship connections rather that those through marriage; see "affinity."
consensus:	A process of decision making based on negotiation and discussion, as opposed to decisions dictated by a single individual or group; usually found in bands and tribes.
cooring:	An Irish term for a pattern of agricultural co-operation and mutual support.
core:	As used in the concept of "culture core" espoused by Julian Steward (1902–1972) to refer to cultural practices linked directly to the exploitation of environmental resources.
coup:	An attested deed of valour among the Aboriginal societies of the Plains.
cross-cousins:	Cousins whose related parents are siblings of unlike sex. Offspring of a person's mother's brother or father's sister.
cultural ecology:	An anthropological approach primarily associated with Julian Steward that focuses on the environmental effects of cultural behaviour in such areas as labour patterns, exchange systems, and socio-political organization.
cultural evolutionism:	Seeks to understand cultural similarities and differences in terms of adaptation through time. Two distinct evolutionary theories have emerged in anthropology, such as the largely discredited unilinear evolutionary perspectives of the nineteenth century, and the more modern ecological approaches of Julian Steward, among others.
cultural materialism:	A theoretical orientation in anthropology that concentrates on cross-cultural similarities and differences in terms of the material and ecological constraints on human activity; is associated with mode of production and mode of reproduction

	as espoused primarily by anthropologist Marvin Harris; see also "nomothetic."
cultural relativism:	See "relativism" and "historical particularism."
culture:	The integrated sum total of learned behaviour traits characteristic of the members of a society.
culture and personality school:	Focuses on the relationship between cultural patterns and personality traits drawing on Freudian psychology; a field of study in anthropology concerned with the cross-cultural variations in personality and psychological traits.
culture area:	A geographical territory within which the cultures tend to be similar in some significant aspects, such as subsistence strategies or social organization.
deductive method:	A form of logical reasoning in which general principles are derived from particular instances; logical analysis in which certain propositions are proposed and resulting consequences are stipulated; contrasts with inductive method.
Dene:	A term used in Athapaskan languages of northwestern Canada, meaning "the people."
descent group:	A social unit in which members claim descent from a common ancestor.
descriptive kinship terminology:	A system of kinship reckoning in which there are many separate terms for different relatives. For example, separate terms are used for "father" and "father's brother," and separate terms distinguish "brother" and "sister" from "cousin"; a kinship system separating collateral and lineal kin.
descriptive linguistics:	Linguistic analysis focusing on the structure and composition of language, such as the study of phonemes and morphemes; contrasts with historical linguistics.
dialectics:	An approach developed by Georg Hegel (1770–1831) to explain the historical movement of ideas; development of sequential stages of thesis-antithesis-synthesis.
dialogical approach:	The use of texts to represent the encounter between native informants and ethnographers; a form of dialogue in which the voice of the Other has a priority.
diffusionism:	A perspective in anthropology in which a central importance is given to the transfer of traits between cultures as the main mechanism of cultural change.
Dionysian:	A term used by Ruth Benedict to refer to the cultural characteristics of such societies as the Kwakiutl, who

are seen as highly competitive and individualistic; contrasts with Apollonian.

double descent: The existence of a maternal and a paternal descent system side by side within the same culture.

dowry: A transfer of goods or money from the bride's family to the bride; representing compensation for the future support of the woman and her future children.

ecology: A field of study pertaining to the interrelationships between living populations and their habitats.

egalitarian society: A population characterized by the near absence of private property, and lacking for the most part in distinctions in power, status, and privilege; societies in which everyone has equal access to productive resources.

emic analysis: A focus on the rules and concepts that are meaningful to the members of a particular society; an insider's point of view; contrasts with etic analysis, or an outsider's viewpoint.

empiricism: A perspective which holds that meaningful knowledge should be based on experience and concrete reality, rather than on mental or intellectual speculation.

enculturation: The process by which the individual learns and assimilates the patterns of a culture; the patterns by which cultural traditions are transmitted from one generation to the next.

endogamy: The rule of marriage that requires a person to marry within a given social group (e.g., clans or classes) of which he or she is a member; contrasts with exogamy.

environmental determinism: A perspective holding that social and cultural phenomenon are determined principally by mechanisms of the natural habitat in which a population is found.

epistemology: The study of the nature of human knowledge; how it is that we know what we know.

ethnocentrism: The making of value judgments concerning other people or their culture on the basis of a belief in the superiority of one's own way of life or cultural standards.

ethnography: A division of anthropology devoted to the descriptive recording of cultures based on research techniques, such as participant observation, carried out through fieldwork.

ethnology: A division of anthropology devoted to the analysis, systematic interpretation, and comparison of cultural material with the intention of producing meaningful generalization about human behaviour.

etic analysis: Pertaining to concepts and rules meaningful to an outsider's point of view (e.g., scientific viewpoint); contrasts with an insider's viewpoint or emic analysis.

evolution, cultural: Modification of culture patterns in a given direction through persistent social change.

evolution, general: A theoretical orientation that purports to express modifications characteristic of all cultures at specific stages of their development.

evolution, multilineal: A theoretical orientation that purports to express modifications only of like cultures.

evolution, specific: A theoretical orientation that purports to express changes characteristic of specific cultures.

evolution, unilinear: The evolution of social forms from a universal and ordered sequence: a theoretical process.

exogamy: Marriage outside of a specific social group of which a person is a member, as required by custom or law; contrasts with endogamy.

explanation: The use of abstract propositions, such as theories, and specific propositions, such as hypotheses, in an attempt to represent the manner in which reality is constituted and represented.

family, conjugal (family of procreation): A social group consisting of spouses and their offspring.

family, consanguine: The kinship group formed by a woman, her children, and her brothers.

family, extended: A social group consisting of near relatives in addition to the mated pair and their offspring.

fictive kinship: The extension of kinship terms to individuals who are not actually relatives either by descent or marriage.

fieldwork: In social anthropology, the main technique used to gather information on human behaviour; usually means living for an extended period of time in a human population and conducting research by participating and observing people in different cultures; see also "ethnography."

functionalism:	A theoretical and methodological approach to anthropology that emphasizes concern with the part each unit within a culture plays in the total existence of the culture; a label for a theoretical perspective developed by British anthropologist Bronislaw Malinowski (1884–1942), which focuses on the function of institutions in fulfilling biological and psychological needs that support the maintenance of the social system; a theoretical approach derived in anthropology from the French sociologist Emile Durkheim (1858–1917), which stressed the role of social institutions in promoting social solidarity and providing security for the individual; see "structural functionalism."
Galton's problem:	Francis Galton posed a question during the meeting of the Royal Society in Britain in 1889 concerning the independence of cultural traits: whether similarities in cultural traits were the result of a common source, or if the observed commonalities were the result of interaction processes, such as diffusion or other forms of cultural borrowing.
generalized reciprocity (or exchange):	From the perspective of French anthropologist Claude Levi-Strauss (1908–2009); refers to the exchange of women among several kinship groups, which strengthens social bonds among such groups.
genitor:	A Latin term referring to the biological male parent of a child. In some societies a distinction is made between the status of the genitor and that of the pater—the legal father—whose status has been established with a marriage to the child's mother. However, in most cases the genitor and the pater are the same individual. See "pater."
glottochronology:	A method for determining the time period for the separation of related languages thought to have a common source or ancestral language, based on certain statistical techniques and assumptions about the rate by which languages change through time; also referred to as lexicostatistical dating.
heuristic (device):	Refers to a concept that may lack meaning by itself, but that can be used to facilitate understanding of other phenomenon, such as the use of a mathematical model, which in itself is an artificial abstraction of nature, but which may prove useful in understanding natural processes.

historical linguistics:	The study of the manner, characteristics, and processes by which languages change over time.
historical particularism:	A theoretical perspective associated with American anthropologist Franz Boas (1858–1942) that is essentially relativistic and anti-scientific; stresses the uniqueness of each individual culture and the historical developments that have led to particular cultural characteristics; see "relativism."
holistic:	An approach used by anthropologists that is comprehensive in scope such that all aspects of human life, biological and cultural, are considered important in understanding behaviour.
hominid (hominidae):	The taxonomic family, including all living and extinct types and races of humans and protohumans, such as the australopithecines and neanderthals.
Homo erectus:	Emerged in Africa and migrated to Europe and Asia. *H. erectus* is succeeded by the oldest member of our species, *H. sapiens*.
Homo habilis:	The earliest species in the genus of hominids, known for manufacturing tools. *Homo habilis* was discovered at many sites in eastern Africa and dates to about 2 million years ago.
Homo sapiens:	Considered an ancestor of modern humans. *Homo sapiens* extended back from Africa, to Europe, and into Asia, and appear in the fossil record about from 1.6 million years ago to 400,000 years ago.
horticulture:	Cultivation of crops using simple hand tools, such as a hoe and digging stick, without fertilization or irrigation. See "slash and burn."
Human Relation Area Files (HRAF):	An anthropological database founded in 1949 at Yale University in New Haven, Connecticut, which is primarily employed to test hypotheses in a cross-cultural perspective.
hypothesis:	A proposition about a set of expectations that can be tested and that are derived from a theory founded on the characteristics of the real world.
inbreeding theory:	A perspective that seeks to explain the adoption of the incest taboo with reference to the harmful genetic effects of mating between closely related individuals in a society.
incest:	Sexual contact between people who are members of the same culturally defined kinship group; sexual relationships between related individuals for whom

such relationships are forbidden by cultural prohibitions or laws.

incest taboo: A rule that is found in all known cultures and which prohibits the marriage or mating of individuals who belong to particular classes or categories of relatives; however, such rules are variable in nature. Among ancient Egyptians, for example, brothers and sisters of royalty were expected to marry, while such marriages were prohibited among the general population. In other cultures cross-cousins were expected to marry, but marriage of parallel cousins would be considered incest.

inductive method: A mode of logical analysis by which propositions are inferred on the basis of specific observations; contrasts with deductive method.

informant: Individuals who provide information to an anthropologists during the conduct of fieldwork, especially those people with expert or specialized knowledge in their culture.

infrastructure: An aspect of the theoretical orientation of cultural materialism, such as the mode of production, which exerts a causal influence on cultural and economic systems.

joking relationship: An institutionalized pattern of privileged familiarity or joking between people of specific social statuses.

kindred: A local group that is composed of bilateral relatives.

kinship system: The customary complex of statuses and roles governing the behaviour of relatives.

kinship terminology: The set of names applied to the various statuses in a kinship system; the linguistic labels used in the classification of kin in particular categories that are used to designate certain genealogical connections between individuals.

Kula ring: The system of inter-tribal ceremonial exchange of shell armbands and necklaces in southwestern Melanesia, especially among the Trobriand Islands, which is based on institutional trading partnerships; described by Bronislaw Malinowski in his classic monograph entitled *Argonauts of the Western Pacific* (1922).

lateral relatives: In kinship studies, people on either one's father's or mother's side of a family, for example, matrilateral or patrilateral relatives; contrasts with lineal relatives.

learned behaviour:	Based on knowledge derived from the passing down of behavioural traits from one generation to the next (enculturation), or those derived from association with one's peers in a particular culture; behaviour not derived from a biological or genetic process.
levirate:	Brother-in-law marriage; the marriage of a woman to her deceased husband's brother.
lexicostatistical dating:	See "glottochronology."
life histories:	Cultural profiles that are created based on details in the lives of particular individuals derived from their experiences and points of view; a research approach characteristic of Boasian ethnography.
lineage:	A unilineal kinship group that traces descent from a known ancestor, who lived not more than five or six generations back.
lineal relatives:	Individuals who are direct descendants of a person's ancestor; contrasts with lateral relatives.
linguistic relativity:	Based on the idea that culture and language are intimately interrelated such that one's thoughts and perceptions are strongly influenced by the language a person speaks; see "Sapir-Whorf hypothesis."
mana:	A term in Polynesian languages referring to the existence of a powerful supernatural force found in objects or people producing good health and fortune.
marriage:	The social institution that regulates the special relations of a mated pair, or other socially recognized couple, to each other, their offspring, their kin, and society at large.
marriage, cross-cousin:	A preferred marriage form that is restricted to cross-cousins, which is to say, the marriage of a man to his mother's brother's daughter or to his father's sister's daughter.
matrilateral:	Pertaining to descent that is reckoned through one's mother's brother; kin on one's mother's side of a family; see "patrilateral kin."
matrilineal (uterine):	Pertaining to descent through the mother or female line; serves to define group membership and inheritance rights.
matrilocal (uxorilocal) residence:	Pertaining to the practice whereby a married couple settles in the domicile of the wife's family.
means of production:	Refers to the tools and technology used during the process of production; a Marxist term.

mode of production:	A concept developed by Marx to refer to the social relations that are established in the context of techno-economic factors between those who control the means of production and those who are the producer-workers; relationships between the forces of production (techno-economic factors) and the relations of production (processes of work); in general terms, the manner in which a society meets its material needs.
mode of reproduction:	Factors relating to technology and the organization of work that affect the size of populations.
model:	Depicts phenomenon through relationships among various components; a hypothetical description of reality that is used to facilitate explanation and further analysis.
moietie (moiety):	A social unit based upon unilineal descent groups comprising clans or phratries that occur when a tribe or other social grouping is divided into two recognized units, usually involving patterns of exchange, co-operation, and mutual support among the members of the different halves; from the French word *moitie.*
monogamy:	Marriage of one man to one woman.
morpheme:	A minimal unit of language that has meaning.
multilinear evolution:	The theoretical orientation espoused by Julian Steward in which social and cultural change is envisioned to occur along a diversity of different lines or paths, depending on various environmental settings.
natural aversion theory:	An attempt to explain the incest taboo by anthropologist Edward Westermarck (1853–1936), who postulated that children raised together tend to develop a natural aversion toward sexual interaction, such that the incest taboo is therefore a manifestation of this aversion; also referred to as the childhood familiarity theory.
Neanderthal:	An extinct fossil variety of man dominant in Europe from the second inter-glacial epoch to the climax of the fourth glacial; *Homo sapiens neandertalensis.*
neo-colonialism:	A modern version of colonial practices in which non-industrial societies are exploited for their labour or natural resources by indirect means, often in the context of multinational corporations.

neo-evolution:	A term used to describe contemporary evolutionary views of social and cultural change, such as multi-linear evolution; contrasts with the unilinear evolutionary perspectives of the nineteenth century.
neolocal residence:	A post-marital residence pattern in which the newly married husband and wife establish their residence without reference to the location of either of the married couple's parents; see also "matrilocal residence" and "patrilocal residence."
nomothetic:	Refers to an approach that is designed to produce scientific laws or generalizations, usually involving a multiplicity of cases in which are expressed causal relationships; in anthropology, a term favoured by Marvin Harris, as used in his theoretical orientation of cultural materialism.
nuclear family:	A social group comprising married parents and their children, usually living in the same residence.
odonah:	An Ojibwa (Anishenabe) word for "town" or "village."
Oedipus complex:	A psychological state of a male characterized by sexual desire for the mother and antagonism toward the father, associated with feelings of guilt and emotional conflict.
ogima:	An Ojibwa (Anishenabe) word for "chief" or "leader."
ontology:	Perspectives or assumptions concerning the nature of reality and existence.
optimal foraging strategy:	The idea that hunters will pursue the largest game animals available to them, such as whales, moose, or giraffe, because there is a better return on their effort than if they pursued only small game; a principle that foragers will seek country food sources in direct proportion to the effort in calories that is used to obtain them.
Other:	In postmodern terminology, "the Other" is a term used to refer to non-Western people and is based on the assumption that each culture produces unique human characteristics; is opposed to the idea of a "pan-human culture."
Paleolithic period:	Literally meaning "the Old Stone Age"; an early evolutionary stage in prehistory.
paleontology:	The scientific study of hominid fossil remains.
paradigm:	A concept developed by Thomas Kuhn (1922–1996) in his work *The Structure of Scientific Revolutions*

(1962), which is associated with a research strategy that is seen to guide the process of scientific investigation during a particular time period.

parallel cousin: A cousin whose related parents are of like sex. The offspring of a person's mother's sister or father's brother.

participant observation: A research technique developed in social anthropology that involves living with the people of a particular culture or community over an extended period of time such that researchers attempt to immerse themselves in the day-to-day activities of the group under study; see "ethnography" and "fieldwork."

pastoralism: A culture marked by a subsistence technique centred on the herding and husbandry of domesticated animals.

pater: A Latin term meaning the authoritarian figure in the Roman family; the legal father of a child, but not necessarily the biological father; see "genitor."

patrilateral kin: Relatives on a person's father's side of a family or descent group; see "matrilateral."

patrilineal (agnatic): Pertaining to unilineal descent through the father or male line, such that group membership and inheritance rights are established and defined.

patrilocal (virilocal) residence: Pertaining to the post-marital residence pattern whereby a married couple settles in or near the domicile of the husband's family; see "matrilocal residence."

phenomenology: An approach to understanding reality that emphasizes sensory information and multiple points of view; contests the idea of a concrete reality; contrasts with positivism.

phoneme: The smallest unit of sound in a language.

phratry: A social unit consisting of two or more linked clans between which exists a special bond of unity as against clans joined in other phratries within a society; usually associated with social bonds for ritual and marriage purposes; see "moietie."

physical (biological) anthropology: The branch of anthropology concerned with the bodily characteristics of *Homo sapiens* and other primates. The scientific study of humans as a biological phenomenon, concerning the characteristics of present-day human populations, the study of the evolution of humans from early and later fossil evidence, and the relationships between humans and other primates.

political economy: A theoretical orientation that stresses the role of political factors, such as power and authority, in the economic organization of production, consumption, and distribution of goods.

polyandry: The marriage of a woman to two or more men simultaneously.

polyandry, fraternal: A polyandrous marriage in which the husbands are brothers.

polygamy: Any multiple marriage.

polygyny: The marriage of a man to two or more women simultaneously.

polyvocal: A postmodern term meaning "multiple voices," as opposed to the "single" voice of the ethnographer.

positivism: An approach to understanding the social and physical world based on a belief that reality is a concrete phenomenon discernible through observation and discoverable laws; a doctrine holding that scientific knowledge is obtained through empirical experience; a philosophical position formulated by August Comte (1798–1857), considered by many to be the founder of sociology, and later espoused by Emile Durkheim; contrasts with phenomenology.

post-marital residence patterns: Cultural rules that specify the location of residence for a newly married couple, which often determine the nature of domestic units in a society; see "ambilocal residence," "matrilocal residence," "neolocal residence," and "patrilocal residence."

postmodernism: In anthropology, a theoretical position that rejects the idea of universal laws and objective knowledge; stresses ethnography as a literary project with multiple "truths."

potlatch: The Northwest coast First Nation institution of ceremonial feasting accompanied by lavish distribution of gifts; a type of redistributive economic and political system usually associated with chiefdoms and centralized authority structures; see "redistribution."

progeny price: The wealth transferred by the relatives of a groom to the kin of his bride in compensation for their release of claim to the children produced in the marriage; also known as bridewealth or bride price.

qualitative research: Methods of gathering information in the social sciences using research strategies of interviewing,

	description, and subjective understanding; see "participant observation" and "fieldwork."
quantitative research:	Strategies of information gathering that stress the collection of quantitative data; the use of statistical analysis and hypothesis testing; see "positivism."
questionnaire:	See "structured interview" and "unstructured interview."
ramage (sept):	A bilaterally extended kinship group, identified with reference to a specific person.
reciprocity:	Economic and social patterns based on the mutual exchange of goods and services that reinforce social ties among the participants in such relationships because of the ethic of obligatory reciprocation.
redistribution:	A social, economic, and political system of exchange in which goods are gathered in a central location and subsequently allocated to participants in elaborate feasts meant to bolster the leaders' claim to status positions within a society; see "potlatch."
relativism:	In anthropology, a perspective stressing the uniqueness and individual characteristics of different cultures, particularly associated with the Boasian orientation of historical particularism.
rite of passage (transition rites):	Ritual complexes associated with important changes in personal status, such as birth, adolescence, marriage, and death; a term associated with Arnold van Gennep (1873–1957), who stressed that such rites involve processes of separation and reincorporation.
role:	The customary complex of behaviour associated with a particular status; see "status."
Sapir-Whorf hypothesis:	See "linguistic relativity."
scapulamancy:	A method of divination used by First Nations peoples of northeastern Canada in which the scapula bone of a caribou is heated over a fire and the resulting burn marks interpreted by a religious specialist in such a way as to determine the location of caribou herds.
sedentary:	A relatively fixed location of residence, usually associated with chiefdoms and states in which a sufficient local supply of food inhibits migratory subsistence patterns.
segmentary lineages:	Systems of unilineal descent groups that are commonly organized in a hierarchical structure such that there are feelings of solidarity among the

members of groups close together in the hierarchy, and feelings of opposition for those groups farther away. Given this hierarchical pattern, when disputes emerge, different descent groups will seek allies among the members of close descent groups in opposition to those farther away in the overall structure.

shaman: A religious specialist who has received his power directly from supernatural sources; synonymous with the colloquial term "medicine man."

sib: A unilineal kinship group, synonymous with "clan."

sibling terminology: A set of kinship terminology pertaining to brother or sister, or extensions of these terms to cross- or parallel cousins.

slash and burn: A form of shifting cultivation in which there is recurrent clearing and burning of cultivation with planting in the burn fields.

social structure: The ways in which groups and individuals are organized and relate to one another; linkages between social roles in a society.

society: An aggregation of human beings (a population) living as a distinct entity and possessing a distinct culture.

socio-biology: An approach to the study of human behaviour that stresses the Darwinian underpinnings of biological or genetic factors.

sodalities: Associations of people who are drawn from different sectors of a society for special-purpose activities such as a club or other type of organization.

sororal polygyny: The simultaneous marriage of two or more sisters to one husband.

sororate: The practice whereby a younger sister marries the widowed husband of her deceased sister.

soulava: The red shell necklaces exchanged in the Melanesian kula.

state: The association within a society that undertakes to direct and organize policy on behalf of and in the name of the entire society; a centralized, hierarchical political, economic, and social organization characteristic of large, sedentary populations; a relatively predictable food supply and a monopoly over the physical use of force.

status: A position or standing in a society that is socially recognized; see "role."

stem family:	Members of a kin group living in the same residence consisting of three generations; usually associated with impartible (not divisible) inheritance and devolution of a farm to the eldest son.
stratigraphy:	Analysis of geological deposits in terms of discernible layers; derivative time sequences are inferred from the relative positions of the strata or layers.
structural functionalism:	A theoretical orientation associated with the British social anthropologist A.R. Radcliffe-Brown (1881–1955) such that the function of an institution is the part it plays in maintaining the viability of the society as a whole; contrasts with the Malinowskian view of functionalism, which stressed the function of an institution in terms of the survival of individual members of a society; see "functionalism."
structuralism:	A style of anthropology associated with the French anthropologist Claude Levi-Strauss, which seeks to understand social systems through patterns associated with the operation of the human mind as, for example, in the study of myths, which reveal binary oppositions that are considered to underlay fundamental processes of human thought.
structured interview:	A research strategy involving the asking of questions in a set pattern or sequence, predetermined beforehand; see "unstructured interview."
subsistence economy:	Production and exchange of food items meant for local consumption; also includes the tools, knowledge, and practices through which such food is secured.
suitor service:	A substitute for, or equivalent of, progeny price, in which the potential groom works for his intended bride's kin.
swidden:	See "slash and burn."
syntax:	Grammatical rules that organize the phonemes and morphemes in a language.
taboo (tabu):	Prohibition of an act, violation of which is punishable by supernatural sanctions.
teepee (tipi):	Conical skin tent, commonly used as a dwelling by the First Nation residents of the North American Plains.
totem:	An object, often an animal or plant, held in special regard by an individual or social group.
totemism:	The institutional complex centring about a totem.

transhumance:	A strategy of pastoralists such that animals are moved to different pasture locations, depending upon fluctuations in weather and the food requirements of the animals.
travois:	A carrying device that has two poles hitched to a draft animal. The free ends of the *travois* drag along the ground.
tribe:	A social group speaking a distinctive language or dialect and possessing a distinctive culture that sets it off from other tribes. It is not necessarily organized politically, nor does it have a centralized decision-making body and is usually based on an organization of kinship units consisting of unilineal descent groups; associated with horticulture or pastoralism as a subsistence strategy.
unilineal:	Pertaining to descent through one parent only.
unilineal evolution:	A perspective that views societies changing along relatively fixed lines, such as through a series of stages from simple to complex socio-technological organization.
unstructured interview:	A method of gathering information using a series of questions that follow one another, not in a predetermined pattern; see "structured interview."

References

Abler, T.S. 1993. "In Memoriam: Sally M. Weaver 1940–1993." *Anthropologica* 35 (1): 117–120.

Abler, T.S., and S.M. Weaver. 1974. *A Canadian Indian Bibliography, 1960–1970*. Toronto: University of Toronto Press.

Aceves, J.B. 1974. *Identity, Survival, and Change*. Morristown: General Learning Press.

Adams, W. 1998. *The Philosophical Roots of Anthropology*. Stanford: CSLI Publications.

Akenson, D.H. 1984. *The Irish in Ontario: A Study of Rural History*. Montreal: McGill-Queen's University Press.

Anderson, M. (Sequin). 2004. "Understanding Tsimshian Potlatch." In R.B. Morrison and C.R. Wilson (eds.), *Native Peoples: The Canadian Experience*. Don Mills: Oxford University Press.

Anderssen, E. 1998. "Nunavut to Be a Welfare Case." *Globe and Mail* (5 June).

Appadurai, A. 1990. "Disjuncture and Difference in the Global Cultural Economy." *Public Culture* 2 (2): 1–24.

Argyrou, V. 1999. "Sameness and the Ethnological Will to Meaning." *Current Anthropology* 40: S29–S41.

Asad, T. (ed.). 1973. *Anthropology and the Colonial Encounter*. Atlantic Highlands: Humanities Press.

Asch, M. 1982. "Capital and Economic Development: A Critical Appraisal of the Recommendations of the Mackenzie Valley Pipeline Commission." *Culture* 2 (3): 3–9.

_____. 1984. *Home and Native Land: Aboriginal Rights and the Canadian Constitution*. Toronto: Methuen.

_____. 2001. "Indigenous Self-Determination and Applied Anthropology in Canada." *Anthropologica* 43 (2): 201–209.

Asimov, I. 1950. *I, Robot*. New York: Gnome Press.

Bailey, A.G. 1937. *The Conflict of European and Eastern Algonkian Cultures, 1504–1700*. Toronto: University of Toronto Press.

Bailey, F.G. 1969. *Strategems and Spoils*. Oxford: Blackwell.

Balikci, A. 1970. *The Netsilik Eskimo*. Prospect Heights: Waveland Press.

Banks, R. 2005. *The Darling*. Toronto: Vintage Canada.

Barak, V. 1988. "Review of: G.E. Marcus and M.J. Fischer, Anthropology as Cultural Critique." *Culture* 8 (2): 100–101.

Barker, J. 1987. "T.F. McIlwraith and Anthropology at the University of Toronto, 1925–1963." *Canadian Review of Sociology and Anthropology* 24: 252–268.

Barnes, J.A. 1962. "African Models in the New Guinea Highlands." *Man* 62 (1–2): 5–9.

Barrett, S.R. 1977. *The Rise and Fall of an African Utopia*. Waterloo: Wilfrid Laurier University Press.

_____. 1984a. "Racism, Ethics, and the Subversive Nature of Anthropological Inquiry." *Philosophy of the Social Sciences* 14: 1–25.

_____. 1984b. *The Rebirth of Anthropological Theory*. Toronto: University of Toronto Press.

_____. 1987. *Is God a Racist? The Right Wing in Canada*. Toronto: University of Toronto Press.

_____. 1996. *Anthropology: A Student's Guide to Theory and Method*. Toronto: University of Toronto Press.

_____. 2002. *Culture Meets Power*. Westport: Praeger.

Barth, F. 1959. *Political Leadership among Swat Pathans*. London School of Economics Monographs on Social Anthropology, no. 19. New York: Humanities Press.

_____. 1966. *Models of Social Organization*. Occasional Paper no. 23. London: Royal Anthropological Institute.

Beattie, J.H.M. 1969. "Understanding and Explanation in Social Anthropology." In R.A. Manners and D. Kaplan (eds.), *Theory in Anthropology*. Chicago: Aldine Publishing.

Beck, B.E.F. 1980. "Asian Immigrants and Canadian Multiculturalism: Current Issues and Future Opportunities." In K.V. Ujimoto and G. Hirabayashi (eds.), *Visible Minorities and Multiculturalism: Asians in Canada*. Toronto: Butterworth.

Benedict, R. 1932. "Configurations of Culture in North America." *American Anthropologist* 34: 1–27.

_____. 1934. *Patterns of Culture*. Boston: Houghton Mifflin.

_____. 1946. *The Chrysanthemum and the Sword*. Boston: Houghton Mifflin.

Bennett, J.W. 1969. *Northern Plainsmen*. Chicago: Aldine Publishing.

_____. 1982. *Of Time and the Enterprise: North American Family Farm Management in a Context of Resource Marginality*. Minneapolis: University of Minnesota Press.

Berdan, F.F. 1982. *The Aztecs of Central Mexico: An Imperial Society*. New York: Holt, Rinehart, and Winston.

Berger, T.R. 1977. *Northern Frontier, Northern Homeland: Report of the Mackenzie Valley Pipeline Inquiry*, 2 vols. Ottawa: Supply and Services Canada.

_____. 1983. "Native Rights and Self-Determination." *Canadian Journal of Native Studies* 3 (2): 363–375.

Bernard, J. 1969. "Observation and Generalization in Cultural Anthropology." In R.A. Manners and D. Kaplan (eds.), *Theory in Anthropology*. Chicago: Aldine Publishing.

Bishop, C. 1974. *The Northern Ojibwa and the Fur Trade*. Toronto: Holt, Rinehart, and Winston.

_____. 1979. "Ethnology: A Canadian Indian Bibliography." *American Anthropologist* 8 (1): 173.

Blaser, M., H. Feit, and G. McRae (eds.). 2004. *In the Way of Development: Indigenous People's Life Projects and Globalization*. New York: Zed Books.

Boas, F. 1888. *The Central Eskimo*. Report of the Bureau of Ethnology, 1884–1885. Washington, D.C.: Smithsonian Institution.

_____. 1897. *The Social Organization and the Secret Societies of the Kwakiutl Indians*. Report of the U.S. National Museum, 1895. Washington, D.C., Smithsonian Institution.

_____. 1898. *The Mythology of the Bella Coola Indians*, vol. 12. New York: American Museum of Natural History.

_____. [1912] 1948. "Changes in the Bodily Form of Descendants of Immigrants." In *Race, Language, and Culture*. New York: Macmillan.

_____. 1966. *Kwakiutl Ethnography*. H. Codere (ed.). Chicago: University of Chicago Press.

Bodley, J.H. 1990. *Victims of Progress*. Menlo Park: Benjamin-Cummings.

Bohannan, P. 1971. "Beyond Civilization." *Natural History* 80 (2): 50–67.

Bohannan, P., and M. Glazer. 1988. "Clifford Geertz." In P. Bohannan and M. Glazer (eds.), *Highpoints in Anthropology*. New York: Alfred Knopf.

Bongaarts, J. 2001. "Household Size and Composition in the Developing World of the 1990s." *Population Studies* 55: 263–279.

Boserup, E. 1970. *Woman's Role in Economic Development*. New York: St. Martin's Press.

Bossen, L. 2002. *Chinese Women and Rural Development*. Lanham: Rowman and Littlefield.

Brody, H. 1973. *Inishkillane: Change and Decline in the West of Ireland*. Harmondsworth: Penguin Books.

_____. 1975. *The People's Land: Eskimos and Whites in the Eastern Arctic*. Harmondsworth: Penguin Books.

Cairns, A.C. 2000. *Citizens Plus: Aboriginal Peoples and the Canadian State*. Vancouver: University of British Columbia Press.

Carrithers, M. 1990. "Is Anthropology Art or Science?" *Current Anthropology* 31 (3): 263–282.

Chagnon, N.A. 1968. *Yanomamo: The Fierce People*. New York: Holt, Rinehart, and Winston.

Chance, N.A. (ed.). 1968. *Conflict in Culture: Problems of Developmental Change among the Cree*. Ottawa: Canadian Research Centre.

Clifford, J., and G.E. Marcus (eds.). 1986. *Writing Culture: The Poetics and Politics of Ethnography*. Berkeley: University of California Press.

Coates, K., and J. Powell. 1989. *The Modern North: Politics and the Rejection of Colonialism*. Toronto: James Lorimer.

Codere, H. 1950. *Fighting with Property*. New York: American Ethnological Society.

Cole, D. 1973. "The Origins of Canadian Anthropology: 1850–1910." *Journal of Canadian Studies* 8 (1): 33–45.

Cole, S. 2000. "Reflections on Anthropology in Canada." *Anthropologica* 42 (2): 123–126.

_____. 2003. *Ruth Landes: A Life in Anthropology*. Lincoln: University of Nebraska Press.

Comte, A. 1896. *The Positive Philosophy*. Trans. and condensed by H. Martineau. London: G. Bell.

Cove, J. 1987. *Shattered Images: Dialogues and Meditations on Tsimshian Narratives*. Ottawa: Carleton University Press.

Crichton, M. 1969. *The Andromeda Strain*. New York: Alfred A. Knopf.

_____. 1972. *The Terminal Man*. New York: Alfred A. Knopf.

_____. 1990. *Jurassic Park*. New York: Alfred A. Knopf.

_____. 1999. *Timeline*. New York: Alfred A. Knopf.

_____. 2006. *Next*. New York: HarperCollins.

Dacks, G. 1981. *A Choice of Futures: Politics in the Canadian North*. Toronto: Methuen.

Daly, M. 2000. "African Genital Mutilation: The Unspeakable Atrocities." In E. Ashton-Jones, G.A. Olson, and M.G. Perry (eds.), *The Gender Reader*. Needham Heights: Allyn and Bacon.

Darnell, R. 1975. "Towards a History of the Professionalization of Canadian Anthropology." *Proceedings of the Canadian Ethnology Society* 3: 399–416.

_____. 1976. "The Sapir Years at the National Museum." In J. Freedman (ed.), *The History of Canadian Anthropology*, 98–121. Proceedings of the Canadian Ethnology Society 3. Ottawa: National Museums of Canada.

_____. 1992. "The Boasian Text Tradition and the History of Canadian Anthropology." *Culture* 17: 39–48.

_____. 1998. "Toward a History of Canadian Departments of Anthropology: Retrospect, Prospect, and Common Cause." *Anthropologica* 40 (2): 153–169.

_____. 2000. "Canadian Anthropologists, the First Nations, and Canada's Self-Image at the Millennium." *Anthropologica* 42 (2): 165–174.

Darwin, C. 1859. *The Origin of Species.* New York: New American Library.

Dawson, K.C.A. 2004. *Original People and Euro-Canadians in Northwestern Ontario.* Thunder Bay: Lakehead University Centre for Northern Studies.

Deutsch, D. 1997. *The Fabric of Reality: The Science of Parallel Universes and Its Implications.* New York: Penguin.

Deutsch, D., and M. Lockwood. 1994. "The Quantum Physics of Time Travel." *Scientific American* (March): 68–74.

Diamond, J. 2008. "The Worst Mistake in the History of the Human Race." In A. Podolefsky and P.J. Brown (eds.), *Applying Cultural Anthropology.* Mountain View: Mayfield Publishing.

DIAND (Department of Indian and Northern Affairs). 2004. *Basic Departmental Data 1999.* Ottawa: Minister of Public Works and Government Services Canada.

Dunk, T.W. 2007. *It's a Working Man's Town: Male Working-Class Culture*, 2nd ed. Montreal: McGill-Queen's University Press.

Dunning, R.W. 1959. *Social and Economic Change among the Northern Ojibwa.* Toronto: University of Toronto Press.

Durkheim, E. [1895] 1938. *The Rules of Sociological Method.* New York: Free Press.

_____. [1897] 1951. *Suicide.* New York: Free Press.

_____. [1912] 1968. *The Elementary Forms of Religious Life.* London: George Allen and Unwin.

Dyck, N. 1980. "Indian, Métis, Native: Some Implications of Special Status." *Canadian Ethnic Studies* 22 (3): 40–55.

Effrat, B., and M. Mitchell. 1974. "The Indian and the Social Scientist: Contemporary Contractual Relations on the Pacific Northwest Coast." *Human Organization* 33 (4): 405–407.

Elkin, F. 1970. *The Family in Canada.* Ottawa: The Vanier Institute of the Family.

Emeneau, M.B. 1937. "Toda Marriage Regulations and Taboos." *American Anthropologist* 39: 103–112.

Ervin, A.M. 1985. "Culture and Agriculture in the North American Context." *Culture* 5 (2): 35–51.

_____. 2001. *Canadian Perspectives in Cultural Anthropology.* Scarborough: Thomson Nelson.

_____. 2005. *Applied Anthropology: Tools and Perspectives for Contemporary Practice.* Boston: Allyn and Bacon.

_____. 2006a. "Applied Anthropology in Canada: Historical Foundations, Contemporary Practice and Policy Potentials." *NAPA Bulletin* 25: 134–155.

_____. 2006b. "Anthropology, Applied." *The Canadian Encyclopedia.* Edmonton: Hurtig.

Evans-Pritchard, E.E. 1940. *The Nuer.* Oxford: Clarendon Press.

_____. 1951. *Kinship and Marriage among the Nuer.* London: Oxford University Press.

Ewers, J.C. 1958. *The Blackfoot: Raiders on the Northwestern Plains.* Norman: University of Oklahoma Press.

Feit, H.A. 2004. "Hunting and the Quest for Power: The James Bay Cree and Whiteman Development." In R.B. Morrison and C.R. Wilson (eds.), *Native Peoples: The Canadian Experience*. Don Mills: Oxford University Press.

Fiske, J. 1988. "Fishing Is Women's Business: Changing Economic Roles of Carrier Women and Men." In B.A. Cox (ed.), *Native People, Native Lands: Canadian Indians, Inuit, and Métis*. Ottawa: Carleton University Press.

Fleras, A., and J.L. Elliot. 1999. *Unequal Relations: Race, Ethnic, and Aboriginal Dynamics in Canada*. Scarborough: Prentice-Hall.

_____. 2002. *Engaging Diversity: Multiculturalism in Canada*. Toronto: Thomson Nelson Canada.

Fluehr-Lobban, C. 1994. "Informed Consent in Anthropological Research: We Are Not Exempt." *Human Organization* 53 (1): 1–10.

Fox, R. 1967. *Kinship and Marriage: An Anthropological Perspective*. Cambridge: Cambridge University Press.

Francis, D., and T. Morantz. 1983. *Partners in Fur: A History of the Fur Trade in Eastern James Bay, 1600–1870*. Montreal: McGill-Queen's University Press.

Freeman, D. 1983. *Margaret Mead and Samoa: The Making and Unmaking of an Anthropological Myth*. Cambridge: Harvard University Press.

Freud, S. 1913. *Totem and Taboo*. New York: Moffat, Yard.

Frideres, J.S. 1998. *Aboriginal Peoples in Canada: Contemporary Conflicts*, 5th ed. Scarborough: Prentice-Hall Canada.

Gagnon, A., and E. Heyer. 2001. "Intergenerational Correlation of Effective Family Size in Early Quebec (Canada)." *American Journal of Human Biology* 13: 645–659.

Garigue, P. 1956. "French Canadian Kinship and Urban Life." *American Anthropologist* 58: 1090–1101.

_____. 1960. "The French-Canadian Family." In M. Wade (ed.), *Canadian Dualism*. Toronto: University of Toronto Press.

Geertz, C. 1973. *The Interpretation of Cultures: Selected Essays*. New York: Basic Books.

_____. 1983. *Local Knowledge: Further Essays in Interpretive Anthropology*. New York: Basic Books.

_____. 1988a. *Works and Lives*. Stanford: Stanford University Press.

_____. 1988b. "Thick Description: Towards an Interpretive Theory of Culture." In P. Bohannan and M. Glazer (eds.), *Highpoints in Anthropology*. New York: Alfred Knopf.

_____. 1990. "Comment: Is Anthropology Art or Science?" *Current Anthropology* 31 (3): 274.

Geertz, C., R.A. Shweder, and B. Good. 2005. *Clifford Geertz and His Colleagues*. Chicago: University of Chicago Press.

Gerber, L.M. 1990. "Multiple Jeopardy: A Socio-economic Analysis of Men and Women among the Indian, Métis, and Inuit Peoples of Canada." *Canadian Ethnic Studies* 22 (3): 69–84.

Globe and Mail (Toronto). 2006. "Obituary of Harry B. Hawthorn" (5 August).

Gluckman, M. [1956]1970. *Custom and Conflict in Africa*. Oxford: Basil Blackwell.

_____. 1963. *Order and Rebellion in Tribal Africa*. London: Cohen and West.

Gmelch, G. 1982. "Baseball Magic." In J. Cole (ed.), *Anthropology for the Eighties*. New York: Free Press.

Gold, G.I., and M.A. Tremblay. 1983. "Steps toward an Anthropology of Quebec, 1960–1980." In F. Manning (ed.), *Consciousness and Inquiry: Ethnology and Canadian Realities*. Ottawa: Canadian Ethnology Service.

Goldstein, L.J. 1968. "The Phenomenological and Naturalistic Approaches to the Social." In R.A. Manners and D. Kaplan (eds.), *Theory in Anthropology*. Chicago: Aldine Publishing.

Graburn, N.H.H. 1969. *Eskimos without Igloos: Social and Economic Development in Sugluk*. Boston: Little, Brown.

Greer, A. 2000. *The Jesuit Relations*. Boston: St. Martin's Press.

Gwynne, M.A. 2003. *Applied Anthropology: A Career-Oriented Approach*. Boston: Allyn.

Haig-Brown, C., and D.A. Nock (eds.). 2006. *With Good Intentions: Euro-Canadian and Aboriginal Relations in Colonial Canada*. Vancouver: University of British Columbia Press.

Hannerz, U. [1969] 2004. *Soulside: Inquiries into Ghetto Culture and Community*. Chicago: University of Chicago Press.

Harris, M. 1968. *The Rise of Anthropological Theory*. New York: Thomas Y. Crowell.

———. 1975. *Cows, Pigs, Wars, and Witches: The Riddles of Culture*. New York: Random House.

———. 1991. *Cultural Anthropology*. New York: HarperCollins.

———. 2001. *Cultural Materialism: The Struggle for a Science of Culture*. Walnut Creek, CA: Alta Mira.

Hawthorn, A. 1993. *A Labour of Love: The Making of the Museum of Anthropology, UBC: The First Three Decades, 1947–1976*. Vancouver: UBC Museum of Anthropology.

Hawthorn, H.B. 1955. *The Doukhobors of British Columbia*. Vancouver: University of British Columbia Press.

———. 1966–1967. *A Survey of the Contemporary Indians of Canada*. Ottawa: Queen's Printer.

Hawthorn, H.B., et al. 1958. *The Indians of British Columbia*. Toronto: University of Toronto Press.

Hedican, E.J. 1976. "Ecologic and Patron–Client Relationships: Algonkians of Eastern Subarctic Canada." *Man in the Northeast* 12 (Fall): 41–50.

———. 1986a. *The Ogoki River Guides: Emergent Leadership among the Northern Ojibwa*. Waterloo: Wilfrid Laurier University Press.

———. 1986b. "Anthropologists and Social Involvement: Some Issues and Problems." *Canadian Review of Sociology and Anthropology* 23 (4): 544–558.

———. 1986c. "Some Issues in the Anthropology of Transaction and Exchange." *Canadian Review of Sociology and Anthropology* 23 (1): 97–117.

———. 1990a. "On the Rail-Line in Northwestern Ontario: Non-reserve Housing and Community Change." *Canadian Journal of Native Studies* 19 (1): 15–32.

———. 1990b. "Algonquian Kinship Terminology: Some Problems of Interpretation." *Man in the Northeast* 40 (Fall): 1–15.

———. 1990c. "The Economics of Northern Native Food Production." In J.I. Bakker (ed.), *The World Food Crisis: Food Security in Comparative Perspective*. Toronto: Canadian Scholars' Press Inc.

———. 1990d. "Richard Salisbury's Anthropology: A Personal Account." *Culture* X (1): 14–18.

———. 1991. "On the Ethno-politics of Canadian Native Leadership and Identity." *Ethnic Groups* 9 (1): 1–15.

_____. 1994. "Epistemological Implications of Anthropological Fieldwork, with notes from Northern Ontario." *Anthropologica* 36: 205–224.

_____. 2001a. *Up in Nipigon Country: Anthropology as a Personal Experience.* Halifax: Fernwood Publishing.

_____. 2001b. "Reflections on the People and the Land of Whitewater Lake, Northwestern Ontario: An Ethnographic Narrative." *Northeast Anthropology* 62 (Fall): 17–30.

_____. 2003. "Irish Farming Households in Eastern Canada: Domestic Production and Family Size." *Ethnology* 42 (1): 15–37.

_____. 2005a. "The Ottawa Valley Irish after the Great Famine, 1851–1881: Re-thinking the Stem Family Debate." *Northeast Anthropology* 69: 87–107.

_____. 2005b. "Review of: *Irish Travellers: Racism and the Politics of Culture.*" *Canadian Review of Sociology and Anthropology* 42 (1): 117–118.

_____. 2006. "What Determines Family Size? Irish Farming Families in Nineteenth-Century Ontario." *Journal of Family History* 31 (4): 315–334.

_____. 2008. *Applied Anthropology in Canada: Understanding Aboriginal Issues*, 2nd ed. Toronto: University of Toronto Press.

_____. 2009. "Ways of Knowing in Anthropology: Alexandre Chayanov and the Perils of 'Dutiful Empiricism.'" *History and Anthropology* 20 (4): 419–433.

Heidenreich, C. 1971. *Huronia: A History and Geography of the Huron Indians, 1600–1650.* Toronto: McClelland & Stewart.

Heider, K.G. 1997. *Grand Valley Dani: Peaceful Warriors.* New York: Holt, Rinehart, and Winston.

Heinlein, R. 1957. *Citizen of the Galaxy.* New York: Ace Books.

_____. 1961. *Stranger in a Strange Land.* New York: Putnam.

Helleiner, J. 2003. *Irish Travellers: Racism and the Politics of Culture.* Toronto: University of Toronto Press.

Helm, J. 1961. *The Lynx Point People: The Dynamics of a Northern Athapascan Band.* Ottawa: National Museums of Canada.

Henry, F. 1973. *Forgotten Canadians: The Blacks of Nova Scotia.* Don Mills: Longman Canada.

_____. 1994. *The Caribbean Diaspora in Toronto: Learning to Live with Racism.* Toronto: University of Toronto Press.

Henry, F., and C. Tator. 2006. *Racial Profiling: Challenging the Myth of a "Few Bad Apples."* Toronto: University of Toronto Press.

_____. 2009. *The Colour of Democracy: Racism in Canadian Society*, 4th ed. Toronto: Nelson, Thomson.

Hier, S.P. 2000. "The Contemporary Structure of Canadian Racial Supremacism: Networks, Strategies, and New Techniques." *Canadian Journal of Sociology* 25: 1–24.

Hoodfar, H. 1997. *Between Marriage and the Market: Intimate Politics and Survival in Cairo.* Berkeley: University of California Press.

Hostetler, J.A., and G.E. Huntington. 1967. *The Hutterites in North America.* New York: Holt, Rinehart, and Winston.

Huxley, A. 1932. *Brave New World.* London: Chatto & Windus.

Jacobson, E.M. 1975. *Bended Elbow: Kenora Talks Back.* Kenora: Central Publications.

Jenness, D. 1932. *The Indians of Canada*. Ottawa: The National Museum of Canada.

———. 1964. *Eskimo Administration: Canada*. Montreal: Arctic Institute of North America.

Jenness, S.E. 2008. *Through Darkening Spectacles: Memoirs of Diamond Jenness*. Mercury Series, History 55. Ottawa: Canadian Museum of Civilization.

Kallen, E. 1977. *Spanning the Generations: A Study in Jewish Identity*. Don Mills: Longman Canada.

———. 1982. *Ethnicity and Human Rights in Canada*. Toronto: Gage Publishing.

Kaplan, A. 1964. *The Conduct of Inquiry: Methodology for Behavioral Science*. San Francisco: Chandler Publishing.

Kaplan, D., and R.A. Manners. 1972. *Culture Theory*. Englewood Cliffs: Prentice-Hall.

Klima, G.J. 1970. *The Barabaig: East African Cattle-Herders*. New York: Holt, Rinehart, and Winston.

Kottak, C.P. 2006. *Assault on Paradise: The Globalization of a Little Community in Brazil*. New York: McGraw-Hill.

Krech, S. 1984. *The Subarctic Fur Trade: Native Social and Economic Adaptations*. Vancouver: University of British Columbia Press.

Kroeber, A.L. 1939. *Cultural and Natural Areas of Native North America*. University of California Publications in American Archaeology and Ethnology, vol. 38.

Kroeber, A.L., and C. Kluckhohn. 1952. *Culture: A Critical Review of Concepts and Definitions*. New York: Vintage Books.

Kuhn, T.S. 1962. *The Structure of Scientific Revolutions*. Chicago: University of Chicago Press.

Kuper, A. 1999. *Anthropology and Anthropologists: The Modern British School*. London: Routledge.

Laing, R.D. 1967. *The Politics of Experience*. Baltimore: Penguin Books.

Lam, V. 2006. *Bloodletting & Miraculous Cures*. Toronto: Anchor Canada.

Lamphere, L., R. Rayna, and G. Rubin. 2007. "Anthropologists Are Talking about Feminist Anthropology." *Ethnos* 72 (3) 408–426.

Landes, R. 1937. *Ojibwa Sociology*. Columbia University Contributions to Anthropology 29. New York: Columbia University Press.

———. 1938. *The Ojibwa Woman*. Columbia University Contributions to Anthropology 31. New York: Columbia University Press.

———. 1947. *The City of Women*. Institute for the Study of Man. New York: Macmillan Co.

———. 1968. *Ojibwa Religion and the Midewiwin*. Madison: University of Wisconsin Press.

———. 1970. *The Prairie Potawatomi: Tradition and Ritual in the Twentieth Century*. Madison: University of Wisconsin Press.

Lapsley, H. 1999. *Margaret Mead and Ruth Benedict: The Kinship of Women*. Amherst: University of Massachusetts Press.

Larocque, S. 2006. *Gay Marriage: The Story of a Canadian Social Revolution*. Toronto: James Lorimer.

Larsen, T. 1983. "Negotiating Identity: The Micmac of Nova Scotia." In A. Tanner (ed.), *The Politics of Indianness: Case Studies of Native Ethnopolitics in Canada*. St. John's: Memorial University of Newfoundland.

LaRusic, I.E. 1979. *Negotiating a Way of Life*. Ottawa: Department of Indian Affairs and Northern Development.

LaViolette, F.E. 1973. *The Struggle for Survival: Indian Cultures and the Protestant Ethic in British Columbia.* Toronto: University of Toronto Press.

Leach, B. 2005. "Agency and the Gendered Imagination: Women's Actions and Local Culture in Steelworker Families." *Identities: Global Studies in Culture and Power* 12: 1–22.

Leach, E.R. (ed.). 1968. *The Structural Study of Myth and Totemism.* London: Tavistock Publications.

_____. 1982. *Social Anthropology.* Oxford: Oxford University Press.

Leacock, E. 1954. *The Montagnais Hunting Territory and the Fur Trade.* Washington, D.C.: American Anthropological Association Memoir, no. 28.

Lee, R.B. 1979. *The !Kung San: Men, Women, and Work in a Foraging Society.* Cambridge: Cambridge University Press.

_____. 1993. *The Dobe Ju/'hoansi.* New York: Harcourt Brace.

Lee, R.B., and I. DeVore (eds.). 1968. *Man the Hunter.* Chicago: Aldine.

_____. 1976. *Kalahari Hunter-Gatherers: Studies of the !Kung San and Their Neighbours.* Cambridge: Harvard University Press.

Legere, A. 1998. "An Assessment of Recent Political Development in Nunavut: The Challenges and Dilemmas of Inuit Self-Government." *Canadian Journal of Native Studies* 18: 271–299.

Lett, J. 1987. *The Human Enterprise: A Critical Introduction to Anthropological Theory.* Boulder: Westview Press.

Levi-Strauss, C. [1958] 1967. *Structural Anthropology.* New York: Anchor Books.

_____. [1964] 1975. *The Raw and the Cooked.* New York: Harper and Row.

_____. 1966. "Anthropology: Its Achievements and Future." *Current Anthropology* 7: 124–127.

_____. 1978. *Myth and Meaning.* Toronto: University of Toronto Press.

Lewis, D. 1973. "Anthropology and Colonialism." *Current Anthropology* 14: 581–602.

Lewis, O. 1951. *Life in a Mexican Village, Tepoztlan Restudied.* Urbana: University of Illinois Press.

_____. 1966a. "The Culture of Poverty." *Scientific American* 215: 19–25.

_____. 1966b. *La Vida: A Puerto Rican Family in the Culture of Poverty—San Juan and New York*: New York: Random House.

Liebow, E. 1967. *Tally's Corner: A Study of Negro Streetcorner Men.* Boston: Little, Brown.

Lienhardt, G. 1978. *Social Anthropology,* 2nd ed. London: Oxford University Press.

Little, K. 1957. "The Role of Volunteer Associations in West African Urbanization." *American Anthropologist* 59: 579–596.

Lock, M., and P. Wakewich-Dunk. 1990. "Nerves and Nostalgia: Expression of Loss among Greek Immigrants in Montreal." *Canadian Family Physician* 36: 253–258.

Long, J. [1791] 1971. *Voyages and Travels of an Indian Interpreter and Trader.* Toronto: Coles Publishing.

Loran, C.T., and T.F. McIlwraith (eds.). 1943. *The North American Indian Today.* Toronto: University of Toronto Press.

Lowie, R. 1920. *Primitive Society.* New York: Boni and Liveright.

MacDonald, G.F. 1968. *Debert: A Paleo-Indian Site in Central Nova Scotia.* Ottawa: National Museums of Canada.

Mackie, C. 1986. "Some Reflections on Indian Economic Development." In J.R. Ponting (ed.), *Arduous Journey: Canadian Indians and Decolonization.* Toronto: McClelland & Stewart.

Mahoney, J. 1999. "On a Frosty Northern Night, Nunavut Is Born." *Globe and Mail* (1 April).

Mair, L. 1968. *An Introduction to Social Anthropology.* Oxford: Oxford University Press.

Malinowski, B. 1922. *Argonauts of the Western Pacific.* New York: E.P. Dutton.

_____. 1924. *Sex and Repression in Savage Society.* London: Routledge and Kegan Paul.

Mandelbaum, D.G. 1941. "Culture Change among the Nilgiri Tribes." *American Anthropologist* 43: 19–26.

Manuel, G., and M. Posluns. 1974. *The Fourth World: An Indian Reality.* Don Mills: Collier-Macmillan.

Marcus, G.E., and M.J. Fischer. 1986. *Anthropology as Cultural Critique.* Chicago: University of Chicago Press.

Marx, K. [1848] 1888. *The Communist Manifesto.* London: W. Reeves.

_____. [1852] 1978. *The Eighteenth Brumaire of Louis Bonaparte.* Peking: Foreign Language Press.

_____. [1859] 1904. *A Contribution to the Critique of Political Economy.* Chicago: International Library Publication.

_____. [1867] 1909. *Capital.* Moscow: Progress Publishers.

Mayer, E. 2002. *The Articulated Peasant: Household Economies in the Andes.* Boulder: Westview Press.

McCallum, J. 1980. *Unequal Beginnings: Agriculture and Economic Development in Quebec and Ontario until 1870.* Toronto: University of Toronto Press.

McCourt, F. 1996. *Angela's Ashes: A Memoir.* New York: Simon and Schuster.

McDonald, M. 1986. "Celtic Ethnic Kinship and the Problem of Being English." *Current Anthropology* 27 (4): 333–347.

McFeat, T. 1976. "The National Museum and Canadian Anthropology." In J. Freedman (ed.), *The History of Canadian Anthropology*, 148–174. Proceedings of the Canadian Ethnology Society, 3.

_____. 1980. *Three Hundred Years of Anthropology in Canada.* Occasional Papers in Anthropology, no. 7. Halifax: Saint Mary's University.

McFee, M. 1972. *Modern Blackfeet: Montanans on a Reservation.* New York: Holt, Rinehart, and Winston.

Mead, M. 1928. *Coming of Age in Samoa.* New York: Morrow.

_____. 1930. *Growing up in New Guinea.* New York: Morrow.

_____. [1935] 1963. *Sex and Temperament in Three Primitive Societies.* New York: Dell Publishing.

_____. 1949. *Male and Female: A Study of the Sexes in a Changing World.* New York: Morrow.

_____. 1972. *Blackberry Winter: My Earlier Years.* New York: Simon and Schuster.

Messenger, J.C. 1971. "Sex and Repression in an Irish Folk Community." In D.S. Marshall and R.C. Suggs (eds.), *Human Sexual Behaviour: Variations in the Ethnographic Spectrum.* New York: Basic Books.

_____. 1983. *Inis Beag: Isle of Ireland.* Long Grove: Waveland Press.

Milton, K. 1979. "Male Bias in Anthropology." *Man* 14 (1): 40–54.

Miner, H. [1939] 1967. *St. Denis: A French-Canadian Parish.* Chicago: University of Chicago Press.

Mitchell, W.E. 1987. *The Bamboo Fire: Field Work with the New Guinea Wape.* Prospect Heights: Waveland Press.

Morgan, L.H. 1851. *League of the Ho-de-no-sau-nee, or Iroquois.* Rochester: Sage and Brothers.

_____. 1870. *Systems of Consanguinity and Affinity of the Human Family.* Washington, D.C.: Smithsonian Institution.

_____. 1877. *Ancient Society.* New York: Henry Holt and Co.

Moses, D.N. 2009. *The Promise of Progress: The Life and Work of Lewis Henry Morgan.* Columbia: University of Missouri Press.

MSNews. 2008. "Caught on Tape: Hospital Patient Left to Die" (9 July).

Murphy, R. 1971. *The Dialectics of Social Life.* New York: Basic Books.

_____. 1979. *An Overture to Social Anthropology.* Englewood Cliff: Prentice-Hall.

Nagengast, C., and C.G. Velez-Ibanez (eds.). 2004. *Human Rights: The Scholar as Activist.* Oklahoma City: Society for Applied Anthropology.

Nash, J. 2001. *Mayan Visions: The Quest for Autonomy in an Age of Globalization.* New York: Routledge.

Neizen, R. 2004. *A World beyond Difference: Cultural Identity in the Age of Globalization.* Oxford: Blackwell Publishing.

New York Times. 1970. "Oscar Lewis, Author and Anthropologist, Dead: U. of Illinois Professor, 55, Wrote of Slum Dwellers" (18 December).

_____. 1991. "Ruth Landes Is Dead; Anthropologist Was 82" (24 February).

_____. 2006. "Clifford Geertz, Cultural Anthropologist, Is Dead at 80" (1 November).

_____. 2008. "A Payoff out of Poverty?" (19 December).

_____. 2010. "'Culture of Poverty' Makes a Comeback" (17 October).

Nowry, L. 1995. *Man of Mana: Marius Barbeau.* Toronto: NC Press.

Ohler, S. 1999. "Nunavut Born with High Hopes, Big Challenges." *National Post* (1 April).

Ohnuki-Tierney, E. 1984. *The Ainu of the Northwest Coast of Southern Sakhalin.* Prospect Heights: Waveland Press.

Orwell, G. 1949. *Nineteen Eighty-Four.* London: Secker & Warburg.

Parman, S. 1990. *Scottish Crofters: A Historical Ethnography of a Celtic Village.* New York: Holt, Rinehart, and Winston.

Patterson, E.P. 1972. *The Canadian Indian: A History Since 1500.* Don Mills, On: Collier-Macmillan.

Peace, A. 1989. "From Arcadia to Anomie: Critical Notes on the Constitution of Irish Society as an Anthropological Object." *Critique of Anthropology* 9 (1): 89–111.

Preston, R.J. 1976. "Marius Barbeau and the History of Canadian Anthropology." In J. Freedman (ed.), *The History of Canadian Anthropology,* 122–135. Proceedings of the Canadian Ethnology Society 3.

_____. 1980. "Reflections on Sapir's Anthropology in Canada." *Canadian Review of Sociology and Anthropology* 17: 367–375.

Price, J.A. 1987. *Applied Anthropology: Canadian Perspectives.* Downsview: Society of Applied Anthropology in Canada.

Purich, D. 1988. *The Métis .* Toronto: James Lorimer.

_____. 1992. *The Inuit and Their Land: The Story of Nunavut.* Toronto: James Lorimer.

Queen, S.A., and R.W. Habenstein. 1974. *The Family in Various Cultures*. Toronto: J.B. Lippincott.

Radcliffe-Brown, A.R. 1918. "Notes on the Social Organization of Australian Tribes." *Journal of the Royal Anthropological Institute* 48: 222–253.

_____. 1922. *The Andaman Islanders*. Cambridge: Cambridge University Press.

_____. 1952. *Structure and Function in Primitive Society*. London: Cohen and West.

Rappaport, R.A. 1967. "Ritual Regulation of Environmental Relations among a New Guinea People." *Ethnology* 6: 17–30.

_____. 1984. *Pigs for the Ancestors: Ritual in the Ecology of a Papuan New Guinea People*, 2nd ed. New Haven: Yale University Press.

Ray, A.J. 1974. *Indians and the Fur Trade: Their Role as Hunters, Trappers, and Middlemen in the Lands Southwest of Hudson Bay, 1660–1870*. Toronto: University of Toronto Press.

Redbird, D. 1980. *We Are Métis: A Métis View of the Development of a Native Canadian People*. Toronto: Ontario Métis and Non-status Indian Association.

Redfield, R. 1930. *Tepoztlan: A Mexican Village*. Chicago: University of Chicago Press.

Renner, E. 1984. "On Geertz's Interpretive Theoretical Program." *Current Anthropology* 25 (4): 538–540.

Richling, B. 1989. "An Anthropologist's Apprenticeship: Diamond Jenness' Papuan and Arctic Fieldwork." *Culture* 9 (1) 71–85.

Richter, D.K. 1985. "Iroquois versus Iroquois: Jesuit Missions and Christianity in Village Politics, 1642–1686." *Ethnohistory* 32 (1): 1–16.

Ridington, R. 1988. *Trail to Heaven: Knowledge and Narrative in a Northern Native Community*. Vancouver: Douglas & McIntyre.

Robinson, A. 2005. *Ta'n Teli-Ktlamsitasit (Ways of Believing): Mi'kmaw Religion in Eskasoni, Nova Scotia*. Canadian Ethnography Series, vol. 3. Toronto: Pearson Education Canada.

Robinson, M. 2006. "Joan Ryan (1932–2005)." *Arctic* 59 (4) 447–448.

Rogers, E.S. 1962. *The Round Lake Ojibwa*. Toronto: Royal Ontario Museum.

Romney, A.K., and P.J. Epling. 1958. "A Simplified Model of Kariera Kinship." *American Anthropologist* 60 (1): 59–74.

Ryan, J. 1978. *Wall of Words: The Betrayal of the Urban Indian*. Toronto: Peter Martin Associates.

_____. 1995. *Doing Things the Right Way: Dene Traditional Justice in Lac La Martre, NWT*. Calgary: University of Calgary Press.

Ryan, J., and M. Robinson. 1990. "Implementing Participatory Action Research in the Canadian North: A Case Study of the Gwich'in Language and Cultural Project." *Culture* 10 (2): 57–71.

_____. 1996. "Community Participatory Research: Two Views from Arctic Institute Practitioners." *Practicing Anthropology* 18 (4): 7–12.

Sacks, K. 1979. *Sisters and Wives: The Past and Future of Social Equality*. Westport: Greenwood Press.

Salisbury, R.F. 1962. *From Stone to Steel: Economic Consequences of a Technological Change in New Guinea*. Melbourne and Cambridge: Melbourne University Publishing and Cambridge University Press.

_____. 1970. *Vunamami: Economic Transformation in a Traditional Society*. Berkeley: University of California Press.

_____. 1973. "Economic Anthropology." *Annual Review of Anthropology* 2: 85–94.

_____. 1977. "The Berger Report: But Is It Social Science?" *Social Sciences in Canada* 5 (3): 10–12.

_____. 1986. *A Homeland for the Cree: Regional Development in James Bay 1971–1981.* Montreal: McGill-Queen's University Press.

Salzman, P.C. 1999. *The Anthropology of Real Life: Events in Human Experience.* Prospect Heights: Waveland Press.

Sanday, P.R. 1973. "Toward a Theory of the Status of Women." *American Anthropologist* 75: 1682–1700.

_____. 1981. *Female Power and Male Dominance: On the Origins of Sexual Inequality.* Cambridge: Cambridge University Press.

Sawchuk, J. 1978. *The Métis of Manitoba: Reformulation of an Ethnic Identity.* Toronto: Peter Martin Associates.

_____. 1982. "Some Early Influences on Métis Political Organization." *Culture* 2 (3): 85–91.

Scheper-Hughes, N. 1979. *Saints, Scholars, and Schizophrenics: Mental Illness in Rural Ireland.* Berkeley: University of California Press.

Scholte, B. 1972. "Toward a Reflective and Critical Anthropology." In D. Hymes (ed.), *Reinventing Anthropology.* New York: Pantheon Books.

Shapere, D. 1964. "The Study of Scientific Revolutions." *The Philosophical Review* 73 (3): 383–394.

Shewell, H. 2004. *Enough to Keep Them Alive: Indian Welfare in Canada, 1873–1965.* Toronto: University of Toronto Press.

Shkilnyk, A.M. 1985. *A Poison Stronger Than Love: The Destruction of an Ojibwa Community.* New Haven: Yale University Press.

Sidky, H. 2004. *Perspectives on Culture: A Critical Introduction to Theory in Cultural Anthropology.* Upper Saddle River: Pearson Prentice-Hall.

Silverman, M. (ed.). 2004. *Ethnography and Development: The Work of Richard F. Salisbury.* Montreal: McGill University Libraries.

Silverman, M., and P.H. Gulliver. 1992. "Historical Anthropology and the Ethnographic Tradition: A Personal, Historical, and Intellectual Account." In M. Silverman and P.H. Gulliver (eds.), *Approaching the Past: Historical Anthropology through Irish Case Studies.* New York: Columbia University Press.

Slobodin, R. 1966. *Métis of the Mackenzie District.* Ottawa: Canadian Research Centre for Anthropology.

Society of Applied Anthropology in Canada (SAAC). 1984. "Ethical Guidelines." 12-page MS.

Solway, J. (ed.). 2003. "Politics and Practice in Critical Anthropology: The Work of Richard B. Lee." Special Issue of *Anthropologica* 44 (1).

Solway, J., and R.B. Lee. 1990. "Foragers, Genuine and Spurious: Situating the Kalahari San in History." *Current Anthropology* 31: 109–146.

Speck, D.C. 1987. *An Error in Judgement: The Politics of Medical Care in an Indian/White Community.* Vancouver: Talon Books.

Spencer, H. 1876. *Principles of Sociology.* New York: D. Appleton.

Spradley, J.P. (ed.). 1972. *Guests Never Leave Hungry: The Autobiography of James Sewid, a Kwakiutl Indian.* Montreal: McGill-Queen's University Press.

Stacey, J. 1988. "Can There Be a Feminist Methodology?" *Women's Studies International Forum* 11: 21–27.

Stearns, M.L. 1981. *Haida Culture in Custody: The Masqet Band.* Vancouver: Douglas & McIntyre.

Steward, J. 1955. *Theory of Culture Change.* Urbana: University of Illinois Press.

Stocking, G. 1974. "Some Problems in the Understanding of Nineteenth-Century Cultural Evolutionism." In R. Darnell (ed.), *Readings in the History of Anthropology.* New York: Harper and Row.

Stout, C.W. 1997. "Nunavut: Canada's Newest Territory in 1999." *Canadian Social Trends* 44 (Spring): 13–18.

Strathern, M. 1987. "An Awkward Relationship: The Case of Feminism and Anthropology." *Signs* 12: 276–292.

Stymeist, D.H. 1975. *Ethnics and Indians: Social Relations in a Northwestern Ontario Town.* Toronto: Peter Martin Associates.

Sugiura, K., and H. Befu. 1962. "Kinship Organization of the Saru Ainu." *Ethnology* 1 (3): 287–298.

Sweet, L. 1976. "What Is Canadian Anthropology?" *American Anthropologist* 78: 844–850.

Sylvain, R. 2005. "Disorderly Development: Globalization and the Idea of 'Culture' in the Kalahari." *American Ethnologist* 32 (3): 354–370.

Szathmary, E.J.E., C. Ritenbaugh, and C.S.M. Goody. 1987. "Dietary Change and Plasma Glucose Levels in an Amerindian Population Undergoing Cultural Transition." *Social Science and Medicine* 24: 791–804.

Tanner, A. 1979. *Bringing Home Animals: Religious Ideology and Mode of Production of the Mistassini Cree Hunters.* St. John's: Memorial University of Newfoundland.

Thwaites, R.G. (ed.). 1896–1901. *The Jesuit Relations and Allied Documents: Travels and Explorations of the Jesuit Missionaries in New France, 1610–1791.* Cleveland: Burrows Brothers.

Times (London). 2006. "Professor Bruce Trigger: Prolific Archaeologist Who Made Authoritative Contributions to Egyptology and Canadian Anthropology" (7 December).

Tooker, E. 1964. *An Ethnography of the Huron Indians, 1615–1649.* Bulletin 190. Washington, D.C.: Smithsonian Institution, Bureau of American Ethnology.

Tremblay, M.A., J. Freedman, and A.M. Ervin. 1990. *Towards the Certification of Canadian Anthropologists.* Ottawa: Report of the Committee on Anthropological Practice of the Canadian Anthropology Society, 28 February 1990.

Trigger, B.G. 1966a. "Sir Daniel Wilson: Canada's First Anthropologist." *Anthropologica* 8: 3–29.

———. 1966b. "Sir John Wilson Dawson: A Faithful Anthropologist." *Anthropologica* 8: 351–359.

———. 1969. *The Huron: Farmers of the North.* Toronto: Holt, Rinehart, and Winston.

———. 1976. *The Children of Aataentsic: A History of the Huron People to 1660.* Montreal: McGill-Queen's University Press.

———. 1985. *Natives and Newcomers: Canada's "Heroic Age" Reconsidered.* Montreal: McGill-Queen's University Press.

———. 1986. "Evolutionism, Relativism, and Putting Native People into Historical Context." *Culture* 6 (2): 65–79.

_____. 1997. "Loaves and Fishes: Sustaining Anthropology at McGill." *Culture* 17: 89–100.

Tsing, A. 2005. "Anthropologists as Public Individuals." *Anthropology News* 46 (1): 10.

Tulchinsky, G. 2008. *Canada's Jews: A People's Journey.* Toronto: University of Toronto Press.

Turnbull, C.M. 1961. *The Forest people: A Study of the Pygmies of the Congo.* New York: Simon and Schuster.

_____. 1983. *The Mbuti Pygmies: Change and Adaptation.* New York: Holt, Rinehart, and Winston.

Turner, E. 1989. "From Shamans to Healers: The Survival of an Inupiaq Eskimo Skill." *Anthropologica* 31 (1): 3–24.

Turner, T. 1993. "Anthropology and Multiculturalism." *Current Anthropology* 8: 411–429.

Tylor, E.B. 1871. *Primitive Culture.* London: John Murray.

Ulin, R.C. 1984. *Understanding Cultures.* Austin: University of Texas Press.

University of Toronto. 2011. "Alumni Profile: Dr. Emoke J.E. Szathmary."

Van West, J.J. 1976. "George Mercer Dawson: An Early Canadian Anthropologist." *Anthropological Journal of Canada* 14: 8–13.

Vigil, J.D. 1997. *Personas Mexicana: Chicano High Schoolers in a Changing Los Angeles.* New York: Harcourt Brace.

Waldram, J.B. 1997. *The Way of the Pipe: Aboriginal Spirituality and Symbolic Healing in Canadian Prisons.* Peterborough: Broadview Press.

Waldram, J.B., D.A. Herring, and T.K. Young. 1995. *Aboriginal Health in Canada: Historical, Cultural, and Epistemological Perspectives.* Toronto: University of Toronto Press.

Warren, C.A. 1988. *Gender Issues in Field Research.* Qualitative Research Methods, vol. 9. Newbury Park: Sage Publications.

Warry, W. 1998. *Unfinished Dreams: Community Healing and the Reality of Aboriginal Self-Government.* Toronto: University of Toronto Press.

Watkins, M. (ed.). 1977. *Dene Nation: The Colony within.* Toronto: University of Toronto Press.

Weaver, S.M. 1972. *Medicine and Politics among the Grand River Iroquois: A Study of the Non-conservatives.* Ottawa: National Museum of Canada, Publications in Ethnology, no. 4.

_____. 1981. *Making Canadian Indian Policy: The Hidden Agenda 1968–1970.* Toronto: University of Toronto Press.

Weber, M. 1949. *The Methodology of the Social Sciences.* New York: The Free Press.

Wells, H.G. 1895. *The Time Machine.* London: W. Heinemann.

Werner, D. 1990. *Amazon Journey: An Anthropologist's Year among Brazil's Mekranoti Indians.* Englewood Cliffs: Prentice-Hall.

Westermarck, E. [1891] 1921. *The History of Human Marriage*, 5th ed. New York: Macmillan.

White, L. 1949. *The Science of Culture.* New York: Grove Press.

_____. 1959. *The Evolution of Culture.* New York: McGraw-Hill.

Whittaker, E. 1994. "Decolonizing Knowledge: Towards a Feminist Ethic and Methodology." In J.S. Grewal and H. Johnston (eds.), *The India–Canada Relationship.* New Delhi: Sage Publications.

Williamson, R.F., and M.S. Bisson (eds.). 2006. *The Archaeology of Bruce Trigger: Theoretical Empiricism.* Montreal: McGill-Queen's University Press.

Wilson, D. 1862. *Prehistoric Man.* London: Macmillan and Co.

Wilson, Rev. E.F. 1874. *The Ojebway Language.* Toronto: Rowsell and Hutchison.

Winnipeg Free Press. 2009. "Tribute Dinner Tonight Honours Emoke Szathmary" (3 November).

Wissler, C. 1913. "Societies and Dance Associations of the Blackfoot Indians." *Anthropological Papers of the American Museum of Natural History* VII (2).

Wolf, E.R. 1955. "Types of Latin American Peasantry: A Preliminary Discussion." *American Anthropologist* 57 (3): 452–471.

_____. 1966. *Peasants.* Englewood Cliffs: Prentice-Hall.

Wright, J.V. 1976. *Six Chapters in Canada's Prehistory.* Ottawa: National Museums of Canada.

Yerbury, J.C. 1986. *The Subarctic Indians and the Fur Trade, 1680–1860.* Vancouver: University of British Columbia Press.

Young, D., G. Ingram, and L. Swartz. 1989. *Cry of the Eagle: Encounters with a Cree Healer.* Toronto: University of Toronto Press.

Young, T.K. 1988. *Health Care and Culture Change: The Indian Experience in the Central Subarctic.* Toronto: University of Toronto Press.

Zechenter, E. 1997. "In the Name of Culture: Cultural Relativism and the Abuse of the Individual." *Journal of Anthropological Research* 53: 319–348.

Index

Copyright Acknowledgements

Chapter 1

Figure 1.1: Cartoon by Kes from www.CartoonStock.com. Reprinted by permission of CartoonStock Ltd.

Photo 1.1: Ken Gigliotti, *Emoke J. Szathmary*, 2009, Winnipeg Free Press, Winnipeg. Reprinted by permission of Winnipeg Free Press.

Figure 1.2: Cartoon by Patrick Hardin from www.CartoonStock.com. Reprinted by permission of CartoonStock Ltd.

Photo 1.2: *Celebrating a tea dance at Treaty time*, Battleford, Saskatchewan, Postcard Views of Early Saskatchewan, LXX-138, University of Saskatchewan, Saskatoon. Reprinted by permission of University of Saskatchewan Library, Special Collections.

Figure 1.3: Cartoon by Loren Fishman from www.CartoonStock.com. Reprinted by permission of CartoonStock Ltd.

Chapter 2

Photo 2.1: *Bruce G. Trigger*, McGill University, Montreal. Reprinted by permission of McGill University.

Figure 2.2: Cartoon by Theresa McCracken from www.CartoonStock.com. Reprinted by permission of CartoonStock Ltd.

Photo 2.2: *Franz Boas posing*, Negative MNH 8304, National Anthropological Archives, Smithsonian Institution, Washington. Reprinted by permission of the Smithsonian Institution.

Photo 2.3: Curtis and Miller, *Diamond Jenness*, C-086412, Rudolph Martin Anderson, Library and Archives Canada, Ottawa. Reprinted by permission of Library and Archives Canada.

Photo 2.4: *Harry Hawthorn with museum artifacts*, 1949, UBC 1.1/9765-11, University of British Columbia Historical Photograph Collection, Vancouver. Reprinted by permission of University of British Columbia Archives.

Photo 2.5: *Totem poles at Totem Park*, 1969, UBC 5.2/158-1, University of British Columbia Historical Photograph Collection, Vancouver. Reprinted by permission of University of British Columbia Archives.

Photo 2.6: Bud Glunz & National Film Board of Canada, *Cree women*, 1946, PA-115408, Photothèque, Library and Archives Canada, Ottawa. Reprinted by permission of Library and Archives Canada.

Photo 2.7: *Joan Ryan in Arctic*, 2006, Arctic Institute of North America, Calgary. Reprinted by permission of the Arctic Institute of America.

Photo 2.8: *The !Kung San being shown to Ju'hoansi by Richard Borshay Lee*, University of Toronto Libraries, Toronto. Reprinted by permission of Richard Lee.

Photo 2.9: David Weaver, *Sally Weaver*, University of Toronto Libraries, Toronto. Reprinted by permission of University of Toronto Libraries.

Chapter 3

Figure 3.1: Cartoon by Aaron Bacall from www.CartoonStock.com. Reprinted by permission of CartoonStock Ltd.

Chapter 4

Photo 4.1: Minnie R. Wyman, *Portrait of Lewis Henry Morgan*, 1945, oil on canvas, 29 ½ in. x 24 ½ in. Schaffer Library Collections of Union College in Schenectady, New York. Reprinted by permission of Schaffer Library at Union College.

Photo 4.2: *Ruth Benedict, half-length portrait*, 1937, LC-USZ62-114649, Library of Congress, Washington. Reprinted by permission of Library of Congress.

Photo 4.3: Bronislaw Malinowski, *Ethnographer with a man in a wig*, MALINOWSKI/3/SOS/68, c1915-1918, London School of Economics Library, London. Reprinted by permission of London School of Economics.

Photo 4.4: *Threshing crew and machinery*, University of Saskatchewan Libraries Special Collections, Postcard Views of Early Saskatchewan, LXX-110. Reprinted by permission of University of Saskatchewan Library, Special Collections.

Photo 4.5: *Mennonite settler returning to farm*, Canada, PA-044418, Department of Interior, Library and Archives Canada, Ottawa. Reprinted by permission of Library and Archives Canada.

Photo 4.6: *Edenbridge Hebrew Colony*, Saskatchewan, C-027467, Louis Rosenberg fonds, Library and Archives Canada, Ottawa. Reprinted by permission of Library and Archives Canada.

Photo 4.7: John Mayall, *Karl Marx*, BG A9/362, Collection IISG (Blumenberg, W.), International Institute of Social History, Amsterdam. Reprinted by permission of International Institute of Social History.

Photo 4.8: *Margaret Mead sitting between two Samoan girls*, 1926, Library of Congress, Washington. Reprinted by permission of Library of Congress.

Chapter 5

Photo 5.1: *The Old Squaw*, c1923-1925, C 267-3, Alexander Isbester family fonds, Archives of Ontario, Toronto. Reprinted by permission of Archives of Ontario.

Photo 5.2: *Early settlers in eastern Canada / The first crude dwelling*, C-002401, Library and Archives Canada, Ottawa. Reprinted by permission of Library and Archives Canada.

Photo 5.3: *Memorial*, PA-136924, Jules-Ernest Livernois Collection, Library and Archives Canada, Ottawa. Reprinted by permission of Library and Archives Canada.

Figure 5.1: *Cartoon depicting the arrival of Mennonites in Canada*, 1918, NA-3055-4, Glenbow Museum, Calgary. Reprinted by permission of Glenbow Museum.

Photo 5.4: *Chinese immigration act*, 30625, Vancouver Public Library - Special Collections, Vancouver. Reprinted by permission of Vancouver Public Library.

Photo 5.5: John Boyd, *Knights of the Ku Klux Klan*, Kingston, August 31, 1927, I0003697, Archives of Ontario, Toronto. Reprinted by permission of the Archives of Ontario.

Chapter 6

Photo 6.1: *Bobbie Crump family in Edmonton, Alberta*, 1918, NA-4210-1, Glenbow Museum, Calgary. Reprinted by permission of Glenbow Museum.

Photo 6.2: A.R. Cogswell, *Mi/kmaq camp*, Nova Scotia Archives, Halifax. Reprinted by permission of Nova Scotia Archives.

Photo 6.3: *Inuit woman drying fish*, PA-129588, Richard Harrington fonds, Library and Archives Canada, Ottawa. Reprinted by permission of Library and Archives Canada.

Photo 6.4: *Inuit men dancing and drumming*, Alaska, c1903-1915, NC-1-12a, Glenbow Museum, Calgary. Reprinted by permission of Glenbow Museum.

Photo 6.5: *Akulack and wife*, 1915, Bathurst Inlet, Nunavut, NA 2306-9, Glenbow Museum, Calgary. Reprinted by permission of Glenbow Museum.

Photo 6.6: *Group of Hutterites*, Alberta, NA-1752-29, Glenbow Museum, Calgary. Reprinted by permission of Glenbow Museum.

Photo 6.7: *Rural mail box*, PA-010668, William James Topley Series, Library and Archives Canada,. Reprinted by permission of Library and Archives Canada.

Photo 6.8: Ronny Jaques, *Workmen*, Hamilton, 1944, P-000762002, National Film Board of Canada, Photothèque, Library and Archives Canada, Ottawa. Reprinted by permission of Library and Archives Canada.

Chapter 7

Photo 7.1: *Amerindians*, PA-135187, Jules-Ernest Livernois Collection, Library and Archives Canada, Ottawa. Reprinted by permission of Library and Archives Canada.

Photo 7.2: Philip H Godsell, *Wabunosa, Ojibwa*, Garden River, Ontario, NA-3878-77, Glenbow Museum, Calgary. Reprinted by permission of Glenbow Museum.

Photo 7.3: *Africville*, Bob Brooks NSARM accession no. 1989-468 vol. 16 image 19, Nova Scotia Archives, Halifax. Reprinted by permission of Nova Scotia Archives.

Photo 7.4: *Africville*, Bob Brooks NSARM accession no. 1989-468 vol. 16 image 27, Nova Scotia Archives, Halifax. Reprinted by permission of Nova Scotia Archives.

Chapter 8

Figure 8.1: Cartoon by Theresa McCracken from www.CartoonStock.com. Reprinted by permission of CartoonStock Ltd.

Photo 8.1: *Cree and Naskapi, in canoe on Kaniapiskau River, Quebec*, c1924-1936, NA-3235-32, Glenbow Museum, Calgary. Reprinted by permission of Glenbow Museum.

Photo 8.2: *Blackfoot warriors*, C-019089, Patent and Copyright Office, Library and Archives Canada, Ottawa. Reprinted by permission of Library and Archives Canada.

Photo 8.3: Edward S. Curtis, *Clayoquot*, 1916, PA-039472, Library and Archives Canada, Ottawa. Reprinted by permission of Library and Archives Canada.

Photo 8.4: *Elders potlatch*, UBC 44.1/608-3, University of British Columbia Archives, Vancouver. Reprinted by permission of University of British Columbia Archives.

Photo 8.5: *Farmers with wheat lined up at elevator*, Piapot, 1912, NA-1382-1, Glenbow Museum, Calgary. Reprinted by permission of Glenbow Museum.

Photo 8.6: *Shanty gang*, Arnprior, 1903, I0010877, Charles Macnamara, Archives of Ontario, Toronto. Reprinted by permission of Archives of Ontario.

Photo 8.7: *Grain elevators*, Thunder Bay, 1980, I0004596, Ministry of Agriculture, Food and Rural Affairs, Archives of Ontario, Toronto. Reprinted by permission of Archives of Ontario.

Photo 8.8: *Log jam on White River near Englehart*, I0006766, Archives of Ontario, Toronto. Reprinted by permission of Archives of Ontario

Chapter 9

Photo 9.1: *Hebrew school picnic at Bowness Park*, Calgary, 1912, NA-2034-1, Glenbow Museum, Calgary. Reprinted by permission of Glenbow Museum.

Photo 9.2: *Calgary Hebrew School graduation ceremonies at Jewish Community Centre*, Calgary, 1959, NA-5093-673c, Glenbow Museum, Calgary. Reprinted by permission of Glenbow Museum.

Photo 9.3: *Councillors of the Métis nation*, 1870, PA-012854, Library and Archives Canada, Ottawa. Reprinted by permission of Library and Archives Canada.

Photo 9.4: *Micmac women*, Notman Studio NSARM accession no. 1983-310 number 69865, Nova Scotia Archives, Halifax. Reprinted by permission of Nova Scotia Archives.

Photo 9.5: *Indian Point*, NSARM Photo Drawer - Indians (Micmac) – Wigwam, Nova Scotia Archives, Halifax. Reprinted by permission of Nova Scotia Archives.

Photo 9.6: *Kenojuak, Inuit Artist*, Cape Dorset, 1961, PA-145170, B. Korda, Library and Archives Canada, Toronto. Reprinted by permission of Library and Archives Canada.

Chapter 10

Figure 10.1: Cartoon by Kresten Forsman from www.CartoonStock.com. Reprinted by permission of CartoonStock Ltd.